D0760182

The Pursuit of Organizational Intelligence

The Pursuit of Organizational Intelligence

James G. March

Copyright © in this collection James G. March 1999.

The right of James G. March to be identified as author of this work has been asserted in accordance with the Copyright, Designs and Patents Act 1988.

First published 1999

Blackwell Publishers Inc.
350 Main Street
Malden, Massachusetts 02148
USA

Blackwell Publishers Ltd
108 Cowley Road
Oxford OX4 1JF
UK

All rights reserved. Except for the quotation of short passages for the purposes of criticism and review, no part of this publication may be reproduced, stored in a retrieval system, or transmitted, in any form or by any means, electronic, mechanical, photocopying, recording or otherwise, without the prior permission of the publisher.

Except in the United States of America, this book is sold subject to the condition that it shall not, by way of trade or otherwise, be lent, resold, hired out, or otherwise circulated without the publisher's prior consent in any form of binding or cover other than that in which it is published and without a similar condition including this condition being imposed on the subsequent purchaser.

Library of Congress Cataloging-in-Publication Data

March, James G.
    The pursuit of organizational intelligence / James G. March.
        p.   cm.
    Includes bibliographical references and index.
    ISBN 0-631-21101-2 (alk. hbk.). — ISBN 0-631-21102-0 (pbk. : alk. paper)
    1. Organization learning.   2. Management.   3. Knowledge management.   I. Title.
    HD58.82.M367   1999
    658.4—dc 21   98-36982
                                                                                    CIP

British Library Cataloguing in Publication Data

A CIP catalogue record for this book is available from the British Library.

Typeset in 10 on 12 pt Sabon by Ace Filmsetting
Printed in Great Britain by TJ International, Padstow, Cornwall
This book is printed on acid-free paper.

CONTENTS

vi | *Contents*

ACKNOWLEDGMENTS

Ten years ago Blackwell Publishers published a collection of my papers in a book entitled *Decisions and Organizations*. The present collection represents a companion volume. As was true of the previous book, this one is hardly a solo effort.

I want to thank my research collaborators for their willingness to have the papers they co-authored with me included in this compendium. These include Daniel A. Levinthal (University of Pennsylvania), Barbara Levitt (Stanford University), Pertti H. Lounamaa (Nokia Electronics), Johan P. Olsen (University of Oslo, Norway), Zur Shapira (New York University), Lee S. Sproull (Boston University), Robert I. Sutton (Stanford University), and Michal Tamuz (Rutgers University). My debt to them extends well beyond their contributions to these papers. I am enriched and sustained by their friendships.

I am grateful to Grove Press for permission to use quotations from Jorge Luis Borges, *Ficciones* (New York, Grove Press, 1962), to Random House for permission to use quotations from Isabel Allende, *Eva Luna* (New York: Bantam Books, 1989), to the Society of Authors, London, for permission to use quotations from George Bernard Shaw, *Saint Joan* (New York: Penguin, 1951), to Educational Technology Publications for permission to use quotations from Harvey A. Averch et al. *How Effective Is Schooling?* (Englewood Cliffs, NJ: Educational Technology Publications, 1974), to W. W. Norton and Co., Inc. for permission to use quotations from Henrik Ibsen, *The Wild Duck* (New York, W. W. Norton, 1968) and from Miguel de Cervantes, *Don Quixote* (New York, W. W. Norton, 1981), and to Penguin Putnam, Inc. for permission to use quotations from Alexander Solzhenitsyn, *One Day in the Life of Ivan Denisovich* (New York: E. P. Dutton/Signet Classic, 1963) and from Leo Tolstoy, *War and Peace* (New York, New American Library/Signet, 1968).

I am also happy to acknowledge the permission of the various publishers and journals that originally published these papers. I owe a collective debt to the community of academic journals and publishers that have supported me and my colleagues over the years and have generously extended that support for this volume.

In a similar way, I have been supported over the years by an academic research community. In my case, a significant part of that support over many years has come from the Spencer Foundation. Over the same years, the Foundation's endowment has grown very substantially. I am reluctant to claim full responsibility for the growth in endowment, but not reluctant at all to thank Spencer both for the resources and for a sustained relationship.

Within the publishing community, Catriona King, the Blackwell editor for this volume, deserves particular mention. Her initiative and her persistence were essential to the project and are much appreciated.

Barbara Beuche, the administrative manager of the Scandinavian Consortium for Organizational Research at Stanford, has done her best to make things happen when they were supposed to happen. With modern information technology, it is unclear whether she works for me or I for her, but either way I am grateful for her presence.

The papers and the collection owe a great deal to my wife, Jayne Dohr March, who has put up with them, and with me, for more than fifty years. I think it is fair to say that she views my work with as much indifference as she does my passion for Susan Sarandon. But (within reason) she tolerates each with benevolent resignation and thereby makes them possible.

For permission to reprint material the author and the publisher are grateful to the following:

2. This chapter originally appeared as "A Preface to Understanding How Decisions Happen in Organizations," in Zur Shapira, ed., *Organizational Decision Making*. New York: Cambridge University Press, 1996. Copyright 1996 by Cambridge University Press.

3. This chapter originally appeared in *Administrative Science Quarterly*, 41 (1996) 278–87. Copyright 1996 Cornell University.

4. This chapter originally appeared in *Governance*, 9 (1996) 247–64. Copyright 1966 by Blackwell Publishers.

5. This chapter originally appeared in *Annual Review of Sociology*, 14 (1988), 319–40. Copyright 1988 by Annual Reviews, Inc.

6. This chapter originally appeared in Joel Baum and Jitendra Singh, eds., *The Evolutionary Dynamics of Organizations*, pp. 39–49, New York: Oxford University Press, 1994. Reproduced by permission of Oxford University Press, Inc.

7. This chapter originally appeared in *Organization Science*, 2 (1991)

71–87. Copyright 1991 by The Institute of Management Sciences (currently INFORMS), 2 Charles Street, Suite 300, Providence, RI 02904 USA.

8. This chapter originally appeared in *Organization Science*, 2 (1991) 1–13. Copyright 1991 by The Institute of Management Sciences (currently INFORMS), 2 Charles Street, Suite 300, Providence, RI 02904 USA.
9. This chapter originally appeared in *Management Science*, 33 (1987) 107–23. Copyright 1987 by The Institute of Management Sciences (currently INFORMS), 2 Charles Street, Suite 300, Providence, RI 02904 USA.
10. This chapter originally appeared in *Organization*, 2 (1995) 427–40.
11. This chapter originally appeared in *Strategic Management Journal*, 14 (1993) 95–112. Copyright 1993 by John Wiley and Sons Limited.
12. This chapter originally appeared in *The Stanford Magazine*, Spring (1988) 61–3.
13. This chapter originally appeared in *Journal of Economic Behavior and Organization*, 9 (1988) 5–24.
14. This chapter originally appeared in *Psychological Review*, 99 (1992) 172–83. Copyright 1992 by the American Psychological Association.
15. This chapter originally appeared in *Psychological Review*, 103 (1996) 309–19. Copyright 1996 by the American Psychological Association.
16. This chapter originally appeared in *Review of Educational Research*, 42 (1973) 413–29. Copyright 1973 by the American Educational Research Association.
17. This chapter originally appeared in *Journal of Applied Communication Research*, 19 (1991) 20–31.
18. This chapter originally appeared in *Organization Science*, 8 (1997) 697–706. Copyright 1997 by The Institute for Operations Research and the Management Sciences (INFORMS), 2 Charles Street, Suite 300, Providence, RI 02904 USA.
19. This chapter originally appeared in *National Research Council in 1979*, pp. 27–36, Washington, DC: National Academy of Sciences, 1980. Copyright 1980 by the National Academy of Sciences.
20. This chapter originally appeared in *Texas Tech Journal of Education*, 2 (1975) 5–16.
21. This chapter originally appeared in *Stanford Business School Magazine*, 64,4 (1996) 10–13. Copyright 1966 by the Board of Trustees of Leland Stanford Junior University. All rights reserved.

CHAPTER ONE

Introduction*

Organizations pursue intelligence. In that pursuit, they process information, formulate plans and aspirations, interpret environments, generate strategies and decisions, monitor experiences and learn from them, and imitate others as they do the same. Organizations seek to serve their interests and conceptions of self, imposing coherence when they can and exploiting the advantages of confusion, chaos, and ambiguity when the opportunity arises. These efforts are disciplined by the presence of other organizations that, in similar pursuit of their own interests and self-conceptions, provide elements of competition and objects for emulation.

This pursuit of intelligence in organizations is never completely successful. To be sure, organizations sometimes manage to achieve impressive levels of intelligence; but organizational intelligence can also be equivocal, ephemeral, and chimerical. Despite all the paraphernalia of intelligence available to them and powerful incentives to avoid errors, organizations often pursue courses that adversely affect some of the interests represented in an organizational coalition. They routinely make blunders, sometimes huge ones. They often fail to survive very long. They frequently discover that actions they thought were unusually clever were actually preludes to disaster. History is filled with organizational stupidity as well as organizational brilliance.

There are reasons for the failures. The pursuit of organizational intelligence appears quite straightforward, but it is not. The difficulties begin with complications in the concept of intelligence itself. In a general way, intelligence refers to the ability to achieve outcomes that fulfill desires as much as possible. We assess the intelligence of a decision procedure by evaluating the outcomes resulting from its use in terms of organizational desires. An intelligent organization is one that adopts procedures that consistently do well (in the organization's own terms) in the face of constraints imposed by such things as scarce resources and competition.

The assessment of organizational intelligence in such terms is complicated by the fact that desires, actions, and outcomes are all distributed across space and time and connected with each other in intricate ways. The outcomes realized from a particular action are not realized instantaneously but are spread over time. Desires also differ across individuals and groups and over time. They change partly in response to the actions and outcomes that they affect. As a result, any assessment of intelligence depends on the time-and-place perspective chosen. What is intelligent from the point of view of one group's desires over one time period may be quite unintelligent from the perspective of another time and set of desires. And what is intelligent from the point of view of preferences activated when action is taken may be quite unintelligent from the point of view of preferences activated later, particularly after preferences adjust to subsequent experience.

If these conceptual problems were not enough, pursuing organizational intelligence, once defined, is made particularly elusive by three elementary problems: The first problem is the problem of *ignorance*. Not everything is known. The future is uncertain. The consequences of taking one action or another are difficult to anticipate precisely. Sometimes they are difficult to anticipate at all. The future depends in part on the actions of many actors, each of whom is simultaneously trying to anticipate the others. Many of the contingencies can be given probabilistic estimates, but such estimates leave considerable range in the possible futures. Moreover, different people in an organization often anticipate dramatically different futures. The past is also uncertain. It is not uncertain because it still remains to be realized but because it is dimly, inaccurately, or differently recalled. The past is experienced in ways that affect both its interpretation and the memories that are retained about it. History is a story, and the story tellers of the past appear to be as variable as the story tellers of the future. Ignorance about the future and the past is organized around ignorance about the causal structure of the world. Interpretations of why things happen in and to organizations are predominately *post hoc*, socially constructed explanations that seem to shift with changing fashions in interpretation and may provide only weak aids to comprehending a future that will reflect new changes.

The second problem is the problem of *conflict*. Organizations seek intelligence in the name of multiple, nested actors over multiple, nested time periods. The preferences or identities embraced by some participants are inconsistent with the preferences or identities of other participants. What is intelligent action from the point of view of one part of an organization is not intelligent from the point of view of another part. These inconsistencies lead to difficulties in exchanging information and cooperation among members of the organization as individuals act intelligently from their own points of view. At the same time, preferences and identities endure or change over time, and the actions that are intelligent from the point of view of one time are inconsistent with actions that are intelligent when viewed from a different time perspective. The complications of weighing the claims of different participants and different time perspectives in organizational intelligence are legendary.

The third problem is the problem of *ambiguity* in the evaluative bases of action. Intelligence presumes some accomplishment of what is desired. The desires may take the form of preferences defined over possible outcomes. They may take the form of conceptions of self that are to be fulfilled. The preferences to be pursued or the identities to be enacted are usually assumed to be clear, stable, and exogenous. In organizations, in fact, they are typically neither clear, nor stable, nor exogenous. Preferences and identities are defined ambiguously and measured crudely. They are not stable. They are likely to change between the time action is taken and the time that its outcomes are realized, so that there is a predictable difference between the intelligence of an action *a priori* and its intelligence *ex post*. Moreover, preferences and identities not only change but are likely to change as a result of the process of trying to act intelligently. As a result, the evaluative bases of action – the criteria of intelligence – are ambiguous.

In the face of these problems, organizations adopt various practices and procedures for taking action. In order to arrive at good procedures, they experiment with alternatives, copy the practices of others, consult decision theorists, and hire consultants. They adopt practices that make a credible claim of leading to intelligent actions and defend actions that lead to disasters as reflecting unfortunate outcomes of good decisions. A claim of intelligence for an action, in these terms, is a claim that it resulted from an intelligent procedure. A claim of intelligence for any particular procedure is a claim that the procedure will, in general, lead to favorable outcomes and that there are no systematic errors that are implicit in the procedure itself.

Thus, for example, the claim that rational action is intelligent is a claim that estimating the future consequences of possible current actions and choosing the one with the highest expected value will generally lead to outcomes that are evaluated as desirable in the long run. The credibility of the claim is supported primarily by an indirect route. It can be shown that, in a specific abstractly specified world, a specific rational decision procedure will yield (on average) the best decisions. The demonstrations are in many ways persuasive, but they tend to beg two questions: First, does the abstract world adequately represent the real world? Second, do real organizations when attempting to follow rational procedures in real situations produce equivalently favorable results?

It would be misleading to say that answers to these questions are firmly established by evidence. In general, the idea that intelligence can be achieved by choosing among alternative courses of action on the basis of prior preferences and estimations of likely consequences is widely accepted, but it is also widely questioned. It is not clear that the abstract world of decision theory adequately represents the real world. And when real organizations attempt to follow rational procedures in real situations it is not clear that their actions can be assured to lead to favorable results. The literature is filled with disastrous results of actions based on calculations of expected consequences. There is a substantial body of commentary that notes the difficulties of knowing what alternatives exist, of estimating the future consequences of possible current action, and of establishing valid measures of the values of those consequences. There is also considerable doubt about the way rational action treats future preferences as equivalent to current preferences. Preferences and identities change, and it is future preferences and identities that are relevant to assessing future outcomes.

Claims of intelligence for procedures based on rule-based action and organizational learning are similarly supported by two kinds of indirect observations, rather than by direct evidence. The first observation is that the processes by which rules are established involve more careful assessments of the collective and long-term consequences of individual action than can be expected from individual actors at a particular time. Specific action occurs under pressures of time and is taken by individuals and organizations with incomplete knowledge and under conditions of compressed attention, thus is unlikely to be intelligent. A system of rules allows a separation of the judgments necessary to define intelligent action from the myopic, decentralized, short-term making of decisions by particular actors. The second observation is that rules reflect the accumulation of knowledge in a way that is impossible for individual calculation. They store past experience, experience that extends over more time, individuals, and situations than any one individual's experience can. Rules retain and extend knowledge through differential survival and growth of organizations using more intelligent rules, and they reproduce by spreading from one organization to another.

There is no question that some of the experiences of organizations with learning have been positive. Organizations have been known to improve by learning from experience. They have been known to transfer knowledge to and from others. They have been known to accumulate knowledge and develop procedures for storing and retrieving it, particularly in standard procedures and rules. The evidence for the contribution of learning to intelligence is, however, mixed. Organizations learn and remember the wrong things as well as the right things. They are prone to superstitious learning. And, sometimes, learning itself produces traps for intelligence.

A persistent theme of the present book is that although they are unquestionably useful, neither rationality nor learning assures favorable outcomes. The point is not simply that outcomes are drawn from a probability distribution thus knowable in advance only up to that distribution. The argument is much more that there are systematic features of rational and learning procedures and systematic features of the interaction between those procedures and key features of organizational life that complicate the realization of intelligence. The pursuit of intelligence is frustrated by irremediable limitations of individuals and organizations, by intrinsic properties of the worlds in which organizations operate, and by unintended traps of adaptive action.

In particular, organizations (like other adaptive systems) are plagued by the difficulty of balancing exploration and exploitation. By exploration is meant such things as search, discovery, novelty, and innovation. It involves variation, risk taking, and experimentation. It commonly leads to disasters but occasionally leads to important new directions and discoveries. By exploitation is meant refinement, routinization, production, and implementation of knowledge. It involves choice, efficiency, selection, and reliability. It usually leads to improvement but often is blind to major redirections.

Both exploration and exploitation are needed for adaptation. Exploration cannot realize its occasional gains without exploitation of discoveries. Exploitation becomes obsolescent without exploration of new directions. Finding a good balance between exploration and exploitation is a recurrent problem of theories of adaptation. In rational choice theories it takes the form of deciding how much should be allocated to search (rather than execution of the currently best alternative). In learning theories it takes the form of deciding how much to experiment with new alternatives (rather than increase competence on old ones). In theories of selection it takes the form of evaluating the rate of generation of new, deviant rules (mutations). Theories of adaptation talk about balancing search and action, balancing efficiency and adaptiveness, balancing variation and selection, balancing change and stability, and balancing diversity and unity.

"Balance" is a nice word, but a cruel concept. Defining an optimum mix of exploration and exploitation is difficult or impossible. It involves trade-offs across time. It also involves trade-offs across people and across levels of a system. The optimum balance may vary from one participant to another. It may vary from an individual to an organization, or from an organization to a population of organizations. We know some things about optimal allocations to exploration and exploitation. For example, in general, the shorter the time horizon and the narrower the domain (the lower the level of integration considered), the more the optimum balance shifts toward exploitation. As that example suggests, however, the optimum is not a simple determination but depends on the time perspective and on the part of the system that is the focus of attention.

Even if it were possible to define an optimum mix of exploitation and exploration, achieving that mix would be difficult or impossible. When costs and benefits extend over time, organizations encounter several important biases. Generally, decisions are more localized than their effects, and decision makers tend to focus on nearby effects, rather than distant ones. Similarly, experiential learning is more responsive to effects that are in the temporal and spatial neighborhood than to effects that are more distant. As a result, ordinary rationality and learning are likely to underinvest in exploration. Moreover, adaptation affects subsequent adaptation. As a particular domain is explored, the pool of prospects is likely to be depleted, thus the likelihood of finding a better alternative is likely to decline over time. Competence increases with experience, thus encouraging the status quo. Aspirations change as a result of one's own experience and the experiences of others. Values shift.

Two conspicuous dynamic threats to the exploration/exploitation balance are especially relevant to organizations. The first is the failure trap, a dynamic of excessive exploration. Experiments usually fail. They fail because, on average, new ideas are poor, because incompetence with new ideas makes even good ideas less productive than they might be, and because new ideas are likely to be oversold in order to be adopted, thus to be burdened with excessive expectations. The result is a cycle of failure and exploration, running through a series of new ideas but failing to persist in any one of them long enough to discover whether it might be good.

The second dynamic threat to the balance is the success (or competency) trap – a dynamic of excessive exploitation. The rewards for exploitation tend to be more certain, nearer in time, and nearer in space than the rewards for exploration. Successful experience leads to more experience which leads to greater competence which leads to more success, and so on. The local positive feedback among experience, competence, and success generates traps of distinctive competence and results in inadequate exploration.

The complications of finding an appropriate balance between exploration and exploitation are legendary. Even if they were not, ignorance, conflict, and ambiguity combine with a changing world to make efforts to achieve intelligence endlessly challenging. This book does not resolve these problems, but examines them. It describes some ways of thinking about the relations among organizational situations, actions, and outcomes. The core of understanding the pursuit of organizational intelligence lies in coming to grips with those relations. In that spirit, the chapters focus on four general topics:

- Chapters 2 to 4 examine ideas about how decisions happen in organizations. They contrast two major conceptions of the bases of action – ideas of choice and ideas of rule-following – and consider the possibilities and limitations of seeking intelligence through such means. They elaborate a modern history of perspectives on action and the various claims made for alternative conceptions of decision making.
- Chapters 5 to 11 examine ideas about organizational learning and other forms of organizational change. They discuss some aspects of the evolution of thinking about social evolution and special features of organizational learning. In particular, these chapters explore a few of the complications involved in specifying and achieving a desirable balance between exploiting what is already known and exploring what might come to be known. They also consider some of the problems involved in comprehending a complex world on the basis of small, biased samples of experience.
- Chapters 12 to 15 examine ideas about risk taking in organizations. They consider the idea of risk preference with its associated notions of risk aversion and risk seeking. They develop a conception of variable risk preferences – risk taking that depends on the relation between aspiration levels and performance – and suggest some reasons why ordinary experiential learning will tend to produce a predilection toward risk aversion for gains and risk seeking for losses. More generally, they develop some conceptions of the role of knowledge, targets, foolishness, and identities in the taking of risks.
- Chapters 16 to 21 discuss some aspects of the giving and taking of advice in organizations. In particular, they consider some complications in consultation and expertise, the dilemmas of wisdom, the limits of cleverness, and the roles of innocence, trust, and senses of self. They examine problems of agency and conflict of interest between advice givers and advice takers. They discuss the limitations and biases of expertise, the possibilities for non-strategic advice giving, and the corruptions of consequentialist thought.

The book straddles a deep canyon that divides studies of organizations. On one side of the canyon are found studies trying to understand how things happen in organizations. Why does an organization do what it does? These studies are variously described as "descriptive," "positive," or "behavioral." They try to report organizations as they actually are. On the other side of the canyon are studies devoted to advising how an organization can be induced to produce better outcomes. How can an organization be improved? These studies are variously described as "prescriptive," "normative," or "instructional." They try to shape organizational actions to conform to models of proper decisions.

Unless you presume that competitive pressures will eliminate all organizations that fail to pursue optimal courses, the two questions are rather different. The first invites the skills and perspectives of behavioral scientists, trying to characterize the way things really are. What are the major phenomena associated with the generation of organizational action? The second invites the skills and perspectives of decision theorists, operations analysts, and economists, trying to show how things might be improved. How can an organization be made more successful or more durable?

The canyon between these two perspectives in deep. A sacred principle of organization studies is the commandment: Thou shalt not confuse behavioral (or descriptive) assertions with normative (or prescriptive) statements. Yet, many writers on organizations straddle this chasm without notable strain. They describe and they advise. Their descriptions slide into their advice (or vice versa) with the ready lubrication of a common terminology, a mixed audience, and a vigorous market for relevance. If the habit of slipping from the language of observers to the language of reformers without changing the words is an academic sin, then academic hell is crowded with students of organization.

The chapters are written primarily from the point of view of describing organizations. They are written by academics who see themselves as observing and reporting organizational life, for the most part, not reforming it. Nevertheless, many of the chapters are in the spirit of straddling the chasm. They describe how organizations operate, but with an eye to how they might be made to operate more intelligently and another eye to the major problems involved in making any assertion about the existence of a guaranteed route to intelligence. Necessarily, such a spirit invites observations of the many ways in which reforms in the name of intelligence may not serve intelligence, of the many possibilities for things that appear obvious to turn out to be misleading or wrong, and of the complexities in establishing that actions, or even outcomes, are desirable.

At the same time, however, the same spirit invites an effort to say something, however tentative, about how things might be better. We ask how to improve the exploitation of what is known; how human beings of limited capabilities for inference can confront incomplete and biased data on history and still make some sense of their experiences; how organizations can cope with the complexities of experience, particularly the way the intelligence of a particular course of action depends on the courses of action adopted by others, as well as the whole history of actions and responses to them; how it is possible to deal with sparse, redundant, confusing data; how the knowledge and actions of others can inform organizational action; how learning can be retained and spread within an organization.

We ask how organizations can improve the exploration of what might come to be known. We examine the proverbial resistance to change in organizations and conclude that knowledge and experience produce systematic biases against exploration, not because of irrational human rigidity or resistance to change but because most new ideas and practices are likely to be inferior to existing ones, particularly in the short run. In the face of this, we ask how organizations can increase the yield from experimentation with new ideas by improving the average quality of new ideas; how they can increase the quantity of new ideas by stimulating experimentation and the taking of risks; how they can increase persistence with new ideas by buffering new ideas from adverse feedback or from responding to it. The fundamental dilemma remains, however, that the quantity of new ideas and persistence in pursuing them can be increased by changing incentives or by encouraging certain forms of willfulness, ignorance, and fantasy; but increasing the number of good new ideas generally leads at the same time to increasing the number of bad new ideas, and specialists in novelty are generally short lived.

We also ask how greater wisdom can arise from the interaction of advice givers and advice takers in organizations. To a substantial extent, the observations on the giving and taking of advice are built around three themes. The first theme elaborates the idea that understanding is necessarily incomplete, that representing the full complexity of the phenomena associated with organizational intelligence would involve a level of complexity that is inaccessible to human communication. The second theme elaborates the idea that intelligent action requires a mixture of knowledge gleaned from an intimate awareness of the fine detail of a specific context and knowledge gleaned from general analytical thinking and that implementing such a mixture requires a high level of self-discipline on the part of both experts and practitioners. The third theme elaborates the idea that the human spirit requires commitment and autonomy and that great commitment comes not so much from anticipation of great consequences or the pursuit of self-conscious cleverness as from a profound sense of self and the obligations of identity.

If organizational intelligence were easier, the tale would be shorter and life would be simpler. Or, possibly, the tale would be simpler and life would be shorter. In either case, it is comforting that consideration of topics as utilitarian as decision making, learning, risk taking, and the giving of advice lead to such deep puzzles as the fundamental bases of human action, the connections between stability and change, the nature of history, the role of imagination, and the place of poetry in ordinary life. The comfort is, however, more the comfort of Søren Kierkegaard than that of Jeremy Bentham. If the chapters in this book suggest anything of a general sort, it is that the pursuit of organizational intelligence is an activity in which knowledge can sometimes produce power but more reliably produces humility.

Acknowledgments

* The research has been supported by the Spencer Foundation.

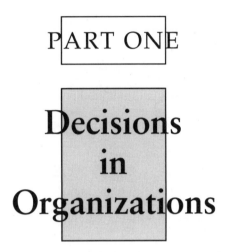

PART ONE

Decisions in Organizations

CHAPTER TWO

Understanding How Decisions Happen in Organizations

A large part of contemporary research on organizational decision making is concerned with how decisions should be made. Such research seeks techniques for improving the intelligence of actions by organizational decision makers. This chapter is, on the other hand, only incidentally concerned with how decisions should be made. It focuses on how decisions actually happen in organizations and how we might think about decision processes. It is an introduction, a sketch of ideas that might be relevant to understanding decision making in organizations.

INTRODUCTION

In one of those extraordinary epigrams that become part of the folklore of a field, James Duesenberry (1960, p. 233) said that "economics [and by analogy psychology] is all about how people make choices; sociology [and by analogy anthropology and political science] is all about how they don't have any choices to make." Students of organizational decisions locate themselves happily in the midst of the distinction, trying to understand decisions as instruments of conflict and consciousness and trying to understand conflict and consciousness as embedded in social relations, rules, norms, and constraints (Allison, 1971; Hickson, 1995; March, 1981, 1988, 1994a; Pennings, 1986; Witte & Zimmerman, 1986; Zey, 1992). They focus on decision-making processes, trying simultaneously to identify the ways in which decisions unfold within them and to understand the processes as forms of social drama and locales for creating stories.

The study of how decisions happen provides a setting for a cluster of contested issues about human action (March, 1994a:viii-ix):

> The first issue is whether decisions are to be viewed as *choice-based* or *rule-based*. Do decision makers pursue a logic of consequence, making choices among alternatives by evaluating their consequences in terms of prior preferences? Or do they pursue a logic of appropriateness, fulfilling identities or roles by recognizing situations and following rules that match appropriate behavior to the situations they encounter?
>
> The second issue is whether decision making is typified more by *clarity* and *consistency* or by *ambiguity* and *inconsistency*. Are decisions occasions in which individuals and institutions achieve coherence and reduce equivocality? Or are they occasions in which inconsistency and ambiguity are exhibited, exploited, and expanded?
>
> The third issue is whether decision making is an *instrumental* activity or an *interpretive* activity. Are decisions to be understood primarily in terms of the way they fit into a problem solving, adaptive calculus? Or are they to be understood primarily in terms of the way they fit into efforts to establish individual and social meaning?
>
> The fourth issue is whether outcomes of decision processes are seen as primarily attributable to the actions of *autonomous actors* or to the systemic properties of an *interacting ecology*. Is it possible to describe decisions as resulting from the intentions, identities, and interests of independent actors? Or is it necessary to emphasize the ways in which individual actors, organizations, and societies fit together?

The easy (and correct) resolution of these issues is to say that decisions, decision making, and decision processes in organizations are all of these things; the largest problem is not to choose among the alternatives but to weave them together in a way that allows each to illuminate the others. This chapter can be seen as an effort to contribute to that weaving and as a modest introduction to fabric design.

DECISIONS AS RATIONAL CHOICES

Virtually all of modern economics and large parts of the rest of social science, as well as the applied fields that build upon them, embrace the idea that human action is the result of human choice and that human choice is intendedly rational. Rational theories picture decision making as based on four things:

A *knowledge of alternatives*. Decision makers have a set of alternatives for action.

A *knowledge of consequences*. Decision makers know the consequences of alternative actions, at least up to a probability distribution.

A consistent preference ordering. Decision makers have consistent values by which alternative consequences of action can be compared in terms of their subjective value.

A decision rule. Decision makers have rules by which they select a single alternative of action on the basis of its consequences for the preferences.

In the most elaborated form of the model, it is assumed that all alternatives, the probability distribution of consequences conditional on each alternative, and the subjective value of each possible consequence are known. A choice is assumed to be made by selecting the alternative with the highest expected value (Schoemaker, 1982). This emphasis on expected value may be moderated by attention to other features of the outcome distribution – for example, the variability (or riskiness) of the distribution (Shapira, 1995).

The durability of this structure is impressive. It is also understandable. Simple rational choice models capture some important elements of truth. Demand curves for consumer products generally have negative slopes, and employees usually are more resistant to wage cuts than to wage increases. Moreover, the core ideas are flexible. When the model seems not to fit, it is often possible to reinterpret preferences or knowledge and preserve the axioms. Finally, choice is a faith as well as a theory. It is linked to the ideologies of the Enlightenment. It is encased in habits of speech to such an extent that ideas of willful, rational choice are the standard terms of discourse for answering the generic questions: Why did it happen? Why did you do it?

Uncertainty

Students of organizational decision making share these basic ideas of anticipatory, consequential choice, but they have modified them considerably over the past 30 years, primarily through consideration of numerous limits to rationality (Cyert & March, 1992; March & Simon, 1993). Insofar as decision making can be understood as stemming from prior preferences and expectations about consequences, it is bounded by significant individual and organizational constraints on finding and implementing an optimal solution.

The earliest empirical challenges to the simple story of rational choice questioned the information assumptions of the theory. Rational actors make two guesses about the future: a guess about the future consequences of current actions and a guess about future sentiments with respect to those consequences. Classical versions of theories of rational choice assume that both guesses are improbably precise. Actual situations in which decisions are made often seem to make each of them problematic.

The first guess – about the uncertain future consequences of current action – has long attracted attention from both students of decision making and choice theorists. Even if estimates of the consequences of alternative actions are formed and action is *intendedly* rational, there are informational and computational limits on human choice. These limits on rationality stem partly from properties of individual humans as information processors. They are unable to see clearly or interpret accurately the decision situations in which they find themselves. They simplify complex situations, using heuristics and frames to cope with information (Kahneman et al., 1982). There are limits on the number of alternatives considered and limits on the amount and accuracy of information that is available. The limits of individual human beings are modified by the organizations in which they function. In some ways, organizations are able to overcome information processing limitations, being more capable of parallel processing, of inventorying knowledge, and of mobilizing expertise (Feldman, 1989). At the same time, however, organizations introduce additional problems, problems of retention of information and communication, of coordination and conflict. As a result, virtually all modern theories of rational choice are theories of limited (or bounded) rationality (Holmstrom & Tirole, 1989; Kreps, 1990).

The core ideas of bounded rationality are elementary and by now familiar. Rather than all alternatives and all information about consequences being known, information has to be discovered through search. The key scarce resource is attention; and theories of limited rationality are, for the most part, theories of the allocation of attention (Cyert & March, 1992; March, 1988). Search is stimulated by a failure to achieve a goal and continues until it reveals an alternative that is good enough to satisfy existing evoked goals. New alternatives are sought in the neighborhood of old ones. Failure focuses search on the problem of attaining goals that have been violated; success allows search resources to move to other domains. Theories of limited rationality are also theories of slack – that is, unexploited opportunities, undiscovered economies, waste, and so on. As long as performance exceeds the goal, search for new alternatives is modest, slack accumulates, and aspirations increase. When performance falls below the goal, search is stimulated, slack is decreased, and aspirations decrease (Antonelli, 1989; Singh, 1986).

This classic system of organizational search and decision does three things to keep performance and goals close. First, it adapts goals to performance: that is, decision makers learn what they should expect. Second, it adapts performance to goals by increasing search in the face of failure and decreasing search when faced with success. And third, it adapts performance to goals by decreasing slack in response to failure and increasing slack in response to success. The result is a system that both provides resilience in the face of adversity and confounds adaptation.

In this tradition, theories of organizational choice draw rather freely from behavioral studies of individual decision making, with their emphasis on framing and human treatment of informational uncertainty (Kahneman et al., 1982; Nisbett & Ross, 1980). These efforts – in combination with concern within economic theories for the problems of incomplete information and information and transaction costs – have turned substantial parts of recent theories of choice into theories of information and attention, that is, into theories of the first guess.

Ambiguity

The second guess – about the uncertain future preferences for the consequences of current actions – has been less considered, yet poses, if anything, greater difficulties for rationality (March, 1988, chap. 13). Consider the following properties of preferences as they appear in standard theories of choice:

Preferences are *stable*. Current action is normally assumed to be taken in terms of current preferences. The implicit assumption is that preferences will be unchanged when the future outcomes of current actions are realized.

Preferences are *consistent* and *precise*. Inconsistencies or ambiguities in preferences are allowed only insofar as they do not affect choice (i.e., only insofar as they are made irrelevant by scarcity or the specification of trade-offs).

Preferences are *exogenous*. Preferences, by whatever process they are imagined to be created, are assumed to be unaffected by the choices they control.

Where preferences are studied through the revelations of a series of choices, preference consistency has been notoriously difficult to establish. Possible reasons come from examination of explicit preferences. Individuals commonly find it possible to express both a preference for something and a recognition that the preference is repugnant. They are often aware of the extent to which some of their preferences conflict with others, yet they do little to resolve those inconsistencies. Many preferences are stated in forms that lack precision. Preferences change over time in such a way that predicting future preferences is often difficult. And while preferences are used to choose among actions, it is also often true at the same time that actions and experience with their consequences affect preferences, as do deliberate efforts to control them (Greber & Jackson, 1993; Mintzberg, 1994).

Such differences between preferences as they are portrayed in theories of choice and preferences as they appear in actual decision making can be interpreted as reflecting some ordinary behavioral wisdom that is not always accommodated within the theory. Human beings seem to believe that the theory of choice exaggerates the relative power of a choice based on two guesses compared with a choice that is itself a guess. They seem to recognize the extent to which preferences are constructed, or developed, through a confrontation between preferences and actions that are inconsistent with them and among conflicting preferences. Though they seek some consistency, they appear to see inconsistency as a normal and necessary aspect of the development and clarification of preferences. They sometimes do something for no better reason than that they must, or that someone else is doing it, or that they "feel" like doing it.

Human beings act as though they recognize the many ways in which talk and action are different domains and the ways in which they serve each other by their inconsistencies (Brunsson, 1989). They accept a degree of personal and social wisdom in simple hypocrisy. They also seem to recognize the political nature of argumentation more clearly and more personally than the theory of choice does. They are unwilling to gamble that God made people who are skilled at rational argumentation uniquely virtuous. They protect themselves from cleverness, in themselves as well as in others, by obscuring and managing their preferences. They construct institutions to shape preferences (March & Olsen, 1989, 1995; Wildavsky, 1987).

Risk preference

The concept of "risk preference," like other concepts of preferences in theories of rational choice, divides students of decision making into two groups. The first group, consisting of many formal theorists of choice, treats risk preference as revealed by choices and associates it with deviations from linearity in a revealed utility for money. For this group, risk has no necessary connection to any observable behavioral rules followed by decision makers. It is simply a feature of a revealed preference function. The second group, consisting of many behavioral students of choice, emphasizes the behavioral processes by which risky choices are made or avoided. This group finds many of the factors in risk taking to be rather remote from any observable preference for taking or avoiding risk (Lopes, 1994; MacCrimmon & Wehrung, 1986; March, 1994c; Shapira, 1995).

To be sure, decision makers often attend to the relationship between opportunities and dangers, and they are often concerned about the latter; but they seem to be relatively insensitive to probability estimates when thinking about taking risks. Although theories of choice tend to treat gambling as a prototypic situation of decision making under risk, decision makers distinguish between risk taking and gambling, saying that although they should take risks, they should never gamble. They react to variability more by trying actively to avoid it or to control it than by treating it as a trade-off with expected value in making a choice (March & Shapira, 1987).

Sometimes decision makers take greater risks than they do at other times, but ideas of risk, risk taking, and risk preference are all, to some extent, inventions of students of decision making. Often the taking of risk is inadvertent, as is the avoiding of risk. The factors that affect risk taking in individuals and organizations can conveniently be divided into three categories. First, decision makers form estimates of the risk involved in a decision. Those estimates are subject to the usual human biases and affect the risk actually taken. Second, decision makers seem to have different propensities to take risks under different conditions. In particular, the propensity to take risks appears to be affected significantly by the context of success and failure in which it occurs. Third, risk taking is affected (unconsciously) by the reliability of organizational actions. Unreliability translates into the taking of risks.

In estimating risk, decision makers typically attribute uncertainty about outcomes to one or more of three different sources: an inherently unpredictable world, incomplete knowledge about the world, and incomplete contracting with strategic actors. Each of these produces efforts to reduce uncertainty. For uncertainties that are thought to arise from inherently uncertain environmental processes, decision makers try to judge the likelihood of events. In general, decision makers do rather well in estimating future probabilities in situations in which they have experience. However, they use estimating heuristics that lead them astray at times. For example, events are judged to be more likely to the extent that they are representative. The most prototypical events are, however, not always the most frequent. In particular, decision makers tend to overlook important information about the base rates of events (Kahneman et al., 1982; Shapira, 1995).

Estimations of risk are systematically biased by the experiences decision makers have in organizations. Individuals are normally elevated to positions of decision-making authority by virtue of their past successes. Success makes them confident about their ability to handle future events, leading them to believe strongly in their wisdom and insight. They have difficulty in recognizing the role of luck in their achievements (Langer, 1975; Taylor & Brown, 1988). As a result, successful decision makers tend to underestimate the risk they have experienced and the risk they currently face, and intentionally risk-averse decision makers may actually be risk seeking in behavior (Kahneman & Lovallo, 1993; Keyes, 1985; March & Shapira, 1987).

For uncertainties that arise from gaps or ambiguities in their knowledge of the environment, decision makers assume that uncertainty can be removed by diligence and imagination. They try to judge and, if possible, improve the quality of information. They have a strong tendency to want their knowledge about what will happen to be couched in terms that deny doubt. They are more likely to seek to confirm their existing information than to acquire or notice disconfirming information. They prefer informa-tion about specific cases to information about general trends. They prefer vivid information to pallid information. They prefer concrete information to abstract statistics. When confronted with inconsistent information, they tend to rely on a few cues and exclude others from consideration (Shapira, 1995).

To deal with uncertainties stemming from incomplete contracting, decision makers develop intelligence systems designed to spy on the intentions of others. They pursue resources to remove dependence on others (Pfeffer & Salancik, 1978). And they try to bind others to desired future actions rather than to predict them probabilistically.

The level of risk taking observed in organizations is affected not only by estimations of risk but also by the propensity of a risk taker to seek or avoid a particular level of expected risk. The evidence for variation among decision makers in individually stable risk-taking propensities is mixed, but it seems plausible to suspect that some such variations exist, that there may be consistent differences among people and even consistent differences among cultures or subcultures. However, the evidence also seems to indicate that, at least within a given culture, the risk-taking effects attributable to trait differences in risk propensity are relatively small compared to other effects.

Probably the best-established situational effect stems from the way decision makers distinguish between situations of success (or expected success) and situations of failure (or expected failure). Risk-taking propensity varies with the relationship between an individual's position and a target or aspiration level, and thus between contexts of success and failure (Payne et al., 1980, 1981; Singh, 1986). When they are in the neighborhood of a target and are given a choice between two items of equal expected value, decision makers tend to choose the less risky alternative if outcomes involve gains and the more risky alternative if outcomes involve losses (Bromiley, 1991; Kahneman & Tversky, 1979).

When individuals find themselves well above the target, they tend to take greater risks – partly presumably because in that position they have little chance of failing and partly because they may be inattentive to their actions as a result of the large cushion. The risk-taking propensities of decision makers who are well below a target are more complicated, especially when their position puts them in danger of not surviving. On the one hand, as they fall further and further below their targets, they tend to take bigger and bigger risks, presumably to increase the chance of achieving their targets. On the other hand, as they come closer and closer to extinction, they tend to become rigid and immobile, repeating previous actions and avoiding risk (Staw et al., 1981). Since falling further from a target and falling closer to extinction are normally correlated, the effect of failure on risk taking appears to depend on whether decision makers focus attention on their hopes or their fears (Lopes, 1987; March & Shapira, 1992).

Risks may also be taken as a consequence of unreliability – breakdowns in competence, communication, coordination, trust, responsibility, or structure. Ignorance is a major source of variability in the distribution of possible outcomes from an action. As decision makers become more knowledgeable, they improve their average performance and reduce their unreliability. Similarly, social controls tend to increase reliability, thus decreasing risk taking. The mechanisms by which controls grow looser and tighter, or become more or less effective, are only marginally connected to conscious risk taking, but they affect the actual level of risk exhibited by decision makers.

DECISIONS AS RULE-BASED ACTIONS

A conception of decision making as resulting from consequential, preference-driven choice is not always accepted as axiomatic. In particular, it has been argued that theories of rational, anticipatory, calculated, consequential action underestimate both the pervasiveness and intelligence of an alternative decision logic – the logic of appropriateness, obligation, duty, and rules (Burns & Flam, 1987; March & Olsen, 1989; March & Simon, 1993). Much of the decision-making behavior we observe reflects the routine way in which people seek to fulfill their identities. For example, most of the time, most people in organizations follow rules even when it is not obviously in their self-interest to do so. Much of the behavior in an organization is specified by standard operating procedures, professional standards, cultural norms, and institutional structures linked to conceptions of identity.

Actual decisions in organizations, as in individuals, seem often to involve finding appropriate rules to follow. The logic of appropriateness differs from the logic of consequence. Rather than evaluating alternatives in terms of the values of their consequences, it matches situations and identities. Thus, it includes the following factors:

Situation. Decision makers classify situations into distinct categories that are associated with identities or rules.

Identity. Decision makers have a conception of their personal, professional, and official identities and evoke particular identities in particular situations.

Matching. Decision makers do what they see as appropriate to their identity in the situation in which they find themselves.

Such identity fulfillment and rule following are not willful in the normal sense. They do not stem from the pursuit of interests and the calculation of future consequences of current choices. Rather, they come from matching a changing (and often ambiguous) set of contingent rules and identities to a changing (and often ambiguous) set of situations (Turner, 1985). The terminology is one of duties and roles rather than anticipatory, consequential choice. Choices are often made without much regard for preferences. Actions reflect images of proper behavior, and human decision makers routinely ignore their own fully conscious preferences. They act not on the basis of subjective consequences and preferences but on the basis of rules, routines, procedures, practices, identities, and roles (Anderson, 1983; Biddle, 1986; March & Simon, 1993). They follow traditions, hunches, cultural norms, and the advice or action of others.

The use of rules and standard operating procedures in routine situations is well known, but their importance is not limited to routine worlds. Behavior in ill-defined situations also often follows from identity-driven conceptions of appropriateness more than from conscious calculations of costs and benefits (Ashforth & Mael, 1989; Schlenker, 1982). Individuals follow heuristics in solving ambiguous problems, and they seek to fulfill identities in novel situations. The uncertainties of decision making are less lack of clarity about the consequences of action and decision-maker preferences than they are lack of clarity about the demands of a logic of appropriateness. Decisions are derived from reasoning about the nature of an identity and a situation, reasoning that invokes cognitive processes of interpretation and social processes of forming accounts (Tetlock, 1992). The rules that match a situation and an identity may be developed through experience, learned from others, or generalized from similar situations.

Rule development

Rules evolve over time, and current rules store information generated by previous experience and analysis in a form not easily retrieved for systematic current evaluation. Seeing rules as coded information has led several recent studies of organizational decision making to focus on the ways in which rules change and develop (Schulz, 1992; Zhou, 1993) and to questions of the long-run intelligence of rule following, thus to some classical puzzles of culture, history, and population biology (March, 1994b).

Four major processes by which rules develop are commonly considered. First, rules can be seen as chosen consciously and accepted rationally by actors who calculate the expected consequences of their actions. From this perspective, rule following can be viewed as contractual, an agreement among rational parties to be bound jointly by a set of norms and conventions of behavior. Such a contractual view has led game theorists to an interest in interpreting norms and institutions as meta-game agreements among rational actors (Shepsle & Weingast, 1987).

Second, it is possible to see an organization or a society as learning from its experience, modifying its rules for action incrementally on the basis of feedback from the environment (Huber, 1991; Levitt & March, 1988). Such experiential learning is often adaptively rational. That is, it allows organizations to find good, even optimal, rules for many choices they are likely to face. However, learning from experience can produce surprises. Learning can be superstitious, and it can lead to local optima that are quite distant from the global optimum. If goals adapt rapidly to experience, outcomes that are good may be interpreted as failures and outcomes that are poor may be interpreted as successes. If technological strategies are learned quickly relative to the development of competence, an organization can easily adopt technologies that are intelligent given the existing levels of competence, but it may fail to invest in enough experience with a suboptimal technology to discover that it would become the dominant choice with additional competence. Such anomalies are frequent and important (Arthur, 1989; Levinthal & March, 1993).

Third, decision making can be seen as reflecting rules that spread through a group of organizations like fads or measles. Decision makers copy each other. Imitation is a common feature of ordinary organizational adaptation (Fligstein, 1985; March, 1991; Sevón, 1996; Westney, 1987). If we want to account for the adoption of accounting conventions, for example, we normally would look to ways in which standard accounting procedures diffuse through a population of accountants. We would observe that individual accountants rather quickly adopt those rules of good practice that are certified by professional associations and implemented by opinion leaders (DiMaggio & Powell, 1983). Like learning and selection, imitation often makes sense, but not always. The processes by which knowledge diffuses and the processes by which fads diffuse are remarkably similar.

Fourth, the population of rules can be seen as an evolving collection of invariant rules (Axelrod, 1984; Baum & Singh, 1994; Hannan & Freeman, 1989; Nelson & Winter, 1982). As with experiential learning, rules are dependent on history, but the mechanism is different. Individual rules are invariant, but the population of rules changes over time through differential survival and extension. Evolutionary arguments about the development of decision rules were originally made to justify the assumption that decision makers maximize expected utility. The argument was simple: Competition for scarce resources resulted in differential survival of decision makers, depending on whether the rules produced decisions that were, in fact, optimal. Thus, it was argued, we could assume that surviving rules (whatever their apparent character) were optimal.

Although the argument about the efficiency of historical processes in discovering optima had a certain charm to it, most close students of selection models have suggested that selection will not reliably guarantee a population of rules that is optimal at any arbitrary point in time (Carroll & Harrison, 1994; March, 1994b). In fact, the intelligence of rules is not guaranteed but depends on a fairly subtle intermeshing of rates of change, consistency, and foolishness. At the least, intelligence seems to require occasional deviation from the rules, some general consistency between adaptation rates and environmental rates of change, and a reasonable likelihood that networks of imitation are organized in a manner that allows intelligent action to be diffused somewhat more rapidly and more extensively than silliness.

Rule implementation

For most students of decision making who emphasize rules, socialization into rules and following them is ordinarily not a case of willful entering into an explicit contract. Rather, it is a set of understandings of the nature of things, of self-conceptions, and of images of proper behavior. These conceptions are often taken for granted. The implementation of taken-for-granted rules is not automatic, however. A rule basis for action ensures neither consistency nor simplicity. Rules are often ambiguous; more than one rule may apply in a particular situation; and the behavior required by the rule may be shaped through interpretation (Bardach, 1977; Pressman & Wildavsky, 1973).

As they try to understand history and self, and as they try to improve the often confusing, uncertain, and ambiguous world they live in, individuals and organizations interpret what rules and identities exist, which ones are relevant, and what different rules and identities demand in specific situations. Individuals may have a difficult time resolving conflicts among contending imperatives of appropriateness, that is, among alternative concepts of the self (Elster, 1986). They may not know what to do. Or they may know what to do but not have the capabilities to do it. They are limited by the resources and competencies they possess.

These indeterminancies lead rule-based theories of action to distinguish between a rule and its realization in a specific case. The processes of constructive interpretation, criticism, and justification through which rules and identities are translated into behavior have to be specified. Implementation of rules can be treated as simply another form of rational action in which choices are made among alternative interpretations in terms of expectations of consequences for the actor's interests. Thus, rules can be seen as interpreted in ways that favor the interpreter and as implemented in ways that favor the implementer (Downs, 1967; Tullock, 1965). In this perspective, ambiguities and conflicts are resolved by calculation, and disagreements over interpretations are results of conflicts of interest.

Although rule interpretation certainly involves various forms of self-interested calculation, it also involves a somewhat different cognitive process – an effort to match rules to situations through analogies and similar forms of recognizing similarities among situations and rules. Identities are clarified by reference to related identities; rules are clarified by reference to comparable rules; situations are clarified by reference to analogous situations. The clarifications are frequently made particularly problematic by the ambiguity of rules, an ambiguity that may itself be a natural result of policy making (Baier et al., 1986; Page, 1976).

DECISION MAKING AND SENSE MAKING

Decision making is intimately linked to sense making. The forming of preferences, identities, rules, situations, and expectations all involve making sense out of a confusing world. As a result, students of decision making are preeminently students of the ways in which individuals and organizations make sense of their pasts, their natures, and their futures (Berger & Luckmann, 1966; Fiske & Taylor, 1984; March et al., 1991). At the same time, decision making contributes to the sense making from which it draws. As individuals and organizations make decisions, they transform their preferences and their identities and shape the worlds they interpret. Thus, it is possible to see the construction of meaning as both an input and an output of decision making.

Sense making as an input to decision making

With the possible but limited exception of theories that emphasize temporal order, all major theories of decision making picture action as thoughtful in the sense that they assume some processes that code situations into terms meaningful to a decision maker. As a result, a description of decision making as "rational" or "rule based" is incomplete without clarifying the ways in which individual and organizational processes shape the premises of either. Theories of rational action assume that decision makers make sense of their situation by forming expectations about future consequences and preferences for those consequences. Theories of rule-based action assume that decision makers make sense of their situation by identifying situations as matching identities and rules and by interpreting the implications of those matches. Decisions are seen as predicated on these meanings that are established prior to action.

Much of the research on a behavioral theory of decision making focuses on how individuals process information in order to provide meaning in decision making (March & Sevón, 1988). Among many other things, this research has shown that individuals frequently edit and simplify situations, ignoring some information and focusing on other information. They frequently try to decompose problems into subproblems, ignoring interactions and working backward from desired outcomes to necessary preconditions. They recognize patterns in situations and apply rules of thumb that are believed to be appropriate for the particular situation. They adopt frames and paradigms that tend to emphasize aspects of a decision problem that are found in their own spatial and temporal neighborhoods. They create "magic numbers" (e.g., "profit," "cost of living") for complex phenomena, treating the numbers as equivalent to the more complex reality they represent. They interpret experience in ways that tend to conserve their prior beliefs and their own importance (Fiske & Taylor, 1984; Kuran, 1988; Nisbett & Ross, 1980).

The research similarly emphasizes the ways in which decision makers give meaning to their aspirations. Which preferences and identities are evoked and in what form? Studies of preferences suggest that information about preferences is simplified in many of the same ways other information is. Not all preferences are considered, and the processes by which some are evoked and others are not is important for decision making. Similarly, evaluation of performance relative to a particular dimension of preferences is simplified by setting targets (levels of aspiration) that define when things are acceptable and reduce attention to gradations of acceptability. Studies of identities indicate that the evocation and interpretation of a particular identity is influenced by social and experiential cues that define some identities as relevant and others as not.

Sense making as an output of decision making

A central commitment of standard conceptions of decision making is to the notion of outcome significance. Both theories of rational decision making and theories of rule-based decision making treat decision outcomes as the primary product of a decision process. Decision makers are assumed to enter the process in order to affect decision outcomes. They establish meaning prior to making decisions in order to reduce uncertainty and ambiguity. The significance of sense making lies in its effects on decision outcomes.

Studies of decision arenas, on the other hand, often seem to describe a set of processes that make little sense in such terms. Decisions often seem to be only loosely linked to the information gathered for making them. Discussions leading to decisions seem to be filled with apparently irrelevant matters, and the postdecision elaboration of justification often seems to be considerably more extensive than the exploration of reasons before a decision. These anomalous observations appear to reflect, at least in part, the extent to which meaning is not only a premise of decision making but also a result of it (March & Sevón, 1984).

Decision making shapes meanings even as it is shaped by them. A choice process provides an occasion for developing and diffusing interpretations of history and current conditions, as well as for mutual construction of theories of life. It is an occasion for defining virtue and truth, discovering or interpreting what is happening, what decision makers have been doing, and what justifies their actions. It is an occasion for distributing glory and blame for what has happened, and thus an occasion for exercising, challenging, and reaffirming friendship and trust relationships, antagonisms, and power and status relationships. Decisions and decision making play a major role in the development of the meaning and interpretations that decisions are based upon (March & Olsen, 1976).

This coevolution of meaning and decisions creates two major complications in understanding decision making. The first complication is connected to the simultaneity of the construction of meaning and the making of decisions. Most theories of choice assume some kind of consistency between actions taken and their premises. Thus, theories of rational choice assume that action will be made consistent with expectations and preferences; and theories of rule-based choice assume that action will be made consistent with a definition of the situation and the demands of identity. Almost without exception, such theories treat the premises as antecedent to the action with which they are associated and consider choice to be primarily a process of making action consistent with the premises.

Observations of decision making suggest a much more interactive relation between action and its premises (March, 1994a). Preferences and identities develop in the context of making choices. Actions come first, and premises are made consistent with them. Individuals and organizations discover their wants by making choices and experiencing the reactions of others as well as of themselves. The idea that decisions are made to reflect beliefs is paired with the idea that beliefs are formed to reflect decisions. This elementary coevolutionary feature of decision making and its premises makes their tendency to consistency both more profound and less helpful as an aid in predicting decision outcomes.

The second complication comes from the recognition that decision making may, in many ways, be better conceived as a meaning factory than as an action factory. Decision outcomes are often not as central to an understanding of decision making as might be expected. Individuals and organizations write history and construct socially acceptable story lines about links between actions and consequences, identities and behaviors. Decision making is a prime arena for developing and enjoying an interpretation of life and one's position in it. As a result, the link between the collection and display of information and its use in affecting decisions is weak (Feldman & March, 1981). Contentiousness in the discussion of alternative policies of an organization is often followed by apparent indifference about the implementation of a decision among them (Christensen, 1976).

The usual terminology in discussions of these apparent anomalies emphasizes the symbolic significance of decision participation, process, and manifest outcomes (Arnold, 1935; Edelman, 1964). For example, individuals fight for the right to participate in decision processes but then do not exercise the right. The rituals and symbols of decision making are important. The meanings involved may be as local as the ego needs of specific individuals and groups. They may be as global as confirming the central ideologies of a society or subculture.

It is hard to imagine a society committed to reason and rational justification that would not exhibit a well-elaborated and ritualized myth of choice, both to sustain social orderliness and meaning and to facilitate change. On the one hand, the processes of choice reassure those involved that a choice has been made intelligently; that it reflects planning, thinking, analysis, and the systematic use of information; and that the choice is sensitive to the concerns of relevant people – that is, that the right people are involved. At the same time, the processes of choice reassure those involved of their own significance. In particular, the symbols are used to reinforce the idea that managers (and managerial decisions) affect the performance of organizations, and do so properly.

Thus, we are led to a perspective that questions the idea, central to many modern theories of action, that life can be conceived as a sequence of choices. The alternative, well articulated in theories of literature but less familiar to theories of action, is that life is more concerned with forming interpretations than with making choices. It is a perspective in which outcomes are seen as less significant – both behaviorally and ethically – than processes. Processes give meaning to life, and meaning is the core of life. The grander forms of such a view glorify symbols, myths, and rituals as fundamental to comprehending the way decisions happen, and particularly the disconnection between decision making and decisions.

DECISION-MAKING ECOLOGIES

By emphasizing the making of decisions, theories of organizational decision making tend to focus on what is happening at a particular place (the decision-making body), in the heads of particular persons (the decision makers), and at a particular time (the time the decision is made). Such portrayals seem to underestimate the systemic properties of decision-making organizations. They tend to ignore the significance of the interactive conflict, confusion, and complexity surrounding actual decision making. The observations are familiar. Many things are happening at once, and they affect each other. Actions in one part of an organization are not coherently coupled to actions in other parts, but they shape each other. Many of the features of decision making are due less to the intentions or identities of individual actors than to the systemic properties of their interactions.

Decision making is embedded in a social context that is itself simultaneously shaped by decision making in other organizations. Premises and actions in one organization coevolve with those in other organizations. This interactive character of decision making extends over time so that the development of beliefs, rules, and expectations in one organization is intertwined with their development in others. Organizational histories, as well as interpretations of those histories, are formed through social interactions that make it difficult to understand decisions in any one organization at any one time without understanding those of other organizations and over time. Competition, cooperation, and imitation lead organizations to shape each other's decisions and decision making (Matsuyama, 1995). Since different parts of the system are connected developmentally in this way, their evolutionary path is more difficult to anticipate than in a world in which the environment can be taken as given and the primary issue is the extent and form of organizational adaptation to it.

Examining these connections and their effects requires what might be called an "ecological" vision of decision making, a vision that considers how the structure of relationships among individual units interacts with the behavior of these units to produce systemic properties not easily attributable to the individual behavior alone. Recent research on organizations has emphasized concepts of decision making that highlight such a vision. These include an emphasis on the interaction among individuals and groups with inconsistent preferences or identities rather than single decision makers; the idea that decision making is organized by time rather than causality; and the idea that the premises of decision making coevolve with the actions based on them.

Interactive inconsistencies

As numerous observers have noted, an obvious difficulty with describing organizational decision making in terms of a theory of autonomous individual choice or rule following is that organizations are not individuals but rather collections of individuals interconnected in many ways. In particular, individual identities and preferences are often mutually inconsistent, producing conflict and confusion (Coleman, 1986; March, 1981).

In standard choice theory, inconsistency among preferences is treated as a problem of assessing trade-offs, establishing marginal rates of substitution among goods. The process *within* individuals is mediated by an unspecified mechanism by which individuals are imagined to be able to make value comparisons among alternatives. The process *among* individuals is mediated by an explicit or implicit price system. In classical theories of the firm, for example, an organization is transformed into an individual by assuming that markets (particularly markets for labor, capital, and products) convert conflicting demands into prices. In this perspective, entrepreneurs are imagined to impose their goals on an organization in exchange for mutually satisfactory wages paid to workers, returns on investment paid to capital, and product characteristics paid to customers. Similarly, inconsistencies among identities or rules are treated as requiring priorities so that some take precedence over others. Organizations arrange priorities through hierarchies that both buffer rules from the consciousness of others and create orders of precedence and subordination among rules and identities.

Such processes can be treated as yielding a series of understandings by which participants divide decision making into two stages (March & Simon, 1993). At the first stage, the individuals negotiate understandings about ways of coordinating their separate behaviors. Each individual negotiates the best possible terms for agreeing to act in ways consistent with another's preferences or rules. At the second stage, individuals execute the understandings. In more sophisticated versions, of course, the understandings are designed so that the terms negotiated at the first stage are self-enforcing at the second. This two-stage vision is characteristic of much of the modern work in agency theory and applications of game theory to economic behavior (Kreps, 1990; Milgrom & Roberts, 1992), as it is of much classical administrative theory (March & Simon, 1993).

Seeing participants as having conflicting preferences and identities is also a basic feature of political visions of decision making. In political treatments, however, the emphasis is less on designing a system of understandings between principals and agents, or partners, than it is on understanding a political process that allows decisions to happen without necessarily resolving inconsistencies among the parties. The usual metaphors are those of "force" or "power," negotiation, exchange, and alliance (March, 1994a). In an exchange process, power comes either from having things that others want or from wanting things that others do not. Thus, it comes from the possession of resources and from the idiosyncrasy of desires, rules, or identities. In a preference pooling process, power comes from having resources and from having preferences near the center of society's preferences, that is, having identities that are broadly consistent with others (March & Olsen, 1989).

Picturing decisions as being based on an ecology of inconsistent preferences and identities seems to come closer to the truth in many situations than does assuming a single, consistent preference function or a collection of consistent identities and rules. Somewhat more problematic is the second feature of many of the behavioral studies of decision making under inconsistency – the tendency for the political aspects of decision making to be interminable. If it were possible to imagine a two-step process in which *first* a set of joint preferences and identities is established through side payments, formation of coalitions, and creation of a hierarchical structure of rules and identities, and *second* action is guided by those preferences and identities, we could treat the first stage as defining the constraints of action and the second stage as acting within them. Such a division has often been tempting (e.g., the distinction between policy making and administration, the distinction between "institutions" and "norms" and decision making within them), but it has rarely been satisfactory as a description of decision making. The decision processes we observe seem to be infused with strategic actions and negotiations at every level and every point (March, 1981). From this character of decision making has come the elaborate complications of what is usually called "implementation" – the relation between decisions as "made" and decisions as "realized" (Bardach, 1977).

In general, the machinations of strategic actors seem likely to produce a complicated concatenation of maneuver in which information has considerably less value than might be expected if strategic considerations were not so pervasive. That this process does not completely destroy meaning in organizational communication is a considerable testimony to the importance of trust in understanding organizational relations. In a conflict system, alliances involve understandings across time. Rarely can agreements be specified with precision. It is not a world of precise contracts but of informal, loose understandings and expectations. As a result, decision making often emphasizes trust and loyalty, in parallel with a widespread belief that these qualities are hard to find and sustain, and power comes from being thought to be trustworthy. Modern research on games of repeated interaction and iterated calculation among rational actors and on norms of enduring relationships has called into question some once standard recommendations for cleverness in bargaining and has moved trust and reputation to a central position in theories of multiactor decision making (Gibbons, 1992; Milgrom & Roberts, 1992).

Temporal orders

The ecological nature of decision making gives it an aura of disorderliness. Pierre Romelaer and I once described organizational decision processes as funny soccer games: "Consider a round, sloped, multigoal field on which individuals play soccer. Many different people (but not everyone) can join the game (or leave it) at different times. Some people can throw balls into the game or remove them. While they are in the game, individuals try to kick whatever ball comes near them in the direction of goals they like and away from goals they wish to avoid" (March & Romelaer, 1976, p. 275).

Observations of the disorderliness in organizational decision making have led some people to argue that there is very little order to it, that it is best described as random. A more common position, however, is that the ways in which organizations bring order to disorder is less hierarchical and less based on means–ends chains than is anticipated by conventional theories. There is order, but it is not conventional order. In particular, it is argued that any decision process involves a collection of individuals and groups who are simultaneously involved in other things. Understanding decisions in one arena requires an understanding of how those decisions fit into the lives of participants.

From this point of view, the loose coupling that we observe in a specific decision situation is a consequence of our theories. The apparent confusion is understandable as resulting from a shifting intermeshing of the demands on the attention and lives of the whole array of actors. It is possible to see any particular decision as the consequence of combining different moments of different lives. A more limited version of the same fundamental idea focuses on the allocation of attention. The idea is simple: Individuals attend to some things and thus do not attend to others. The attention devoted to a particular decision by a particular potential participant depends on alternative claims on attention.

Since those alternative claims are not homogeneous across participants and change over time, the attention any particular decision receives can be both unstable and remarkably independent of the properties of the decision (Kingdon, 1984). The same decision will attract much attention or little, depending on the other things that possible participants might be doing. The apparently erratic character of decision making is made somewhat more explicable by placing it in this context of multiple, changing claims on attention.

Such ideas have been generalized to deal with flows of solutions and problems, as well as with participants in what has come to be called a "garbage-can decision process" (Cohen & March, 1986; March & Olsen, 1976). In a garbage-can process, it is assumed that there are exogenous, time-dependent arrivals of choice opportunities, problems, solutions, and decision makers. Problems and solutions are attached to choices, and thus to each other, not because of their means–ends linkage but in terms of their temporal proximity. At the limit, for example, almost any solution can be associated with almost any problem – provided that they are contemporaries. The temporal pooling is, however, constrained by social and organizational structures (Levitt & Nass, 1989; March & Olsen, 1986).

CONCLUSION

Research on organizational decision making has influenced contemporary ideas about action throughout the social sciences. The grandest tradition of research, however, is to increase ignorance at the same time as it increases knowledge. Any consideration of the study of organizational decision making would have to conclude that it is well within that tradition. We know more than we used to know, and some of the things we know are now well encased in theoretical forms. In particular, simple ideas about rational actors and role players that were used to represent decision making 50 years ago have been elaborated and extended substantially. Ideas that emphasize limits on rationality and inconsistency in preferences and identities have become the received doctrine underlying most theories of organizational decision making.

The price of such knowledge is consciousness of other difficulties. Awareness of the instability, inconsistency, and endogeneity of preferences and identities; of the sense-making complications in acting according to either a logic of consequence or a logic of appropriateness; of the importance of decision processes for the construction of meaning; of the interactive, ecological nature of decision making; and of the potential inefficiency of history in ensuring unique optima in behavior or rules is now widely stated and some progress in dealing with such things is observable, but we are a long way from being able to deal with all of them.

Acknowledgments

This chapter is based substantially on March (1994a). The research has been supported financially by the Spencer Foundation and the Stanford

Graduate School of Business, and in many other ways by the Scandinavian Consortium for Organizational Research.

References

Allison, G. T. (1971). *Essence of decision: Explaining the Cuban missile crisis*. Boston: Little, Brown.

Anderson, J. R. (1983). *The architecture of cognition*. Cambridge, MA: Harvard University Press.

Antonelli, C. (1989). A failure-induced model of research and development expenditure: Italian evidence from the early 1980s. *Journal of Economic Behavior and Organization, 12,* 159–80.

Arnold, T. (1935). *The symbols of government*. New Haven, CT: Yale University Press.

Arthur, W. B. (1989). Competing technologies, increasing returns, and lock-ins by historical events. *Economic Journal, 99,* 116–31.

Ashforth, B. E., & Mael, F. (1989). Social identity theory and the organization. *Academy of Management Review, 14,* 20–39.

Axelrod, R. M. (1984). *The evolution of cooperation*. New York: Basic Books.

Baier, V. E., March, J. G., & Sætren, H. (1986). Implementation and ambiguity. *Scandinavian Journal of Management Studies, 2,* 197–212.

Bardach, E. (1977). *The implementation game*. Cambridge, MA: MIT Press.

Baum, J., & Singh, J. (Eds). (1994). *The evolutionary dynamics of organizations*. New York: Oxford University Press.

Berger, P. L., & Luckmann, T. (1966). *The social construction of reality: A treatise in the sociology of knowledge*. New York: Doubleday.

Biddle, B. J. (1986). Recent developments in role theory. *Annual Review of Sociology, 12,* 67–92.

Bromiley, P. (1991). Testing a causal model of corporate risk-taking and performance. *Academy of Management Journal, 34,* 37–59.

Brunsson, N. (1989). *The organization of hypocrisy*. Chichester, England: Wiley.

Burns, T. R., & Flam, H. (1987). *The shaping of social organization: Social rule system theory with applications*. London: Sage.

Carroll, G. R., & Harrison, J. R. (1994). On the historical efficiency of competition between organizational populations. *American Journal of Sociology, 100,* 720–49.

Christensen, S. (1976). Decision making and socialization. In J. G. March & J. P. Olsen, *Ambiguity and choice in organizations* (pp. 351–85). Bergen, Norway: Universitetsforlaget.

Cohen, M. D., & March, J. G. (1986). *Leadership and ambiguity: The American college president* (2nd ed.) Boston: Harvard Business School Press.

Coleman, J. S. (1986). *Individual interests and collective action*. Cambridge: Cambridge University Press.

Cyert, R. M., & March, J. G. (1992). *A behavioral theory of the firm* (2nd edn). Oxford: Blackwell.

DiMaggio, P. J., & Powell, W. W. (1983). The iron cage revisited: Institutional isomorphism and collective rationality in organizational fields. *American Sociological Review, 48,* 147–60.

Downs, A. (1967). *Inside bureaucracy*. Boston: Little, Brown.

Duesenberry, J. (1960). Comment on

"An economic analysis of fertility." In National Bureau Committee for Economic Research. *Demographic and Economic Change in Developed Countries* (pp. 231–4). Princeton, NJ: Princeton University Press.

Edelman, M. (1964). *The symbolic uses of politics*. Urbana, IL: University of Illinois Press.

Elster, J. (1986). *The multiple self*. Cambridge: Cambridge University Press.

Feldman, M. S. (1989). *Order without design: Information production and policy making*. Stanford, CA: Stanford University Press.

Feldman, M. S., & March, J. G. (1981). Information in organizations as signal and symbol. *Administrative Science Quarterly*, 26, 171–86.

Fiske, S. T., & Taylor, S. E. (1984). *Social cognition*. Reading, MA: Addison-Wesley.

Fligstein, N. J. (1985). The spread of the multidivisional form among large firms, 1919–1979. *American Sociological Review*, 50, 377–91.

Gibbons, R. (1992). *Game theory for applied economists*. Princeton, NJ: Princeton University Press.

Greber, E. R., & Jackson, J. E. (1993). Endogenous preferences and the study of institutions. *American Political Science Review*, 87, 639–56.

Hannan, M. T., & Freeman, J. (1989). *Organizational ecology*. Cambridge, MA: Harvard University Press.

Hickson, D. J. (Ed.). (1995). *Managerial decision making*. Dartmouth, NH: Aldershot.

Holmstrom, B. R., & Tirole, J. (1989). The theory of the firm. In R. Schmalensee and R. D. Willig (Eds), *Handbook of industrial organization* (vol. 1, pp. 61–133). New York: Elsevier.

Huber, G. P. (1991). Organizational learning: The contributing processes and the literature. *Organization Science*, 2, 88–115.

Kahneman, D., & Lovallo, D. (1993). Timid choice and bold forecasts: A cognitive perspective on risk taking. *Management Science*, 39, 17–31.

Kahneman, D., Slovic, P., & Tversky, A. (eds). (1982). *Judgment under uncertainty: Heuristics and biases*. Cambridge: Cambridge University Press.

Kahneman, D., & Tversky, A. (1979). Prospect theory: An analysis of decision under risk. *Econometrica*, 47, 263–91.

Keyes, R. (1985). *Chancing it*. Boston: Little, Brown.

Kingdon, J. W. (1984). *Agendas, alternatives, and public policies*. Boston: Little, Brown.

Kreps, D. M. (1990). *A course in microeconomic theory*. Princeton, NJ: Princeton University Press.

Kuran, T. (1988). The tenacious past: Theories of personal and collective conservatism. *Journal of Economic Behavior and Organization*, 10, 143–71.

Langer, B. J. (1975). The illusion of control. *Journal of Personality and Social Psychology*, 32, 311–28.

Levinthal, D. A., & March, J. G. (1993). The myopia of learning. *Strategic Management Journal*, 14, 95–112.

Levitt, B., & March, J. G. (1988). Organizational learning. *Annual Review of Sociology*, 14, 319–40.

Levitt, B., & Nass, C. (1989). The lid on the garbage can: Institutional constraints on decision making in the technical core of college-text publishers. *Administrative Science Quarterly*, 34, 190–207.

Lopes, L. L. (1987). Between hope and fear: The psychology of risk. *Advances in Experimental Social Psychology*, 20, 255–95.

Lopes, L. L. (1994). Psychology and

economics: Perspectives on risk, co-operation, and the marketplace. *Annual Review of Psychology*, 45, 197–227.

MacCrimmon, K. R., & Wehrung, D. A. (1986). *Taking risks: The management of uncertainty.* New York: Free Press.

March, J. G. (1981). Decisions in organizations and theories of choice. In A. Van de Ven and W. Joyce (eds), *Perspectives on organizational design and performance* (pp. 205–44). New York: Wiley.

March, J. G. (1988). *Decisions and organizations.* Oxford: Blackwell.

March, J. G. (1991). Organizational consultants and organizational research. *Journal of Applied Communications Research*, 19, 20–31.

March, J. G. (1994a). *A primer on decision making: How decisions happen.* New York: Free Press.

March, J. G. (1994b). The evolution of evolution. In J. Baum & J. Singh (eds), *The evolutionary dynamics of organizations* (pp. 39–49). New York: Oxford University Press.

March, J. G. (1994c). *Three lectures on efficiency and adaptiveness in organizations.* Helsinki: Svenska Handelshögskolan.

March, J. G., & Olsen, J. P. (1976). *Ambiguity and choice in organizations.* Bergen, Norway: Universitetsforlaget.

March, J. G., & Olsen, J. P. (1986). Garbage can models of decision making in organizations. In J. G. March & R. Weissinger-Baylon (eds), *Ambiguity and command* (pp. 11–36). Cambridge, MA: Ballinger.

March, J. G., & Olsen J. P. (1989). *Rediscovering organizations: The organizational basis of politics.* New York: Free Press.

March, J. G., & Olsen, J. P. (1995). *Democratic governance.* New York: Free Press.

March, J. G., & Romelaer, P. (1976). Position and presence in the drift of decisions. In J. G. March & J. P. Olsen. *Ambiguity and choice in organizations* (pp. 251–75). Bergen, Norway: Universitetsforlaget.

March, J. G., & Sevón, G. (1984). Gossip, information, and decision making. In J. G. March (ed.), *Decisions and organizations* (pp. 429–42). Oxford: Blackwell.

March, J. G., & Sevón, G. (1988). Behavioral perspectives on theories of the firm. In W. F. van Raaij, G. M. van Veldhoven, & K. E. Wärneryd (eds), *Handbook of economic psychology* (pp. 369–402). Dordrecht, the Netherlands: Kluwer.

March, J. G., & Shapira, Z. (1987). Managerial perspectives on risk and risk taking. *Management Science*, 33, 1404–18.

March, J. G., & Shapira, Z. (1992). Variable risk preferences and the focus of attention. *Psychological Review*, 99, 172–83.

March, J. G., & Simon, H. A. (1993). *Organizations* (2nd ed.). Oxford: Blackwell.

March, J. G., Sproull, L. S., & Tamuz, M. (1991). Learning from samples of one or fewer. *Organization Science*, 2, 1–13.

Matsuyama, K. (1995). Complementarities and cumulative processes in models of monopolistic competition. *Journal of Economic Literature*, 33, 701–29.

Milgrom, P., & Roberts, J. (1992). *Economics, organization and management.* Englewood Cliffs, NJ: Prentice-Hall.

Mintzberg, H. (1994). *The rise and fall of strategic planning: Reconceiving roles for planning, plans, planners.*

New York: Free Press.

Nelson, R. R., & Winter, S. G. (1982). *An evolutionary theory of economic change*. Cambridge, MA: Harvard University Press.

Nisbett, R., & Ross, L. (1980). *Human inference: Strategies and shortcomings of social judgment*. Englewood Cliffs, NJ: Prentice-Hall.

Page, B. I. (1976). The theory of political ambiguity. *American Political Science Review, 70*, 742–52.

Payne, J. W., Laughhann, D. J., & Crum, R. L. (1980). Translation of gambles and aspiration level effects in risky choice behavior. *Management Science, 26*, 1039–60.

Payne, J. W., Laughhann, D. J., & Crum, R. L. (1981). Further tests of aspiration level effects in risky choice behavior. *Management Science, 27*, 953–8.

Pennings, J. M. (ed.). (1986). *Decision making: An organizational behavior approach*. New York: M. Weiner.

Pfeffer, J., & Salancik, G. R. (1978). *The external control of organizations*. New York: Harper & Row.

Pressman, J. L., & Wildavsky, A. B. (1973). *Implementation*. Berkeley: University of California Press.

Schlenker, B. R. (1982). Translating actions into attitudes: An identity-analytic approach to the explanation of social conduct. *Advances in Experimental Social Psychology, 15*, 194–248.

Schoemaker, P. J. H. (1982). The expected utility model: Its variants, purposes, evidence and limitations. *Journal of Economic Literature, 20*, 529–63.

Schulz, M. (1992). A depletion of assets model of organizational learning. *Journal of Mathematical Sociology, 17*, 145–73.

Sevón, G. (1996). Organizational imitation in identity transformation. In B. Czarniawska & G. Sevón (eds), *Translating organizational change* (pp. 49–67). Berlin: De Gruyter.

Shapira, Z. (1995). *Risk taking: A managerial perspective*. New York: Russell Sage.

Shepsle, K. A., & Weingast, B. (1987). The institutional foundations of committee power. *American Political Science Review, 81*, 85–104.

Singh, J. V. (1986). Performance, slack, and risk taking in organizational decision making. *Academy of Management Journal, 29*, 562–85.

Staw, B. M., Sandelands, L. E., & Dutton, J. E. (1981). Threat-rigidity effects in organizational behavior: A multilevel analysis. *Administrative Science Quarterly, 26*, 501–24.

Taylor, S. E., & Brown, J. D. (1988). Illusion and well-being: A social psychological perspective on mental health. *Psychological Bulletin, 103*, 193–210.

Tetlock, P. E. (1992). The impact of accountability on judgment and choice: Toward a social contingency model. *Advances in Experimental Social Psychology, 25*, 331–76.

Tullock, G. (1965). *The politics of bureaucracy*. Washington, DC: Public Affairs Press.

Turner, J. C. (1985). Social categorization and the self concept: A social cognitive theory of group behavior. In E. J. Lawler (ed.), *Advances in group processes* (vol. 2, pp. 77–122). Greenwich, CT: JAI Press.

Westney, D. E. (1987). *Imitation and innovation: The transfer of Western organizational patterns to Meiji Japan*. Cambridge, MA: Harvard University Press.

Wildavsky, A. (1987). Choosing preferences by constructing institutions: A cultural theory of preference formation. *American Political Science Review, 81*, 3–22.

Witte, E., & Zimmermann, H. -J. (eds). (1986). *Empirical research on organizational decision making.* Amsterdam: Elsevier.

Zey, M. (ed.). (1992). *Decision making.* Newbury Park, CA: Sage.

Zhou, X. (1993). The dynamics of organizational rules. *American Journal of Sociology, 98*, 1134–66.

CHAPTER THREE

Continuity and Change in Theories of Organizational Action

Most theories of adaptation assume that effective learning requires a balance between exploration and exploitation but that such a balance is continually threatened by tendencies for both exploration and exploitation to be self-reinforcing. I tell a morality tale within such a frame about the past 40 years in the study of organizations. The tale emphasizes the struggle of students of organizational action to maintain a rough balance between openness and discipline, thus proclaiming both the possibility of a balanced virtue and its rewards – a truly romantic story.*

The writing of history is a conceit of survivors. Since survival is temporary, history is ephemeral; but we exercise our fleeting right to authoritative voice. So, I will tell a story. It is not the only such story that could be told in the world of organization studies, but it happens to be one I know. It is embedded in the context of a particular time, the 40 years between 1956 and 1996, and a particular set of experiences. It has a moral, not perhaps a very profound moral, but a comfortably uncomplicated one. And it is romantic enough for the present occasion.

A LITTLE CONTEXT: 1956–1996

The intellectual foundations for the systematic study of organizations are scattered over much of the early twentieth century, especially the years between the two world wars, but the period that began shortly after the end of World War II propelled the field into importance. The early part of that period was a time of growth and innocent excitement, when scholars built their pretenses from optimistic hopes for scholarship and found little time for angst. The *Administrative Science Quarterly* was a creation of those times. Its survival for 40 years is testimony to an ability to sustain that innocence while paying the bills.

Plus ça change, plus c'est même chose

In an introduction to the *Handbook of organizations* (March, 1965), I attempted a brief description of the state of studies of organizations at the start of the 1960s, for all practical purposes at the time the *ASQ* began. The introduction made three general points: First, the study of organizations honors prior research through appropriate citations, but there is no clearly defined family tree. Citations show rather little genealogical structure. There is only a modest sharing of "classics," the "classics" draw from a diffuse collection of general social science sources, and the multiple generation citation lineage of current work is obscure. Second, although students of organizations have increasingly differentiated themselves into a distinct semidiscipline with its own professional associations, journals, academic departments, and traditions, the field remains one that depends heavily on more established disciplines for ideas, personnel, and legitimation. And third, the growth of the study of organizations has paralleled the growth of organizational and managerial techniques and has been entwined with the teaching of management in universities and consultancies, but a clear link between research and teaching is elusive. Many well-known organizational techniques have little or no research basis; many research findings have little or no impact on organizational techniques.

Although I think that each of these propositions would require some shading and qualification, the same conclusions could easily be repeated in 1996. In that sense at least, nothing has changed very dramatically in 40 years. Yet to describe organization studies in terms of such stabilities would be quite misleading. The world of organization studies has been altered in ways that are striking. Many of these changes are either due directly to, or have been shaped significantly by, sheer growth in the size of the enterprise. Proliferation of people, papers, pulpits, and predictions has resulted in an intellectual world that is more luxurious, more crowded, more differentiated, and more competitive. Any one of several subfields can sustain academic programs, conferences, and reviews of current knowledge on scales that would not have been possible 40 years ago, even in the field as a whole.

Along the way, the content of the field has changed conspicuously. Any later handbook of organizational research would have to have a different table of contents.[1] Some of the chapters in the old handbook still are marvelous "reads" (e.g., Starbuck on organizational growth and development, Stinchcombe on social structure and organizations, Weick on laboratory experimentation), but most of them would require extensive reworking and additions to reflect changes in research findings, conceptions, and language.

Some topics that were included then would not warrant as much attention now, but the more conspicuous changes are in the number of substantial new domains that have pushed their way into our consciousness.[2] Since the early 1960s, the sociological, economic, and political science versions of institutional perspectives on organizations have been rediscovered and elaborated. Transaction cost economics has similarly become obviously significant. The links between hierarchical organizations and markets and between hierarchies and other forms of networks, as well as the role of such networks in understanding organized human behavior, have all become important. A variety of approaches that emphasize humanistic, interpretive, and ethnographic visions of organizational research have become common. Studies of organizational change and learning have been extended into studies of the evolution of populations of organizations, organizational forms, and organizational rules, and into the dynamics of ecologies of mutual learning. The simple observation that organizations involve conflicts of interest has become the basis for extensive applications of game theory and related concepts to questions of information exchange, bargaining, contracts, and problems of agency. Issues of gender, ethnicity, and culture have attracted students of organizations with a wide variety of methodological styles, as they have scholars throughout the social sciences.

Judged by any reasonable historical standard, the record reflects an extraordinary outburst of research energy. And although disagreements about criteria of research excellence are as characteristic of the study of organizations as they are of other areas in social science, it requires unusual perversity to compare the first two or three volumes of the *Administrative Science Quarterly* with the last two or three without being impressed by the marked improvement in average quality. The mean is up. Just as clearly, I think, the variance is down. There has been considerable long-term movement toward serious professional standards and standardization. Although casual observations and unsupported imaginations have maintained a certain place and even secured a kind of breathless cachet, they have for the most part been replaced by trained competencies. It is an exchange that has its costs, but on the whole, the vapidity of many contemporary contributions seems to me less a source of dismay than is the vacuousness of many earlier ones.

This history represents an achievement of enormous proportions, one that can perhaps only be fully appreciated by those of us who have survived it. It is, of course, not a unique history. The 40 years from 1956 were years in which scholarship in all of the social and behavioral sciences expanded significantly both in the numbers of practitioners and in the amount and quality of research productivity.

Expansion, fractionation, and reintegration

This unparalleled flowering of scholarship has not always been accompanied by easy conversations among the gardeners. As the field has grown and elaborated new perspectives, it has continually been threatened with becoming not so much a new integrated semidiscipline as a set of independent, self-congratulatory cultures of comprehension. This is evident with five of the more lively subfields of contemporary studies of organizations: the economics of organizations, the institutional basis of organizations, the interpretive, critical theory of organizations, the network analysis of intra- and interorganizational life, and the study of the evolutionary/learning adaptation of ecologies of organizations. Although these subfields have been particularly successful in augmenting our understanding of organizations over the past 40 years, they have exhibited persistent symptoms of isolation, engaging in intermittent internecine worldview cleansing. In the name of technical purity and claims of universality, energized subfields have tended to seal themselves off, each seemingly eager to close further the minds of the already converted, without opening the minds of others. There is, to be sure, a certain grim necessity in the process. Exploiting interesting ideas often thrives on commitment more than thoughtfulness, narrowness more than breadth, cohesiveness more than openness. These advantages tend to be self-sustaining and to cumulate into a balkanization of a field.

The balkanization of organization studies has, however, been limited by two traditions that developed early and have been maintained. The first is a tradition of intellectual openness, of relatively promiscuous borrowing across disciplines and across subfields. For example, although students of adaptation and interpretation have tended to huddle in their separate domains, the rudiments of evolutionary and cultural theories have penetrated many parts of contemporary organizational thought as easily as did the rudiments of Marxist and systems theories earlier. The second tradition is one of intellectual path dependence, of maintaining continuity in ideas. Thus, for example, conceptions of organizational structure that characterized some of the earlier writings on organizations have been sustained and elaborated by subsequent ideas of networks and transaction cost efficiency without losing their connections to earlier thought. These elements of continuity have helped to counterbalance the centrifugal forces of localized excitements.

I propose to illustrate the traditions of openness and continuity in organizational research by a brief look at the development of theories of organizational action. Since it is a domain in which I have labored from time to time, my romanticism may reasonably be suspect, but I think it is a domain in which contributions from several different modern perspectives have become conspicuous over the past forty years. Those perspectives have been combined with earlier ideas to create a polyphonic fugue that is often discordant but occasionally achieves a certain modicum of delicate harmony (Zey, 1992; March, 1994; Hickson, 1995; Shapira, 1996).

A SHORT STORY: THEORIES OF ACTION

In the past 40 years, theories of organizational action have developed in a systematic way from a base that existed well before 1956 but was profoundly shaped by the early papers of Herbert A. Simon (1955, 1956). Without completely reconstructing that base, significant contributions from the economics of organizations, institutional theory, interpretive theory, network analysis, and theories of evolution have been incorporated into contemporary conceptions. Students of organizational action form a community within which economists, sociologists, historians, political scientists, psychologists, and humanists meet frequently and even occasionally constructively – a kind of Switzerland of ideas. It is also, as these things are usually measured, a success story of sorts. Students of organizational decision making have contributed obviously and significantly to understandings of decision making more generally, whether by individuals or by larger social and political systems.

Autonomous consequential action

In the beginning, more or less, there was a theory of autonomous consequential choice. It was built on the assumption that action stemmed from choice, and choice stemmed from two guesses about the future: (1) a guess about the consequences that would stem from a particular choice, thus about expectations, and (2) a guess about the subjective value that would be associated with those consequences when they were realized, thus about preferences.

Elements of such a theory can be found earlier, but it became part of standard Western intellectual discourse in the seventeenth and early-eighteenth centuries with the triumph of rationalist and utilitarian thought, typified most purely perhaps by the writings of Jeremy Bentham. The elaborations of the first part of the twentieth century built on this structure in two primary ways: First, they tied a probabilist perspective to the utilitarian structure to create (statistical) decision theory. Second, they established an axiomatics that derived cardinal utility functions from collections of consistent choices among lotteries. The two elaborations became the basic canon of twentieth-century theories of consequentialist thought.

The last half of the twentieth century has witnessed considerable effort to revise the theory to reflect observations drawn from studies of human, particularly organizational, decision making. The oldest and best-established modification of the classical canon of human choice recognizes that the two basic guesses of consequential choice are problematic. First, alternatives and their consequences are not given but have to be discovered and estimated. Identifying alternatives and anticipating their consequences requires information, calculative capabilities, and attention, all of which are scarce resources. As a result, theories of choice became intertwined with theories of search, and the field of behavioral decision theory grew very substantially. Second, human preferences are systematically different from the preferences anticipated by classical theories of choice. Instead of being refined into a coherent, continuous utility function, they are often better represented by a series of aspiration levels, or targets. Instead of being consistent, stable, and exogenous, they are often inconsistent, unstable, and endogenous.

These observations have led to considerable reconstruction of theories of autonomous consequential choice. Modern theories are often better characterized as theories of heuristics, attention, search, and learning than of comprehensive calculative rationality. They fold into a broad decision-making frame ideas about the updating of expectations, behavioral biases, sequential attention to targets, search, the temporal sorting of problems and solutions, adaptive aspirations, variable risk preferences, and the costs and benefits of information.

Autonomous rule-based action

Ideas of autonomous consequential choice developed in parallel to a second set of ideas, also with a long history. These ideas share the assumption that an actor, whether individual or collective, is an autonomous system. But the logic of choice is a logic of appropriateness rather than a logic of consequences. Action is seen as resulting from a matching of rules to situations. The actor is seen as a collection of identities that dictate appropriate action in particular situations. The problematics of choice are seen as lying in the definition of the salient identity and the classification of the situation.

The idea of rule-based decision making has a long history in sociological, economic, and jurisprudential theories of action. The importance of such ideas for theories of autonomous action was emphasized by students of organizational decision making who observed the ubiquity of standard operating procedures, professional rules, social norms, and rules of thumb in organizational action. Action, for example, the adoption of a new technology or organizational form, was portrayed as driven not by estimation of its consequences for productivity but by an association with the demands of an identity or by an attempt to gain legitimacy. Theories of choice became theories of situation recognition, socialization, institutionalization, and imitation and developed stronger links with theories of cognitive processes, artificial intelligence, and diffusion than with theories of calculation. They also became theories of evolution, for if standard operating procedures and other institutionalized features of organizations could be imagined to endure, provide reliability, and to have the capability of transferring from one organization to another, they could be imagined to be the "genes" of an evolutionary theory of organizational action.

The basic idea that has come to be accepted rather broadly is that rules are products of a process combining learning from an organization's own experience, learning from others, and selection stemming from differential organizational growth and survival. The mix of rules changes over time, but the sequence of changes that occurs is not assured to be adaptive in the sense of leading inexorably to a unique equilibrium that is optimal. In that sense, learning is myopic and history is inefficient.

The erosion of confidence in historical efficiency has become a problem for those parts of organization theory that involve the comparative statics of rules and institutions (e.g., contingency theory, transaction cost analysis, contract theory). If historical processes do not reliably result in contracts, forms, rules, institutions, and practices that are at equilibria uniquely defined by their survival advantages, the theoretical underpinnings of functional analysis are in doubt. Historical inefficiency is, however, less of a problem for the study of rules as a basis for action. On the contrary, it has stimulated studies of rule making, rule endurance and change, and rule imitation that make up a significant part of recent studies of rule-based autonomous action.

Ecologies of action

Whether action is treated as stemming from expectations and preferences using a logic of consequences or from the application of rules to situations using a logic of appropriateness, it must be fit into an ecological context. An organization reacts to the actions of others that are reacting to it. Much of what happens is attributable to those interactions and thus is not easily explicable as the consequence of autonomous action.

The earliest significant recognition of the ecological context of action came in treatments of rational strategic action, as typified by classical theories of competition and their modern elaboration through the theory of games. As students of politics and economics had long noted, rational choice is embedded in an environment that consists of other rational actors, an environment in which each actor anticipates the rationality of the other and is aware that the other is doing likewise. As the analysis of games became a well-developed art form, it cast new light on the importance of repetitive encounters, time horizons, reputations, and trust in encounters among rational actors and led to new insights into the complications of communication, control, and cooperation in the face of conflict of interest.

The vision of rational actors leaping into Nash equilibria is, however, only a part of theories of decision conflict. Elements of self-conscious rationality and strategic action are ancient foundations of political treatments of conflict, finding modern expression particularly in various forms of exchange (resource dependence) theories of power. Students of politics have given a somewhat greater role, however, to the ways in which action stems from coalitions bound together by traditional allegiances and rules, from conflict stimulated by misestimations, misperceptions, and emotions of anger and shame, from the happenstance of attention allocation in a world of scarce attention resources, and from the framing of political encounter by the constraints of ideology and history. Although some of these traditions lead to theories of grand mono-causal sweep, most of them emphasize the ways in which collective decisions stem from an intricate mosaic of individual actors and actions.

Interactive perspectives on conflict are significant contributors to an ecological perspective on organizational action, but they are not by any means the entire ecological story. Preferences (in theories of consequential choice) and identities (in theories of rule-based choice) are more ecological than their usual representation. Ideas of autonomous consequential choice treat preferences as exogenous to the making of decisions. Preferences (utilities, tastes, values, goals) are imagined to exist prior to and independent of the making of a choice. Similarly, ideas of autonomous rule-based choice generally treat identities as exogenous to the exercise of an identity. Identities and the associated rules are imagined to exist prior to and independent of the application of a rule to a situation. Neither treatment is satisfactory. The ecology of action shapes desires. Tastes and conceptions of self are modified in the process of acting in their names.

Similarly, the components of action are linked in ecological networks of imitation. Large parts of the sociological and political study of institutions, the economic and sociological study of knowledge, the economic study of technology, and the managerial study of organizational practice and knowledge are testaments to the idea that imitation is a major principle of human action. All of the major components of decisions – information, alternatives, expectations, desires, identities, definitions of situations, rules – spread through populations of organizations. Aspirations adapt not only to an actor's past performance but also to the past performance of other actors who are defined as relevant. This other-referential character of aspirations makes a difference to decisions, search, and risk taking. Norms and practices diffuse from one actor to another. The diffusion of institutions through a population of organizations makes a difference. Knowledge developed in one organization spreads to another. This appropriation of knowledge makes a difference. All of these processes of imitation make theories of organizational action attentive to the network structures through which diffusion takes place and to the dynamics of their change.

Interest in interactive ecologies extends into more general issues of coevolution and mutual learning. Even in the absence of fully rational consciousness, organizations exist in systems of competition and cooperation through which the actions of one affect the realizations of actions of another. Niche crowding is one example. Another is the armaments race (or red queen) effect, familiar both to evolutionary theory and to students of advertising and other explosive competitions. Another is the symbiosis between suppliers and manufacturers or between labor unions and labor political parties. Similarly, relations among organizations in a knowledge domain can create important cooperative (as well as competitive) effects. Some successes have been achieved in modeling these complications, but difficult puzzles remain.

Action, ambiguity, and interpretation

The idea that the bases of action are not "reality" but perceptions of reality is close to a received doctrine these days, though there are ample controversies about the nature of the perceptions and the sense in which a more autonomous reality also exists. Almost all students of action grant actors some kind of subjective control over the normative and perceptual factors guiding their actions, though they differ in their assumptions about the extent to which subjective judgments and "objective reality" diverge. Some theorists would claim to have discovered or defined a generic preference structure; others would presume that expectations (at least on average) approximate reality, at least after some time; and others would suggest that beliefs and perceptions may be more or less automatically enacted into reality. With these important qualifications, however, there is some general consensus that what we see or believe may at times deviate from what is true.

The ambiguities of knowledge and desires reflect partly the cognitive limitations of individuals and organizations. Such a conception leads both to an interest in improving the capabilities of human actors to approximate the decision-theory ideal and to a fascination with systematic bias in judgments and in collective decisions. Ambiguity can, however, also be seen as a fundamental feature of life, one that endures despite the best efforts of reformers and may even be portrayed as having survival advantages. For example, the capability of a collective to satisfy requirements of agreement may depend on exploiting the ambiguities of preferences and meaning.

It is also received doctrine that the premises of action are socially constructed. Preferences, expectations, identities, and definitions of situations are seen as arising from interactions within a social system, thus as embedded in social norms and cultural conventions of discourse. In this view, explanations of action gain legitimacy by invoking shared understandings of proper narrative. Shared understandings are the result of social exchange mediated by a full panoply of social elements – social structure, language, myth, resource distributions. While such exchange may result in divergence of belief, as, for example, in the exchange between enemies or in processes of individualization, more of the recent interest has been in convergent diffusion processes by which perceptions, desires, and rules tend to become shared.

The stories that are told by decision makers can be viewed as instrumental premises of action, as they are by most students of decision making. In such a view, interpretations of history are instrumental to the making of decisions and thus important; but there is no fundamental interest in a theory of interpretation, or story telling. For example, it is clear that certain "magic numbers," such as performance measures or summary statistics, often guide organizational action. Thus, the theory of action has come to emphasize theories of the politics and technology of numbers and the social construction of accounting. Grander derivatives of a subjectivist stance, however, identify humanity not so much with action as with interpretation, with explanations of action, history, and the self. Story telling is seen as more elemental. It is sometimes portrayed as independent of action and thus as a separate domain. Alternatively, action is pictured as an instrument in the development of interpretation, rather than the other way around.

Out of such conceptions have come notions of loose coupling between the processes of decision making and its outcomes. Decision-making processes are seen as signals and symbols of legitimacy, and thus valuable in their own right, regardless of any consequences for decision outcomes. The community of talk is seen as distinct from the community of action, with different rules and different audiences. As a result, organizations can talk about some things about which they cannot act and can act on some things about which they cannot talk. The symbolic meaning of decisions has come to be recognized as a vital aspect of decision making that is not necessarily linked to decision implementation. The basic technology of organization is described as a technology of narrative, as well as a technology of production. The contested terrain of organizations is seen as a terrain of meaning.

A MINOR MORAL

The moral is a moral of intellectual adaptiveness. Adaptation requires a balance between exploration and exploitation but is continually threatened by the tendency of each to extinguish the other. Recent history of the study of organizations exemplifies the tendency. Parts of the field seem to be dedicated to exploring indefinitely the remote corollaries of a particular set of assumptions, becoming more and more competent in a less and less useful way. Other parts seem to be random walks of fads, never becoming notably competent at much of anything.

The risks of both traps are conspicuous in the history of studies of organizational action. It would have been possible simply to take the ideas that were current in 1956 and make them ever more precise, teasing finer points from that structure. Much of the development of modern information and organizational economics is testimony to the attractiveness of such a strategy. Similarly, it would have been possible simply to abandon the earlier work and to embrace new visions. Each new theoretical enthusiasm has its coterie of true believers ready to proclaim a new intellectual messiah or the resurrection of an old one.

For the most part, students of organizational action have managed to avoid both traps. The field has been relatively open with respect to the various new excitements in studies of organizations. Network analysis, institutional sociology and political science, interpretive analysis, and evolutionary and learning theories have all found their places and have all illuminated understandings of organizational action. The openness, however, has not prevented a certain skepticism. The new messiahs have not been condemned, but neither have they been embraced fully. The new wine has been accommodated in old bottles and has been affected by the containers.

The overall result is neither unique nor mysterious, but it may possibly be instructive. The first essence of intellectual history is that things change, that important parts of what is believed today will not be believed tomorrow. The second essence of intellectual history is that there is continuity, that threads of the past are woven into fabrics of the future. History is ephemeral, but the tellers of history and their subjects are not free to elaborate arbitrary fables. They are obliged to tie new interpretations to ones that have gone before. The links may well be contested, but they are a reminder that we seek not only to construct a clever story but also one connecting us to a chain of coherence that began long before us and will continue long after us.

The achievement of an effective mixing of continuity and change is made possible by intellectual and social structures that sustain a tension between the delights of exploitation and the delights of exploration. It is the good fortune of much of the study of organizations that by simultaneously occupying small parts of many disciplines and existing as its own semidiscipline, it participates both in the rigorous excitements of refining good ideas and in the risky enjoyments of experimenting with novel ones to find the occasional jewel lurking among the many disappointments. Such good fortune can hardly be viewed as just, but it can be enjoyed, at least briefly.

Acknowledgment

*The research has been supported by the Spencer Foundation and the Stanford Graduate School of Business.

Notes

1. These changes are reflected in two subsequent handbooks edited by Nystrom and Starbuck (1981) and Clegg et al. (1996). Like the 1965 volume, each of these reflects both the idiosyncracies of its editors and their commitments to universality. If one discounts for the former and focuses on the latter, I think their tables of contents are consistent with the observations here.
2. To avoid cluttering the text with innumerable citations, I have minimized references in the present chapter. It should be obvious that the history I report is a history of many researchers who are thereby slighted by a possibly misguided effort to maintain readability.

References

Clegg, Stewart, Cynthia Hardy, and Walter Nord (eds.) 1996 Handbook of Organization Studies. London: Sage.

Hickson, David J. (ed.) 1995 Managerial Decision Making. Aldershot: Dartmouth.

March, James G. 1965 Handbook of Organizations Chicago: Rand McNally.

March, James G. 1994 A Primer on Decision Making: How Decisions Happen. New York: Free Press.

Nystrom, Paul C., and William H. Starbuck (eds.) 1981 Handbook of Organizational Design. Oxford: Oxford University Press.

Shapira, Zur (ed) 1996 Organizational

Decision Making. New York: Cambridge University Press.

Simon, Herbert A. 1955 "A behavioral model of rational choice." Quarterly Journal of Economics, 69: 99–118.

Simon, Herbert A. 1956 "Rational choice and the structure of the environment." Psychological Review, 63: 129–138.

Zey, Mary (ed) 1992 Decision Making. Newbury Park, CA: Sage.

CHAPTER FOUR

Institutional Perspectives on Political Institutions

with Johan P. Olsen

This chapter examines some basic assumptions about the nature of political institutions, the ways in which practices and rules that comprise institutions are established, sustained, and transformed, and the ways in which those practices and rules are converted into political behavior through the mediation of interpretation and capability. We discuss an institutional approach to political life that emphasizes the endogenous nature and social construction of political institutions, identities, accounts, and capabilities.[1]

Political science as a field is defined less by a set of theoretical concepts than by an empirical focus on concrete political institutions and processes. Legislatures, bureaucracies, legal systems, political parties, mass media, and all the other institutions of contemporary politics are objects of study. Although political scientists occasionally examine other institutions, such as business firms, churches, or armies, and use various forms of political analysis to interpret them, the discipline persistently retreats from attempts to generate distinctive theoretical tools and returns to concerns about identifiable political institutions.

Historically, theoretical political science has been more an interweaving of metaphors than a theoretically coherent discipline or even an arena for competition among alternative metaphors. It has combined the traditions of Aristotle and Tocqueville with those of Hobbes and Bentham and grafted on to those roots various elements of the wisdom of Freud, Marx, Durkheim, Adam Smith, and Darwin. In recent years, this pragmatic approach to ideas has been expressed most conspicuously in efforts to reconcile an exchange conception of politics drawn particularly from ideas of social contracts, the utilitarians, and modern microeconomics with an institutional conception that builds on jurisprudence, sociological and psychological conceptions of identity, and modern organization theory.

This chapter is in that tradition of political science. We examine some basic assumptions about the nature of political institutions, the ways in which the practices and rules that comprise institutions are established, sustained, and transformed, and the ways in which those practices and rules are converted into political behavior through the mediation of interpretation and capability. Without denying the elements of exchange in politics and the many ways in which politics aggregates exogenous individual preferences and responds to exogenous distributions of resources and capabilities, we discuss an institutional approach to political life – one that emphasizes the endogenous nature and social construction of political institutions, identities, accounts, and capabilities.

TELLING STORIES ABOUT POLITICS

The stories of politics are stories attached to real political events in real political institutions. Why did the Weimar Republic fail? How do we account for the historical divergence of the political institutions of Canada and the United States? What explains post-communist political developments in Hungary? The stories about such events and institutions constructed within political science are organized around a few themes of how political institutions work. Politics is organized by (and helps to organize) these stories of history.

There are two conventional stories of democratic politics. The first story sees politics as a market for trades in which individual and group interests are pursued by rational actors. It emphasizes the negotiation of coalitions and "voluntary" exchanges. The second story is an institutional one. It characterizes politics in a more integrative fashion, emphasizing the creation of identities and institutions as well as their structuring effects on political life.

Politics as arranging exchanges

Politics can be seen as aggregating individual preferences into collective actions by some procedures of bargaining, negotiation, coalition formation, and exchange (Riker, 1962; Coleman, 1966; Downs, 1967; March, 1970; Niskanen, 1971). In such a view, individual actors have prior desires (preferences, interests) which they use to determine the attractiveness of expected consequences. Collective action depends on the negotiation of bargains and side-payments among potential trading partners. Exchange stories of politics and governance have roots in the doctrines of social contract theory which arose in the seventeenth century. The political community is seen as atomistic. Society is constituted of individuals for the fulfillment of individual ends. Individuals have rights but no obligations or bonds, except those created through consent and contracts based on calculated advantage (Taylor, 1985, pp. 187–229).

The ability of any particular actor to realize his or her desires in such a system of exchange depends on what the desires are, what exchangeable resources that actor possesses, and what political rights he or she has. Wants that are consistent with the wants of others are more easily satisfied than wants that compete with others. The greater the exchangeable resources (initial endowments) and the more rights to political voice, the stronger the trading position. One version of the exchange story emphasizes the pareto-optimal qualities of exchange and gains from trade – the achievement of outcomes that make at least some people better off and no one worse off than before the exchanges. A second version of the exchange story emphasizes the coercive qualities of exchange when initial endowments are unequal, the way in which "voluntary exchange" results in one group of actors imposing its will on other groups (Moe, 1990; Sened, 1991; Olsen, 1992).

Politics as creating and sustaining institutions

An alternative story emphasizes the role of institutions. The exchange vision of human nature as static and universal and unaffected by politics is replaced by a view of the political actor as flexible, varied, malleable, culture-dependent and socially constructed. Intentional, calculative action is embedded in rules and institutions that are constituted, sustained, and interpreted in a political system. The core notion is that life is organized by sets of shared meanings and practices that come to be taken as given for a long time. Political actors act and organize themselves in accordance with rules and practices which are socially constructed, publicly known, anticipated and accepted. Actions of individuals and collectivities occur within these shared meanings and practices, which can be called institutions and identities (Meyer and Rowan, 1977; March and Olsen, 1984, 1989; North, 1990).

In the institutional story, people act, think, feel and organize themselves on the basis of exemplary or authoritative (and sometimes competing or conflicting) rules derived from socially constructed identities, belongings and roles. Institutions organize hopes, dreams, and fears as well as purposeful actions. Institutionalized rules proscribe or prescribe emotions and expression of emotions (Flam, 1990a, 1990b). Sentiments of love, loyalty, devotion, respect, friendship, as well as hate, anger, fear, envy, and guilt are made appropriate to particular identities in particular situations.

Institutions constitute and legitimize political actors and provide them with consistent behavioral rules, conceptions of reality, standards of assessment, affective ties, and endowments, and thereby with a capacity for purposeful action (Douglas, 1986; Thompson et al., 1990; March and Olsen, 1995). Along the way, political institutions create rules regulating the possession and use of political rights and resources. Even the conception of an autonomous agent with a particularistic way of feeling, acting, and expression is an acquired identity, a socialized understanding of self and others (Taylor, 1985, p. 205).

Action is taken on the basis of a logic of appropriateness associated with roles, routines, rights, obligations, standard operating procedures and practices. The perspective is more behavioural than moral but it echoes an Aristotelian judgment: "As man is the best of all animals when he has reached his full development, so he is the worst of all when divorced from law and morals" (Aristotle, 1980, p. 29).

INSTITUTIONAL PERSPECTIVES

The word "institutional" has come to mean rather different things to different authors.[2] The institutional alternatives to voluntary exchange stories about politics with which we are concerned here are infused with two basic themes:

1. a theme that pictures political action as driven less by anticipation of its uncertain consequences and preferences for them than by a logic of appropriateness reflected in a structure of rules and conceptions of identities;
2. a theme that pictures political change as matching institutions, behaviors, and contexts in ways that take time and have multiple, path-dependent equilibria, thus as being susceptible to timely interventions to affect the meander of history and to deliberate efforts to improve institutional adaptiveness.

Institutional conceptions of political action

Institutional theories supplement exchange theories of political action in two primary ways: first, they emphasize the role of institutions in defining the terms of rational exchange. Rational action depends on subjective perceptions of alternatives, their consequences, and their evaluations.

Pictures of reality and feelings about it are constructed within social and political institutions (Cyert and March, 1992; March and Simon, 1993). Second, without denying the reality of calculations and anticipations of consequences, institutional conceptions see such calculations and anticipations as occurring within a broader framework of rules, roles, and identities (North, 1981, 1990; Shepsle and Weingast, 1987; Shepsle, 1989, 1990). Indeed, at the limit, self-interested calculation can be seen as simply one of many systems of rules that may be socially legitimized under certain circumstances (Taylor, 1985; Nauta, 1992).

Institutional bases of rational exchange

In exchange theories, political action (decision-making, resource allocation) is a result of bargains negotiated among individual actors pursuing individual interests. The theories presume that individuals pursue their interests by considering alternative bargains in terms of their anticipated consequences for individual preferences and choosing those combinations of bargains that serve their preferences best. Political actors are imagined to be endowed with preferences or interests that are consistent, stable, and exogenous to the political system. They act on the basis of incomplete and possibly biased information. In short, exchange theories of politics are special cases of rational actor theories of human behavior.

Institutional theories focus on the behavioral and social bases of information and preferences in a theory of rational choice. They picture preferences as inconsistent, changing, and at least partly endogenous, formed within political institutions. Interests and cleavages are seen as created by institutional arrangements and maintained by institutional processes of socialization and cooptation (Selznick, 1949; Lipset and Rokkan, 1967; Eisenstadt and Rokkan, 1973; Wildavsky, 1987; Sunstein, 1990; Greber and Jackson, 1993). Institutional theories similarly emphasize the ways in which institutions shape the definition of alternatives and influence the perception and construction of the reality within which action takes place. Institutional capabilities and structures affect the flow of information, the kinds of search undertaken, and the interpretations made of the results (Cyert and March, 1963; March and Olsen, 1989, 1995; Olsen and Peters, 1996).

Awareness of the limits of rationality and of the embedding of rationality in an institutional context has led to a considerable restructuring of theories of rational exchange, including political theories based on an exchange perspective. This restructuring has come to picture rational exchange as framed by and dependent on political norms, identities, and institutions. Insofar as political actors act by making choices, they act within definitions of alternatives, consequences, preferences (interests), and strategic options that are strongly affected by the institutional context in which the actors find themselves. Exploring the ways in which institutions affect the definition of alternatives, consequences, and preferences, the cleavages that produce conflict, and the enforcement of bargains have become major activities within modern choice theory (Laitin, 1985).

Rules and identities

Institutional conceptions of action, however, differ from rational models in a more fundamental way. Most people in politics and political institutions follow rules most of the time if they can (Searing, 1991). The uncertainties they face are less uncertainties about consequences and preferences than they are uncertainties about the demands of identity. Actions are expressions of what is exemplary, natural, or acceptable behavior according to the (internalized) purposes, codes of rights and duties, practices, methods, and techniques of the constituent group and of the self. As a result, the institutional axiomatics for political action begin not with subjective consequences and preferences but with rules, identities, and roles (Friedrich, 1950; Tussman, 1960).

Political institutions matter. Institutionalized identities create individuals: citizens, officials, engineers, doctors, spouses (Dworkin, 1986). Rule-following can be viewed as contractual – an implicit agreement to act appropriately in return for being treated appropriately. Such a contractual view has led game theorists and some legal theorists to interpret norms and institutions as meta-game agreements (Shepsle, 1990; Gibbons, 1992), but the term "contract" is potentially misleading. The terms are often unclear enough to be better called a "pact" (Selznick, 1992) than a "contract," and socialization into rules and their appropriateness is ordinarily not a case of willful entering into an explicit contract.

Within an institutional framework, "choice," if it can be called that, is based more on a logic of appropriateness than on the logic of consequence that underlies conceptions of rational action. Institutionalized rules, duties, rights, and roles define acts as appropriate (normal, natural, right, good) or inappropriate (uncharacteristic, unnatural, wrong, bad). The impact of rules of appropriateness and standard operating procedures in routine situations is well known (March and Simon, 1958; Cyert and March, 1963). But the logic of appropriateness is by no means limited to repetitive, routine worlds. It is also characteristic of human action in ill-defined, novel situations (Dynes, 1970; Quarantelli and Dynes, 1977). Civil unrest, demands for comprehensive redistribution of political power and welfare, as well as political revolutions and major reforms often follow from identity-driven conceptions of appropriateness more than conscious calculations of costs and benefits (Lefort, 1988; Elster, 1989b). Appropriateness has overtones of morality, but it is in this context primarily a cognitive, or perhaps teleological, concept. Rules of action are derived from reasoning about the nature of the self. People act from understandings of the nature of things, from self-conceptions and conceptions of society, and from images of proper behavior. Identities define the nature of things and are implemented by a cognitive process of interpretation (March and Olsen, 1989, 1994).

Neither the definition of an identity nor its achievement is necessarily trivial. Fulfilling an identity through following appropriate rules involves matching a changing (and often ambiguous) set of contingent rules to a changing (and often ambiguous) set of situations. As a result, institutional approaches to behavior make a distinction between a rule and its behavioral realization in a particular instance (Apter, 1991; Thelen and Steinmo, 1992, p. 15). Identities and rules assure neither consistency nor simplicity (Biddle, 1986; Berscheid, 1994). The elements of openness in their interpretation mean that while institutions structure politics, they ordinarily do not determine political behavior precisely. The processes through which rules are translated into actual behavior through constructive interpretation and available resources have to be specified.

As they try to understand history and self, and as they try to improve the often confusing, uncertain, and ambiguous world they live in, individuals and collectivities interpret what rules and identities exist, which ones are relevant, and what different rules and identities demand in specific situations or spheres of behavior. Individuals may have a difficult time resolving conflicts among contending imperatives of appropriateness, among alternative concepts of the self. They may not know what to do. They may also know what to do but not have the capabilities to do it. They are limited by the complexities of the demands upon them and by the distribution and regulation of resources, competencies and organizing capacities – that is by the capability for acting appropriately.

Processes of constructive interpretation, criticism and justification of rules and identities are processes familiar to the intellectual traditions of the law (Dworkin, 1986; Sunstein, 1990; Teubner, 1993). Such processes are highly relevant for the ambiguities of identities, rules and factual situations. They give specific content in specific situations both to such heroic identities as patriot or statesman and to such everyday identities as those of an accountant, police officer, or citizen (Kaufman, 1960; Maanen, 1973; Spradley and Mann, 1975).

Identities, interests, and the common good

Some of the more celebrated differences between exchange theories of politics and institutional theories concern the concept of the "common good," the idea that individuals might, under some circumstances, act not in the name of individual or group interest but in the name of the good of the community. Exchange traditions downplay the significance or meaning of virtue in the values of the citizenry and doubt the relevance of social investment in citizenship. The assumption is that interests cannot (and should not) be eliminated or influenced. The object is to provide a neutral arena for voluntary exchange among them. If leaders wish to control the outcomes of this self-seeking behavior, they do so by designing incentives that induce self-interested individuals to act in desired ways as much as possible (Hart and Holmström, 1987; Levinthal, 1988). Political norms are seen as negotiated constraints on fundamental processes of self-serving rationality rather than constitutive (Coleman, 1986; Shepsle, 1990). From this perspective, a community of virtuous citizens is Gemein-schaftschwermerei – a romantic dream (Yack, 1985). The fantasy in some democratic thought that modern society can be held together by, and that conflicts can be resolved through, reference to either a moral consensus or a shared conception of the common good is deemed to be wrong as a description and pernicious as an objective.[3]

In virtually all institutional theories of politics, on the other hand, humans (through their institutions) are seen as able to share a common life and identity, and to have concern for others. Either what is good for one individual is the same as what is good for other members of the community, or actions are supposed to be governed by what is best for the community as a whole. Although the idea of a common good is plagued by the difficulty of defining what is meant by the term and by the opportunities for exploitation of individual gullibility that lie in an uncritical embrace of hopes for community values, many institutional theorists criticize presumptions of individual self-interested behavior that are standard in the rational tradition (Mansbridge, 1990; Mulhall and Swift, 1992; Chapman and Galston, 1992).

Indeed, the civic basis of identities is often intrinsic to the concept of a person, citizen, or public official. Giving priority to private interests and preferences is not merely a corruption of the political process but also a corruption of the soul and a fall from grace. Social identities are the building blocks of the self. Anyone incapable of achieving an identity based on constitutive attachments – if such a person could be imagined – should not be described as a free and rational agent, but as a being without character or moral depth, a non-person (Sandel, 1982, 1984).

This folding of communitarian values into institutional theories of politics is almost universal in modern discussions of political democracy, and it leads to a tendency to confuse two related but distinct notions. The first notion is the idea that political democracy requires a sense of community. Exactly what constitutes a sense of community varies a bit from one communitarian author to another, but a common element is the idea that individuals might (and should) have empathy for the feelings and desires of others and under some circumstances might (and should) subordinate their own individual or group interests to the collective good of the community (Sabine, 1952; Olsen, 1990).

The second notion is the idea that democracy is built upon visions of civic identity and a framework of rule-based action – what we have called a logic of appropriateness. Embedded in this notion are ideas about the obligations of citizenship and office, the commitment to fulfill an identity without regard to its consequences for personal or group preferences or interests. The self becomes central to personhood, and civic identity becomes central to the self (Turner, 1990).

The two notions share some common presumptions, but they have quite different perspectives about the fundamental basis for democratic action. The communitarian ideal of shared preferences, including a preference for the common good, presumes that individual action is based on individual values and preferences. The model is one of individual, consequential, preference-based action. Strategies for achieving democracy emphasize constructing acceptable preferences.

On the other hand, the civic identity ideal presumes, that action is rule-based, that it involves matching the obligations of an identity to a situation. Pursuit of the common good is not so much a personal value as a constitutive part of democratic political identities and the construction of a meaningful person. The community is created by its rules, not by its intentions. Strategies for achieving democracy emphasize molding rules and identities and socializing individuals into them (Elster and Slagstad, 1988; Elster, 1989a).

The distinctions are worth maintaining. When they are confounded, there is a tendency to see the problems of modern polities as lying primarily in the value premises of individual preference-based action rather than in a structure of political rules, institutions, and identities. In fact, many of the greatest dangers to the democratic polity come not from particularistic individual self-seeking but from deep, group-based identities that are inconsistent with democracy, for example, strong feelings of religious, class, and national identities. And efforts to build a personal set of communitarian values enhancing concern for the common good will be of little use – even if successful – if anti-democratic action stems primarily not from preferences and their associated values but from commitments to identities that are inconsistent with democratic institutions.

Institutional conceptions of political change

Exchange theories of political change are largely theories of the adjustment of political bargains to exogenous changes in interests, rights, and resources. When values change, political coalitions change. For example, when attitudes with respect to the role of women in society shift, so also do political parties. When resources are redistributed, political coalitions change. For example, when the age composition of society shifts in the direction of older citizens, so also do political programs. The presumption is that political bargains adjust quickly and in a necessary way to exogenous changes.

In contrast to political accounts drawn from an exchange tradition, which are organized primarily around stories of how resources and interests shape the outcomes of politics, students of political institutions are generally less confident of the efficiency of history in matching political outcomes to exogenous pressures. They see the match between an environment of interests and resources on the one hand and political institutions on the other as less automatic, less continuous, and less precise. They see a world of historical possibilities that includes multiple stable equilibria. They see the pressures of survival as sporadic rather than constant, crude rather than precise. They see institutions and identities as having lives and deaths of their own, sometimes enduring in the face of apparent inconsistency with their environments, sometimes collapsing without obvious external cause (Krasner, 1988; March and Olsen, 1989).

The nature of history

Although their many different manifestations allow numerous variations on theories of history, institutional and exchange conceptions of politics tend to be divided by a grand debate in historical interpretation. On one side in that debate is the idea that politics follows a course dictated uniquely by exogenous factors. From such a perspective, history is efficient in the sense that it matches political institutions and outcomes to environments uniquely and relatively quickly. This side of the debate is typical of exchange theories and theories of rational choice.

Some version of an efficient history assumption also underlies traditional comparative statics as applied to political institutions. Why do political institutions differ from one country to another? It is because the social and economic environments of the countries differ. How does one explain specific differences in institutions? It is by pointing to specific differences in their environments. As long as history is efficient in the sense of driving institutions to a unique equilibrium quickly, variations in institutional structures can be predicted without identifying the underlying processes of change (Furubotn and Richter, 1984).

On the other side of the debate is the idea typical of institutional theories that history follows a less determinate, more endogenous course. They generally presume that the conditions under which political development is driven quickly to a unique outcome in which the match between a political system and the political environment has some properties of unique survival advantage seem relatively restricted (Kitcher, 1985; Baum and Singh, 1994). There is no guarantee that the development of identities and institutions will instantaneously or uniquely reflect functional imperatives or demands for change. Political institutions and identities develop in a world of multiple viable possibilities. Moreover, the paths they follow seem determined in part by internal dynamics only loosely connected to changes in their environments.

Even in an exogenous environment, there are lags in matching an environment, multiple equilibria, path dependencies, and interconnected networks of diffusion. In addition, environments are rarely exogenous. Environments adapt to institutions at the same time as institutions adapt to environments. Institutions and their linkages coevolve. They are intertwined in ecologies of competition, cooperation, and other forms of interaction. And institutions are nested, so that some adapting institutions (e.g., bureaus) are integral parts of other adapting institutions (e.g., ministries).

The complications tend to convert history into a meander (March, 1994b). There are irreversible branches, involving experimentation, political alliances, communication contacts, and fortuitous opportunities. The direction taken at any particular branch sometimes seems almost chance-like, yet it is likely to be decisive in its effect on subsequent history (Brady, 1988; Lipset, 1990). Institutional histories require an understanding of both the origins of an institution and the paths by which it has developed (Berman, 1983).

The path of development is produced by a comprehensible process, but because of its indeterminate meander the realized course of institutional development is difficult to predict very far in advance. Wars, conquests, and occupation are significant in changing the political maps of the world (Tilly, 1975, 1993; Giddens, 1985). "Timely interventions" at historical junctions may make a difference. This ability to create change, however, does not guarantee either that any arbitrary change can be made at any time or that changes will turn out to be consistent with prior intentions (March, 1981). Institutions may be established to serve the interests of a specific group, but the long run results may be quite deleterious to the same interests (Rothstein, 1992).

In general, neither competitive pressure nor current conditions uniquely determine institutional options or outcomes (Herzog, 1989; North, 1990). Institutional development depends not only on satisfying current environmental and political conditions but also on an institution's origin and history (Berman, 1983). Political technologies and practices are stabilized by positive local feedback leading to the endurance of institutions, competency traps, and misplaced specialization (Levitt and March, 1988). The adaptation of identities and institutions to an external environment is shaped and constrained by internal dynamics by which identities and institutions modify themselves endogenously.

Autonomous institutional development

Politics is not simply a matter of negotiating coalitions of interests within given constraints of rights, rules, preferences, and resources. Politics extends to shaping those constraints, to constructing accounts of politics, history, and self that are not only bases for instrumental action but also central concerns of life.

Autonomous identities

Identities are responsive to external forces. Religious movements, great social and economic transformations, war, conquest, and migration all leave their marks (Tilly, 1975; Flora, 1983). But political identities, such as those of the citizen or the public official, also evolve endogenously within a political process that includes conflict, public discourse, civic education, and socialization. Politics develops values and identities. In the context of political life, citizens struggle to understand "who they are, where they come from historically, what they stand for, and what is to be done about the perils and possibilities that lie ahead of them as a people" (Wolin, 1989, p. 14).

In the course of that struggle, individuals come to define identities such as that of the democratic citizen and public official and to mold those identities to a specific set of historical and political experiences and conditions. Clearly, there are limits. It has been argued that there are eradicable and irreconcilable differences among cultures, making some immigrants "unassimilable." For instance, the processes that used to turn foreigners into Frenchmen are faltering (Brubaker, 1992; Hoffmann, 1993, p. 66). Nevertheless, the self is not so much a premise of politics as it is one of its primary creations (Sandel, 1982, 1984).

Autonomous institutions

The story of institutional change is a story of many failed experiments. At every level of adaptation – at the level of interpretations, rules, institutional forms, and specific institutions – changes usually lead to increased vulnerability. Nevertheless, in the struggle to survive, institutions transform themselves. Changes may be discontinuous, contested, and problematic (Skowronek, 1982; Orren and Skowronek, 1994). They may represent "punctuated equilibrium" (Krasner, 1988) and "critical junctions" (Collier and Collier, 1991), and be linked to "performance crises" (March and Olsen, 1989) which stimulate departures from established routines and practices. Many important institutional changes have been associated with the rare cataclysms and metamorphoses at breaking points in history where considerable resources are mobilized and one definition of appropriateness replaces another (Krasner, 1988; March and Olsen, 1989).

However, change also occurs through mundane processes of interpretation, reasoning, education, imitation and adaptation. Institutions create elements of temporary and imperfect order and historical continuity. They give rules communicable meaning so they can be diffused and passed on to new generations. Indeed, institutions are usually associated with routinization and repetition, persistence and predictability, rather than with political change and flexibility, agency, creativity and discretion. Surviving institutions seem to stabilize their norms, rules, and meanings so that procedures and forms adopted at birth have surprising durability (Stinchcombe, 1965; Hannan and Freeman, 1989).

The processes of securing stability, however, introduce two important sources of change. First, the same institutional stability that provides advantage (and may even be essential to survival in the short run) can easily become a source of vulnerability. Institutional competence and reliability become a barrier to change, thus a likely precursor of long-run obsolescence (Levinthal and March, 1993). Second, communicable meaning is subject to reinterpretation. Institutions change as individuals learn the culture (or fail to), forget (parts of) it, revolt against it, modify it or reinterpret it (McNeil and Thompson, 1971; Lægreid and Olsen, 1978, 1984). The resulting drifts in meaning lead to changes that explore alternative political paths and create the divergences of politics.

The pursuit of intelligence

The logic of consequence and the logic of appropriateness are equally logics of thoughtfulness, and the cognitive demands for each are substantial. In the case of a logic of consequence, there are requirements for knowledge about the future and for consistency and clarity in preferences. In the case of a logic of appropriateness, there are requirements for knowledge about the situation and for consistency and clarity in identities. Under appropriate circumstances action based on either logic can lead to achieving outcomes that are judged to be attractive or contribute (over some time horizon) to survival advantage. However, neither rational exchange nor rule-following (and the learning and selection of rules that lies behind it) is assured of being intelligent (March, 1994a). The intelligence of each depends on the ways in which their imperatives are interpreted and on the extent to which capabilities for meeting them exist.

IMPLICATIONS FOR A RESEARCH AGENDA

Institutional perspectives on political institutions and politics provide a set of ideas for thinking about research that is different from ideas drawn from an exchange perspective. Emphasis on modeling the bargaining of exchanges among self-interested individuals within constraints of prior preferences, resources, and rights is replaced by a broader conception that includes attention to the constraints, indeed places them at the center of attention.

Such a framework invites research on the ways in which a political order of rights, rules, and institutions is constructed and maintained through active education and socialization of citizens and officials; on the ways individual and collective capabilities for action evolve endogenously through the allocation of resources and capabilities; on the ways conceptions of identity are developed and shared; on the construction of meaning, including an understanding of history and self, through political and social experience; and on histories in which institutions, behaviors, and contexts are matched in ways that take time and have multiple, path-dependent equilibria.

Within such a conception, research might focus particularly on four grand factors in political development:

First, politics depends on the *identities* of citizens and communities in the political environment. Preferences, expectations, beliefs, identities, and interests are not exogenous to political history. They are created and changed within that history. Political actors act on the basis of identities that are themselves shaped by political institutions and processes. When they act in ways that support a democratic system, they do so because they have come to see such action as part of their own identities.

Second, politics depends on the distribution of *capabilities* for appropriate political action among citizens, groups, and institutions. Acting appropriately to fulfill an identity requires not only the will to do so but also the ability. Those capabilities are not just imposed on a political system or the individuals in it but are distributed and developed within the system as well. It is possible to study the ways individuals and institutions garner the rights, authorities, resources, competencies, and organizing capacities necessary to do what is expected of them and the processes by which they achieve or fail to achieve the fruits of those capabilities.

Third, politics depends on *accounts* of political events and responsibility for them, interpretations of political history. Accounts form the basis for defining situations within which identities are relevant. Meanings and histories are socially constructed. Political myths are developed and transmitted. Accountability is established. It is possible to study the processes by which a current situation is defined or history is understood and by which political events and possibilities are interpreted, as well as the possibilities for transmission, retention, and retrieval of the lessons of history.

Fourth, politics depends on the ways in which a political system *adapts* to changing demands and changing environments. Such adaptiveness involves a balance between exploring new possibilities and exploiting existing capabilities, a balance that is easily upset by dynamics leading to excessive experimentation or excessive stability. Studies of the ways in which political systems reinterpret the meaning of stable identities and institutions and the circumstances and manner in which they are transformed are essential to a comprehension of political continuity and change.

Notes

1. An earlier version of this chapter was presented at the International Political Science Association World Congress, Berlin, August 1994. It draws extensively from March and Olsen, 1994, 1995. The research has been supported by the Spencer Foundation, the Stanford Graduate School of Business, the Norwegian Research Centre in Organization and Management, the Center for Advanced Study in the Behavioral Sciences at Stanford, and the ARENA-program (Advanced Research on the Europeanization of the Nation-State) financed by the Norwegian Research Council.

2. Compare for instance, the various uses of "institution" in political science (Shepsle and Weingast, 1987; Lepsius, 1988; March and Olsen, 1989; Shepsle, 1989; Moe, 1990; Apter, 1991; Grafstein, 1992; Steinmo et al., 1992; Weaver and Rockman, 1993; Orren and Skowronek, 1994) as well as in sociology (Meyer and Rowan, 1977; Scott, 1987; Thomas et al., 1987; Hechter et al., 1990; Powell and DiMaggio, 1991), anthropology (Douglas, 1986), economics (Furubotn and Richter, 1984, 1993; North, 1990; Eggertsson, 1990), and law (Broderick, 1970; MacCormick and Weinberger, 1986; Smith, 1988).

3. Both Habermas and Rawls suggest that we have to avoid models which overburden citizens ethically by assuming a political community united by a comprehensive substantive doctrine. At the same time, both seem to suggest that citizens may share some aims and ends which do not make up a comprehensive doctrine, as well as basic rules for regulating their political coexistence in the face of persistent disagreements and different ways of life (Habermas, 1992, 1994; Rawls, 1993).

References

Apter, D. A. 1991. Institutionalism Reconsidered. *International Social Science Journal* 8:463–81.

Aristotle. 1980. *Politics*. Harmonds-worth: Penguin.

Baum, J. and J. Singh, eds. 1994. *The Evolutionary Dynamics of Organizations*. New York: Oxford University

Press.

Berman, H. J. 1983. *Law and Revolution. The Formation of the Western Legal Tradition.* Cambridge, MA: Harvard University Press.

Berscheid, E. 1994. Interpersonal Relationships. *Annual Review of Psychology* 45:79–129.

Biddle, B. J. 1986. Recent Developments in Role Theory. *Annual Review of Sociology* 12:67–92.

Brady, D. W. 1988. *Critical Elections and Congressional Policy Making.* Stanford CA: Stanford University Press.

Broderick, A. 1970. *The French Institutionalists.* Cambridge MA: Harvard University Press.

Brubaker, R. 1992. *Citizenship and Nationhood in France and Germany.* Cambridge MA: Harvard University Press.

Chapman, J. W. and W. A. Galston, eds. 1992. *Virtue.* Nomos XXXIV. New York: New York University Press.

Coleman, J. S. 1966. The Possibility of a Social Welfare Function. *American Economic Review* 56:1105–22.

Coleman, J. S. 1986. *Individual Interests and Collective Action.* Cambridge: Cambridge University Press.

Collier, R. B. and D. Collier. 1991. *Shaping the Political Arena: Critical Junctures, the Labor Movement, and Regime Dynamics in Latin America.* Princeton NJ: Princeton University Press.

Cyert, R. M. and J. G. March. 1963. *A Behavioral Theory of the Firm.* Englewood Cliffs NJ: Prentice-Hall (2d. ed. 1992: Blackwell).

Douglas, M. 1986. *How Institutions Think.* Syracuse: Syracuse University Press.

Downs, A. 1967. *Inside Bureaucracy.* Boston: Little, Brown.

Dworkin, R. 1986. *Law's Empire.* Cambridge MA: Belknap, Harvard University Press.

Dynes, R. R. 1970. *Organized Behavior in Disaster.* Lexington MA: Heath Lexington Books.

Eggertsson, T. 1990. *Economic Behavior and Institutions.* Cambridge MA: Cambridge University Press.

Eisenstadt, S. and S. Rokkan, eds. 1973. *Building States and Nations* (I,II). Beverly Hills: Sage.

Elster, J. 1989a. *The Cement of Society.* Cambridge MA: Cambridge University Press.

Elster, J. 1989b. Demokratiets verdigrunnlag og verdikonflikter. In *Vitenskap og politikk*, ed. J. Elster. Oslo: Universitetsforlaget.

Elster, J. and R. Slagstad, eds. 1988. *Constitutionalism and Democracy.* Oslo: Norwegian University Press.

Flam, H. 1990a. Emotional Man and the problem of Collective Action. *International Sociology* 5:39–56.

Flam, H. 1990b. Emotional Man II: Corporate Actors as Emotion-motivated Emotion Managers. *International Sociology* 5:225–234.

Flora, P. 1983. *State, Economy, and Society in Western Europe 1815–1975.* Frankfurt: Campus Press.

Friedrich, C. J. 1950. *Constitutional Government and Democracy* (rev. ed.). Boston MA: Ginn and Company.

Furubotn, E. G. and R. Richter, eds. 1984. The new institutional economics. A symposium. Special Issue: *Zeitschrift für die gesamte Staatswissenschaft* 140 (1).

Furubotn, E. G. and R. Richter eds. 1993. The new institutional economics. Recent progress; expanding frontiers. Special Issue, *Zeitschrift für die gesamte Staatswissenschaft* 149 (1).

Gibbons, R. 1992. *Game Theory for Applied Economists.* Princeton NJ:

Princeton University Press.

Giddens, A. 1985. *The Nation-State and Violence*. Berkeley: University of California Press.

Grafstein, R. 1992. *Institutional Realism*. New Haven: Yale University Press.

Greber, E. R. and J. E. Jackson. 1993. Endogenous Preferences and the Study of Institutions. *American Political Science Review* 87:639–56.

Habermas, J. 1992. *Faktizität und Geltung: Beiträge zur Diskurstheorie des rechts und des demokratischen Rechtsstaats*. Frankfurt am Main: Suhrkamp.

Habermas, J. 1994. Three Normative Models of Democracy (manuscript).

Hannan, M. T. and J. Freeman. 1989. *Organizational Ecology*. Cambridge MA: Harvard University Press.

Hart, O. and B. Holmström. 1987. The Theory of Contracts. In T. Bewley, ed. *Advances in Economic Theory*. Cambridge: Cambridge University Press.

Hechter, M., K-D Opp and R. Wippler. 1990. *Social Institutions. Their Emergence, Maintenance and Effects*. New York: deGruyter.

Herzog, Don. 1989. *Happy Slaves. A Critique of Consent Theory*. Chicago: The University of Chicago Press.

Hoffmann, S. 1993. Thoughts on the French Nation Today. *Dædalus* 122:63–79.

Kaufman, H. 1960. *The Forest Ranger*. Baltimore MD: Johns Hopkins University Press.

Kitcher, P. 1985. *Vaulting Ambition*. Cambridge MA: MIT Press.

Krasner, S. D. 1988. Sovereignty: An institutional perspective. *Comparative Political Studies* 21:66–94.

Laitin, D. D. 1985. Hegemony and Religious Conflict: British Imperial Control and Political Cleavages in

Yorubaland. In P.B. Evans, D. Rueschemeyer and T. Skocpol eds. *Bringing the State Back In*, Cambridge: Cambridge University Press.

Lefort, C. 1988. *Democracy and Political Theory*. Cambridge: Polity Press.

Lepsius, M. R. 1988. *Interessen, Ideen und Institutionen*. Opladen: Westdeutscher Verlag.

Levinthal, D. A. 1988. A Survey of Agency Models of Organizations. *Journal of Economic Behavior and Organization* 9:153–85.

Levinthal, D. A. and J. G. March. 1993. The Myopia of Learning. *Strategic Management Journal* 14:95–112.

Levitt B. and J. G. March. 1988. Organizational Learning. *Annual Review of Sociology* 14:319–40.

Lipset, S. M. 1990. *Continental Divide*. New York: Routledge.

Lipset, S. M. and S. Rokkan. 1967. Cleavage Structures, Party Systems and Voter Alignments: An Introduction. In *Party Systems and Voter Alignments*, eds. S. M. Lipset and S. Rokkan. New York: Free Press.

Lægreid, P. and J. P. Olsen. 1978. *Byråkrati og beslutninger*. Bergen: Universitetsforlaget.

Lægreid, P. and Olsen, J. P. 1984. Top Civil Servants in Norway: Key Players – on Different Teams. In *Bureaucrats & Policy Making*, ed. E. N. Suleiman. New York: Holmes & Meier.

Maanen, J. van. 1973. Observations on the Making of Policemen. *Human Organization* 32:407–18.

MacCormick, N. and O. Weinberger. 1986. *An Institutional Theory of Law*. Dordrecht: D. Reidel.

Mansbridge, J. J., ed. 1990. *Beyond Self-Interest*. Chicago: University of Chicago Press.

McNeil, K. and J. D. Thompson. 1971. The Regeneration of Social Organizations. *American Sociological Review* 36:624–37.

March J. G. 1970. Politics and the City. In *Urban Processes as Viewed by the Social Sciences*, eds. K. Arrow; J. S. Coleman, A. Downs, and J. G. March. Washington DC: The Urban Institute Press.

March, J. G. 1981. Footnotes to Organizational Change. *Administrative Science Quarterly* 26:563–77.

March, J. G. 1991. Exploration and Exploitation in Organizational Learning. *Organizational Science* 2:71–87.

March, J. G. 1994a. *A Primer on Decision-Making*. New York: Free Press.

March, J. G. 1994b. The evolution of evolution. In *Evolutionary Dynamics of Organizations*, eds. J. Baum and J. Singh. New York: Oxford University Press.

March, J. G. and J. P. Olsen. 1984. The New Institutionalism: Organizational Factors in Political Life. *American Political Science Review* 78:734–49.

March, J. G. and J. P. Olsen 1989. *Rediscovering Institutions*. New York: Free Press.

March, J. G. and J. P. Olsen 1994. Institutional Perspectives on Governance. In *Systemrationalität und Partialinteresse*, eds. H. U. Derlien, U. Gerhardt and F. W. Scharpf. Baden-Baden: Nomos.

March, J. G. and J. P. Olsen. 1995. *Democratic Governance*. New York: Free Press.

March, J. G. and H. A. Simon. 1958. *Organizations*. New York: Wiley (2d edn 1993: Blackwell).

Meyer, J. W. and B. Rowan. 1977. Institutionalized Organizations: Formal Structure as Myth and Ceremony. *American Journal of Sociology* 83:340–63.

Moe, T. M. 1990. Political Institutions: The Neglected Side of the Story. *Journal of Law, Economics, and Organizations* 6:213–66.

Mulhall, S. and A. Swift. 1992. *Liberals and Communitarians*. Oxford: Blackwell.

Nauta, L. 1992. Changing Conceptions of Citizenship. *Praxis International* 12:20–34.

Niskanen, W. A. 1971. *Bureaucracy and Representative Government*. Chicago: Rand McNally.

North, D. C. 1981. *Structure and Change in Economic History*. New York: Norton.

North, D. C. 1990. *Institutions, Institutional Change and Economic Performance*. Cambridge: Cambridge University Press.

Olsen, J. P. 1990. *Demokrati på svenska*. Stockholm: Carlssons.

Olsen, J. P. 1992. Analyzing Institutional Dynamics. *Staatswissenschaften und Staatspraxis* 2:247–71.

Olsen, J. P. and B. G. Peters, eds. 1996. *Lessons from Experience Experiential Learning in Administrative Reforms in Eight Democracies*. Oslo: Scandinavian University Press.

Orren, K. and S. Skowronek. 1994. Beyond the Iconography of Order: Notes for a "New Institutionalism." In *The Dynamics of American Politics*, eds. L. C. Dodd and C. Jillson. Boulder: Westview Press.

Powell, W. W. and P. J. DiMaggio, eds. 1991. *The New Institutionalism in Organizational Analysis*. Chicago: The University of Chicago Press.

Quarantelli, E. L. and R. R. Dynes. 1977. Responses to Social Crisis and Disaster. *Annual Review of Sociology* 3:23–49.

Rawls, J. 1993. *Political Liberalism*. New York: Columbia University Press.

Riker, W. H. 1962. *The Theory of*

Political Coalitions. New Haven: Yale University Press.

Rothstein, B. 1992. Labor-Market Institutions and Working Class Strength. In *Structuring Politics. Historical Institutionalism in Comparative Analysis*, eds. S. Steinmo, K. Thelen and F. Longstreeth. Cambridge: Cambridge University Press.

Sabine, G. H. 1952. The Two Democratic Traditions. *The Philosophical Review* 5:493–511.

Sandel, M. J. 1982. *Liberalism and the Limits of Justice*. Cambridge: Cambridge University Press.

Sandel, M. J. 1984. The Procedural Republic and the Unencumbered Self. *Political Theory* 12:81–96.

Scott, W. R. 1987. The Adolescence of Institutional Theory. *Administrative Science Quarterly* 32:493–511.

Searing, D. D. 1991. Roles, Rules and Rationality in the New Institutionalism. *American Political Science Review* 85:1239–60.

Selznick, P. 1949. *TVA and the Grass Roots*. Berkeley: University of California Press.

Selznick, P. 1992. *The Moral Commonwealth*. Berkeley: University of California Press.

Sened, I. 1991. Contemporary Theory of Institutions in Perspective. *Journal of Theoretical Politics* 3:379–402.

Shepsle. K. A. 1989. Studying Institutions. Some Lessons from the Rational Choice Approach. *Journal of Theoretical Politics* 1:131–47.

Shepsle, K. A. 1990. *Perspectives on Positive Economy*. Cambridge: Cambridge University Press.

Shepsle, K. A. and B. Weingast. 1987. The Institutional Foundations of Committee Power. *American Political Science Review* 81:85–104.

Skowronek, S. 1982. *Building a New American State*. Cambridge: Cambridge University Press.

Smith, R. M. 1988. Political Jurisprudence, the "New Institutionalism" and the Future of Public Law. *American Political Science Review* 82:89–108.

Spradley, J. P. and B. J. Mann. 1975. *The Cocktail Waitress*. New York: Wiley.

Steinmo, S., K. Thelen and F. Longstreeth, eds. 1992. *Structuring Politics. Historical Institutionalism in Comparative Analysis*. Cambridge: Cambridge University Press.

Stinchcombe, A. L. 1965. Social Structure and Organizations. In *Handbook of Organizations*, ed. J. G. March. Chicago: Rand McNally.

Sunstein, C. 1990, *After the Rights Revolution*. Cambridge MA: Harvard University Press.

Taylor, C. 1985. *Philosophy and the Human Sciences*. Cambridge: Cambridge University Press.

Teubner, G. 1993. *Lew as an Autopoietic System*. Oxford: Blackwell.

Thelen, K. and S. Steinmo. 1992. Historical Institutionalism in Comparative Politics. In *Structuring Politics. Historical Institutionalism in Comparative Analysis*, eds. S. Steinmo, K. Thelen and F. Longstreeth. Cambridge: Cambridge University Press.

Thomas, G. M. et al. 1987. *Institutional Structure, Constituting State, Society, and the Individual*. Beverly Hills CA: Sage.

Thompson, M., R. Ellis and A. Wildavsky, 1990. *Cultural Theory*. Boulder: Westview Press.

Tilly, C., ed. 1975. *The Formation of National States in Western Europe*. Princeton NJ: Princeton University Press.

Tilly, C. 1993, rev. ed. *Coercion, Capital, and European States*. Oxford:

Blackwell.

Turner, B. S. 1990. Outline of a Theory of Citizenship. *Sociology* 24:189–217.

Tussman, J. 1960. *Obligation and the Body Politic*. London: Oxford University Press.

Weaver, R. K. and B. A. Rockman, eds. 1993. *Do Institutions Matter?* Washington DC: Brookings.

Wildavsky, A. 1987. Choosing Preferences by Constructing Institutions: A Cultural Theory of Preference Formation. *American Political Science Review* 81:3–22.

Wolin, S. S. 1989. *The Presence of the Past. Essays on the State and the Constitution*. Baltimore: The Johns Hopkins University Press.

Yack, B. 1985. Concept of Political Community in Aristotle's Philosophy. *The Review of Politics* 47:92–112.

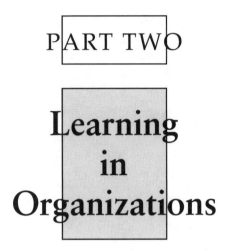

PART TWO

Learning in Organizations

CHAPTER FIVE

Organizational Learning
with Barbara Levitt

This chapter reviews the literature on organizational learning. Organizational learning is viewed as routine-based, history-dependent, and target-oriented. Organizations are seen as learning by encoding inferences from history into routines that guide behavior. Within this perspective on organizational learning, topics covered include how organizations learn from direct experience, how organizations learn from the experience of others, and how organizations develop conceptual frameworks or paradigms for interpreting that experience. The section on organizational memory discusses how organizations encode, store, and retrieve the lessons of history despite the turnover of personnel and the passage of time. Organizational learning is further complicated by the ecological structure of the simultaneously adapting behavior of other organizations, and by an endogenously changing environment. The final section discusses the limitations as well as the possibilities of organizational learning as a form of intelligence.

INTRODUCTION

Theories of organizational learning can be distinguished from theories of analysis and choice which emphasize anticipatory calculation and intention (Machina, 1987), from theories of conflict and bargaining which emphasize strategic action, power, and exchange (Pfeffer, 1981), and from theories of variation and selection which emphasize differential birth and survival rates of invariant forms (Hannan & Freeman, 1977). Although the actual behavioral processes and mechanisms of learning are sufficiently intertwined with choice, bargaining, and selection to make such theoretical distinctions artificial at times, ideas about organizational learning are distinct from, and framed by, ideas about the other processes (Grandori, 1987; Scott, 1987).

Our interpretation of organizational learning builds on three classical observations drawn from behavioral studies of organizations. The first is that behavior in an organization is based on routines (Cyert & March 1963; Nelson & Winter, 1982). Action stems from a logic of appropriateness or legitimacy more than from a logic of consequentiality or intention. It involves matching procedures to situations more than it does calculating choices. The second observation is that organizational actions are history-dependent (Lindblom, 1959; Steinbruner, 1974). Routines are based on interpretations of the past more than anticipations of the future. They adapt to experience incrementally in response to feedback about outcomes. The third observation is that organizations are oriented to targets (Simon, 1955; Siegel, 1957). Their behavior depends on the relation between the outcomes they observe and the aspirations they have for those outcomes. Sharper distinctions are made between success and failure than among gradations of either.

Within such a framework, organizations are seen as learning by encoding inferences from history into routines that guide behavior. The generic term "routines" includes the forms, rules, procedures, conventions, strategies, and technologies around which organizations are constructed and through which they operate. It also includes the structure of beliefs, frameworks, paradigms, codes, cultures, and knowledge that buttress, elaborate, and contradict the formal routines. Routines are independent of the individual actors who execute them and are capable of surviving considerable turnover in individual actors.

The experiential lessons of history are captured by routines in a way that makes the lessons, but not the history, accessible to organizations and organizational members who have not themselves experienced the history. Routines are transmitted through socialization, education, imitation, professionalization, personnel movement, mergers, and acquisitions. They are recorded in a collective memory that is often coherent but is sometimes jumbled, that often endures but is sometimes lost. They change as a result of experience within a community of other learning organizations. These changes depend on interpretations of history, particularly on the evaluation of outcomes in terms of targets.

In the remainder of the present chapter we examine such processes of organizational learning. The perspective is narrower than that used by some (Starbuck, 1976; Hedberg, 1981; Fiol & Lyles, 1985) and differs conceptually from that used by others. In particular, both the emphasis on routines and the emphasis on ecologies of learning distinguish the present formulation from treatments that deal primarily with individual learning within single organizations (March & Olsen, 1975; Argyris &

Schön, 1978) and place this chapter closer to the traditions of behavioral theories of organizational decision-making (Winter, 1986; House & Singh, 1987), and to population level theories of organizational change (Carroll, 1984; Astley, 1985).

LEARNING FROM DIRECT EXPERIENCE

Routines and beliefs change in response to direct organizational experience through two major mechanisms. The first is trial-and-error experimentation. The likelihood that a routine will be used is increased when it is associated with success in meeting a target, decreased when it is associated with failure (Cyert & March, 1963). The underlying process by which this occurs is left largely unspecified. The second mechanism is organizational search. An organization draws from a pool of alternative routines, adopting better ones when they are discovered. Since the rate of discovery is a function both of the richness of the pool and of the intensity and direction of search, it depends on the history of success and failure of the organization (Radner, 1975).

Learning by doing

The purest example of learning from direct experience is found in the effects of cumulated production and user experience on productivity in manufacturing (Dutton et al., 1984). Research on aircraft production, first in the 1930s (Wright, 1936) and subsequently during World War II (Asher, 1956), indicated that direct labor costs in producing airframes declined with the cumulated number of airframes produced. If C_i is the direct labor cost of the ith airframe produced, and a is a constant, then the empirical results are approximated by: $C_n = C_1 n^{-a}$. This equation, similar in spirit and form to learning curves in individuals and animals, has been shown to fit production costs (in constant dollars) reasonably well in a relatively large number of products, firms, and nations (Yelle, 1979). Much of the early research involved only simple graphical techniques, but more elaborate analyses have largely confirmed the original results (Rapping, 1965). Estimates of the learning rate, however, vary substantially across industries, products, and time (Dutton & Thomas, 1984).

Empirical plots of experience curves have been buttressed by three kinds of analytical elaborations. First, there have been attempts to decompose experience curves into several intercorrelated causes and to assess their separate contributions to the observed improvements in manufacturing costs. Although it has been argued that important elements of the improvements come through feedback from customers who use the products, particularly where those products are complex (Rosenberg, 1982), most of the research on experience curves has emphasized the direct effects of cumulative experience on production skills. Most studies indicate that the effects due to cumulative production are greater than those due to changes in the current scale of production, transformation of the technology, increases in the experience of individual production workers, or the passage of time (Preston & Keachie, 1964; Hollander, 1965; Argote et al., 1987); but there is evidence that the latter effects are also involved (Dutton & Thomas, 1984, 1985). Second, there have been attempts to use experience curves as a basis for pricing strategies. These efforts have led to some well-publicized successes but also to some failures attributable to an inadequate specification of the basic model, particularly as it relates to the sharing of experience across organizations (Day & Montgomery, 1983; Dutton & Freedman, 1985). Third, there have been attempts to define models that not only predict the general log-linear result but also accommodate some of the small but theoretically interesting departures from that curve (Muth, 1986). These efforts are, for the most part, variations on themes of trial-and-error learning or organizational search.

Competency traps

In simple discussions of experiential learning based on trial-and-error learning or organizational search, organizations are described as gradually adopting those routines, procedures, or strategies that lead to favorable outcomes; but the routines themselves are treated as fixed. In fact, of course, routines are transformed at the same time as the organization learns which of them to pursue, and discrimination among alternative routines is affected by their transformations (March, 1981; Burgelman, 1988).

The dynamics are exemplified by cases in which each routine is itself a collection of routines, and learning takes place at several nested levels. In such multilevel learning, organizations learn simultaneously both to discriminate among routines and to refine the routines by learning within them. A familiar contemporary example is the way in which organizations learn to use some software systems rather than others and simultaneously learn to refine their skills on the systems that they use. As a result of such learning, efficiency with any particular procedure increases with use, and differences in success with different procedures reflect not only differences in the performance potentials of the procedures but also an organization's current competences with them.

Multilevel learning typically leads to specialization. By improving competencies within frequently used procedures, it increases the frequency with which those procedures result in successful outcomes and thereby increases their use. Provided this process leads the organization both to improve the efficiency and to increase the use of the procedure with the highest potential, specialization is advantageous. However, a competency trap can occur when favorable performance with an inferior procedure leads an organization to accumulate more experience with it, thus keeping experience with a superior procedure inadequate to make it rewarding to use. Such traps are well-known both in their new technology version (Cooper & Schendel, 1976) and in their new procedures version (Zucker, 1977).

Competency traps are particularly likely to lead to maladaptive specialization if newer routines are better then older ones. One case is the sequential exposure to new procedures in a developing technology (Barley, 1988). Later procedures are improvements, but learning organizations have problems in overcoming the competences they have developed with earlier ones (Whetten, 1987). The likelihood of such persistence in inferior procedures is sensitive to the magnitude of the difference between the potentials of the alternatives. The status quo is unlikely to be stable if the differences in potential between existing routines and new ones are substantial (Stinchcombe, 1986). The likelihood of falling into a competency trap is also sensitive to learning rates. Fast learning among alternative routines tends to increase the risks of maladaptive specialization, while fast learning within a new routine tends to decrease the risks (Herriott et al., 1985).

The broader social and evolutionary implications of competency traps are considerable. In effect, learning produces increasing returns to experience (thus typically to scale) and leads an organization, industry, or society to persist in using a set of procedures or technologies that may be far from optimal (Arthur, 1984). Familiar examples are the standard typewriter keyboard and the use of the internal combustion gasoline engine to power motor vehicles. Since they convert almost chance actions based on small differences into stable arrangements, competency traps result in organizational histories for which broad functional or efficiency explanations are often inadequate.

INTERPRETATION OF EXPERIENCE

The lessons of experience are drawn from a relatively small number of observations in a complex, changing ecology of learning organizations. What has happened is not always obvious, and the causality of events is difficult to untangle. What an organization should expect to achieve, and thus the difference between success and failure, is not always clear. Nevertheless, people in organizations form interpretations of events and come to classify outcomes as good or bad (Thompson, 1967).

Certain properties of this interpretation of experience stem from features of individual inference and judgment. As has frequently been observed, individual human beings are not perfect statisticians (Kahneman et al., 1982). They make systematic errors in recording the events of history and in making inferences from them. They overestimate the probability of events that actually occur and of events that are available to attention because of their recency or saliency. They are insensitive to sample size. They tend to overattribute events to the intentional actions of individuals. They use simple linear and functional rules, associate causality with spatial and temporal contiguity, and assume that big effects must have big causes. These attributes of individuals as historians are important to the present topic because they lead to systematic biases in interpretation, but they are reviewed in several previous publications (Slovic et al., 1977; Einhorn & Hogarth, 1986; Starbuck & Milliken, 1988) and are not discussed here.

Stories, paradigms, and frames

Organizations devote considerable energy to developing collective understandings of history. These interpretations of experience depend on the frames within which events are comprehended (Daft & Weick, 1984). They are translated into, and developed through, story lines that come to be broadly, but not universally, shared (Clark, 1972; Martin et al., 1985). This structure of meaning is normally suppressed as a conscious concern, but learning occurs within it. As a result, some of the more powerful phenomena in organizational change surround the transformation of givens, the redefinition of events, alternatives, and concepts through consciousness raising, culture building, double-loop learning, or paradigm shifts (Argyris & Schön, 1978; Brown, 1978; Beyer, 1981).

It is imaginable that organizations will come to discard ineffective interpretive frames in the very long run, but the difficulties in using history to discriminate intelligently among alternative paradigms are profound. Where there are multiple, hierarchically arranged levels of simultaneous learning, the interactions among them are complex, and it is difficult to evaluate higher order alternatives on the basis of experience. Alternative frames are flexible enough to allow change in operational routines without affecting organizational mythology (Meyer & Rowan, 1977; Krieger, 1979), and organizational participants collude in support of interpretations that sustain the myths (Tirole, 1986). As a result, stories, paradigms, and beliefs are conserved in the face of considerable potential disconfirmation (Sproull, 1981); and what is learned appears to be influenced less by history than by the frames applied to that history (Fischhoff, 1975; Pettigrew, 1985).

Although frameworks for interpreting experience within organizations are generally resistant to experience – indeed, may enact that experience (Weick, 1979) – they are vulnerable to paradigm peddling and paradigm politics. Ambiguity sustains the efforts of theorists and therapists to promote their favorite frameworks, and the process by which interpretations are developed makes it relatively easy for conflicts of interest within an organization to spawn conflicting interpretations. For example, leaders of organizations are inclined to accept paradigms that attribute organizational successes to their own actions and organizational failures to the actions of others or to external forces, but opposition groups in an organization are likely to have the converse principle for attributing causality (Miller & Ross, 1975). Similarly, advocates of a particular policy, but not their opponents, are likely to interpret failures less as a symptom that the policy is incorrect than as an indication that it has not been pursued vigorously enough (Ross & Staw, 1986). As a result, disagreements over the meaning of history are possible, and different groups develop alternative stories that interpret the same experience quite differently.

The ambiguity of success

Both trial-and-error learning and incremental search depend on the evaluation of outcomes as successes or failures. There is a structural bias toward postdecision disappointment in ordinary decision making (Harrison & March, 1984), but individual decision makers often seem to be able to reinterpret their objectives or the outcomes in such a way as to make themselves successful even when the shortfall seems quite large (Staw & Ross, 1978).

The process is similar in organizational learning, particularly where the leadership is stable and the organization is tightly integrated (Ross & Staw, 1986). But where such conditions do not hold, there are often differences stemming from the political nature of an organization. Goals are ambiguous, and commitment to them is confounded by their relation to personal and subgroup objectives (Moore & Gates, 1986). Conflict and decision advocacy within putatively rational decision processes lead to inflated expectations and problems of implementation and thus to disappointments (Olsen, 1976; Sproull et al., 1978). Different groups in an organization often have different targets and evaluate the same outcome differently. Simple euphoria is constrained by the presence of individuals and groups who opposed the direction being pursued, or who at least feel no need to accept responsibility for it (Brunsson, 1985). New organizational leaders are inclined to define previous outcomes more negatively than are the leaders who preceded them (Hedberg, 1981). As a result, evaluations of outcomes are likely to be more negative or more mixed in organizations than they are in individuals.

Organizational success is ordinarily defined in terms of the relation between performance outcomes and targets. Targets, however, change over time in two ways. First, the indicators of success are modified. Accounting definitions change (Burchell et al., 1985); social and policy indicators are redefined (MacRae, 1985). Second, levels of aspiration with respect to any particular indicator change. The most common assumption is that a target is a function of some kind of moving average of past achievement, the gap between past achievement and past targets, or the rate of change of either (Cyert & March, 1963; Lant, 1987).

Superstitious learning

Superstitious learning occurs when the subjective experience of learning is compelling, but the connections between actions and outcomes are misspecified. Numerous opportunities exist for such misunderstandings in learning from experience in organizations. For example, it is easy for technicians to develop superstitious perceptions of a new technology from their experience with it (Barley, 1988). Cases of superstition that are of particular interest to students of organizations are those that stem from special features of life in hierarchical organizations. For example, the promotion of managers on the basis of performance produces self-confidence among top executives that is partly superstitious, leading them to overestimate the extent to which they can control the risks their organizations face (March & Shapira, 1987).

Superstitious learning often involves situations in which subjective evaluations of success are insensitive to the actions taken. During very good times, or when post-outcome euphoria reinterprets outcomes positively, or when targets are low, only exceptionally inappropriate routines will lead an organization to experience failure. In like manner, during very bad times, or when post-outcome pessimism reinterprets outcomes negatively, or when targets are high, no routine will lead to success. Evaluations that are insensitive to actions can also result from adaptive aspirations. Targets that adapt very rapidly will be close to the current performance level. This makes being above or below the target an almost chance event. Very slow adaptation, on the other hand, is likely to keep an organization either successful for long periods of time or unsuccessful for long periods of time. A similar result is realized if targets adapt to the performance of other organizations. For example, if each firm in an industry sets its target equal to the average performance of firms in that industry, some firms are likely to be persistently above the target and others persistently below (Levinthal & March, 1981; Herriott et al., 1985).

Each of these situations produces superstitious learning. In an organization that is invariantly successful, routines that are followed are associated with success and are reinforced; other routines are inhibited. The organization becomes committed to a particular set of routines, but the routines to which it becomes committed are determined more by early (relatively arbitrary) actions than by information gained from the learning situation (Nystrom & Starbuck, 1984). Alternatively, if failure is experienced regardless of the particular routine that is used, routines are changed frequently in a fruitless search for some that work. In both cases, the subjective feeling of learning is powerful, but it is misleading.

ORGANIZATIONAL MEMORY

Organizational learning depends on features of individual memories (Hastie et al., 1984; Johnson & Hasher, 1987), but our present concern is with organizational aspects of memory. Routine-based conceptions of learning presume that the lessons of experience are maintained and accumulated within routines despite the turnover of personnel and the passage of time. Rules, procedures, technologies, beliefs, and cultures are conserved through systems of socialization and control. They are retrieved through mechanisms of attention within a memory structure. Such organizational instruments not only record history but shape its future path, and the details of that path depend significantly on the processes by which the memory is maintained and consulted. An accounting system, whether viewed as the product of design or the residue of historical development, affects the recording and creation of history by an organization (Johnson & Kaplan, 1987; Røvik, 1987). The ways in which military routines are changed, maintained, and consulted contribute to the likelihood and orchestration of military engagement (Levy, 1986).

Recording of experience

Inferences drawn from experience are recorded in documents, accounts, files, standard operating procedures, and rule books; in the social and physical geography of organizational structures and relationships; in standards of good professional practice; in the culture of organizational stories; and in shared perceptions of "the way things are done around here." Relatively little is known about the details by which organizational experience is accumulated into a structure of routines, but it is clearly a process that yields different kinds of routines in different situations and is only partly successful in imposing internal consistency on organizational memories.

Not everything is recorded. The transformation of experience into routines and the recording of those routines involve costs. The costs are sensitive to information technology, and a common observation is that modern computer-based technology encourages the automation of routines by substantially reducing the costs of recording them. Even so, a good deal of experience is unrecorded simply because the costs are too great. Organizations also often make a distinction between outcomes that will be considered relevant for future actions and outcomes that will not. The distinction may be implicit, as for example when comparisons between projected and realized returns from capital investment projects are ignored (Hägg, 1979). It may be explicit, as for example when exceptions to the rules are declared not to be precedents for the future. By creating a set of actions that are not precedents, an organization gives routines both short-term flexibility and long-term stability (Powell, 1986).

Organizations vary in the emphasis placed on formal routines. Craft-based organizations rely more heavily on tacit knowledge than do bureaucracies (Becker, 1982). Organizations facing complex uncertainties rely on informally shared understandings more than do organizations dealing with simpler, more stable environments (Ouchi, 1980). There is also variation within organizations. Higher level managers rely more on ambiguous information (relative to formal rules) than do lower level managers (Daft & Lengel, 1984).

Experiential knowledge, whether in tacit form or in formal rules, is recorded in an organizational memory. That memory is orderly, but it exhibits inconsistencies and ambiguities. Some of the contradictions are a consequence of inherent complications in maintaining consistency in inferences drawn sequentially from a changing experience. Some, however, reflect differences in experience, the confusions of history, and conflicting interpretations of that history. These latter inconsistencies are likely to be organized into deviant memories, maintained by subcultures, subgroups, and subunits (Martin et al., 1985). With a change in the fortunes of the dominant coalition, the deviant memories become more salient to action (Martin & Siehl, 1983).

Conservation of experience

Unless the implications of experience can be transferred from those who experienced it to those who did not, the lessons of history are likely to be lost through turnover of personnel. Written rules, oral transitions, and systems of formal and informal apprenticeships implicitly instruct new individuals in the lessons of history. Under many circumstances, the transfer of tradition is relatively straightforward and organizational experience is substantially conserved. For example, most police officers are socialized successfully to actions and beliefs recognizable as acceptable police behavior, even in cases where those actions and beliefs are substantially different from those that were originally instrumental in leading an individual to seek the career (Van Maanen, 1973).

Under other circumstances, however, organizational experience is not conserved. Knowledge disappears from an organization's active memory (Neustadt & May, 1986). Routines are not conserved because of limits on the time or legitimacy of the socializing agents, as for example in deviant subgroups or when the number of new members is large (Sproull et al., 1978); because of conflict with other normative orders, as for example with new organization members who are also members of well-organized professions (Hall, 1968); or because of the weaknesses of organizational control, as for example in implementation across geographic or cultural distances (Brytting, 1986).

Retrieval of experience

Even within a consistent and accepted set of routines, only part of an organization's memory is likely to be evoked at a particular time, or in a particular part of the organization. Some parts of organizational memory are more available for retrieval than others. Availability is associated with the frequency of use of a routine, the recency of its use, and its organizational proximity. Recently used and frequently used routines are more easily evoked than those that have been used infrequently. Thus, organizations have difficulty retrieving relatively old, unused knowledge or skills (Argote et al., 1987). In cases where routines are nested within more general routines, the repetitive use of lower level routines tends to make them more accessible than the more general routine to which they are related (Merton, 1940). The effects of proximity stem from the ways the accumulation of history is linked to regularized responsibility. The routines that record lessons of experience are organized around organizational responsibilities and are retrieved more easily when actions are taken through regular channels than when they occur outside those channels (Olsen, 1983). At the same time, organizational structures create advocates for routines. Policies are converted into responsibilities that encourage rule zealotry (Mazmanian & Nienaber, 1979).

Availability is also partly a matter of the direct costs of finding and using what is stored in memory. Particularly where there are large numbers of routines bearing on relatively specific actions, modern information technology has reduced those costs and made the routinization of relatively complex organizational behavior economically feasible, for example in the preparation of reports or presentations, the scheduling of production or logistical support, the design of structures or engineering systems, or the analysis of financial statements (Smith & Green, 1980). Such automation of the recovery of routines makes retrieval more reliable. Reliability is, however, a mixed blessing. It standardizes retrieval and thus typically underestimates the conflict of interest and ambiguity about preferences in an organization. Expert systems of the standard type have difficulty capturing the unpredictable richness, erratic redundancy, and casual validity checking of traditional retrieval procedures, and they reduce or eliminate the fortuitous experimentation of unreliable retrieval (Simon, 1971; Wildavsky, 1983). As a result, they are likely to make learning more difficult for the organization.

LEARNING FROM THE EXPERIENCE OF OTHERS

Organizations capture the experience of other organizations through the transfer of encoded experience in the form of technologies, codes, procedures, or similar routines (Dutton & Starbuck, 1978). This diffusion of experience and routines from other organizations within a community of organizations complicates theories of routine-based learning. It suggests that understanding the relation between experiential learning and routines, strategies, or technologies in organizations will require attention to organizational networks (Håkansson, 1987) as well as to the experience of the individual organization. At the same time, it makes the derivation of competitive strategies (e.g. pricing strategies) more complex than it would otherwise be (Hilke & Nelson, 1987).

Mechanisms for diffusion

The standard literature on the epidemiology of disease or information distinguishes three broad processes of diffusion. The first is diffusion involving a single source broadcasting a disease to a population of potential, but not necessarily equally vulnerable, victims. Organizational examples include rules promulgated by governmental agencies, trade associations, professional associations, and unions (Scott, 1985). The second process is diffusion involving the spread of a disease through contact between a member of the population who is infected and one who is not, sometimes mediated by a host carrier. Organizational examples include routines diffused by contacts among organizations, by consultants, and by the movement of personnel (Biggart, 1977). The third process is two-stage diffusion involving the spread of a disease within a small group by contagion and then by broadcast from them to the remainder of a population. Organizational examples include routines communicated through formal and informal educational institutions, through experts, and through trade and popular publications (Heimer, 1985a). In the organizational literature, these three processes have been labeled *coercive, mimetic,* and *normative* (DiMaggio & Powell, 1983). All three are involved in a comprehensive system of information diffusion (Imai et al., 1985).

Dynamics of diffusion

The possibilities for learning from the experience of others, as well as some of the difficulties, can be illustrated by looking at the diffusion of innovations among organizations. We consider here only some issues that are particularly important for organizational learning. For more general reviews of the literature, see Rogers & Shoemaker (1971) and Kimberly (1981).

Although it is not easy to untangle the effects of imitation from other effects that lead to differences in the time of adoption, studies of the spread of new technologies among organizations seem to indicate that diffusion through imitation is less significant than is variation in the match between the technology and the organization (Mansfield, 1968), especially as that match is discovered and molded through learning (Kay, 1979). Imitation, on the other hand, has been credited with contributing substantially to diffusion of city manager plans among American cities (Knoke, 1982) and multidivisional organizational structures among American firms (Fligstein, 1985). Studies of the adoption of civil service reform by cities in the United States (Tolbert & Zucker, 1983) and of high technology weaponry by air forces (Eyre et al., 1987) both show patterns in which features of the match between the procedures and the adopting organizations are more significant for explaining early adoptions than they are for explaining later ones, which seem better interpreted as due to imitation. The latter result is also supported by a study of the adoption of accounting conventions by firms (Mezias, 1987).

The underlying ideas in the literature on the sociology of institutionalization are less epidemiological than they are functional, but the diffusion of practices and forms is one of the central mechanisms considered (Zucker, 1987). Pressure on organizations to demonstrate that they are acting on collectively valued purposes in collectively valued ways leads them to copy ideas and practices from each other. The particular professions, policies, programs, laws, and public opinion that are created in the process of producing and marketing goods and services become powerful institutionalized myths that are adopted by organizations to legitimate themselves and ensure public support (Meyer & Rowan, 1977; Zucker, 1977). The process diffuses forms and procedures and thereby tends to diffuse organizational power structures as well (Fligstein, 1987).

The dynamics of imitation depend not only on the advantages that come to an organization as it profits from the experience of others, but also on the gains or losses that accrue to those organizations from which the routines or beliefs are drawn (DiMaggio & Powell, 1983). In many (but not all) situations involving considerations of technical efficiency, diffusion of experience has negative consequences for organizations that are copied. This situation is typified by the case of technical secrets, where sharing leads to loss of competitive position. In many (but not all) situations involving considerations of legitimacy, diffusion of experience has positive consequences for organizations that are copied. This situation is typified by the case of accounting practices, where sharing lead to greater legitimacy for all concerned.

The critical factor for the dynamics is less whether the functional impetus is a concern for efficiency or legitimacy than whether the feedback effects are positive or negative (Wiewel & Hunter, 1985). Where concerns for technical efficiency are associated with positive effects of sharing, as for example in many symbiotic relations within an industry, the process will unfold in ways similar to the process of institutionalization. Where concerns for legitimacy are associated with negative effects of sharings as for example in cases of diffusion where mimicking by other organizations of lower status reduces the lead organization's status, the process will unfold in ways similar to the spread of secrets.

ECOLOGIES OF LEARNING

Organizations are collections of subunits learning in an environment that consists largely of other collections of learning subunits (Cangelosi & Dill, 1965). The ecological structure is a complication in two senses. First, it complicates learning. Because of the simultaneously adapting behavior of other organizations, a routine may produce different outcomes at different times, or different routines may produce the same outcome at different times. Second, an ecology of learners complicates the systematic comprehension and modeling of learning processes. Environments change endogenously, and even relatively simple conceptions of learning become complex.

Learning in a world of learners

Ecologies of learning include various types of interactions among learners, but the classical type is a collection of competitors. Competitors are linked partly through the diffusion of experience, and understanding learning within competitive communities of organizations involves seeing how experience, particularly secrets, are shared (Sitkin, 1986), and how organizational actors come to trust one another, or not (Zucker, 1986). Competitors are also linked through the effects of their actions on each other. One organization's action is another organization's outcome. As a result, even if learning by an individual organization were entirely internal and direct, it could be comprehended only by specifying the competitive structure.

Suppose competitors learn how to allocate resources to alternative technologies (strategies, procedures) in a world in which the return received by each competitor from the several technologies is a joint consequence of the potentials of the technologies, the changing competences of the several competitors within the technologies, and the allocations of effort by the several competitors among the technologies (Khandwalla, 1981). In a situation of this type, it has been shown that there are strong ecological effects (Herriott et al., 1985). The learning outcomes depend on the number of competitors, the rates at which they learn from their own experience, the rates at which they adjust their targets, the extent to which they learn from the experience of others, and the differences in the potentials of the technologies. There is a tendency for organizations to specialize and for faster learners to specialize in inferior technologies.

Learning to learn

Learning itself can be viewed as one of the technologies within which organizations develop competence through use and among which they choose on the basis of experience. The general (nonecological) expectation is that learning procedures will become common when they lead to favorable outcomes and that organizations will become effective at learning when they use learning routines frequently. The ecological question is whether there are properties of the relations among interacting organizations that lead some of them to learn to learn and others not to do so.

In competitive situations, small differences in competence at learning will tend to accumulate through the competency multiplier, driving slower learners to other procedures. If some organizations are powerful enough to create their own environments, weaker organizations will learn to adapt to the dominant ones, that is they will learn to learn (Heimer, 1985b). By the same token, powerful organizations, by virtue of their ability to ignore competition, will be less inclined to learn from experience and less competent at doing so (Engwall, 1976). The circumstances under which these learning disabilities produce a disadvantage, rather than an advantage, are more complicated to specify than might appear, but there is some chance that a powerful organization will become incapable of coping with an environment that cannot be arbitrarily enacted (Hannan & Freeman, 1984).

LEARNING AS A FORM OF INTELLIGENCE

Organizational learning from experience is not only a useful perspective from which to describe organizational change; it is also an important instrument of organizational intelligence. The speculation that learning can improve the performance, and thus the intelligence, of organizations is confirmed by numerous studies of learning by doing, by case observations, and by theoretical analyses. Since we have defined learning as a process rather than as an outcome, the observation that learning is beneficial to organizations is not empty. It has become commonplace to emphasize learning in the design of organizations, to argue that some important improvements in organizational intelligence can be achieved by giving organizations capabilities to learn quickly and precisely (Starbuck & Dutton, 1973; Duncan & Weiss, 1979). As we have seen, however, the complications in using organizational learning as a form of intelligence are not trivial.

Nor are those problems due exclusively to avoidable individual and organizational inadequacies. There are structural difficulties in learning from experience. The past is not a perfect predictor of the future, and the experimental designs generated by ordinary life are far from ideal for causal inference (Brehmer, 1980). Making organizational learning effective as a tool for comprehending history involves confronting several problems in the structure of organizational experience: (a) The paucity of experience problem: Learning from experience in organizations is compromised by the fact that nature provides inadequate experience relative to the complexities and instabilities of history, particularly when the environment is changing rapidly or involves many dangers or opportunities each of which is very unlikely. (b) The redundancy of experience problem: Ordinary learning tends to lead to stability in routines, to extinguish the experimentation that is required to make a learning process effective. (c) The complexity of experience problem: Organizational environments involve complicated causal systems, as well as interactions among learning organizations. The various parts of the ecology fit together to produce learning outcomes that are hard to interpret.

Improving the structure of experience

The problems of paucity, redundancy, and complexity in experience cannot be eliminated, but they can be ameliorated. One response to the paucity of experience is the augmentation of direct experience through the diffusion of routines. Diffusion increases the amount of experience from which an organization draws and reduces vulnerability to local optima. However, the sharing of experience through diffusion can lead to remarkably incomplete or flawed understandings. For example, if the experiences that are combined are not independent, the advantages of sharing are attenuated, and organizations are prone to exaggerate the experience base of the encoded information. Indeed, part of what each organization learns from others is likely to be an echo of its own previous knowledge (Anderson, 1848).

Patience is a virtue. There is considerable evidence that organizations often change through a sequence of small, frequent changes and inferences formed from experience with them (Zald, 1970). Since frequent changes accentuate the sample size problem by modifying a situation before it can be comprehended, such behavior is likely to lead to random drift rather than improvement (Lounamaa & March, 1987). Reducing the frequency or magnitude of change, therefore, is often an aid to comprehension, though the benefits of added information about one situation are purchased at a cost of reduction in information about others (Levinthal & Yao, 1988).

The sample size problem is particularly acute in learning from low probability, high consequence events. Not only is the number of occurrences small, but the organizational, political, and legal significance of the events, if they occur, often muddies the making of inferences about them with conflict over formal responsibility, accountability, and liability. One strategy for moderating the effects of these problems is to supplement history by creating hypothetical histories of events that might have occurred (Tamuz, 1987). Such histories draw on a richer, less politically polarized set of interpretations, but they introduce error inherent in their hypothetical nature.

Difficulties in overcoming the redundancy of experience and assuring adequate variety of experience is a familiar theme for students of organizational change (Tushman & Romanelli, 1985). Organizational slack facilitates unintentional innovation (March, 1981), and success provides self-confidence in managers that leads to risk-taking (March & Shapira, 1987); but in most other ways success is the enemy of experimentation (Maidique & Zirger, 1985). Thus, concern for increasing experimentation in organizations focuses attention on mechanisms that produce variations in the failure rate, preferably independent of the performance level. One mechanism is noise in the measurement of performance. Random error or confusion in performance measurement produces arbitrary experiences of failure without a change in (real) performance (Hedberg & Jönsson, 1978). A second mechanism is aspiration level adjustment. An aspiration level that tracks past performance (but not too closely) produces a failure rate – thus a level of search and risk taking – that is relatively constant regardless of the absolute level of performance (March 1988).

A second source of experimentation in learning comes from imperfect routine-maintenance – failures of memory, socialization, or control. Incomplete socialization of new organizational members leads to experimentation, as do errors in execution of routines or failures of implementation (Pressman & Wildavsky, 1973). Although it seems axiomatic that most new ideas are bad ones (Hall, 1976), the ideology of management and managerial experience combine to make managers a source of experimentation. Leaders are exhorted to introduce change; they are supposed to make a difference (MacCrimmon & Wehrung, 1986). At the same time, individuals who have been successful in the past are systematically more likely to reach top level positions in organizations than are individuals who have not. Their experience gives them an exaggerated confidence in the chances of success from experimentation and risk taking (March & Shapira, 1987).

Overcoming the worst effects of complexity in experience involves improving the experimental design of natural experience. In particular, it involves making large changes rather than small ones and avoiding multiple simultaneous changes (Miller & Friesen, 1982; Lounamaa & March, 1987). From this point of view, the standard version of incrementalism with its emphasis on frequent, multiple, small changes cannot be, in general, a good learning strategy, particularly since it also violates the patience imperative discussed above (Starbuck, 1983). Nor, as we have suggested earlier, is it obvious that fast, precise learning is guaranteed to produce superior performance. Learning that is somewhat slow and somewhat imprecise often provides an advantage (Levinthal & March, 1981; Herriott et al., 1985).

The intelligence of learning

The concept of intelligence is ambiguous when action and learning occur simultaneously at several nested levels of a system (March, 1987). For example, since experimentation often benefits those who copy successes more than it does the experimenting organization, managerial illusions of control, risk taking, and playful experimentation may be more intelligent from the point of view of a community of organization than from the point of view of organizations that experiment. Although legal arrangements, such as patent laws, attempt to reserve certain benefits of experimentation to those organizations that incur the costs, these complications seem, in general, not to be resolved by explicit contracts but through sets of evolved practices that implicitly balance the concerns of the several levels (March, 1981). The issues involved are closely related to similar issues that arise in variation and selection models (Holland, 1975; Gould, 1982).

Even within a single organization, there are severe limitations to organizational learning as an instrument of intelligence. Learning does not always lead to intelligent behavior. The same processes that yield experiential wisdom produce superstitious learning, competency traps, and erroneous inferences. Problems in learning from experience stem partly from inadequacies of human cognitive habits, partly from features of organization, partly from characteristics of the structure of experience. There are strategies for ameliorating some of those problems, but ordinary organizational practices do not always generate behavior that conforms to such strategies.

The pessimism of such a description must, however, be qualified by two caveats. First, there is adequate evidence that the lessons of history as encoded in routines are an important basis for the intelligence of organizations. Despite the problems, organizations learn. Second, learning needs to be compared with other serious alternatives, not with an ideal of perfection. Processes of choice, bargaining, and selection also make mistakes. If we calibrate the imperfections of learning by the imperfections of its compettitors, it is possible to see a role for routine-based, history-dependent, target-oriented organizational learning. To be effective, however, the design of learning organizations must recognize the difficulties of the process and in particular the extent to which intelligence in learning is often frustrated, and the extent to which the comprehension of history may involve slow rather than fast adaptation, imprecise rather than precise responses to experience, and abrupt rather than incremental changes.

Acknowledgments

This research has been supported by grants from the Spencer Foundation, the Stanford Graduate School of Business, and the Hoover Institution. We are grateful for the comments of Robert A. Burgelman, Johan P. Olsen, W. Richard Scott, and William H. Starbuck.

References

Anderson, H. C. 1848. Det er ganske vist. In *H. C. Andersens Eventyr*. ed. P. Høybe, pp. 72–75. Copenhagen: Forlaget Notabene.

Argote, L., Beckman, S., Epple, D. 1987. The persistence and transfer of learning in industrial settings. Paper presented at the St. Louis meetings of the Institute of Management Sciences (TIMS) and the Operations Research Society of America (ORSA).

Argyris, C., Schön, D. 1978. *Organizational Learning*. Reading: MA: Addison-Wesley.

Arthur, W. B. 1984. Competing technologies and economic prediction. *IIASA Options* 2:10–13.

Asher, H. 1956. *Cost-Quantity Relationships in the Airframe Industry*. Santa Monica, CA: Rand.

Astley, W. G. 1985. The two ecologies: population and community perspectives on organizational evolution. *Admin. Sci. Q.* 30:224–41.

Barley, S. R. 1988. The social construction of a machine: ritual, superstition, magical thinking and other pragmatic responses to running a CT Scanner. In *Knowledge and Practice in Medicine: Social Cultural and Historical Approaches*, ed. M. Lock, D. Gordon. Hingham, MA: Reidel.

Becker, H. S. 1982. *Art Worlds*. Berkeley, CA: Univ. Calif. Press.

Beyer, J. M. 1981. Ideologies, values, and decision making in organizations. See Nystrom & Starbuck 1981, 2:166–202.

Biggart, N. W. 1977. The creative-destructive process of organizational change: the case of the post office. *Admin. Sci. Q.* 22:410–26.

Brehmer, B. 1980. In one word: not from experience. *Acta Psychol.* 45:223–41.

Brown, R. H. 1978. Bureaucracy as

praxis: toward a political phenomenology of formal organizations. *Admin. Sci. Q.* 23:365–82.

Brunsson, N. 1985. *The Irrational Organization: Irrationality as a Basis for Organizational Action and Change.* Chichester, UK: Wiley.

Brytting, T. 1986. The management of distance in antiguity. *Scand. J. Mgmt. Stud.* 3:139–55.

Burchell, S., Colin, C., Hopwood, A. G. 1985. Accounting in its social context: towards a history of value added in the United Kingdom. *Account. Organ. Soc.*, 10:381–413.

Burgelmen, R. A. 1988. Strategy-making as a social learning process: the case of internal corporate venturing. *Interfaces* 18:74–85.

Cangelosi, V. E., Dill, W. R. 1965. Organizational learning: observations toward a theory. *Admin. Sci. Q.* 10:175–203.

Carroll, G. R. 1984. Organizational ecology. *Ann. Rev. Sociol.* 10:71–93.

Clark, B. R. 1972. The organizational saga in higher education. *Admin. Sci. Q.* 17:178–84.

Cooper, A. C., Schendel, D. E. 1976. Strategic responses to technological threats. *Bus. Horizons* Feb: 19(1):61–3.

Cyert, R. M., March, J. G. 1963. *A Behavioral Theory of the Firm.* Englewood Cliffs, NJ: Prentice-Hall.

Daft, R. L., Lengel, R. H. 1984. Information richness: a new approach to managerial behavior and organization design. In *Research in Organizational Behavior.* ed. B. M. Staw, L. L. Cummings, 6:191–223. Greenwich, CT: JAI Press.

Daft, R. L., Weick, K. E. 1984. Toward a model of organizations as interpretation systems. *Acad. Mgmt. Rev.* 9:284–95.

Day, G. S., Montgomery, D. B. 1983.

Diagnosing the experience curve, *J. Mark.* 47:44–58.

DiMaggio, P. J., Powell, W. W. 1983. The iron cage revisited: institutional isomorphism and collective rationality in organizational fields. *Am. Sociol. Rev.* 48:147–60.

Duncan, R., Weiss, A. 1979. Organizational learning: implications for organizational design. In *Research in Organizational Behavior*, ed. B. M. Staw, 1:75–123. Greenwich, CT: JAI Press.

Dutton, J. M., Freedman, R. D. 1985. External environment and internal strategies: calculating, experimenting, and imitating in organizations. In *Advances in Strategic Management*, ed. R. B. Lamb 3:39–67. Greenwich, CT: JAI.

Dutton, J. M., Starbuck, W. H. 1978. Diffusion of an intellectual technology. In *Communication and Control in Society.* ed. K. Krippendorff, pp. 489–511. New York: Gordon & Breach.

Dutton, J. M., Thomas, A. 1984. Treating progress functions as a managerial opportunity. *Acad. Mgmt. Rev.* 9:235–47.

Dutton, J. M., Thomas, A. 1985. Relating technological change and learning by doing. In *Research on Technological Innovation, Management and Policy.* ed. R. S. Rosenbloom, 2:187–224. Greenwich, CT: JAI.

Dutton, J. M., Thomas, A., Butler, J. E. 1984. The history of progress functions as a managerial technology. *Bus. Hist. Rev.* 58:204–33.

Einhorn, E. J., Hogarth, R. M. 1986. Judging probable cause. *Psychol. Bull.* 99:3–19.

Engwall, L. 1976. Response time of organizations. *J. Mgmt. Stud.* 13:1–15.

Eyre, D. P., Suchman, M. C., Alexander, V. D. 1987. The social construction of weapons procurement: proliferation as rational myth. Pap. pres. Ann. Meet. Am. Sociol. Assoc. Chicago.

Fiol C. M., Lyles, M. A. 1985. Organizational learning. *Acad. Mgmt. Rev.* 10:803–13.

Fischhoff, B. 1975. Hindsight or foresight: The effect of outcome knowledge on judgement under uncertainty. *J. Exper. Psychol.* 1:288–99.

Fligstein, N. 1985. The spread of the multidivisional form among large firms, 1919–1979. *Am. Sociol. Rev.* 50:377–91.

Fligstein, N. 1987. The intraorganizational power struggle: rise of finance personnel to top leadership in large corporations, 1919–1979. *Am. Sociol. Rev.* 52:44–58.

Gould, S. J. 1982. Darwinism and the expansion of evolutionary theory. *Science* 216: 380–7.

Grandori, A. 1987. *Perspectives on Organization Theory.* Cambridge, MA: Balling.

Hägg, I. 1979. Reviews of capital investments: empirical studies. *Finn. J. Bus. Econ.* 28:211–25.

Håkansson, H. 1987. *Industrial Technological Development: A Network Approach.* London: Croom Helm.

Hall, R. H. 1968. Professionalization and bureaucratization. *Am. Sociol. Rev.* 33:92–104.

Hall, R. I. 1976. A system pathology of an organization: the rise and fall of the old Saturday Evening Post. *Admin. Sci. Q.* 21:185–211.

Hannan, M. T., Freeman, J. 1977. The population ecology of organizations. *Am. J. Sociol.* 82:929–64.

Hannan, M. T., Freeman, J. 1984. Structural inertia and organizational change. *Am. Sociol. Rev.* 49:149–64.

Harrison, J. R., March, J. G. 1984. Decision making and post-decision surprises. *Admin. Sci. Q.* 29:26–42.

Hastie, R., Park, B., Weber, R. 1984. Social memory. In *Handbook of Social Cognition.* ed. R. S. Wyer, T. K. Srull, 2:151–212. Hillsdale, NJ: Eribaum.

Hedberg, B. L. T., Jönsson, S. 1978. Designing semi-confusing information systems for organizations in changing environments. *Account. Organ. Soc.* 3:47–64.

Hedberg, B. L. T. 1981. How organizations learn and unlearn. See Nystrom & Starbuck 1981, 1:3–27.

Heimer, C. A. 1985a. *Reactive Risk and Rational Action: Managing Moral Hazard in Insurance Contracts.* Berkeley, CA: Univ. Calif. Press.

Heimer, C. A. 1985b. Allocating information costs in a negotiated information order: interorganizational constraints on decision making in Norwegian oil insurance. *Admin. Sci. Q.* 30:395–417.

Herriott, S. R., Levinthal, D., March, J. G. 1985. Learning from experience in organizations. *Am. Econ. Rev.* 75: 298–302.

Hilke, J. C., Nelson, P. B. 1987. Caveat innovator: strategic and structural characteristics of new product innovations. *J. Econ. Behav. Organ.* 8:213–29.

Holland, J. H. 1975. *Adaptation in Natural and Artificial Systems: An Introductory Analysis with Applications to Biology, Control and Artificial Intelligence.* Ann Arbor, MI: Univ. Mich. Press.

Hollander, S. 1965. *The Sources of Increased Efficiency: A Study of Du-Pont Rayon Manufacturing Plants.* Cambridge, MA: MIT Press.

House, R. J., Singh, J. V. 1987. Organizational behavior: some new directions for i/o psychology. *Ann. Rev.*

Psychol. 38:669–718.

Imai, K., Nonaka, I., Takeuchi, H. 1985. Managing the new product development process: how Japanese companies learn and unlearn. In *The Uneasy Alliance*, ed. K. Clark, R. Hayes, C. Lorentz, pp. 337–75. Boston: Harvard Grad. Sch. Bus.

Johnson, H. T., Kaplan, R. S. 1987. *Relevance Lost: The Rise and Fall of Management Accounting.* Boston, MA: Harvard Bus. Sch. Press.

Johnson, M. K., Hasher, L. 1987. Human learning and memory. *Ann. Rev. Psychol.* 38:631–68.

Kahneman, D., Slovic, P., Tversky, A., eds. 1982. *Judgment under Uncertainty: Heuristics and Biases.* Cambridge: Cambridge Univ. Press.

Kay, N. M. 1979. *The Innovating Firm: A Behavioral Theory of Corporate R&D.* New York: St. Martin's Press.

Khandwalla, P. N. 1981. Properties of competing organizations. See Nystrom & Starbuck 1981, 1:409–32.

Kimberly, J. R. 1981. Managerial innovation See Nystrom & Starbuck 1981, 1:84–104.

Knoke, D. 1982. The spread of municipal reform: temporal, spatial, and social dynamics. *Am. J. Sociol.* 87:1314–39.

Krieger, S. 1979. *Hip Capitalism.* Beverly Hills, CA: Sage.

Lant, T. K. 1987. *Goals, search, and risk taking in strategic decision making.* PhD thesis. Stanford Univ.

Levinthal, D. A., March, J. G. 1981. A model of adaptive organizational search. *J. Econ. Behav. Organ.* 2:307–33.

Levinthal, D. A., Yao, D. A. 1988. The search for excellence: organizational inertia and adaptation. *Unpubl. ms.* Carnegie-Mellon Univ.

Levy, J. S. 1986. Organizational routines and the causes of war. *Int. Stud. Q.* 30:193–222.

Lindblom, C. E. 1959. The "science" of muddling through. *Public Admin. Rev.,* 19:79–88.

Lounamas, P. H., March, J. G. 1987. Adaptive coordination of a learning team. *Mgmt. Sci.* 33:107–23.

Machins, M. J. 1987. Choice under uncertainty: problems solved and unsolved. *J. Econ. Perspect.* 1:121–54.

MacCrimmon, K. R., Wehrung, D. A. 1986 *Taking Risks: The Management of Uncertainty.* New York: Free Press.

MacRae, D. 1985. *Policy Indicators.* Chapel Hill, NC: Univ. North Carolina Press.

Maidique, M. A., Zirger, B. J. 1985. The new product learning cycle. *Res. Policy* 14:299–313.

Mansfield, E. 1968. *The Economics of Technological Change.* New York: Norton.

March, J. G. 1981. Footnotes to organizational change. *Admin. Sci. Q.* 26:563–77.

March, J. G. 1987. Ambiguity and accounting: the elusive link between information and decision making. *Account. Organ. Soc.* 12:153–68.

March, J. G. 1988. Variable risk preferences and adaptive aspirations. *J. Econ. Behav. Organ.* 9:5–24.

March, J. G., Olsen, J. P. 1975. The uncertainty of the past: organizational learning under ambiguity. *Eur. J. Polit. Res.* 3:147–71.

March, J. G., Shapira, Z. 1987. Managerial perspectives on risk and risk taking. *Mgmt. Sci.* 33:1404–18.

Martin, J., Siehl, C. 1983. Organizational culture and counterculture: an uneasy symbiosis. *Organ. Dynam.* Autumn:52–64.

Martin, J., Sitkin, S. B., Boehm, M. 1985. Founders and the elusiveness of a culture legacy. In *Organizational Culture*, ed. P. J. Frost, L. F. Moore, M. R. Louis, C. C. Lundberg, J. Martin, pp. 99–124. Beverly Hills, CA: Sage.

Mazmanian, D. A., Nienaber, J. 1979. *Can Organizations Change? Environmental Protection, Citizen Participation, and the Corps of Engineers*. Washington, DC: The Brookings Inst.

Merton, R. K. 1940. Bureaucratic structure and personality. *Soc. Forces* 18:560–8.

Meyer, J. W., Rowan, B. 1977. Institutionalized organizations: formal structure as myth and ceremony. *Am. J. Sociol.* 83:340–63.

Mezias, S. J. 1987. *Technical and Institutional Sources of Organizational Practices: The Case of a Financial Reporting Method*. PhD thesis. Stanford Univ.

Miller, D., Friesen, P. 1982. Structural change and performance: quantum vs. piecemeal-incremental approaches. *Acad. Mgmt. J.* 25:867–92.

Miller, D. T., Ross, M. 1975. Self-serving biases in the attribution of causality. *Psychol. Bull.* 82:213–25.

Moore, M. H., Gates, M. J. 1986. *Inspector-General: Junkyard Dogs or Man's Best Friend?* New York: Russell Sage Found.

Muth, J. F. 1986. Search theory and the manufacturing progress function. *Mgmt. Sci.* 32:948–62.

Nelson, R. R., Winter, S. G. 1982. *An Evolutionary Theory of Economic Change*. Cambridge, MA: Harvard Univ.

Neustadt, R. E., May, E. R. 1986. *Thinking in Time: The Uses of History for Decision Makers*. New York, NY: Free Press.

Nystrom, N. C., Starbuck, W. H., eds. 1981. *Handbook of Organizational Design*. Oxford: Oxford Univ. Press.

Nystrom, N. C., Starbuck, W. H. 1984. To avoid organizational crisis, unlearn. *Organ. Dynam.* Spring: 53–65.

Olsen, J. P. 1976. The process of interpreting organizational history. In *Ambiguity and Choice in Organizations*. ed. J. G. March, J. P. Olsen, pp. 338–50. Bergen, Norway: Universitetsforlaget.

Olsen, J. P. 1983. *Organized Democracy*. Bergen, Norway: Universitetsforlaget.

Ouchi, W. G. 1980. Markets, bureaucracies and clans. *Admin. Sci. Q.* 25:129–41.

Pettigrew, A. M. 1985. *The Awakening Giant: Continuity and Change in Imperial Chemical Industries*. Oxford: Blackwell.

Pfeffer, J. 1981. *Power in Organizations*. Marshfield, MA: Pitman.

Powell, W. W. 1986. How the past informs the present: the uses and liabilities of organizational memory. Paper read at the Conference on Communication and Collective Memory, Annenberg School, University of Southern California.

Pressman, J. L., Wildavsky, A. B. 1973. *Implementation*. Berkeley: Univ. Calif. Press.

Preston, L., Keachie, E. C. 1964. Cost functions and progress functions: an integration. *Am. Econ. Rev.* 54:100–7.

Radner, R. 1975. A behavioral model of cost reduction. *Bell J. Econ.* 6:196–215.

Rapping, L. 1965. Learning and World War II production functions. *Rev. Econ. Stat.* 47:81–6.

Rogers, E. M., Shoemaker, F. F. 1971. *Communication of Innovations*. New York: Free Press.

Rosenberg, N. 1982. *Inside the Black Box: Technology and Economics*. Cambridge: Cambridge Univ. Press.

Ross, J., Staw, B. M. 1986. Expo 86: an escalation prototype. *Admin. Sci. Q.* 31:274–97.

Røvik, K. -A. 1987. Laeringssystemer og Laeringsatferd i offentlig Forvaltning: En Studie av Styringens Kunnskapsgrunnlag. Unpublished MS. Universitetet i Tromsø (Norway).

Scott, W. R. 1985. Conflicting levels of rationality: regulators, managers, and professionals in the medical care sector. *J. Health Admin. Educ.* 3:113–31.

Scott, W. R. 1987. *Organizations: Rational, Natural, and Open Systems.* Englewood Cliffs: NJ: Prentice-Hall. 2nd ed.

Siegel, S. 1957. Level of aspiration and decision making. *Psychol. Rev.* 64:253–62.

Simon, H. A. 1955. A behavioral model of rational choice. *Q. J. Econ.* 69:99–118.

Simon, H. A. 1971. Designing organizations for an information rich world. In *Computers. Communications and the Public Interest.* ed. M. Greenberger, pp. 37–52. Baltimore, MD: Johns Hopkins Univ. Press.

Sitkin, S. B. 1986. *Secrecy in Organizations: Determinants of Secrecy Behavior among Engineers in Three Silicon Valley Semiconductor Firms.* PhD thesis. Stanford Univ.

Slovic, P., Fischhoff, B., Lichtenstein, S. 1977. Behavioral decision theory. *Ann. Rev. Psychol.* 28:1–39.

Smith, H. T., Green, T. R. G., eds. 1980. *Human Interaction with Computers.* New York: Academic.

Sproull, L. S. 1981. Beliefs in organizations. See Nystrom & Starbuck 1981, 2:203–24.

Sproull, L. S., Weiner, S., Wolf, D. 1978. *Organizing an Anarchy: Belief, Bureaucracy, and Politics in the*

National Institute of Education. Chicago, IL: Univ. Chicago Press.

Starbuck, W. H. 1976. Organizations and their environments. In *Handbook of Industrial and Organizational Psychology.* ed. M. D. Dunnette, pp. 1067–123. Chicago: Rand McNally.

Starbuck, W. H. 1983. Organizations as action generators. *Am. Sociol. Rev.* 48:91–102.

Starbuck, W. H., Dutton, J. M. 1973. Designing adaptive organizations. *J. Bus. Policy* 3:21–8.

Starbuck, W. H., Milliken, F. J. 1988. Executives perceptual filters; what they notice and how they make sense. In *Executive Effect: Concepts and Methods for Studying Top Managers,* ed. D. Hambrick. Greenwich, CT: JAI.

Staw, B. M., Ross, J. 1978. Commitment to a policy decision: a multitheoretical perspective. *Admin. Sci. Q.* 23:40–64.

Steinbruner, J. D. 1974. *The Cybernetic Theory of Decision.* Princeton, NJ: Princeton Univ. Press.

Stinchcombe, A. L. 1986. *Stratification and Organization.* Cambridge: Cambridge Univ. Press.

Tamuz, M. 1987. The impact of computer surveillance on air safety reporting. *Columbia J. World Bus.* 22:69–77.

Thompson, J. D. 1967. *Organizations in Action.* New York: McGraw-Hill.

Tirole, J. 1986. Hierarchies and bureaucracies: on the role of collusion in organizations. *J. Law Econ. Organ.* 2:181–214.

Tolbert, P. S., Zucker, L. G. 1983. Institutional sources of change in the formal structure of organizations: the diffusion of civil service reform, 1880–1935. *Admin. Sci. Q.* 28:22–39.

Tushman, M. L., Romanelli, E. 1985. Organizational evolution: a metamorphosis model of convergence and reorientation. In *Research in Organizational Behavior*, ed. L. L. Cummings, B. M. Staw, 7:171–222. Greenwich, CT: JAI Press.

Van Maanen, J. 1973. Observations on the making of policemen. *Hum. Organ.* 32:407–18.

Weick, K. E. 1979. *The Social Psychology of Organizing*. Reading. MA: Addison-Wesley. 2nd ed.

Whetten, D. A. 1987. Organizational growth and decline processes. *Ann. Rev. Sociol.* 13:335–58.

Wiewel, W., Hunter, A. 1985. The interorganizational network as a resource: a comparative case study on organizational genesis. *Admin. Sci. Q.* 30:482–96.

Wildavsky, A. 1983. Information as an organizational problem. *J. Mgmt. Stud.* 20:29–40.

Winter, S. G. 1986. The research program of the behavioral theory of the firm: orthodox critique and evolutionary perspective. In *Handbook of Behavioral Economics*, ed. B. Gilad, S. Kaish, 1:151–87. Greenwich, CT: JAI Press.

Wright, T. P. 1936. Factors affecting the cost of airplanes. *J. Aeronautical Sci.* 3:122–8.

Yelle, L. E. 1979. The learning curve: historical review and comprehensive survey. *Decision Sci.* 10:302–28.

Zald, M. N. 1970. *Organizational Change: The Political Economy of the YMCA*. Chicago, IL: Univ. Chicago Press.

Zucker, L. G. 1977. The role of institutionalization in cultural persistence. *Am. Sociol. Rev.* 42:726–43.

Zucker, L. G. 1986. Production of trust: institutional sources of economic structure, 1840 to 1920. In *Research in Organizational Behavior.* ed. L. L. Cummings, B. M. Staw, 8:55–111. Greenwich, CT: JAI Press.

Zucker, L. G. 1987. Institutional theories of organization. *Ann. Rev. Sociol.* 13:443–64.

CHAPTER SIX

The Evolution of Evolution

In the organizational research literature the word "evolution" is ordinarily used in a relatively narrow sense, referring to a set of ideas about change in a population through variation and selection of a particular sort. In the present chapter, that usage is located in an older and larger context in order to explore some implications of the evolution of evolution that are not limited to Darwinian natural selection models but extend to a wide range of theories of organizational adaptation.

The arguments are simple: As ideas about evolution have developed, they have moved from outcome conceptions of evolution to process conceptions. They have moved from conceptions of evolutionary processes as "efficient" instruments of adaptation to an appreciation of their "inefficiencies." And they have moved from an emphasis on using evolutionary theories to predict history to an emphasis on the engineering of history.

EVOLUTION AS OUTCOME AND PROCESS

Evolution as an outcome of history

One traditional meaning of "evolution" is ordered change in species, individuals, or social systems. Within this meaning, historical sequences are not arbitrary. Rather, the state of an organism, organization, technology, or society at any particular time is a "natural" step in a historical path. Evolutionary history is described in terms of such natural developments, and theories of evolution are theories of these ordered paths.

In this spirit, we describe the development of the human embryo, observing how it evolves along a path toward a recognizable human being.

Or we describe the development of the human species, observing how it evolves along a path of increasing capability. Or we describe the development of organizations, human civilizations, technologies, science, or knowledge as evolving through a set of orderly stages that can be observed in histories of similar units of adaptation. These paths of development can be seen as unfolding toward a destiny that is implicit in the unit that is developing or in its environment or both.

In theories of historical progress or in theories that trace the elaboration of a technology from a vague idea to a finished and economically successful product, the destinies reflect relatively exalted states. Ordered change is described as leading from relatively simple structures to more complex ones, from relatively crude practices to relatively sophisticated ones. Evolution is described as following a path of greater and greater elaboration, beauty, civility, or fit with the environment. The essential element, however, is not that development leads to higher and higher states but that it inexorably leads somewhere. For example, theories of entropy, as found in some theories of information "development" by transmission through a series of channels, are theories of inexorable degradation. They presume that the evolutionary destiny of information is noise.

Evolution as a process of history

"Evolution" is also used to refer to the processes that produce history. The development of a species, individual, organization, or society occurs through a set of historical mechanisms. Much of contemporary interest in evolution is in describing the mechanisms that generate a path of history. These include reproduction, learning, choice, imitation, and competition.

Many of the most common ideas about the evolution of institutions and organisms have historically been ideas that describe the present state of an institution as implicit in its future. For example, the evolution of the embryo can be seen as an unfolding in the biological present of the future destiny of the infant. The forms and procedures that an organization uses in the present can be seen as shaped by expectations and intentions for the future.

The logic is anticipatory. Change stems from the imposition of the future on the present. Engines for the process are found in conceptions of destinies and necessary steps toward their fulfillment. The destinies may be imagined to be inventions of human actors, in which case the theory is one of rational individual or institutional choice, reflecting wills, desires, and intentions. Alternatively, the destinies are sometimes portrayed as extrahuman, in which case evolution is seen as teleologically linked to usefulness within some ultimate purpose or design.

The idea that organisms evolve in order to achieve their destinies is embedded deeply in the history of thinking about evolution and still retains vitality in contemporary talk about evolution. Most such ideas were originally linked to conceptions of "God's will" or "the unity of nature," and evolution was associated with improvement in the fit between organisms and institutions and God's vision. More recently, God's will has been replaced for the most part by the will of individual humans. The idea that the expectations and willful actions of human beings enact the future into the present is a central presumption of much of modern social science. It is reflected in theories of rational action, including theories of rational conflict (e.g., game theory), in theories of strategic action, and in theories of power. The substitution of the intentions of individual human actors for the intentions of God retains a conception of history as being a realization in the present of necessary steps toward a preexistent destiny.

A second set of ideas about the evolution of organisms and institutions emphasizes the ways in which the present is a residue of the past. Present organisms and institutions are summaries of past experience. For example, the evolution of a population can be seen as the coding in the biological present of the past reproductive experience of members of the population. An organizational past can be seen as imposing itself on the present through retention of organizational experience in organizational routines.

The logic is not anticipatory but historical. The past is retained in rules that guide the present. The possible adaptive units in history-based evolution are any that can be imagined to accumulate information from history, but the more familiar examples in practice include such elements as gene pools, individual organisms, organizational forms and routines, cultures, institutions, or systems of knowledge. The fact that some of these evolving units are nested in other evolving units is a troublesome complexity.

Historical processes by which the present encapsulates the past are the mechanisms of modern theories of evolution, as found in theories of learning, culture, and natural selection. The theories differ, most conspicuously in how they imagine the informational consequences of history to be sustained and diffused within a population of evolving units, but they belong to a common family. In each case, the past is experienced through a combination of exploration and exploitation. Exploration produces variety in experience (experimentation, variation, diversity). Exploitation produces reliability in experience (selection, consistency, unity). The engines of evolution include mechanisms for interpreting, retaining, transmitting, and retrieving these lessons of the experienced past.

THE EFFICIENCY OF HISTORY

Expectations about the future and experiences of the past are both ordinarily seen as instruments of the environment. They match attributes of the unit of adaptation to attributes of the environment so that the former can be predicted from a knowledge of the latter. If (on average) expectations about the environment come to match the true environment, actions based on such expectations are implicit in the environment. If (on average) experience in the world leads to forms and actions that come to match the environment, such forms and actions are implicit in the environment. This is, of course, the first thing that a child learns about any kind of evolutionary theory, namely, that an organism or institution adapts to its environment.

In early forms of evolutionary theory (e.g., in the ideas of Alfred Russel Wallace) the environment was seen as imposing itself primarily through scarcity. Where an environment was relatively munificent, environmental pressure was weak and the tie between an organism or institution on the one hand and its environment on the other was loose. In organization theory, this notion has its counterpart in concepts of environmental munificence and organizational slack. Slack buffers an organization from fluctuations in resource availability in its environment, thus weakening immediate environmental pressure. One of the major contributions of Malthus and subsequently Darwin was to recognize the role of competition for environmental resources in tightening the control of the environment over the evolution of species. Competition plays a similar role in organization theory, but its effects are often complicated by the extent to which organizations use satisficing, rather than optimizing, decision rules.

For much of the history of evolutionary thinking, the competitive processes of history were seen as efficient. That is, they were seen as leading to unique and stable equilibria that were (in some relatively uncomplicated sense) optimal. As a result, evolutionary outcomes were treated as unambiguously implicit in environmental conditions, and the distinction between talking about evolution as a process by which experience is encoded and used (learning, development) and talking about evolution as a mechanism for maximizing fit (performance, maturity) was unimportant. A process that encoded experience in a reasonably systematic and adaptive way was assumed to lead to improvement in fit and ultimately to the one best fit. This was Spencer's vision, and it continues to be a familiar one in the modern literature.

The litanies are familiar. Given competition among intentional actors trying to do well, rationality drives organisms or institutions to behavior that is both uniquely determined by the environment and optimal. Given competition among learning actors trying to improve, learning drives organisms or institutions to uniquely optimal behavior. Given competition among actors selected by differential reproduction, selection drives a population of organisms or institutions to a mix of behaviors uniquely matching the environment. Although the manifest procedures may appear to reflect any number of kinds of adaptive processes, the competitive coercion of the environment assures that evolutionary outcomes are implicit in the environment and are optimal.

INEFFICIENT HISTORIES

Assumptions of efficient histories are appealing, but they are assumptions that have long been suspect. Many of the developments in modern understandings of evolutionary processes involve identifying the inefficiencies of history, the many ways in which evolutionary outcomes are not implicit in evolutionary environments or are not optimal. They highlight the dangers in confusing outcome and process meanings of evolution.

Histories in exogenous environments

The history by which organisms or institutions evolve within exogenous environments makes the realization of uniquely required optimal outcomes problematic. There are *lags in matching*. Evolutionary adaptation (e.g., incremental learning, selection) takes time. Although we might imagine that evolutionary processes act to improve the match between the current form of an organism or institution and the environment, there is no guarantee that convergence will have been achieved by any particular time. If the environment changes, there is not even any assurance that adaptation will be fast enough to improve the match.

There are *multiple equilibria*. Most theories of learning or selection are theories of local adaptation. They assume a process in which relevant factors are localized in time and space. Considerations that are close in time and close in cognitive or organizational distance dominate those that are more distant. Such adaptation is essentially "hill-climbing," responding to local feedback, and is subject to becoming stranded at any one of a number of local (rather than global) maxima.

There is *path dependency*. Many models of evolutionary processes represent them as branching processes. The outcomes in a particular environment depend not only on that environment but also on previous environments and the ways in which they have been experienced. The historical path makes some outcomes unrealizable in the future, including some previously realized. Relatively unlikely events, if they occur, change the structure in permanent ways. History is nonrecursive, dynamic, and nonlinear.

There are networks of *diffusion*. Outcomes depend on the ways in which the information from historical experience spreads. Evolutionary processes of diffusion (e.g., sexual reproduction, networks of management consultants) create information structures that isolate some parts of the population and produce outcomes (e.g., speciation, cultural differentiation) attributable to elements of isolation and integration. In the organizational context, this makes the outcomes of an evolutionary process sensitive to patterns of connection in information networks, to changes in information technology, and to the ease with which information is incorporated into receiving organizations.

Histories in endogenous environments

One of the more important post-Aristotelian developments in evolutionary theory is the emphasis on endogenous environments, on the ways in which the convergence between an evolving unit and its environment is complicated by the fact that the environment is not only changing but changing partly as part of a process of coevolution.

There is *mutual adaptation* between the unit of evolution and the environment. Rats learn from experimenters, but experimenters also learn from rats at the same time. Through experience, organisms learn what parts of the environment are exploitable by them. But the exploitability of the environment changes as a result of the experience. Organizations receive social approval or disapproval as a function of adopting particular practices. But the level of approval or disapproval shifts as the number of organizations adopting the practices changes. These forms of mutual adaptation are likely to lead to stable outcomes that are not uniquely predicted by the initial environment.

Units of adaptation are located within *ecologies* of other units. Organisms and institutions exist in communities of other organisms and institutions. Their histories are intertwined by competition, cooperation, and other forms of interaction. These interactions considerably complicate the idea of evolution. History cannot be seen as simply a product of the organism and its own exogenous environment. Species coevolve, as do institutions.

Units of adaptations are *nested*, so that some adapting units (e.g., individuals) are integral parts of other adapting units (e.g., organizations). The structure of relations among them arises from an interaction among the various nested units responding to a shifting environment and their own internal dynamics. These features of organization considerably complicate any multilevel evolutionary story.

Implications of inefficient histories

The idea that history is a locally adaptive, branching process with multiple equilibria is a central feature of modern biological theories as well as theories of organizational change. There is considerable ecological complexity, and how the various units of evolution fit together is significant to the development of each and to the collective course of history.

History is portrayed as a meander. There are irreversible branches, thus path-dependence and decisive minor moments. The branch-points, involving such factors as mutations, mating, communication contacts, and fortuitous opportunities often seem almost chancelike in their resolution, yet decisive in their effects on subsequent history. Though the path of development is explicable in terms of a comprehensible process, the realized course of natural evolution is difficult to predict.

When history is pictured as a path-dependent drift rather than a unique developmental path implicit in the environment, the link between evolution as an outcome and evolution as a process has to be demonstrated rather than assumed. History as a process is not guaranteed to have a unique, optimal result. It may have a unique equilibrium that is nonoptimal. It may have multiple "optimal" (in a Pareto sense) equilibria. Rationality (as a process) may or may not lead to decisions uniquely required by the decision situation. Conflict (as a process) may or may not lead to uniquely predicted resolutions. Learning (as a process) may or may lead to forms and practices uniquely required by the environment. Knowledge accumulation (as a process) may or may not lead to a uniquely appropriate comprehension. Natural selection (as a process) may or may not lead to uniquely adapted species.

This innocent change has some significance for thinking in history and social science. Much of the style of social science is basically comparative statics, the exploration of the ways in which individual behavior, institutional practices, and cultural norms match the demands of the environments in which they are found. The basic strategy is to predict features of the units of adaptation (organisms, institutions, cultures) from attributes of their environments. The "invisible hand" of evolution is imagined to provide the link. Conspicuous examples in organization theory are the various forms of contingency theory, from studies of technology and structure to transaction cost analysis.

A meandering, locally adaptive history provides only a relatively weak link between attributes of the environment being adapted to and attributes of the units doing the adapting. Differences among institutions are traceable not only to differences among their contemporary environments but also to a history of interaction with a changing environment. That history is one in which each step is both problematic and decisive in defining possibilities at the next step.

A connection between environmental conditions and evolved forms remains, and under some circumstances the process may yield a match that is broadly predictable. For example, despite a speciation process resulting in considerable history-dependent species heterogeneity, there are observable consistent differences between water-based species and land-based species. Similarly, despite cultural differentiation resulting in considerable history-dependent organizational heterogeneity, there are observable consistent differences between market-based organizations and those based on political constituencies.

These consistent differences are important, but inefficient histories undermine the strong "functionalist" tone of many modern interpretations of comparative institutions. Implicit presumptions of historical efficiency underlie much of the literature on organizational structure, comparative organizations, the economics of organizations, and organizational change. Their inferences depend on a unique matching between evolutionary processes and evolutionary outcomes that is not assured.

THE ENGINEERING OF EVOLUTIONARY HISTORY

A meandering evolutionary history is not easily predicted. Its course depends on the sequence of particular historical branches that are realized along the way. Precisely for this reason, however, it is possible to imagine decisive intervention in history. The classic case is the breeding of species. By managing mating, critical branch-points of biological evolutionary history, breeders change species in decisive ways. Similar examples can be drawn from the evolution of cultures (e.g., colonial intervention), the evolution of knowledge (e.g., the introduction of the printing press), and the evolution of political systems (e.g., the introduction of instruments of governance). In each case, relatively conscious attempts have been made to transform units of evolution by intervening in the evolutionary process. In each case, there have been major effects. History has been changed.

Engineering basics

The natural speculation is that organizations, like species, can be engineered. The idea is not that any imaginable organization can be designed and built but that natural developmental processes of organizational histories can be affected significantly by relatively small, timely interventions. The engineering of evolution involves understanding those processes well enough to intervene in history and produce organizational effects.

Our theories of organizational evolution provide some basic strategies for intervening in history. They include three broad kinds of interventions. The first involves altering the possibilities for *transmission, retention, and retrieval* of the lessons of history. The invention of the printing press, the construction of computer databases, and the institutionalization of professional standards are conspicuous examples. The second kind of strategic intervention involves altering the *structure of interactions* among units of evolution. Increasing the intensity of competition or the patterns of cooperation is a conspicuous example, as is the building or breaching of organizational boundaries. By shifting the structure of interactions, we change the advantages that accrue to alternative organizational forms or practices. The third kind of strategic intervention involves managing the *exploration/exploitation balance*. Manipulating the level of risk taking, or the salience of diversity relative to unity, or the amount of organizational slack is a conspicuous example of the ways by which history can be affected by changing the level of variation or the effectiveness by which lessons and opportunities of the environment are exploited.

Ambiguities of improvement

Producing effects is necessary for engineering, but it is not sufficient. Engineering is not simply the art of making changes. It is the art of improvement. The engineering of transportation is an effort to improve outcomes by intervening in the processes of movement. The engineering of health is an effort to improve outcomes by intervening in the processes of disease. The engineering of history is an effort to improve outcomes by intervening in the processes of history. We ask not only whether we can produce change – which within a branching, meandering history may be relatively easy – but whether we can produce change that can be relied on to be an improvement.

Engineering traditions have ordinarily treated the definition and measurement of improvement as unproblematic. In fact, of course, improvement is difficult to define and measure, and every experienced engineer knows it. If one accepts the dictum that an engineer is simply an agent of a client, there nevertheless are numerous occasions on which engineering involves trying to persuade a client that a desired change involves long-term or second-order consequences that may be unacceptable. If one adds the stricture that good engineering also involves attention to broader social concerns and virtue, the conception of improvement becomes murky indeed. The history of engineering is cluttered with examples of steps that seemed to offer short-run improvements in some domains but in retrospect were deemed to have created greater problems in the long run or in other domains. Engineering history is filled with effects. It is also filled with unanticipated and complicated consequences.

Theories of evolution elaborate these ambiguities more than they resolve them. A central feature of evolutionary history is the way in which local or short-term improvements often turn out to be distant or long-term disasters. In ecologies of interacting and evolving units, improvements in the short-run survival prospects of one part of the system do not reliably lead to improvements in the survival prospects over the longer run or of another part.

These "social welfare" aspects of defining an objective function for evolutionary engineering are implicit in the "unit of adaptation" problem. That problem, as it is usually discussed, is seen as a problem for a descriptive theory of evolution. What is it that adapts to the environment? The individual organism? The gene pool? The species? The ecological community? Or in the case of economic organizations: The individuals? The firm? The industry? The market? The society?

The choice of unit is complicated by the fact that the units are nested in space and in time. Firms are nested in industries which, in turn, are nested in societies. The short-run future is nested in the long-run future. Adaptation involves a complicated mosaic of evolution over time by interacting nested units within an environment that is also evolving. Characteristically, the survival of a unit at one level and at one time is affected by the survival of a unit at another level or at another time. Contemporary disputes over "altruism" and over the role of phenotypic organization in evolutionary models are symptomatic of the difficulties.

These are profound problems for developing a descriptive theory of evolution. They are also profound problems for developing an engineering improvement or history. If evolutionary engineers are supposed to improve prospects for survival, they need to know for what part of a nested system they should make improvements, and over what portion of a nested future. Specifically, in an organizational context, it is not obvious that improvement is achieved by preserving any particular organization or organizational form. And there is no obvious metric for comparing long-run and short-run consequences. Theories of evolution make the difficulties clear without providing any clearer specification of improvements than do concepts of Pareto "optimality" in welfare economics or justice in political philosophy.

Strengthening evolutionary processes

Evolutionary engineers seem to be left with two possible approaches to improvement, neither fully satisfactory. The first is to emphasize strengthening evolutionary processes without any commitment to particular outcomes. This approach suffers a bit from obscurity about what it means to "strengthen" the processes, but a few things can be said.

For example, it is possible to argue that organizational engineering involves simultaneously improving the processes by which organizations seek out or generate new options (exploration) and improving their capabilities for implementing options that prove effective (exploitation). Organizations are engineered so as to facilitate experimentation and protect deviant ideas from premature elimination. At the same time, they are engineered to allow the identification, routinization, and extension of known good ideas. With inadequate exploration, an organization suffers from not having experiments with new options from which it can learn about new possibilities. With inadequate exploitation, an organization suffers from not eliminating bad experiments and not utilizing good ones.

An engineering strategy of maintaining a balance between exploration and exploitation is an attractive goal. Unfortunately, some of the more obvious mechanisms of adaptation accentuate, rather than reduce, imbalances between exploration and exploitation. Organizations can be trapped in either excessive exploration or excessive exploitation through short-term adaptive responses to experience.

Exploration can become a trap for a failing organization. If failure usually leads to exploration and exploration usually leads to failure, an adaptive unit can be trapped in a cycle of exploration, trying one new thing after another without spending enough time exploiting any innovation to secure the gains from experience that are necessary to make it fruitful. When adaptive processes lead to a string of inadequately exploited experiments, they are likely to be improved by interventions that inhibit exploration.

Exploitation can also become a trap. The returns to exploitation tend to be more certain, more immediate in time, and more proximate organizationally than are those to exploration. Consequently, strategies of exploitation that lead to locally positive outcomes are likely to come to dominate exploratory strategies that are globally better. In this way, adaptive processes can easily tip the balance in favor of exploitation, toward excessive stability of organizational practices, forms, and technologies. In such cases, adaptive processes are likely to be improved by interventions that protect or stimulate exploration.

Although determining the optimal balance to be sought between exploitation and exploration is not ordinarily feasible in an organizational setting, it may be possible to anticipate some of these ways in which adaptive dynamics lead to imbalances. Such awareness is a basis for timely interventions based on knowledge about risk preferences, communication, and conflict in organizations.

Visions of destiny

A second approach to defining objectives for evolutionary engineering involves identifying a desired course of history – a vision of progress. Few concepts in social theory are currently as disreputable as the concept of progress. Conceptions of human progress suffer from a consciousness of the many ways in which progress has historically been defined to confirm the virtue of a particular historical meander and particular historical accidents of survival, dominance, and subordination.

Moreover, the self-referential quality of evolutionary theory undermines the meaningfulness of conscious engineering for progress. Evolutionary engineers are part of the process in which they intervene – and their desires to intervene are as easily seen as a consequence of the process and as a factor in changing it. Seeing visions of progress as themselves part of the process that they are imagined to evaluate or control weakens their status as prescriptive commands.

Nevertheless, one point that seems obvious about human evolution is the persistence of human hope for engineering significance. For the most part, we have abandoned creationist myths and metaphors of God's will. But the will to intervene in history in pursuit of a vision of destiny is built deeply into our souls (or wherever such information codes are retained). Destiny myths of direction (the idea of vision and its implementation, the idea of strategic action) are important parts of contemporary human belief.

Conceptions of destiny do not exist in an evolutionary vacuum. For example, they can be pictured as having coevolved with human rational consciousness. In the presence of a myth of rationality, a myth of human destiny becomes a vehicle for exploration, and the two myths are jointly favored in a world in which exploration is precious. Such a coevolution argument provides a speculative explanation for the evolutionary dominance of ideas of destiny within our specific ideological path, but it is difficult to find justification for any particular vision of future destiny within a meandering theory of history. Indeed, the role of conceptions of destiny as vehicles of exploration would seem to speak to the desirability of conflict over changing conceptions of destiny rather than convergence on one.

Neither ideas of strengthening evolutionary processes nor ideas tied to specific visions of destiny can claim profound justification. Consequently, although evolutionary engineering often seems able to change the course of history, it cannot give assurance that the changes will be desirable. Relative to *post hoc* assessments of improvement, our interventions in history seem likely to be almost as haphazard as mutations.

WHERE WE HAVE BEEN AND WHERE WE ARE

Theories of evolution have become well-recognized frames for organizational analysis. The frames include theories of rational action, theories of rational conflict, theories of experiential learning, theories of confrontation and contradiction, theories of the development of knowledge, theories of variation and selection. They can be well specified; they can be translated into well-defined sets of procedures for observing and analyzing empirical data; they have been associated with a number of reasonable data sets.

These evolutionary theories carry their histories with them, and traces of those histories are sustained within our current thinking. Three conspicuous historical ideas have been mentioned: the idea of a prototypic developmental path with a preexistent destiny, the idea that process and outcome are closely connected, and the idea that evolutionary histories can (and ought to) be engineered.

For the most part, the meandering drift of thinking about evolution has moved away from the idea of a prototypic destiny and the idea that evolutionary processes have unique outcomes. Although there are regularities within an evolutionary process (e.g., the development of the embryo, the elaboration of forms of life), the course of history has no destiny and no fixed path. And although the evolutionary process involves processes of matching between environments and units of evolution, the outcomes of those processes are not uniquely defined by the environmental context. Nevertheless, conceptions of destiny and uniqueness are part of our linguistic and worldview baggage. Their marks remain in life-cycle stage theories of development and in the generality of comparative statics and functionalism as fundamentals of contemporary social science.

The evolution of evolution has, on the other hand, sustained and supported a vision of evolutionary engineering. Evolutionary theories of history are invitations to interventions in history. By emphasizing the path-dependent branching and local feedback of historical processes, evolutionary theories define opportunities for changing the course of history by relatively modest interventions at decisive places and moments. The possibilities have attracted people from cattle breeders to philosophers of science, from environmental and political activists to consultants in strategic management.

Small, precise changes can be imagined to be achievable by modest, timely interventions and to produce large, permanent effects. Small structural changes in organizations can be imagined to change the likelihood of such interventions and of their having significant consequences to the realized path of history. It is an appealing notion that grants a role to consciousness and thus fits comfortably within a human-centered ideology.

At least in the realm of organizations, however, we have to suspect that our judgments about which changes would be desirable are not likely to be very good. A conspicuous feature of our current condition is that we know enough about evolutionary processes to affect history significantly without knowing enough to be confident that the effects we produce will be intelligent ones. The complications of resolving the trade-offs across space and time are formidable, as is the frequency with which our models of evolutionary complexity are incomplete. Much of modern technological, biological, and social history is testimony both to those problems and to the capabilities of human beings for underestimating them.

Acknowledgments

Research for this chapter, first presented as a talk at New York University, was supported by the Spencer Foundation and the Stanford Graduate School of Business. I am grateful for the comments of Derek Scissors and Jitendra Singh. The style of a talk, without references, has been retained here.

CHAPTER SEVEN

Exploration and Exploitation in Organizational Learning

This chapter considers the relation between the exploration of new possibilities and the exploitation of old certainties in organizational learning. It examines some complications in allocating resources between the two, particularly those introduced by the distribution of costs and benefits across time and space, and the effects of ecological interaction. Two general situations involving the development and use of knowledge in organizations are modeled. The first is the case of mutual learning between members of an organization and an organizational code. The second is the case of learning and competitive advantage in competition for primacy. The chapter develops an argument that adaptive processes, by refining exploitation more rapidly than exploration, are likely to become effective in the short run but self-destructive in the long run. The possibility that certain common organizational practices ameliorate that tendency is assessed.

A central concern of studies of adaptive processes is the relation between the exploration of new possibilities and the exploitation of old certainties (Schumpeter, 1934; Holland, 1975; Kuran, 1988). Exploration includes things captured by terms such as search, variation, risk taking, experimentation, play, flexibility, discovery, innovation. Exploitation includes such things as refinement, choice, production, efficiency, selection, implementation, execution. Adaptive systems that engage in exploration to the exclusion of exploitation are likely to find that they suffer the costs of experimentation without gaining many of its benefits. They exhibit too many undeveloped new ideas and too little distinctive competence. Conversely, systems that engage in exploitation to the exclusion of exploration are likely to find themselves trapped in suboptimal stable equilibria. As a result, maintaining an appropriate balance between exploration and exploitation is a primary factor in system survival and prosperity.

This chapter consider some aspects of such problems in the context of organizations. Both exploration and exploitation are essential for organizations, but they compete for scarce resources. As a result, organizations make explicit and implicit choices between the two. The explicit choices are found in calculated decisions about alternative investments and competitive strategies. The implicit choices are buried in many features of organizational forms and customs, for example, in organizational procedures for accumulating and reducing slack, in search rules and practices, in the ways in which targets are set and changed, and in incentive systems. Understanding the choices and improving the balance between exploration and exploitation are complicated by the fact that returns from the two options vary not only with respect to their expected values, but also with respect to their variability, their timing, and their distribution within and beyond the organization. Processes for allocating resources between them, therefore, embody intertemporal, interinstitutional, and interpersonal comparisons, as well as risk preferences. The difficulties involved in making such comparisons lead to complications in specifying appropriate trade-offs, and in achieving them.

THE EXPLORATION/EXPLOITATION TRADE-OFF

Exploration and exploitation in theories of organizational action

In rational models of choice, the balance between exploration and exploitation is discussed classically in terms of a theory of rational search (Radner and Rothschild, 1975; Hey, 1982). It is assumed that there are several alternative investment opportunities, each characterized by a probability distribution over returns that is initially unknown. Information about the distribution is accumulated over time, but choices must be made between gaining new information about alternatives and thus improving future returns (which suggests allocating part of the investment to searching among uncertain alternatives), and using the information currently available to improve present returns (which suggests concentrating the investment on the apparently best alternative). The problem is complicated by the possibilities that new investment alternatives may appear, that probability distributions may not be stable, or that they may depend on the choices made by others.

In theories of limited rationality, discussions of the choice between exploration and exploitation emphasize the role of targets or aspiration levels in regulating allocations to search (Cyert and March, 1963). The usual assumption is that search is inhibited if the most preferred alternative is above (but in the neighborhood of) the target. On the other hand, search is stimulated if the most preferred known alternative is below the target. Such ideas are found both in theories of satisficing (Simon, 1955) and in prospect theory (Kahneman and Tversky, 1979). They have led to attempts to specify conditions under which target-oriented search rules are optimal (Day, 1967). Because of the role of targets, discussions of search in the limited rationality tradition emphasize the significance of the adaptive character of aspirations themselves (March, 1988).

In studies of organizational learning, the problem of balancing exploration and exploitation is exhibited in distinctions made between refinement of an existing technology and invention of a new one (Winter, 1971; Levinthal and March, 1981). It is clear that exploration of new alternatives reduces the speed with which skills at existing ones are improved. It is also clear that improvements in competence at existing procedures make experimentation with others less attractive (Levitt and March, 1988). Finding an appropriate balance is made particularly difficult by the fact that the same issues occur at levels of a nested system – at the individual level, the organizational level, and the social system level.

In evolutionary models of organizational forms and technologies, discussions of the choice between exploration and exploitation are framed in terms of balancing the twin processes of variation and selection (Ashby, 1960; Hannan and Freeman, 1987). Effective selection among forms, routines, or practices is essential to survival, but so also is the generation of new alternative practices, particularly in a changing environment. Because of the links among environmental turbulence, organizational diversity, and competitive advantage, the evolutionary dominance of an organizational practice is sensitive to the relation between the rate of exploratory variation reflected by the practice and the rate of change in the environment. In this spirit, for example, it has been argued that the persistence of garbage-can decision processes in organizations is related to the diversity advantage they provide in a world of relatively unstable environments, when paired with the selective efficiency of conventional rationality (Cohen, 1986).

The vulnerability of exploration

Compared to returns from exploitation, returns from exploration are systematically less certain, more remote in time, and organizationally more distant from the locus of action and adaption. What is good in the long run is not always good in the short run. What is good at a particular historical moment is not always good at another time. What is good for one part of an organization is not always good for another part. What is good for an organizations is not always good for a larger social system of which it is a part. As organizations learn from experience how to divide resources between exploitation and exploration, this distribution of consequences across time and space affects the lessons learned. The certainty, speed, proximity, and clarity of feedback ties exploitation to its consequences more quickly and more precisely than is the case with exploration. The story is told in many forms. Basic research has less certain outcomes, longer time horizons, and more diffuse effects than does product development. The search for new ideas, markets, or relations has less certain outcomes, longer time horizons, and more diffuse effects than does further development of existing ones.

Because of these differences, adaptive processes characteristically improve exploitation more rapidly than exploration. These advantages for exploitation cumulate. Each increase in competence at an activity increases the likelihood of rewards for engaging in that activity, thereby further increasing the competence and the likelihood (Argyris and Schön, 1978; David, 1985). The effects extend, through network externalities, to others with whom the learning organization interacts (Katz and Shapiro, 1986; David and Bunn, 1988). Reason inhibits foolishness; learning and imitation inhibit experimentation. This is not an accident but is a consequence of the temporal and spatial proximity of the effects of exploitation, as well as their precision and interconnectedness.

Since performance is a joint function of potential return form an activity and present competence of an organization at it, organizations exhibit increasing returns to experience (Arthur, 1984). Positive local feedback produces strong path dependence (David, 1990) and can lead to suboptimal equilibria. It is quite possible for competence in an inferior activity to become great enough to exclude superior activities with which an organization has little experience (Herriott et al., 1985). Since long-run intelligence depends on sustaining a reasonable level of exploration, these tendencies to increase exploitation and reduce exploration make adaptive processes potentially self-destructive.

The social context of organizational learning

The trade-off between exploration and exploitation exhibits some special features in the social context of organizations. The next two sections of this chapter describe two simple models of adaptation, use them to elaborate the relation between exploitation and exploration, and explore some implications of the relation for the accumulation and utilization of knowledge in organizations. The models identify some reasons why organizations may want to control learning and suggest some procedures by which they do so.

Two distinctive features of the social context are considered. The first is the mutual learning of an organization and the individuals in it. Organizations store knowledge in their procedures, norms, rules, and forms. They accumulate such knowledge over time, learning from their members. At the same time, individuals in an organization are socialized to organizational beliefs. Such mutual learning has implications for understanding and managing the trade-off between exploration and exploitation in organizations. The second feature of organizational learning considered here is the context of competition for primacy. Organizations often compete with each other under conditions in which relative position matters. The mixed contribution of knowledge to competitive advantage in cases involving competition for primacy creates difficulties for defining and arranging an appropriate balance between exploration and exploitation in an organizational setting.

MUTUAL LEARNING IN THE DEVELOPMENT OF KNOWLEDGE

Organizational knowledge and faiths are diffused to individuals through various forms of instruction, indoctrination, and exemplification. An organization socializes recruits to the languages, beliefs, and practices that comprise the organizational code (Whyte, 1957; Van Maanen, 1973). Simultaneously, the organizational code is adapting to individual beliefs. This form of mutual learning has consequences both for the individuals involved and for an organization as a whole. In particular, the trade-off between exploration and exploitation in mutual learning involves conflicts between short-run and long-run concerns and between gains to individual knowledge and gains to collective knowledge.

A model of mutual learning

Consider a simple model of the development and diffusion of organizational knowledge. There are four key features to the model:

1. There is an external reality that is independent of beliefs about it. Reality is described as having m dimensions, each of which has a value of 1 or -1. The (independent) probability that any one dimension will have a value of 1 is 0.5.
2. At each time period, beliefs about reality are held by each of n individuals in an organization and by an organizational code of received truth. For each of the m dimensions of reality, each belief has a value of 1, 0, or -1. This value may change over time.
3. Individuals modify their beliefs continuously as a consequence of

socialization into the organization and education into its code of beliefs. Specifically, if the code is 0 on a particular dimension, individual belief is not affected. In each period in which the code differs on any particular dimension from the belief of an individual, individual belief changes to that of the code with probability, p_1. Thus, p_1 is a parameter reflecting the effectiveness of socialization, i.e., learning *from* the code. Changes on the several dimensions are assumed to be independent of each other.

4. At the same time, the organizational code adapts to the beliefs of those individuals whose beliefs correspond with reality on more dimensions than does the code. The probability that the beliefs of the code will be adjusted to conform to the dominant belief within the superior group on any particular dimension depends on the level of agreement among individuals in the superior group and on p_2.[1] Thus, p_2 is a parameter reflecting the effectiveness of learning *by* the code. Changes on the several dimensions are assumed to be independent of each other.

Within this system, initial conditions include: a reality *m*-tuple (*m* dimensions, each of which has a value of 1 or −1, with independent equal probability); an organizational code *m*-tuple (*m* dimensions, each of which is initially 0); and *n* individual *m*-tuples (*m* dimensions, with values equal 1, 0, or −1, with equal probabilities).

Thus, the process begins with an organizational code characterized by neutral beliefs on all dimensions and a set of individuals with varying beliefs that exhibit, on average, no knowledge. Over time, the organizational code affects the beliefs of individuals, even while it is being affected by those beliefs. The beliefs of individuals do not affect the beliefs of other individuals directly but only through affecting the code. The effects of reality are also indirect. Neither the individuals nor the organizations experience reality. Improvement in knowledge comes by the code mimicking the beliefs (including the false beliefs) of superior individuals and by individuals mimicking the code (including its false beliefs).

Basic properties of the model in a closed system

Consider such a model of mutual learning first within a closed system having fixed organizational membership and a stable reality. Since realizations of the process are subject to stochastic variability, repeated simulations using the same initial conditions and parameters are used to estimate the distribution of outcomes. In all of the results reported here, the number of dimensions of reality (*m*) is set at 30, the number of individuals (*n*) is set at 50, and the number of repeated simulations is 80. The quantitative levels of the results and the magnitude of the stochastic fluctuations reported depend on these specifications, but the qualitative results are insensitive to values of m and n.

Since reality is specified, the state of knowledge at any particular time period can be assessed in two ways. First, the proportion of reality that is correctly represented in the organizational code can be calculated for any period. This is the knowledge level of the code for that period. Second, the proportion of reality that is correctly represented in individual beliefs (on average) can be calculated for any period. This is the average knowledge level of the individuals for that period.

Within this closed system, the model yields time paths of organizational and individual beliefs, thus knowledge levels, that depend stochastically on the initial conditions and the parameters affecting learning. The basic features of these histories can be summarized simply: each of the adjustments in beliefs serves to eliminate differences between the individuals and the code. Consequently, the beliefs of individuals and the code converge over time. As individuals in the organization become more knowledgeable, they also become more homogeneous with respect to knowledge. An equilibrium is reached at which all individuals and the code share the same (not necessarily accurate) belief with respect to each dimension. The equilibrium is stable.

Effects of learning rates

Higher rates of learning lead, on average, to achieving equilibrium earlier. The equilibrium level of knowledge attained by an organization also depends interactively on the two learning parameters. Figure 7.1 shows the results when we assume that p_1 is the same for all individuals. Slower socialization (lower p_1) leads to greater knowledge at equilibrium than does faster socialization, particularly when the code learns rapidly (high p_2). When socialization is slow, more rapid learning by the code leads to greater knowledge at equilibrium; but when socialization is rapid, greater equilibrium knowledge is achieved through slower learning by the code. By far the highest equilibrium knowledge occurs when the code learns rapidly from individuals whose socialization to the code is slow.

The results pictured in figure 7.1 confirm the observation that rapid learning is not always desirable (Herriott et al., 1985; Lounamaa and March, 1987).

In previous work, it was shown that slower learning allows for greater exploration of possible alternatives and greater balance in the development of specialized competences. In the present model, a different version of the same general phenomenon is observed. The gains to individuals from adapting rapidly to the code (which is consistently closer to reality

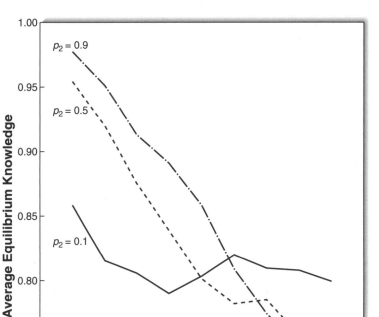

Figure 7.1 Effect of Learning Rates (p_1, p_2) on Equilibrium Knowledge $m = 30$; $n = 50$; 80 Iterations.

than the average individual) are offset by second-order losses stemming from the fact that the code can learn only from individuals who deviate from it. Slow learning on the part of individuals maintains diversity longer, thereby providing the exploration that allows the knowledge found in the organizational code to improve.

Effects of learning rate heterogeneity

The fact that fast individual learning from the code tends to have a favorable first-order effect on individual knowledge but an adverse effect on improvement in organizational knowledge and thereby on long-term individual improvement suggests that there might be some advantage to having

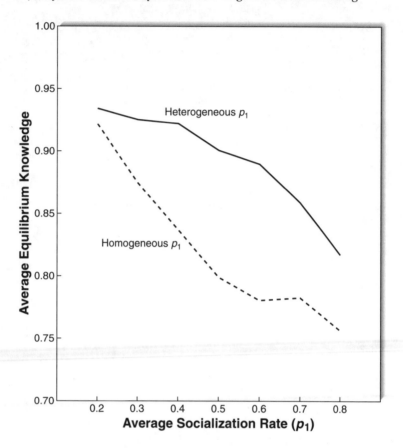

Figure 7.2 Effect of Heterogeneous Socialization Rates (p_1 = 0.1, 0.9) on Equilibrium Knowledge m = 30; n = 50; p_2 = 0.5; 80 Iterations.

a mix of fast and slow learners in an organization. Suppose the population of individuals in an organization is divided into two groups, one consisting of individuals who learn rapidly from the code (p_1 = 0.9) and the other consisting of individuals who learn slowly (p_1 = 0.1).

If an organization is partitioned into two groups in this way, the mutual learning process achieves an equilibrium in which all individuals and the code share the same beliefs. As would be expected from the results above with respect to homogeneous socialization rates, larger fractions of fast learners result in the process reaching equilibrium faster and in lower levels of knowledge at equilibrium than do smaller fractions of fast learners. However, as figure 7.2 shows, for any average rate of learning from the code, it is better from the point of view of equilibrium knowledge to

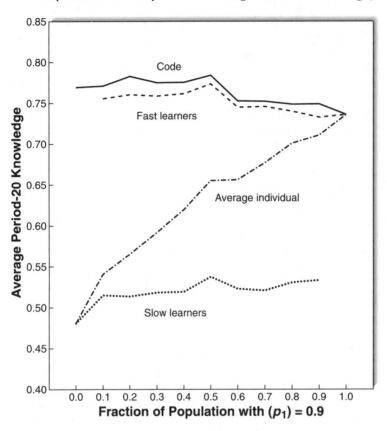

Figure 7.3 Effect of Heterogeneous Socialization Rates (p_1 = 0.1, 0.9) on Period-20 Knowledge m = 30; n = 50; p_1 = 0.1, 0.9; p_2 = 0.5; 80 Iterations.

have that average reflect a mix of fast and slow learners rather than a homogeneous population. For equivalent average values of the socialization learning parameter (p_1), the heterogeneous population consistently produces higher equilibrium knowledge.

On the way to equilibrium, the knowledge gains from variability are disproportionately due to contributions by slow learners, but they are disproportionately realized (in their own knowledge) by fast learners. Figure 7.3 shows the effects on period-20 knowledge of varying the fraction of the population of individuals who are fast learners (p_1 = 0.9) rather than slow learners (p_1 = 0.1). Prior to reaching equilibrium, individuals with a high value for p_1, gain from being in an organization in which there are individuals having a low value for p_1, but the converse is not true.

These results indicate that the fraction of slow learners in an organization is a significant factor in organizational learning. In the model, that fraction is treated as a parameter. Disparities in the returns to the two groups and their interdependence make optimizing with respect to the fraction of slow learners problematic if the rates of individual learning are subject to individual control. Since there are no obvious individual incentives for learning slowly in a population in which others are learning rapidly, it may be difficult to arrive at a fraction of slow learners that is optimal from the point of view of the code if learning rates are voluntarily chosen by individuals.

Basic properties of the model in a more open system

These results can be extended by examining some alternative routes to selective slow learning in a somewhat more open system. Specifically, the role of turnover in the organization and turbulence in the environment are considered. In the case of turnover, organizational membership is treated as changing. In the case of turbulence, environmental reality is treated as changing.

Effects of personnel turnover

In the previous section, it was shown that variability is sustained by low values of p_1. Slow learners stay deviant long enough for the code to learn from them. An alternative way of producing variability in an organization is to introduce personnel turnover. Suppose that in each time period each individual has a probability, p_3, of leaving the organization and being replaced by a new individual with a set of naive beliefs described by an m-tuple, having values equal to 1, 0, or −1, with equal probabilities. As might be expected, there is a consistent negative first-order effect of turnover on average individual knowledge. Since there is a positive relation between length of service in the organization and individual knowledge, the greater the turnover, the shorter the average length of service and the lower the average individual knowledge at any point. This effect is strong.

The effect of turnover on the organizational code is more complicated and reflects a trade-off between learning rate and turnover rate. Figure 7.4 shows the period-20 results for two different values of the socialization rate (p_1). If p_1 is relatively low, period-20 code knowledge declines with increasing turnover. The combination of slow learning and rapid turnover leads to inadequate exploitation. However, if p_1 is relatively high, moderate amounts of turnover improve the organizational code. Rapid socialization of individuals into the procedures and beliefs of an organization tends to reduce exploration. A modest level of turnover, by introduc-

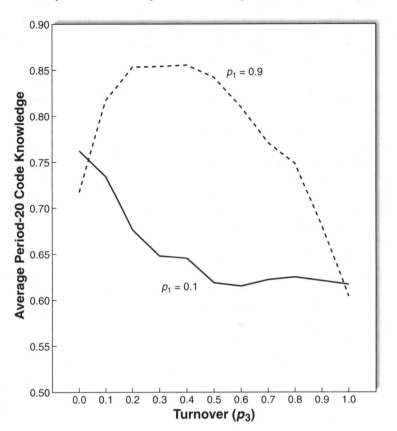

Figure 7.4 Effect of Turnover (p_3) and Socialization Rate (p_1) on Period-20 Code Knowledge. $m = 30$; $n = 50$; $p_2 = 0.5$; 80 Iterations.

ing less socialized people, increases exploration, and thereby improves aggregate knowledge. The level of knowledge reflected by the organizational code is increased, as is the average individual knowledge of those individuals who have been in the organization for some time. Note that this effect does not come from the superior knowledge of the average new recruit. Recruits are, on average, less knowledgeable than the individuals they replace. The gains come from their diversity.

Turnover, like heterogeneity in learning rates, produces a distribution problem. Contributions to improving the code (and subsequently individual knowledge) come from the occasional newcomers who deviate from the code in a favorable way. Old-timers, on average, know more, but what they know is redundant with knowledge already reflected in the code. They are less likely to contribute new knowledge on the margin. Novices know less on average, but what they know is less redundant with the code and occasionally better, thus more likely to contribute to improving the code.

Effects of environmental turbulence

Since learning processes involve lags in adjustment to changes, the contribution of learning to knowledge depends on the amount of turbulence in the environment. Suppose that the value of any given dimension of reality shifts (from 1 to −1 or −1 to 1) in a given time period with probability p_4. This captures in an elementary way the idea that understanding the world may be complicated by turbulence in the world. Exogenous environmental change makes adaptation essential, but it also makes learning from experience difficult (Weick, 1979). In the model, the level of knowledge achieved in a particular (relatively early) time period decreases with increasing turbulence.

In addition, mutual learning has a dramatic long-run degenerate property under conditions of exogenous turbulence. As the beliefs of individuals and the code converge, the possibilities for improvement in either decline. Once a knowledge equilibrium is achieved, it is sustained indefinitely. The beliefs reflected in the code and those held by all individuals remain identical and unchanging, regardless of changes in reality. Even before equilibrium is achieved, the capabilities for change fall below the rate of change in the environment. As a result, after an initial period of increasing accuracy, the knowledge of the code and individuals is systematically degraded through changes in reality. Ultimately, the accuracy of belief reaches chance (i.e., where a random change in reality is as likely to increase accuracy of beliefs as it is to decrease it). The process becomes a random walk.

The degeneracy is avoided if there is turnover. Figure 7.5 plots the average level of code knowledge over time under conditions of turbulence (p_4 = 0.02). Two cases of learning are plotted, one without turnover ($p_3 = 0$), the other with moderate turnover ($p_3 = 0.1$). Where there is turbulence without turnover, code knowledge first rises to a moderate level, and then declines to 0, from which it subsequently wanders randomly. With turnover, the degeneracy is avoided and a moderate level of code knowledge is sustained in the face of environmental change. The positive effects of moderate turnover depend, of course, on the rules for selecting new recruits. In the present case, recruitment is not affected by the code. Replacing departing individuals with recruits closer to the current organizational code would significantly reduce the efficiency of turnover as a source of exploration.

Turnover is useful in the face of turbulence, but it produces a disparity between code knowledge and the average knowledge of individuals in the organization. As a result, the match between turnover rate and level of turbulence that is desirable from the point of view of the organization's

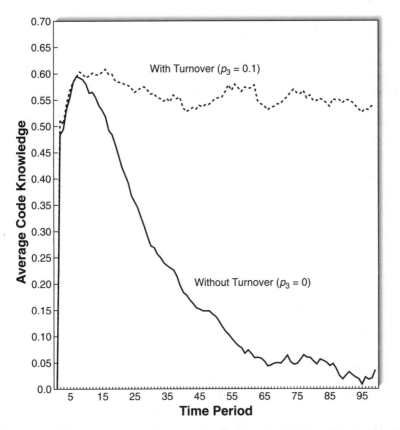

Figure 7.5 Effect of Turbulence (p_4) on Code Knowledge over Time with and Without Turnover (p_3) $m = 30$; $n = 50$; $p_1 = 0.5$; $p_2 = 0.5$; $p_4 = 0.02$; 80 Iterations.

knowledge is not necessarily desirable from the point of view of the knowledge of every individual in it, or individuals on average. In particular, where there is turbulence, there is considerable individual advantage to having tenure in an organization that has turnover. This seems likely to produce pressures by individuals to secure tenure for themselves while restricting it for others.

KNOWLEDGE AND ECOLOGIES OF COMPETITION

The model in the previous section examines one aspect of the social context of adaptation in organizations, the ways in which individual beliefs and an organizational code draw from each other over time. A second major feature of the social context of organizational learning is the competitive ecology within which learning occurs and knowledge is used. External competitive processes pit organizations against each other in pursuit of scarce environmental resources and opportunities. Examples are competition among business firms for customers and governmental subsidies. Internal competitive processes pit individuals in the organization against each other in competition for scarce organizational resources and opportunities. Examples are competition among managers for internal resources and hierarchical promotion. In these ecologies of competition, the competitive consequences of learning by one organization depend on learning by other organizations. In this section, these links among learning, performance, and position in an ecology of competition are discussed by considering some ways in which competitive advantage is affected by the accumulation of knowledge.

Competition and the importance of relative performance

Suppose that an organization's realized performance on a particular occasion is a draw from a probability distribution that can be characterized in terms of some measure of average value (x) and some measure of variability (v). Knowledge, and the learning process that produces it, can be described in terms of their effects on these two measures. A change in an organization's performance distribution that increases average performance (i.e., makes $x' > x$) will often be beneficial to an organization, but such a result is not assured when relative position within a group of competing organizations is important. Where returns to one competitor are not strictly determined by that competitor's own performance but depend on the relative standings of the competitors, returns to changes in knowledge depend not only on the magnitude of the changes in the expected value but also on changes in variability and on the number of competitors.

To illustrate the phenomenon, consider the case of competition for primacy between a reference organization and N other organizations, each having normal performance distributions with mean = x and variance = v. The chance of the reference organization having the best performance within a group of identical competitors is $1/(N + 1)$. We compare this situation to one in which the reference organization has a normal performance distribution with mean = x' and variance = v'. We evaluate the probability, P^*, that the (x', v') organization will outperform all of the N (x, v) organizations. A performance distribution with a mean of x' and a variance of v' provides a competitive advantage in a competition for primacy if P^* is greater than $1/(N + 1)$. It results in a competitive disadvantage if P^* is less than $1/(N + 1)$.

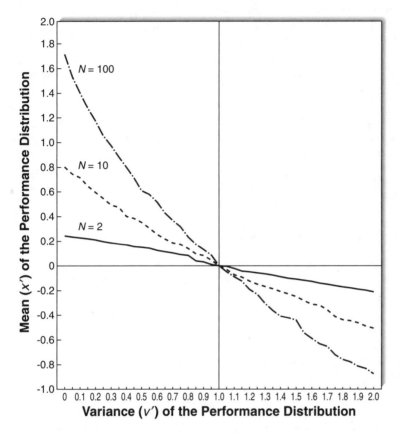

Figure 7.6 Competitive Equality Lines ($P^* = 1/(N + 1)$) for One ($x'v'$) Organization Competing with N (0, 1) Organizations (Normal Performance Distributions).

If an organization faces only one competitor ($N = 1$), it is easy to see that any advantage in mean performance on the part of the reference organization makes P^* greater than $1/(N + 1) = 0.5$, regardless of the variance. Thus, in bilateral competition involving normal performance distributions, learning that increases the mean always pays off, and changes in the variance – whether positive or negative – have no effect.

The situation changes as N increases. Figure 7.6 shows the competitive success (failure) of an organization having a normal performance distribution with a mean = x' and a variance = v', when that organization is faced with N identical and independent competitors whose performance distributions are normal with mean = 0 and variance = 1. Each point in the space in Figure 7.6 represents a different possible normal performance distribution (x', v'). Each line in the figure is associated with a particular

N and connects the (x', v') pairs for which $p^* = 1/(N + 1)$.[2] The area to the right and above a line includes (x', v') combinations for which P^* is greater than $1/(N + 1)$, thus that yield a competitive advantage relative to $(0, 1)$. The area to the left and below a line includes (x', v') combinations for which P^* is less than $1/(N + 1)$, thus that yield a competitive disadvantage relative to $(0, 1)$.

The pattern is clear. If N is greater than 1 (but finite), increases in either the mean or the variance have a positive effect on competitive advantage, and sufficiently large increases in either can offset decreases in the other. The trade-off between increases in the mean and increases in the variance is strongly affected by N. As the number of competitors increases, the contribution of the variance to competitive advantage increases until at the limit, as N goes to infinity, the mean becomes irrelevant.

Learning, knowledge, and competitive advantage

The effects of learning are realized in changes in the performance distribution. The analysis indicates that if learning increases both the mean and the variance of a normal performance distribution, it will improve competitive advantage in a competition for primacy. The model also suggests that increases in the variance may compensate for decreases in the mean; decreases in the variance may nullify gains from increases in the mean. These variance effects are particularly significant when the number of competitors is large.

The underlying argument does not depend on competition being only for primacy. Such competition is a special case of competition for relative position. The general principle that relative position is affected by variability, and increasingly so as the number of competitors increases, is true for any position. In competition to achieve relatively high positions, variability has a positive effect. In competition to avoid relatively low positions, variability has a negative effect.

Nor does the underlying argument depend on the assumption of normality or other symmetry in the performance distributions. Normal performance distributions are special cases in which the tails of the distribution are specified when the mean and variance are specified. For general distributions, as the number of competitors increases, the likelihood of finishing first depends increasingly on the right-hand tail of the performance distribution, and the likelihood of finishing last depends increasingly on the left-hand tail (David, 1981). If learning has different effects on the two tails of the distribution, the right-hand tail effect will be much more important in competition for primacy among many competitors. The left-hand tail will be much more important in competition to avoid finishing last.

Some learning processes increase both average performance and variability. A standard example would be the short-run consequences from adoption of a new technology. If a new technology is so clearly superior as to overcome the disadvantages of unfamiliarity with it, it will offer a higher expected value than the old technology. At the same time, the limited experience with the new technology (relative to experience with the old) will lead to an increased variance. A similar result might be expected with the introduction of a new body of knowledge or new elements of cultural diversity to an organization, for example, through the introduction of individuals with untypical skills, attitudes, ethnicity, or gender.

Learning processes do not necessarily lead to increases in both average performance and variation, however. Increased knowledge seems often to reduce the variability of performance rather than to increase it. Knowledge makes performance more reliable. As work is standardized, as techniques are learned, variability, both in the time required to accomplish tasks and in the quality of task performance, is reduced. Insofar as that increase in reliability comes from a reduction in the left-hand tail, the likelihood of finishing last in a competition among many is reduced without changing the likelihood of finishing first. However, if knowledge has the effect of reducing the right-hand tail of the distribution, it may easily decrease the chance of being best among several competitors even though it also increases average performance. The question is whether you can do exceptionally well, as opposed to better than average, without leaving the confines of conventional action. The answer is complicated, for it depends on a more careful specification of the kind of knowledge involved and its precise effects on the right-hand tail of the distribution. But knowledge that simultaneously increases average performance and its reliability is not a guarantee of competitive advantage.

Consider, for example, the case of modern information and decision technology based on computers. In cases where time is particularly important, information technology has a major effect on the mean, less on the variance. Some problems in environmental scanning for surprises, changes, or opportunities probably fall into such a category. Under such conditions, appropriate use of information technology seems likely to improve competitive position. On the other hand, in many situations the main effect of information technology is to make outcomes more reliable. For example, additional data, or more detailed analyses, seem likely to increase reliability in decisions more rapidly than they will increase their average returns. In such cases, the effects on the tails are likely to dominate the effects on the mean. The net effect of the improved technology on the chance of avoiding being the worst competitor will be positive, but the effect on the chance of finishing at the head of the pack may well be negative.

Similarly, multiple, independent projects may have an advantage over a single, coordinated effort. The average result from independent projects is likely to be lower than that realized from a coordinated one, but their right-hand side variability can compensate for the reduced mean in a competition for primacy. The argument can be extended more generally to the effects of close collaboration or cooperative information exchange. Organizations that develop effective instruments of coordination and communication probably can be expected to do better (on average) than those that are more loosely coupled, and they also probably can be expected to become more reliable, less likely to deviate significantly from the mean of their performance distributions. The price of reliability, however, is a smaller chance of primacy among competitors.

Competition for relative position and strategic action

The arguments above assume that the several individual performances of competitors are independent draws from a distribution of possible performances, and that the distribution cannot be arbitrarily chosen by the competitors. Such a perspective is incomplete. It is possible to see both the mean and the reliability of a performance distribution (at least partially) as choices made strategically. In the long run, they represent the result of organizational choices between investments in learning and in consumption of the fruits of current capabilities, thus the central focus of this chapter. In the short run, the choice of mean can be seen as a choice of effort or attention. By varying effort, an organization selects a performance mean between an entitlement (zero-effort) and a capability (maximum-effort) level. Similarly, in the short run, variations in the reliability of performance can be seen as choices of knowledge or risk that can be set willfully within the range of available alternatives.

These choices, insofar as they are made rationally, will not, in general, be independent of competition. If relative position matters, as the number of competitors increases, strategies for increasing the mean through increased effort or greater knowledge become less attractive relative to strategies for increasing variability. In the more general situation, suppose organizations face competition from numerous competitors who vary in their average capabilities but who can choose their variances. If payoffs and preferences are such that finishing near the top matters a great deal, those organizations with performance distributions characterized by comparatively low means will (if they can) be willing to sacrifice average performance in order to augment the right-hand tails of their performance distributions. In this way, they improve their chances of winning, thus force their more talented competitors to do likewise, and thereby convert the competition into a right-hand tail "race" in which average performance (due to ability and effort) becomes irrelevant. These dynamics comprise powerful countervailing forces to the tendency for experience to eliminate exploration and are a reminder that the learning dominance of exploitation is, under some circumstances, constrained not only by slow learning and turnover but also by reason.

LITTLE MODELS AND OLD WISDOM

Learning, analysis, imitation, regeneration, and technological change are major components of any effort to improve organizational performance and strengthen competitive advantage. Each involves adaptation and a delicate trade-off between exploration and exploitation. The present argument has been that these trade-offs are affected by their contexts of distributed costs and benefits and ecological interaction. The essence of exploitation is the refinement and extension of existing competences, technologies, and paradigms. Its returns are positive, proximate, and predictable. The essence of exploration is experimentation with new alternatives. Its returns are uncertain, distant, and often negative. Thus, the distance in time and space between the locus of learning and the locus for the realization of returns is generally greater in the case of exploration than in the case of exploitation, as is the uncertainty.

Such features of the context of adaptation lead to a tendency to substitute exploitation of known alternatives for the exploration of unknown ones, to increase the reliability of performance rather more than its mean. This property of adaptive processes is potentially self-destructive. As we have seen, it degrades organizational learning in a mutual learning situation. Mutual learning leads to convergence between organizational and individual beliefs. The convergence is generally useful both for individuals and for an organization. However, a major threat to the effectiveness of such learning is the possibility that individuals will adjust to an organizational code before the code can learn from them. Relatively slow socialization of new organizational members and moderate turnover sustain variability in individual beliefs, thereby improving organizational and average individual knowledge in the long run.

An emphasis on exploitation also compromises competitive position where finishing near the top is important. Knowledge-based increases in average performance can be insufficient to overcome the adverse effects produced by reductions in variability. The ambiguous usefulness of learning in a competitive race is not simply an artifact of representing knowledge in terms of the mean and variance of a normal distribution. The key factor is the effect of knowledge on the right-hand tail of the performance distribution. Thus, in the end, the effects stem from the relation between knowledge and discovery. Michael Polanyi, commenting on one of his contributions to physics, observed (Polanyi, 1963, p. 1013) that "I would never have conceived my theory, let alone have made a great effort to verify it, if I had been more familiar with major developments in physics that were taking place. Moreover, my initial ignorance of the powerful, false objections that were raised against my ideas protected those ideas from being nipped in the bud."

These observations do not overturn the renaissance. Knowledge, learning, and education remain as profoundly important instruments of human well-being. At best, the models presented here suggest some of the considerations involved in thinking about choices between exploration and exploitation and in sustaining exploration in the face of adaptive processes that tend to inhibit it. The complexity of the distribution of costs and returns across time and groups makes an explicit determination of optimality a nontrivial exercise. But it may be instructive to reconfirm some elements of folk wisdom asserting that the returns to fast learning are not all positive, that rapid socialization may hurt the socializers even as it helps the socialized, that the development of knowledge may depend on maintaining an influx of the naive and ignorant, and that competitive victory does not reliably go to the properly educated.

Notes

1. More precisely, if the code is the same as the majority view among those individuals whose overall knowledge score is superior to that of the code, the code remains unchanged. If the code differs from the majority view on a particular dimension at the start of a time period, the probability that it will be unchanged at the end of period is $(1-p_2)^k$, where k ($k>0$) is the number of individuals (within the superior group) who differ from the code on this dimension minus the number who do not. This formulation makes the effective rate of code learning dependent on k, which probably depends on n. In the present simulations, n is not varied.
2. The lines are constructed by estimating, for each value of v' from 0 to 2 in steps of 0.05, the value of x' for which $P^*=1/(N+1)$. Each estimate is based on 5000 simulations. Since if $x' = 0$ and $v' = 1$, $P^* = 1/(N+1)$ for any N, each of the lines is constrained to pass through the $(0,1)$ point.

Acknowledgments

This research has been supported by the Spencer Foundation and the Graduate School of Business, Stanford University. The author is grateful for the assistance of Michael Pich and Suzanne Stout and for the comments of Michael Cohen, Julie Elworth, Thomas Finholt, J. Michael Harrison, J. Richard Harrison, David Matheson, Martin Schulz, Sim Sitkin, and Lee Sproull.

References

Argyris, C. and D. Schön (1978), *Organizational Learning*. Reading, MA: Addison-Wesley.

Arthur, W. B. (1984), "Competing Technologies and Economic Prediction," *IIASA Options*, 2, 10–13.

Ashby, W. R. (1960), *Design for a Brain*. (2nd ed.). New York: Wiley.

Cohen, M. D. (1986), "Artificial Intelligence and the Dynamic Performance of Organizational Designs," in J. G. March and R. Weissinger-Baylon (eds.), *Ambiguity and Command: Organizational Perspectives on Military Decision Making*. Boston, MA: Ballinger, 53–71.

Cyert, R. M. and J. G. March (1963), *A Behavioral Theory of the Firm*. Englewood Cliffs, NJ: Prentice Hall.

David, H. A. (1981), *Order Statistics*. (2nd ed.). New York: John Wiley

David, P. A. (1985), "Clio and the Economics of QWERTY," *American Economic Review*, 75, 332–7.

David, P. A. (1990), "The Hero and the Herd in Technological History: Reflections on Thomas Edison and 'The Battle of the Systems'," in P. Higgonet and H. Rosovsky (eds.), *Economic Development Past and Present: Opportunities and Constraints*. Cambridge, MA: Harvard University Press.

David, P. A. and J. A. Bunn (1988), "The Economics of Gateway Technologies and Network Evolution," *Information Economics and Policy*, 3, 165–202.

Day R. H. (1967), "Profits, Learning, and the Convergence of Satisficing to Marginalism," *Quarterly Journal of Economics*, 81, 302–11.

Hannan, M. T. and J. Freeman (1987), "The Ecology of Organizational Foundings: American Labor Unions, 1836–1985," *American Journal of Sociology*, 92, 910–43.

Herriott, S. R., D. A. Levinthal and J. G. March (1985), "Learning from Experience in Organizations," *American Economic Review*, 75, 298–302.

Hey, J. D. (1982), "Search for Rules for Search," *Journal of Economic Behavior and Organization*, 3, 65–81.

Holland, J. H. (1975), *Adaptation in Natural and Artifcial Systems*. Ann Arbor, MI: University of Michigan Press.

Kahneman, D. and A. Tversky (1979), "Prospect Theory: An Analysis of Decision under Risk," *Econometrica*, 47, 263–91.

Katz, M. L. and C. Shapiro (1986), "Technology Adoption in the Presence of Network Externalities," *Journal of Political Economy*, 94, 822–41.

Kuran, T. (1988), "The Tenacious Past: Theories of Personal and Collective Conservatism," *Journal of Economic Behavior and Organization*, 10, 143–71

Levinthal, D. A. and J. G. March (1981), "A Model of Adaptive Organizational Search," *Journal of Economic Behavior and Organization*, 2, 307–33.

Levitt, B. and J. G. March (1988), "Organizational Learning." *Annual Review of Sociology*, 14, 319–40.

Lounamaa, P. H. and J. G. March (1987), "Adaptive Coordination of a Learning Team," *Management Science*, 33. 107–23.

March, J. G. (1988), "Variable Risk Preferences and Adaptive Aspirations," *Journal of Economic Behavior and Organization*, 9, 5–24.

Polanyi, M. (1963), "The Potential Theory of Adsorption: Authority in

Science Has Its Uses and Its Dangers," *Science,* 141, 1010–13.

Radner, R. and M. Rothschild (1975), "On the Allocation of Effort," *Journal of Economic Theory,* 10, 358–76.

Schumpeter, J. A. (1934), *The Theory of Economic Development.* Cambridge, MA: Harvard University Press.

Simon, H. A. (1955), "A Behavioral Model of Rational Choice," *Quarterly Journal of Ecomics,* 69, 99–118.

Van Maanen, J. (1973), "Observations on the Making of Policemen," *Human Organization,* 32, 407–18.

Weick, K. E. (1979), *The Social Psychology of Organizing.* (2nd ed.). Reading, MA: Addison-Wesley.

Whyte, W. H., Jr. (1957), *The Organization Man.* Garden City, NY: Doubleday.

Winter, S. G. (1971), "Satisficing, Selection, and the Innovating Remnant," *Quarterly Journal of Economics,* 85, 237–61.

CHAPTER EIGHT

Learning from Samples of One or Fewer

with Lee S. Sproull and Michal Tamuz

Organizations learn from experience. Sometimes, however, history is not generous with experience. We explore how organizations convert infrequent events into interpretations of history, and how they balance the need to achieve agreement on interpretations with the need to interpret history correctly. We ask what methods are used, what problems are involved, and what improvements might be made. Although the methods we observe are not guaranteed to lead to consistent agreement on interpretations, valid knowledge, improved organizational performance, or organizational survival, they provide possible insights into the possibilities for and problems of learning from fragments of history.

LEARNING FROM SAMPLES OF ONE OR FEWER

Organizations learn from experience, but learning seems problematic when history offers only meager samples of experience. Historical events are observed, and inferences about historical processes are formed, but the paucity of historical events conspires against effective learning. We consider situations in which organizations seek to learn from history on the basis of very small samples of experience. For example:

Case 1. A military organization has rarely fought in a battle. Yet it wants to learn from its history how to improve its ability to engage in warfare.

Case 2. A business firm has little experience with foreign acquisitions. Yet it wants to learn from its history whether and how to make such investments.

Case 3. An airline rarely has fatal accidents. Yet it wants to learn from its history how to reduce the chances of such disasters.

Case 4. A business firm rarely makes major marketable discoveries. Yet it wants to learn from its history how to increase the chances of such innovations.

Case 5. A power company rarely has nuclear accidents. Yet it wants to learn from its history how to minimize the chances of such catastrophes.

In the next section, we examine how organizations convert meager experience into interpretations of history by experiencing infrequent events richly. We then examine processes for simulating hypothetical histories. Following this, we examine some justifications for these two learning strategies and some of the problems involved.

EXPERIENCING HISTORY RICHLY

Historical events are unique enough to make accumulating knowledge difficult. Each event is a single, unrepeated data point, and accumulation seems to require pooling across diverse contexts. Organizations attempt such pooling, but they also seek to increase the information extracted from their own limited historical experience by treating unique historical incidents as detailed stories rather than single data points. They elaborate experience by discovering more aspects of experience, more interpretations of experience, and more preferences by which to evaluate experience.

Experiencing more aspects of experience

Characterizing history as small samples of unique occurrences overlooks the wealth of experience that is represented in each historical event. The apparent stinginess of history is moderated by attending to more aspects of experience (Campbell, 1979). For example, learning about a decision involves monitoring its outcomes. But long before an organization experiences many of the outcomes of a typical decision, it experiences a variety of collateral consequences associated with the making of the decision and its implementation. Learning and evaluation occur through these experiences prior to outcome-based learning. For example, participants appreciate collateral experiences such as "a bold move" or "a good meeting."

When early collateral experiences are positive, organizations, like individuals, are prone to exhibit self-reinforcing decision behavior. Especially when outcome feedback is slow or unclear, an organization is likely to repeat decisions simply because it has made them before. Thus, in a study of decisions about foreign direct investments by Finnish firms, Björkman (1989) found that, prior to receiving information on the results of their first investments and simply as a result of their experience in making the first decisions, firms increased their propensity to make more investments. This did not appear to be a consequence of any explicit intention to spread risk. Apparently, the organizations extracted lessons from the choice process itself, lessons about the competence and character of relevant actors and the pleasure of deciding to invest. Learning was embedded richly in the taking of action, rather than simply in considering its ultimate consequences.

Making a decision also induces anticipations of its future costs and benefits (Merton, 1968). The anticipations are experienced prior to the consequences and are an independent basis for learning. Since expectations for chosen alternatives will generally be positive, they ordinarily reinforce a repetition of the action. On the other hand, negative expectations might be experienced in situations involving coercion or peril, or when learning takes place in an alienated part of the organization, or among opposition groups. In such cases, the effect of making a decision reduces the propensity to repeat it. In general, decision processes in organizations lead to overly optimistic expectations and thus are vulnerable to subsequent disappointment with results (Harrison and March, 1984). These optimistic errors in anticipations are likely to make the short-run lessons of experience more reinforcing of action than the long-run lessons. The inconsistency in learning is reduced by the tendency for actual experience to be both delayed and more ambiguous than anticipations, thus allowing optimistic expectations about experience to be confirmed by retrospective sense-making of it (Aronson, 1968; Salancik, 1977).

Organizations also enhance the richness of history by focusing intensively on critical incidents. For example, when a large section of the metal skin of an Aloha Airlines aircraft peeled away in mid-air, the event attracted considerable attention and triggered a major modification in FAA-mandated maintenance programs. Close examination of what happened revealed significant features of aircraft engineering and maintenance that had not been noted earlier. By identifying those features and their implications, the organizations learned. Similarly, when a computer science graduate student propagated a "virus" among many computer networks, producing breakdowns in hundreds of systems, and considerable publicity, the incident stimulated analyses that identified weaknesses in the underlying computer code and in how people and systems were organized to respond to such events.

Three aspects of an event seem to make it critical. The first is its place in the course of history. Events that change the world are critical incidents. They are branching points of historical development. From such an incident, one learns about changed implications for the future rather than about how to predict or control similar occurrences in the future. A classic example is the invention of the printing press.

The second aspect of an event that makes it critical is its place in the development of belief. Events that change what is believed about the world are critical incidents. In a way consistent with conventional ideas about the relation between surprise and information value (Raiffa, 1968), criticality is associated with the surprise an event evokes for current belief. A single incident is typically unsurprising because it can be interpreted as consistent with sampling variation within existing theories (Fischhoff, 1975; Fischhoff and Beyth, 1975). But sometimes a solitary event provides an unexpected contradiction to our beliefs, as for example in the Aloha Airlines and computer virus cases.

A third aspect that makes an event critical is its metaphorical power. Events that evoke meaning, interest, and attention for organizational participants are critical incidents. Anecdotes and stories are standard features of pedagogical practice. Skill at story telling is a major factor in endowing experience with metaphorical force. But the raw material of experience also affects the development of stories. Critical incidents have a quality of simplicity and representativeness that is not entirely imposed on them. Some historical events are better vehicles for meaning than others.

Experiencing more interpretations

Organizations often augment history by attending to multiple observers or interpretations. The consequences of an action are experienced differently throughout the organization. Conflicts of interest or differences in culture, in particular, stimulate multiple interpretations. Because different individuals and groups experience historical events differently, they learn different lessons from the same experience (Dearborn and Simon, 1958; Sproull and Hofmeister, 1986). As a result, organizational experience leads to a variety of interpretations, and an organization's repertoire may come to include several different, possibly contradictory, story lines. Differences in perspectives lead to differences in interpretations and create a mosaic of conflicting lessons.

To be sure, efforts to make multiple interpretations consistent are also routine in organizations. Formal proceedings, findings, informal conversations, and the diffusion of stories tend to create a shared, interpretive history. Interpretations of individual or group responsibility for mistakes or failures (or brilliant moves or successes) come to be shared. However, such efforts are not always successful (Brunsson, 1989). The structure of internal competition and conflict divides many organizations into advocates and opponents for organizational policies and actions. The contending groups interpret history differently and draw different lessons from it.

Experiencing more preferences

Organizations discover values, aspirations, and identities in the process of experiencing the consequences of their actions. They learn how to distinguish success from failure, and thus affect considerably the other lessons they take from their experience. While the interpretation of a particular outcome as a success or failure is not arbitrary, neither is it always self-evident. The preferences and values in terms of which organizations distinguish successes from failures are themselves transformed in the process of learning. By acting, reflecting, and interpreting, organizations learn what they are. By observing their own actions, they learn what they want (Weick, 1979). Whether these changes are seen as learning new implications of alternative actions for stable preferences, or as transforming preferences, is partly a matter of intellectual taste (Becker and Stigler, 1977).

For any given dimension of organizational preferences, aspiration levels change in response to an organization's own experience and to the experience of other organizations to which it compares itself (Cyert and March, 1963; Lant and Montgomery, 1987), thereby loosening the link between performance and outcomes, on the one hand, and evaluations of success and failure (and thus learning), on the other. Because experiencing an outcome as a success or failure depends on the relation between the outcome and adaptive aspirations for it, what is learned from any particular kind of experience can vary substantially across time and across organizations. Consider, for example, the efforts of a business firm to learn from its marketing experience. Whether a particular marketing strategy is viewed as a success (to be reinforced) or a failure (to be extinguished) will depend as much on the organization's aspirations as on the marketing outcomes. In a similar way, election results are experienced by political parties and movements in terms of a comparison between outcomes and aspirations rather than simply in terms of the former.

The dimensions of preferences also change. As we have noted above, a rich examination of an individual case uncovers a variety of features and consequences of action. These experiences become bases for organizational interpretations not only of the world and its rewards but also of the organization, particularly its preferences, values, and character (Zald and Denton, 1963). For example, when the Coca-Cola Company reinstated old coke as Coca-Cola Classic (after having first withdrawn it from the market in favor of a replacement), it learned from its behavior that it was a "flexible company that listened to its customers" (Oliver, 1986). Anything that predisposes parts of an organization to find pleasure in consequences, for example, an upbeat mood (Isen et al., 1978) or a sense of responsibility for action (March and Olsen, 1975), tends to increase the likelihood of identifying positive aspects of unanticipated consequences, thus of transforming preferences.

SIMULATING EXPERIENCE

In trying to understand unique experiences, organizations make implicit choices between two alternative perspectives on history. In the first perspective, realized events are seen as necessary consequences of antecedent historical conditions. In the second perspective, realized events are seen as *draws* from a distribution of possible events. If historical events are (possibly unlikely) draws from a wealth of possibilities, an understanding of history requires attention to the whole distribution of possible events, including those that did not occur (Fischhoff, 1980; Hogarth, 1983). The organizational problem is to infer an underlying distribution of possible events from a series of realized events having varying, but possibly quite low, probabilities. The merging of empirical and theoretical knowledge required to understand these underlying distributions raises some complicated problems of inference and method.

We consider two closely related techniques for organizational simulation of hypothetical events: the first technique is to define and elaborate a class of historical non-events that can be called near-histories – events that almost happened. The second technique is to define and elaborate a class of historical non-events that can be called hypothetical histories – events that might have happened under certain unrealized but plausible conditions.

Near-histories

If a basketball game is decided by one point, one team wins and the other team loses, with consequences that may be vital for a championship. But the outcome will normally be interpreted by experts as a draw from some probability distribution over possible outcomes rather than simply as a "win" by one team and a "loss" by the other. In general, if a relatively small change in some conditions would have transformed one outcome into another, the former will be experienced to some degree as having been the latter. In such a spirit, the National Research Council (1980) has defined a safety "incident" as an event that, under slightly different circumstances, could have been an accident.

Air traffic systems illustrate how organizations learn from near-histories or "incidents" (Tamuz, 1987). By collecting information about near-accidents from pilots and air traffic controllers, air safety reporting systems considerably enlarge the sample of events that can be treated as relevant to understanding aviation safety. Information on near-accidents augments the relatively sparse history of real accidents and has been used to redesign aircraft, air traffic control systems, airports, cockpit routines, and pilot training procedures.

Near-histories are useful antidotes to a tendency to overgeneralize from the drama of great disasters or victories (Fischhoff, 1982). For example, students of the Battle of Midway have suggested a number of quite likely alternative scenarios for that battle that would have led to notably different outcomes (Prange, 1982). Future admirals learn not only from the battle but also from its near-histories. Standard folkloric observations that great failures often are the consequence of bad luck or timing and great successes the consequence of good luck or timing suggest an implicit distribution of possible outcomes around the observed outliers. They emphasize that the near-histories of genius and foolishness are more similar than their realized histories.

Hypothetical histories

Near-histories are a special case of a more general approach – the construction of hypothetical histories. Hypothetical histories play a role in organizational learning similar to that of mental models or simulations in studies of individual learning (Kahneman and Tversky, 1982a; Johnson-Laird, 1983). Organizations use small samples of specific historical events to construct theories about events, and then simulate hypothetical histories that can be treated as having interpretive significance comparable to, or even greater than, the history actually experienced. In this process, the analysis of unique historical outcomes emphasizes identifying the underlying distribution from which that realization was drawn rather than explaining the particular draw (Stinchcombe, 1978).

A pervasive contemporary version of hypothetical histories is found in the use of spreadsheets to explore the implications of alternative assumptions or shifts in variables in a system of equations that portrays organizational relations. More generally, many modern techniques of planning in organizations involve the simulation of hypothetical future scenarios, which in the present terms are indistinguishable from hypothetical histories (Hax and Majluf, 1984). The logic is simple: small pieces of experience are used to construct a theory of history from which a variety of unrealized, but possible, additional scenarios are generated. In this way, ideas about historical processes drawn from detailed case studies are used to develop distributions of possible futures.

Organizations expand their comprehension of history by making experience richer, by considering multiple interpretations of experience, by using experience to discover and modify their preferences, and by simulating near-events and hypothetical histories. They try to learn from samples of one or fewer. Many of the techniques organizations use to learn from small samples of history, however, are clearly suspect. They can lead to learning false lessons, to superstitious learning, to exaggerated confidence in historical understandings. As a result, discussions of organizational learning from small samples tend to be framed by a mood of despair over the futility of the effort. We now turn to an examination of how such learning might be understood, evaluated, and improved.

ASSESSING AND IMPROVING LEARNING FROM SMALL HISTORIES

We have described some of the ways organizations learn from fragments of history. In this section, we assess their effectiveness in terms of two common criteria: reliability and validity. A reliable learning process is one by which an organization develops common understandings of its experience and makes its interpretations public, stable, and shared. A valid learning process is one by which an organization is able to understand, predict, and control its environment. Neither reliability nor validity is assured. Because different people and groups in an organization approach historical experience with different expectations and beliefs, shared understandings cannot be assumed. And because historical events are produced by particular (and often complicated) combinations of factors occurring in non-repetitive contexts, learning validly from small samples of historical experience is difficult (Brehmer, 1980, Kiesler and Sproull, 1982).

If individual beliefs converge to an accurate understanding of reality, then they become simultaneously shared and valid. Such a convergence might be expected in worlds of stable knowledge and cumulative discovery. Alternatively, if socially constructed beliefs are enacted into reality (Weick, 1979), the enactment brings high levels of both reliability and validity. For example, organizational beliefs about power, legitimacy, competence, and responsibility are based upon interpretations of shared experiences that are themselves considerably affected by the beliefs.

The more general situation, however, is one of partial conflict between the dual requirements of reliability and validity. Stable, shared knowledge interferes with the discovery of contrary experience from which valid learning arises, and the exploration of novel ideas interferes with the reliable maintenance and sharing of interpretations (March, 1990). As a result, organizational learning involves balancing the two. The trade-offs between reliability and validity made by the learning procedures we observe are less a result of conscious choice than a collection of evolving practices, imperfectly justified and incompletely comprehended. For example, the extent and character of subgroup differentiation in organizations and the mechanisms by which they are sustained or changed are important means by which the trade-off between reliability and validity is made.

The reliability of learning: The construction and sharing of belief

Stability in shared understandings is important for organizational effectiveness and survival (Beyer, 1981; March and Olsen, 1989), as it is for social systems (Durkheim, 1973) and knowledge in general (Rorty, 1985). However, the ambiguities of history make common understandings of organizational experience difficult to sustain. Meaning is not self-evident but must be constructed and shared. Many different interpretations are both supportable and refutable.

Some standard mechanisms of individual sense-making contribute to reliability. The retrieval of history from memory exaggerates the consistency of experience with prior conceptions (Fischhoff, 1975; Pearson et al., 1990). Incorrect predictions are not noticed or are interpreted as irrelevant anomalies or measurement errors (Einhorn and Hogarth, 1978; Lord et al., 1979). Missing data are experienced as consistent with the model and are remembered as real (Cohen and Ebbesen, 1979; Loftus, 1979).

The apparatus of organizational information processing and decision making supplements these individual and social cognitive processes. Information is gathered and distributed more to interpret decisions than to inform them (Feldman and March, 1981; March and Sevón, 1984). Meetings are organized more to share stories and explanations than to take action (Brunsson, 1985; 1989). Organizations develop robust understandings that are resilient to contradictory information (Sproull et al. 1978; Starbuck, 1983). Conceptions of identity in organizations tend also to be conserved by interpretations of experience. Decision makers in organizations discover what they are and how they should behave by taking actions (Weick, 1979). Making a decision leads to defining a personal and organizational identity consistent with that decision. Similarly, the social construction of aspirations tends to be conservative, to reinforce shared behavioral preferences.

Pressures toward reliability are easily orchestrated within an emphasis on critical incidents. Defining an event as critical focuses attention on interpreting and responding to the event. Because of the ambiguities associated with any single incident, responses and interpretations tend to be adopted more as a result of their temporal proximity, cognitive availability, or political convenience than by virtue of their obvious validity (Cyert et al., 1958; Cohen et al., 1972).

The learning process is generally conservative, sustaining existing structures of belief, including existing differences, while coping with surprises in the unfolding of history. Organizations create the same kinds of coherent systems of belief that in science are called knowledge, in religion are called morality, and in other people's societies are called myths. Experience is used to strengthen and elaborate previously believed theories of life.

Such a description is, however, incomplete. There are limits to the conservation of belief (Martin and Siehl, 1983, Higgins and Bargh, 1987). Both success and failure contain the seeds of change. A persistent subjective sense of success leads to a sense of competence and a willingness to experiment (March and Shapira, 1987). A persistent subjective sense of failure produces instability in beliefs and disagreement among organizational participants with respect to both preferences and action (Sproull et al., 1978). In addition, pressures toward subgroup homogeneity lead to internal differentiation and limit organizational homogeneity (Cangelosi and Dill, 1965, Lawrence and Lorsch, 1967).

The validity of learning: The construction of causal belief

The confusions of history often obscure what happened, why it happened, and how we should learn from it. The general problem is not simply one of eliminating known biases in historical interpretation by organizations. The experimental design and sample sizes of history are inadequate for making inferences about it (Lounamaa and March, 1987; Levitt and March, 1988). Estimation from historical events is subject to two major kinds of variability. The first stems from the fact that some of the processes by which history is produced may be genuinely stochastic. Understanding those processes requires approximating the underlying distributions from which a realized event is drawn. The expected error in estimation can be decreased by aggregating over several events, but history limits the number of comparable events. Lacking multiple events, organizations use whatever information they can extract from single cases to discern the historical processes that determine those underlying distributions.

The second kind of variability in estimation stems from the measurement and interpretation of historical events by observers. Measurement error, model misspecification, and system complexity introduce substantial noise into observations and interpretations. With large samples of events, organizations can tolerate a relatively large amount of noise, aggregating over events to extract a signal. With small samples, however, aggregation is a less powerful procedure. Two organizational responses are common. First, since variability in interpretation with respect to any information is partly a function of the effort expended in examining it, the expected error can be decreased through a more intense examination of the individual case. Second, since the processes of measurement and interpretation yield a distribution of possible observations, the expected error can be decreased by aggregating over multiple observers.

Most of the ways organizations increase the validity of learning from historical experience can be seen as reflecting such considerations. Organizations attempt to overcome the limitations in the experimental design and sample sizes of history by enhancing the knowledge they have. They attempt to experience history more richly, to formulate more interpretations of that experience, and to supplement history by experiencing more of the events that did not occur but could have.

Consider, first, efforts to experience history more richly. Every unique historical event is a collection of micro events, each of which can be experienced. In this sense, the learning potential of any historical event is indeterminate. Because both the scope of an event and the depth of its decomposition into elements are arbitrary, so also is the richness of experience. By considering additional aspects of experience and new dimensions of preferences, an organization expands the information gained from a particular case. The pursuit of rich experience, however, requires a method for absorbing detail without molding it. Great organizational histories, like great novels, are written, not by first constructing interpretations of events and then filling in the details, but by first identifying the details and allowing the interpretations to emerge from them. As a result, openness to a variety of (possibly irrelevant) dimensions of experience and preference is often more valuable than a clear prior model and unambiguous objectives (Maier, 1963; March, 1978; 1987).

Moving from rich experiences of history to valid inferences about history involves a logic that is not very well defined but is different from the logic of classical statistical inference. It assumes that the various micro events associated with an event are in some way interconnected. They are clearly not independent samples of some universe in the standard statistical sense. But they provide scraps of information about an underlying reality that cumulate, much the way various elements of a portrait cumulate to provide information about its subject.

Consider, second, efforts to interpret experience in more ways. Imagination in generating alternatives of interpretation reduces the standard confirmatory bias of experience, at the cost of also reducing the speed at which a correct interpretation is recognized and confirmed. Janis and Mann (1977) and George (1980) have each pointed out the advantages of pooling perceptions and judgments across individuals who interpret history differently. A similar argument is made into a methodological point by Allison (1971) and Neustadt and May (1986). Such observations suggest an important trade-off in attempts to improve the precision of estimates: an organizations can opt to increase the number of events to be observed and interpreted or, alternatively, to increase the number and diversity of observers for a single event. Whether it is better to invest in additional events or in additional observers depends both on the relative cost of the two and on the relative magnitudes of the two sources of variability. But in pursuing an understanding of organizational history, greater reduction in uncertainty can often be achieved by pooling observers rather than by pooling events, particularly if the observers are relatively independent.

Consider, third, efforts to experience more of the events that did not happen. The presumption is that the processes of history are both more stable than their realized outcomes and more susceptible to understanding through rich descriptions. Near-histories and hypothetical histories produce distributions of unrealized, possible events. By treating events that did not occur as having significance similar to those that did occur, hypothetical histories exploit the information contained in rich descriptions of historical processes to provide a more judicious assessment of the probability distribution of future events.

In addition to providing a wider range of experience from which to draw, near-histories may be more easily interpreted than realized history. Tamuz (1988) suggests that understanding actual aviation accidents is heavily compromised by the legal and financial contexts which provide individual and organizational incentives for discovering particular self-interested interpretations. She argues that although the reporting of near-accidents is affected by publicity, politics, and perceived reporting incentives, the analysis of these near-accidents often introduces fewer biases than those of accidents, thus producing understandings that are more consistent with broader social constructions and theories of evidence.

Although near-histories make useful contributions to learning, supplementing realized events with hypothetical ones introduces certain complications. First, constructing hypothetical histories can be expensive. Sometimes the substantial costs of such activities are shared by professional associations and governmental agencies, as they are in the air transportation industry. But often the ordinary branchings of history make it difficult to gather and interpret information on consequences of hypothetical histories that are not immediate. Imagine an organization that wanted to compare the ultimate careers and productivity of its employees with those job applicants it almost hired, or of applicants to whom it offered employment but who chose to work elsewhere. Assembling information on such a collection of historical branches involving outsiders, and interpreting the information, are substantial tasks.

Second, the impact of hypothetical histories ordinarily cannot compare with the dramatic power of realized history (Fischhoff and Beyth, 1975; Kiesler and Sproull, 1982). It is difficult to match the powerful effect of actual events (for example, the 1987 Challenger explosion) on beliefs. As a result, a vital part of the telling of history is the evocation of imagination (Tolstoy, 1869). The probable dependence of imagination on vividness (Shedler and Manis, 1986) and rich detail (Krieger, 1983) provides at least a partial reason for emphasizing such stories in organizations (Clark, 1972; Martin, 1982). In the stories of Three-Mile Island, the Aloha Airlines flight, and the Cornell computer virus, vivid historical events were used to dramatize a hypothetical story of even greater potential disaster. The drama mobilized attention and learning across a wide spectrum of groups.

Third, hypothetical histories may be ambiguous and thus unpersuasive. Where organizations face possible events of great consequence but small likelihood, the use of near-histories to augment simple experience is sometimes controversial. If the probability of disaster is very low, near-histories will tend to picture greater risk than will be experienced directly by most organizations or individuals in a reasonable length of time. In such case, near-histories are likely to be treated as generating too pessimistic a picture. For example, long before the fatal Challenger flight, the spacecraft flew a series of successful missions despite its faulty O-rings. Some engineers interpreted the indications of O-ring problems during these early flights as symptoms that past successes had been relatively lucky draws from a distribution in which the probability of disaster was relatively high (Bell and Esch, 1987; Boisjoly, 1987). Others, including some key personnel in NASA, considered these estimates of danger as exaggerated because, in the realized history, the system had been robust enough to tolerate such problems (Starbuck and Milliken, 1988).

Conversely, if the probability of success is very low, most short sequences of realized experience will contain no successes. The direct experience of most organizations and individuals with projects offering very low probability of very high return will be less favorable than will an analysis of near-successes. In such cases, near-histories are likely to be treated as providing too optimistic a picture. One such case involves organizations searching unsuccessfully for major innovations and treating assertions of "near-discoveries" as an unduly optimistic basis for sustaining investment in research.

As these examples suggest, the most obvious learning problem with near-histories is the necessary ambiguity of their interpretation. If an organization is concerned with product quality and uses an inspection system to reject items that do not meet standards, every rejected item provides information on two things – the likelihood of substandard production and the likelihood of discovering the inadequacy. Each event, therefore, is both a failure and a success. Similarly, every time a pilot avoids a collision, the event provides evidence both for the threat and for its irrelevance. It is not clear whether the learning should emphasize how close the organization came to a disaster, thus the reality of danger in the guise of safety, or the fact that disaster was avoided, thus the reality of safety in the guise of danger.

FOUR QUESTIONS

Organizational efforts to learn reliably and validly from small histories are marked by two conspicuous things: first, we try to learn from them, often believing that we do so (Allison, 1971; George and McKeown, 1985), or can do so (Fischhoff, 1982; Kahneman and Tversky 1982b), and often believing that we do not and cannot (Fischhoff, 1980; Dawes et al., 1989). Second, we do not have a shared conception of how we learn from small histories or what distinguishes single cases that are informative from those that are not (Herbst, 1970; Mohr, 1985).

We have not invented a general logic for learning from history that can fully rationalize what we have described, nor do we imagine that such a total rationalization is possible. Many of the ways in which organizations treat small histories are difficult to justify as either leading to shared beliefs, exhibiting intelligence, or producing competitive advantage. Learning processes sometimes result in confusion and mistakes.

Nevertheless, we are disposed to see elements of intelligence in organizational efforts to organize, construct, and interpret experience, so as to move toward a shared understanding of it. We think organizations learn from their histories in ways that are, at times, remarkably subtle adaptations to the inferential inadequacies of historical experience. We recognize some advantages in having stable, shared beliefs about experience even if misinterpretations are embedded in those beliefs. We see possibilities for expanding and enhancing unique, ambiguous events, so as to learn more richly and validly from them. We believe that usable knowledge can be extracted from fragments of history and that intensive examinations of individual cases can be used imaginatively to construct meaningful hypothetical histories.

Such beliefs depend ultimately on confidence in being able to resolve some fundamental issues in historical inference. These include four critical questions:

1. What is the evidential standing of imagination? Organizations use near-histories and hypothetical histories to learn from samples of one or fewer. The procedures seem to have elements of intelligence in them, but they mix theoretical and empirical knowledge in ways that are not considered comprehensively in our theories of inference.
2. What is a proper process for combining prior expectations and interrelated, cumulated aspects of a rich description into an interpretation of history? Organizations develop and modify stories about history on the basis of detailed examinations of individual cases. It is clear that radically different stories may be told about the same history. But it also seems clear that the evaluation of stories is not arbitrary, that there are criteria for differentiating between good and bad stories.
3. What is the proper trade-off between reliability and validity in historical interpretation? As organizations develop theories of their experiences, they balance gains and losses in validity against gains and losses in reliability. The metric and the procedures for the trade-off are ill-defined, but there seems little doubt that an intelligent organization will sometimes sacrifice conventional notions of validity in order to achieve or sustain reliability in interpretation.
4. What are the relative values of multiple observations of events and multiple interpretations of them? Improving precision in estimates involves pooling over observations and over observers. Theories of historical inference tend to emphasize pooling over observations. Pooling over observers appears to have advantages in some common situations, but in the absence of a clearer formulation of the gains and losses involved, it is hard to specify the precise conditions favoring one strategy or the other.

These questions invite heroic philosophical and methodological efforts to clarify and extend the uses of historical experience in the construction and sharing of meaning. The problems involved are not trivial. Nevertheless, we think modest progress can be made without waiting for a revolution in epistemology and within reasonably conventional modes of thinking about historical inference and learning from experience. This chapter is in that spirit. By examining the ways organizations actually seek to learn from small histories, and by trying to make sense of some of the things they do, we have tried to suggest some possible directions for understanding how meaning is extracted from sample sizes of one or fewer.

Acknowledgments

The research has been supported by the National Science Foundation, the Spencer Foundation, the Stanford Graduate School of Business, the

System Development Foundation, and the Xerox Corporation. We are grateful for the comments of Michael Cohen, Robyn Dawes, Kristian Kreiner, Arie Lewin, Allyn Romanow, Sim Sitkin, and Suzanne Stout.

References

Allison, G. T. (1971), *Essence of Decision*, Boston, MA: Little, Brown.

Aronson, E. (1968), "Disconfirmed Expectancies and Bad Decisions – Discussion: Expectancy vs. Other Motives," in R. P. Abelson, E. Aronson, W. McGuire, T. Newcombe, M. Rosenberg, and P. H. Tannenbaum (eds), *Theories of Cognitive Consistency*. Chicago, IL: Rand McNally, 491–3.

Becker, G. S. and G. J. Stigler (1977), "De Gustibus non est Disputandum," *Am. Econ. R.*, 67, 76–90.

Bell, T. E. and K. Esch (1987), "The Fatal Flaw in Flight 51-L," *IEEE Spectr.*, 24, 2, 36–51.

Beyer, J. M. (1981), "Ideologies, Values and Decision-making in Organizations," in P. C. Nystrom and W. H. Starbuck (eds), *Handbook of Organizational Design*, Vol. 2. Oxford: Oxford University Press, 166–202.

Björkman, I. (1989), *Foreign Direct Investments: An Empirical Analysis of Decision Making in Seven Finnish Firms*. Helsinki: Svenska Handelhögskolan.

Boisjoly, R. (1987), "Ethical Decisions – Morton Thiokol and the Space Shuttle Challenger Disaster," *Am. Soc. Mech. Eng. J.*, 87-WA/TS-4, 1–13.

Brehmer, B. (1980), "In One Word: Not from Experience," *Acta Psychol.*, 45, 223–41.

Brunsson, N. (1985), *The Irrational Organization: Irrationality as a Basis for Organizational Action and Change*. Chichester, England: Wiley.

Brunsson, N. (1989), *The Organization of Hypocrisy*. Chichester, England: Wiley.

Campbell, D. (1979), "Degrees of Freedom and the Case Study," in T. D. Cook and C. S. Reichardt (eds), *Qualitative and Quantitative Methods in Evaluations Research*. Beverly Hills: Sage.

Cangelosi, V. and W. R. Dill (1965), "Organizational Learning: Observations toward a Theory," *Adm. Sci. Q.*, 10, 175–203.

Clark, B. R. (1972), "The Organizational Saga in Higher Education," *Adm. Sci. Q.*, 17, 178–84.

Cohen, C. E. and E. B. Ebbesen (1979), "Observational Goals and Schema Activation: A Theoretical Framework for Behavior Perception," *J. Exper. Social Psychol.*, 15, 305–29.

Cohen, M. D., J. G. March and J. P. Olsen (1972), "A Garbage Can Model of Organizational Choice," *Adm. Sci. Q.*, 17, 1–25.

Cyert, R. M. and J. G. March (1963), *A Behavioral Theory of the Firm*. Englewood Cliffs, NJ: Prentice-Hall.

Cyert, R. M., W. Dill and J. G. March (1958), "The Role of Expectations in Business Decision Making," *Adm. Sci. Q.*, 3, 307–40.

Dawes, R. M., D. Faust and P. E. Meehl (1989), "Clinical versus Actuarial Judgment," *SCI*, 243, 1668–74.

Dearborn, D. C. and H. A. Simon (1958), "Selective Perception: A Note on the Departmental Identification of Executives," *Sociom.*, 21, 140–4.

Durkheim, E. (1973), *On Morality and*

Society. Translated by R. N. Bellah. Chicago, IL: University of Chicago Press.

Einhorn, H. and R. Hogarth (1978), "Confidence in Judgment: Persistence in the Illusion of Validity." *Psychol. R.*, 85, 395–416.

Feldman, M. S. and J. G. March (1981), "Information as Signal and Symbol," *Adm. Sci. Q.*, 26, 171–86.

Fischhoff, B. (1975), "Hindsight/Foresight: The Effect of Outcome Knowledge on Judgment under Uncertainty," *J. Exper. Psych.: Human Perception and Performance*, 1, 288–99.

Fischhoff, B. (1980), "For Those Condemned to Study the Past: Reflections on Historical Judgment," in R. A. Shweder and D. W. Fiske (eds), *New Directions for Methodology of Behavioral Science*. San Fransisco, CA: Jossey-Bass, 79–93.

Fischhoff, B. (1982), "Debiasing," in D. Kahneman, P. Slovic, and A. Tversky (eds), *Judgment Under Uncertainty: Heuristics and Biases*. Cambridge: Cambridge University Press, 422–44.

Fischhoff, B. and R. Beyth (1975), " 'I knew it would happen' – Remembered Probabilities of Once-future Things," *Organizational Behavior and Human Performance*, 13, 1–16.

George, A. L. (1980), *Presidential Decision Making in Foreign Policy: The Effective Use of Information and Advice*, Boulder, CO: Westview.

George, A. L. and T. McKeown (1985), "Case Studies and Theories of Organizational Decision Making," in R. F. Coulam and R. A. Smith (eds), *Advances in Information Processing in Organizations*, vol. 2. Greenwich, CT: JAI Press, 21–58.

Harrison, J. R. and J. G. March (1984), "Decision-making and Postdecision Surprises," *Adm. Sci. Q.*, 29, 26–42.

Hax, A. C. and N. S. Majluf (1984), *Strategic Management: An Integrated Perspective*. Englewood Cliffs, NJ: Prentice Hall.

Herbst, P. G. (1970), *Behavioral Worlds: The Study of Single Cases*. London: Tavistock.

Higgins, E. T. and J. A. Bargh (1987), "Social Cognition and Social Perception," *Ann. R. Psych.*, 38, 369–425.

Hogarth, R. (1983), "Small Probabilities: Imagination as Experience," Working Paper, University of Chicago Center for Decision Research.

Isen, A. M., T. E. Schalker, M. Clark and L. Karp (1978), "Affect Accessibility of Material in Memory, and Behavior: A Cognitive Loop?", *J. Pers. Soc. Psych.*, 36, 1–12.

Janis, I. L. and L. Mann (1977), *Decision-Making: A Psychological Analysis of Conflict, Choice and Commitment*. New York, NY: Free Press.

Johnson-Laird, P. N. (1983), *Mental Models: Towards a Cognitive Science of Language, Inference, and Consciousness*. Cambridge, MA: Harvard University Press.

Kahneman, D. and A. Tversky (1982a), "The Simulation Heuristic," in D. Kahneman, P. Slovic, and A. Tversky (eds), *Judgment Under Uncertainty: Heuristics and Biases*. Cambridge: Cambridge University Press, 201–28.

Kahneman, D. and A. Tversky (1982b), "Intuitive Prediction: Biases and Corrective Procedures," in D. Kahneman, P. Slovic, and A. Tversky (eds), *Judgment Under Uncertainty: Heuristics and Biases*. Cambridge: Cambridge University Press, 414–21.

Kiesler, S. and L. S. Sproull (1982), "Managerial Response to Changing Environments: Perspectives on Problem Sensing from Social Cognition," *Adm. Sci. Q.*, 27, 548–70.

Krieger, S. (1983), "Fiction and Social

Science," in S. Krieger, *The Mirror Dance: Identity in a Women's Community*. Philadelphia, PA: Temple University Press, 173–99.

Lant, T. K. and D. B. Montgomery (1987), "Learning from Strategic Success and Failure," *J. Bus. Res.*, 15, 503–18.

Lawrence, P. and J. Lorsch (1967), *Organization and Environment: Managing Differentiation and Integration*. Boston: Harvard Graduate School of Business Administration.

Levitt, B. and J. G. March (1988), "Organizational Learning," *Ann. R. Sociol.*, 14, 319–40.

Loftus, E. (1979), *Eyewitness Testimony*. Cambridge, MA: Harvard University Press.

Lord, C., M. R. Lepper and L. Ross (1979), "Biased Assimilation and Attitude Polarization: The Effects of Prior Theories on Subsequently Considered Evidence," *J. Pers. Soc. Psych.*, 37, 2098–110.

Lounamaa, P. H. and J. G. March (1987), "Adaptive Coordination of a Learning Team," *Man. Sci.*, 33, 107–23.

Maier, N. R. F. (1963), *Problem-solving Discussions and Conferences: Leadership Methods and Skills*. New York, NY: McGraw-Hill.

March, J. G. (1978), "Bounded Rationality, Ambiguity, and the Engineering of Choice," *Bell J. Econ.*, 9, 587–608.

March, J. G. (1987), "Ambiguity and Accounting: The Elusive Link between Information and Decision Making," *AOS*, 12, 153–68.

March, J. G. (1990), "Exploration and Exploitation in Organizational Learning." *Organ. Sci.*, 2, 1, 71–87.

March, J. G. and J. P. Olsen (1975), "The Uncertainty of the Past: Organizational Learning under Ambiguity,"

Europ. J. Polit. Res., 3, 147–71.

March, J. G. and J. P. Olsen (1989), *Rediscovering Institutions: The Organizational Basis of Politics*. New York, NY: Free Press.

March, J. G. and G. Sevón (1984), "Gossip, Information, and Decision Making," in L. S. Sproull and J. P. Crecine (eds), *Advances in Information Processing in Organizations*. vol. 1. Greenwich, CT: JAI Press, 95–107.

March, J. G. and Z. Shaphira (1987), "Managerial Perspectives on Risk and Risk Taking," *Man. Sci.*, 33, 1404–18.

Martin, J. (1982), "Stories and Scripts in Organizational Settings," in A. H. Hasdorf and A. M. Isen (eds), *Cognitive Social Psychology*. New York, NY: Elsevier-North Holland, 255–305.

Martin, J. and C. Siehl (1983), "Organizational Culture and Counter Culture: An Uneasy Symbiosis," *Organ. Dynam.*, Autumn, 52–64.

Merton, R. (1968), *Social Theory and Social Structure*, New York, NY: The Free Press.

Mohr, L. B. (1985), "The Reliability of the Case Study as a Source of Information," in R. F. Coulam and R. A. Smith (eds), *Advances in Information Processing in Organizations*, vol. 2. Greenwich, CT: JAI Press, 65–94.

National Research Council (Assembly of Engineering Committee on FAA Airworthiness Certification Procedures) (1980), *Improving Aircraft Safety: FAA Certification of Commercial Passenger Aircraft*. Washington, DC: National Academy of Sciences.

Neustadt, R. E. and E. R. May (1986), *Thinking in Time: The Uses of History for Decision-makers*. New York, NY: Free Press.

Oliver, T. (1986), *The Real Coke, The*

Real Story. New York, NY: Penguin Books.

Pearson, R. W., M. Ross and R. M. Dawes (1990), "Personal Recall and the Limits of Retrospective Questions in Surveys," in J. Tanur (ed.), *Questions about Survey Questions*. Beverly Hills, CA: Sage.

Prange, G. W. (1982), *Miracle at Midway*. New York, NY: McGraw-Hill.

Raiffa, H. (1968), *Decision Analysis*. Reading. MA: Addison-Wesley.

Rorty, R. (1985), "Solidarity and Objectivity," in J. Rajchman and C. West (eds), *Post-Analytic Philosophy*. New York. NY: Columbia University Press, 3–19.

Salancik, G. R. (1977), "Commitment and Control of Organizational Behavior and Belief," in B. M. Staw and G. R. Salancik (eds), *New Directions in Organizational Behavior*. Chicago, IL: St. Clair, 1–54.

Shedler, J. and M. Manis (1986), "Can the Availability Heuristic Explain Vividness Effects?", *J. Pers. Soc. Psychol.*, 51, 26–36.

Sproull, L. S. and K. R. Hofmeister (1986), "Thinking about Implementation," *J. Manage.*, 12, 43–60.

Sproull, L. S., S. Weiner and D. Wolf (1978), *Organizing an Anarchy: Belief, Bureaucracy, and Politics in the National Institute of Education*. Chicago, IL: University of Chicago Press.

Starbuck, W. H. (1983), "Organizations as Action Generators." *Amer. Sociol. R.*, 48, 91–102.

Starbuck, W. H. and F. J. Milliken (1988), "Challenger: Fine-Tuning the Odds until Something Breaks." *J. Manag. Stu.*, 25, 4, 319–40.

Stinchcombe, A. (1978). *Theoretical Methods in Social History*. New York. NY: Academic Press.

Tamuz, M. (1987), "The Impact of Computer Surveillance on Air Safety Reporting." *Columbia J. World Bus.*, 22, 69–77.

Tamuz, M. (1988), "Monitoring Dangers in the Air: Studies in Ambiguity and Information." Ph.D. thesis, Stanford University.

Tolstoy, L. N. (1869). *War and Peace*. Translated by R. Edmonds. Harmondsworth, England: Penguin.

Weick, K. (1979). *The Social Psychology of Organizing*. 2d ed. Reading. MA: Addison-Wesley.

Zald, M. N. and P. Denton (1963), "From Evangelism to General Service: The Transformation of the YMCA," *Adm. Sci. Q.*, 8, 214–34.

CHAPTER NINE

Adaptive Coordination of a Learning Team

with Pertti H. Lounamaa

Contemporary research on organizations has cast doubt on the extent to which organizations can be expected to adapt to their environments through rational, anticipatory action. Incremental experiential learning has been suggested as an alternative form of organizational intelligence, less demanding cognitively yet capable of considerable power. This chapter examines such learning in the context of a model of a team involving two learning members, each of whom modifies beliefs about the other on the basis of experience, and an adaptive coordinator who adjusts a coordination control variable. It is shown that although learning is a powerful mechanism for improving organizational performance, it can often be confounded by the effects of attributional biases on the part of members, by the interactions of simultaneous learning by the members and the coordinator, and by errors in perceiving or interpreting experience. These complications lead to consideration of possible heuristics to overcome such learning liabilities. It is suggested that the effectiveness of incremental learning can often be improved by slowing the rate of learning and adaptation, by reducing the simultaneity of behavioral changes, and by scaling the size of the changes.

THE INTELLIGENCE OF LEARNING

The ability to act intelligently in a changing environment is a key factor in the survival and success of an organization. In modern times, organizations have been presumed to achieve intelligence primarily through anticipatory, rational action. That is, it is assumed that organizations act by estimating the future consequences of alternative actions, forecasting future preferences with respect to those consequences, and choosing the course of action that offers the best expected outcome (Raiffa, 1968). Research on organizational behavior has cast doubt on whether organizations do, in fact, act in this way, whether they could do so if they wanted to, and whether they should want to do so if they could. Numerous empirical studies have shown that organizational decision processes are substantially less "rational" than the conventional model suggests, though they often contain important elements of rationality in them (Cyert and March, 1963; Kay, 1979). Moreover, students of organizational decision making have questioned whether anticipatory rationality is even imaginable in an organization, noting the limitations of information processing capabilities, and the significant ways in which organizational memory, attention, and coherence deviate from the requirements for acting in such a way (March and Simon, 1958; Nelson and Winter, 1982). Finally, some observers of organizations have questioned whether rationality is a particularly good normative model for choice in organizations, citing various limitations of the model (Elster, 1979; 1983; March, 1978).

Recognition of the limitations of anticipatory reason as a model for organizational decision making has led to interest in history-dependent routes to intelligence in organizations, most notably learning from experience. Organizations have been described as adapting to their environments by monitoring their experience and repeating past actions that appear successful, changing actions that appear unsuccessful. Incremental trial-and-error learning of this sort seems capable of leading to intelligent behavior without requiring improbable capacities for securing and processing information. Such adaptation has been pictured as being more consistent with organizational capabilities as we know them, or can anticipate them, than is rational, anticipatory action (Lindblom, 1959; 1965; Cyert and March, 1963).

The inclination to embrace learning because of discontent with the demands of calculated rationality should, however, be moderated by an awareness of our ignorance and the potential traps. Discussions of incremental adaptation in the behavioral literature are generally at a qualitative level. Primary attention is given to the basic idea that organizations adapt to their environments through small steps, observing the consequences of incremental movement and making marginal adjustments. The failure to specify the mechanisms of adaptation with greater precision makes discussions of organizational learning as a form of intelligence somewhat difficult to evaluate. On the face of it, simple learning is no more assured to be sensibly intelligent than is anticipatory reason. Where incremental adaptive mechanisms have been specified more precisely, as in some parts of engineering, they are most often based either on stochastic search or on advanced stochastic control theory, neither of which is more plausible behaviorally than is anticipatory rationality. For example, stochastic control theory assumes that the forms of the system, objective function, or control laws are known.

Some recent analyses of experiential learning have explored a set of learning mechanisms that seem consistent with cognitive limitations on rationality. Although they differ in detail, these mechanisms can be characterized as myopic, incremental, and ignorant. They are *myopic* in the sense that they are not based on estimating the long-term effects of current changes. They are *incremental* in the sense that only the performance effect of the immediately previous change is considered in modifying beliefs or making a change in controls. They are *ignorant* in the sense that they are based on only minimal, implicit information about the structure of the system or of the performance function. Analyses of models based on myopic, incremental, and ignorant learning mechanisms indicate that such learning is often effective, but that it is also often confounded by the way in which learning of competences, goals, and strategies interact (Levinthal and March, 1981; Herriott et al., 1985). In addition, that work suggests, but does not pursue, the possibility that simultaneous learning at multiple levels in an organizational hierarchy may reduce overall learning effectiveness.

The work reported here considers experiential learning in the context of a simple team problem, examining particularly the interaction produced by simultaneous learning at two levels in an organization. The model is based on a dynamic model of team behavior (Lounamaa, 1985). The model organization is composed of a coordinator and two agents. Such an organization is both abstract and minimal. It does not capture the detail of a real bureaucracy, but is intended simply to present the problems of organizational learning in their most elementary form. Thus, it is not easy to identify a concrete example of an organizational setting that fits the model. A possible approximation is to think of a Chief Executive Officer (CEO) as the coordinator of division managers responsible for producing substitute products, for example, the large automobile division and the small automobile division of an automobile manufacturer. A problem of coordination arises because sales by either division affect sales by the other.

The model specifies learning procedures closely related to linear learning rules and adaptive control procedures closely related to hill-climbing search algorithms. It includes one control variable, coordination, and one state variable, a team member's belief about the strength of interaction between the two members. Each of these variables is assumed to change in response to experience, and performance outcomes are affected by the interaction between them. As a reminder that the two mechanisms of adjustment are somewhat different, we will call changes in the members' beliefs "learning" and changes in the control variable "adaptation"; but they are both incremental adjustments based on experience. The key organizational parameters are the members' learning rates and the rules for adapting coordination to experience. The key environmental parameter is noise in performance signals.

In the remainder of this chapter, we develop and explore this model in order to examine adaptive intelligence in an organizational setting. First, we sketch the decision process that is assumed in the model. Second, assumptions about the learning of beliefs are specified and some benchmark simulation results reported. Third, some alternative ways for modeling the adaptation of control strategies are discussed and the basic adaptation mechanism is formulated. Fourth, the interaction of changes in beliefs (learning) and the control variable (adaptation) are analyzed within a deterministic version of the model. The effects on performance of varying key parameters are discussed. Fifth, the examination of learning and adaptation is extended to a stochastic environment. Sixth, the general implications of the results are reviewed. In particular, we ask how experiential adjustments can be managed so as to improve performance if learning and adaptation occur through simple incremental procedures.

A MODEL OF A SIMPLE ORGANIZATION

The organization, or team, is assumed to consist of two lower level decision makers, called members, and one higher level decision maker, called the coordinator. Since we wish to explore the impact of innocent cognitive bias rather than self-conscious strategic behavior, we assume that each member seeks to maximize overall organizational performance. The task of each lower level decision maker, $i = 1,2$, in each time period t, is to determine a personal level of activity, d_{it}, such that the sum of the performances of the two members (overall organizational performance) is maximized. Thus,

$$W_t = \sum_{i=1}^{2} W_{it} \qquad (9.1)$$

for each time period t.

Although there is no conflict of interest, each member's performance depends on both members' levels of activity. Consequently, the members need both to exchange information about beliefs and to coordinate their activities. A simple way of capturing this need for communication and coordination is to use a quadratic performance function:

$$W_{it} = \mu_i d_{it} - q_{ij} d_{it} d_{jt} - d^2_{it} \qquad (9.2)$$

Each member has an independent effect on organizational performance via the linear term $\mu_i d_{it}$. The parameter of the linear term, μ_i, can be viewed as the importance of member i. In addition, there is an interaction between the agents which requires communication and cooperation. This interaction is represented by the other two terms. The parameter q_{ij} can be called the strength of interaction between members i and j. The term d^2_{it} can be thought of as the "cost of effort" and reflects an assumption that beyond some point the cost of increased effort exceeds the increased benefit from it. The true performance parameters, μ_i, q_{ij}, are assumed to be constant. That is, the environment is assumed to be static.

To further simplify the model, we assume the true performance parameters are identical for the two members $\mu_i = \mu$ and $q_{ij} = q$. Importance is restricted to $\mu = 1$. The strength of interaction is assumed to satisfy $0 \leq q \leq 1$. This ensures that the unique solution of the first order necessary conditions is a maximum. Given these assumptions, the optimal decision for both members is:

$$d^* = \frac{1}{2(1 + q)} \qquad (9.3)$$

The performance parameters are assumed to be unknown to the members, and information relevant to estimating them is assumed to be decentralized. Each member has estimates of the parameters that affect that member's performance. The superscript i is used to denote estimates (or beliefs) by member i. Thus, μ^i_{it} and q^i_{ijt} are the beliefs of member i at time t. To achieve the overall optimum for the organization the members need to coordinate their levels of activity. In order to do that, each member needs to estimate her impact on the other. Thus, the need for experiential inferences about beliefs. The dual needs for coordination and inferences about beliefs are the fundamental problems to which learning and adaptation are addressed.

The process we assume is a form of gradient search. In each time period a search consisting of several steps in undertaken. At each step each member proposes a personal activity level based on personal beliefs. Let $d_{it}(p)$ denote the suggested level of activity at step p of time t. Let $\partial W_{it}/\partial d_i$ and $\partial W_{jt}/\partial d_i$ denote the derivative of W_{it} and W_{jt} with respect to d_{it} evaluated at $d_{it} = d_{it}(p)$ and $d_{it} = d_{it}(p)$. With h_i as a step size parameter, the decision process proceeds according to:

$$d_{it}(p + 1) = d_{it}(p) + h_i\left(\frac{\partial W_i}{\partial d_i} + \frac{\partial W_j}{\partial d_i}\right) \qquad (9.4)$$

until an equilibrium is reached. The information exchanged through this process is the derivative $\partial W_j/\partial d_i = -q^i_{jit}d_{it}(p)$. The only information exchange needed at each step p is $d_{it}(p)$. The believed impact q_{jt}^i is only communicated once each time t. This gradient search mechanism satisfies the optimality requirement within the information constraints (Marschak and Radner, 1972). That is, if the members' beliefs are accurate, the iterative exchange leads to a maximum.

A problem arises, however, if there are errors in the beliefs. Consciously self-interested biases are excluded by the assumption that all members seek to maximize overall organizational performance, but we assume that nonstrategic biases are common. Because a central management ordinarily cannot know more about the detailed performance determinants of a specific member than the member himself, there is no direct way to exercise intelligent managerial control over bias. We assume the central management achieves control indirectly by specifying the appropriate coordination factor, that is, how much each member should take into account his impact on the other. Let c_{jt} denote the coordination factor specified for member $i \neq j$ in time period t. Each member is assumed to take the coordination factor into account by changing (9.4) to:

$$ d_{it}\,(p + 1) = d_{it}(p) + h_i\left(\frac{\partial W_i}{\partial d_i} + c_{jt}\frac{\partial W_j}{\partial d_i}\right) \tag{9.5} $$

Since the coordination factor depends on the accuracy of beliefs, it may be interpreted as a counter-bias introduced with respect to member j.

The idea of coordination in the model can be illustrated within the example given earlier of the coordination between two divisions, one manufacturing small automobiles, the other manufacturing large automobiles. Suppose the coordination factor is equal to one initially, so that each division takes the other into account, specifically that the small automobile division takes into account the negative impact that the sales of small automobiles have on the sales of the other division. Suppose, however, that the manager of the large car division has a positive bias, believing that the demand for large automobiles is larger than the demand for small automobiles.[1] By lowering the coordination factor, that is by lowering the degree to which the smaller automobile division manager takes into account the negative impact of small car sales on big car profits, the CEO can induce behavior that increases overall company profits. In effect, the CEO introduces a counter-bias to the bias of the large automobile manager.

Since the results that we will discuss in this chapter can be illustrated with the special case of identical members with identical error terms, we assume identity. In that case, it is straightforward to show that the gradient mechanism will achieve the symmetric unique equilibrium given by:

$$d_t = \frac{\mu_t}{2 + (1 + c_t)q_t} \tag{9.6}$$

where μ_t stands for μ_{it}^i, q_t for q_{ijt}^i, d_t for d_{it} and c_t for c_{it}.[2] Thus, hereafter, perceived values have a time subscript, true values do not. If the beliefs are accurate, then the optimal coordination factor is one, which yields (9.3).

The primary purpose of this chapter is to study how this gradient search procedure within a team is affected by the interplay of biased learning of beliefs by members and adaptive control by the coordinator. In order to pursue that objective, the next two sections specify a learning process by which μ_t and q_t are modified by members and an adaptation process by which c_t is modified by the coordinator. Subsequently, we consider how these two experience-based processes interact.

Learning by Members

The level of activity of a member is determined by (9.6). Overall organizational performance is defined by (9.1). The true relationship between the two depends on the values of μ and q. We assume that organizational members form estimates, μ_t and q_t, each time period, changing those estimates on the basis of experience. Thus, they modify their beliefs about causal relationships between their own actions and organizational outcomes. Each time period each member forecasts how well he will perform. Since the two members are identical and each estimates the quadratic effect accurately via the term d_t^2,

$$\hat{W}_t = \mu_t d_t - d_t^2 - q_t d_t^2 \tag{9.7}$$

To model ambiguity in organizational perceptions of performance (March and Olsen, 1976), we assume that each member perceives personal performance as:

$$W_t^0 = W_t(1 + \varepsilon_t) \tag{9.8}$$

where $W_t = (1 - (1 + q)d_t)d_t$ is the true performance of the member at time t. Note that this is also the overall performance divided by two. The noise term, ε_t, represents the error by a member in perceiving performance and is a random variable with zero mean.

Learning in the model takes place by members attributing the difference $W_t^0 - \hat{W}_t$ to their beliefs about μ, the importance of a member, and q, the strength of interaction. There is empirical basis for anticipating bias in attribution by the members (Nisbett and Ross, 1980). We explore the effects of two simple propositions about learning bias that are common in the empirical literature. The first proposition is that $\mu_t > \mu$, i.e., members exaggerate their own significance. As Kiesler and Sproull (1982) observe, "members of a subunit perceive the world in a way that enhances the importance of their subunit." In the present model, the true importance of an individual member is represented by $\mu = 1$. We assume $\mu_t = 1 + b$, where $b > 0$. The second proposition is that errors in estimation are attributed to q_t. Studies of attribution processes have shown a consistent tendency for human subjects to attribute unexpected failures to extrinsic causes (Jones and Nisbett, 1972). We reflect this attribution bias by assuming that errors in estimation are attributed to q, the strength of interaction, rather than μ, the importance of the member. The learning in the model can thus be formalized as:[3]

$$q_{t+1} = q_t + a \frac{\hat{W}_t - W_t^0}{d_t^2} \qquad (9.9)$$

The initial value for q_t is assumed to be zero. With experience, each member comes to modify her estimate of the impact of the actions of the other member on her own performance, and the value for q_t is changed.

To explore the implications of the model, we first analyze the deterministic version. The model consists of one difference equation (9.9) which, by using (9.6) and (9.1), leaving out the noise term, and recalling that $d_t = (1 + b)/[2 + (1 + c_t)q_t]$, may be written as:

$$q_{t+1} = q_t + a \frac{2b + (1 + b)q + (c_t b - 1)q_t}{1 + b} \qquad (9.10)$$

In this form, the model has three parameters, the learning rate, α, the true strength of interaction, q, and the bias, b.

Figure 9.1 shows the belief and performance trajectories for four cases under noiseless conditions.[4] The cases correspond to high and low coordination combined with fast and slow learning members. The strength of interaction is medium ($q = 0.5$) and members overestimate their importance by 70 percent ($b = 0.7$) in all runs. The basic result is that the beliefs tend to grow overly high in the long run, causing low performance unless coordination is low. Long-run beliefs tend to be higher than the true values because the members attribute unexpected poor performance to the interactions. Furthermore, the impact of the coordination signal is not only static, i.e., reducing coordination, but also dynamic, i.e., reducing the long-run beliefs of the members. If $c_t b > 1$ then q_t grows toward infinity. Thus, when biases are strong ($b = 1$) the learning dynamics are quite sensitive to the level of coordination.

The value for the coordination factor that maximizes average performance cannot be derived. However, by setting (9.6) equal to (9.3) and using

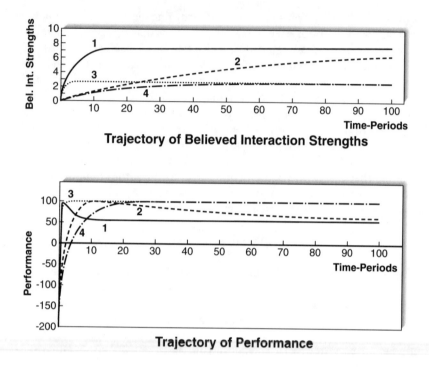

Trajectory of Believed Interaction Strengths

Trajectory of Performance

Figure 9.1 Dynamics of member learning, where $b = 0.7$ and $q = 0.5$. The curves are labeled as follows: (1) $a = 1.0$, $c = 1.0$; (2) $a = 0.1$, $c = 0.1$; (3) $a = 1.0$, $c = 0.2$; (4) $a = 0.1$, $c = 0.2$.

the equilibrium of (9.10) as the value for q_t, the level of coordination that maximizes final performance is shown to be $q/[2b + (1 + 2b)q]$. Thus, the greater the bias, the smaller the optimal coordination factor. On the other hand, the greater the interactions, the larger the optimal coordination (in equilibrium). This equilibrium analysis has been pursued in more detail by Lounamaa (1985).[5]

Where there is no noise in the observations of performance and coordination is fixed, simulations[6] show that the model is robust to learning rates. Final performance is the same for learning rates between 0.1 and 1.0. In general, faster learning leads to better average performance; but the optimal level of coordination is independent of the learning rate, except when short-run performance is emphasized and the learning rate is very low. A coordination value of 0.2 is the best, within 0.05, for both final and average performance and for all learning rates, when averaging over bias values 0, 0.5, 1.0 and interaction values 0.1, 0.55, 1.0.[7] The only exception to this result is that a slightly higher coordination factor (0.3) results in higher average performance when the learning rate is 0.1. In this case, a low learning rate leads to a low q_t, which is compensated by a higher c_t. Since the case of short-run performance with a low learning rate may be important, this exception is not to be ignored. It suggests that the dynamics of individual member learning can have implications even for static organizational coordination.

Noise has no impact on the optimal (fixed) level of coordination.[8] For all learning rates, the optimal value of c_t is still 0.2. With noisy observations, the slower the learning, the higher the final performance is. Slow learning avoids the spurious tracking of noise. These differences are, however, not great. With a learning rate of 0.1, final performance reaches 99 percent of the optimal performance determined by (9.3); with a learning rate of 1.0, the final performance is 95 percent of the optimal. With respect to average performance, a medium rate of learning is best when observations of performance are subject to noise. There is a trade-off between speed and accuracy of learning. If learning is too slow, the interactions are ignored in the decision making; if it is too fast, learning follows the noise too closely. However, the difference between the most effective learning rate and a learning rate of 1.0 is less than 2 percent. Thus, learning is relatively robust to noise when coordination is fixed.

ADAPTATION BY THE COORDINATOR

The simulation results above indicate that 0.2 is a good (fixed) value for the coordination factor when averaging over a variety of biases in the learning of beliefs by members. On the other hand, it is clear that considerable improvement in performance can be realized for any particular bias and learning rate. For example, when there is no bias, $c_t = 1$ is best. This suggests the possibility that just as the members adjust their beliefs on the basis of experience, the coordinator can use information gathered from experience to modify the coordination factor.

Before turning to an examination of the interaction between adaptation by the coordinator and learning by members, we consider the case in which the members' beliefs are fixed. A classic operations research approach to a problem like this involves dynamic programming and the updating of the decision variable each time period on the basis of expectations, conditional on current information. We examine an alternative approach that seems more consistent with the capabilities and standard behavior of human decision makers. The alternative emphasizes the incremental adaptation of coordination using a single candidate level of coordination.[9] We assume a hill-climbing process[10] that considers the apparent effect of changes in the control variable, c_t, on performance:

$$c_{t+1} = c_t + h \frac{W^0_t - W^0_{t-1}}{c_t - c_{t-1}} \tag{9.11}$$

where h is a step size parameter.[11]

We assume initial values of $c_0 = 1.0$ and $c_1 = 0.9$. Since $c_t = 1$ is optimal when members are unbiased, these initial conditions can be interpreted as an assumption that the coordinator initially considers the members to be unbiased and immediately tries out the effect of decreasing coordination.[12] Provided the interaction effects are not too small, this basic hill-climbing process for modifying coordination is quite successful in an organization where no learning of beliefs by members takes place and performance observations are made without error. A performance level equal to 99 percent of the optimum is reached in an average of 30 periods for $h = 1$ and $q_0 = 3$.[13] Higher values of h lead to achieving 99 percent performance very rapidly when interaction effects are high, e.g. $q > 1.0$.

However, hill-climbing with higher h performs poorly when interaction effects are low, e.g., $q < 0.1$. If we solve for the optimal coordination factor by setting (9.6) equal to (9.3), we see that the optimal value is negative for weak interactions ($q = 0.1$) and the assumed beliefs ($b = 1$ and $q_t = 3$). When h is high the coordination factor overshoots and becomes at some point more negative than optimal. At that point, the activity level based on (9.6) becomes high, causing in turn a negative performance. The sudden negative performance causes a very large increase in the coordination factor, due to the high h. A high coordination factor causes a very low activity level (9.6) and subsequent changes in the coordination factor, even if substantial, produce only small changes in the decision and thus also in performance. As a result, the process is trapped at a value far from the optimum. A reasonable trade-off between speed and stability of search is achieved by setting $h = 1$, and that value is used in all simulations reported below.

INTERACTIVE LEARNING WITH ACCURATE OBSERVATIONS

Our major interest is neither in the case in which members are constant and only the coordinator adjusts, nor in the case where the coordinator is fixed and only the members adjust. We wish to assess the consequences for organizational performance of simultaneous learning by members and adaptation by the coordinator. In this section, we consider the case in which performance observations are accurate. In the next section, we examine the implications of random errors in observing performance. Since it is assumed that the coordinator has no detailed understanding of the impact of a member's learning on performance, we can expect that the impact will tend to confuse the adaptation of the coordinator. Similarly, since the members are assumed to have no detailed understanding of the impact of changes in coordination on performance, we can expect that the impact will tend to confuse the learning of members. Furthermore, based on the previous results, we can expect that the coordinator will not be efficient in finding the optimal coordination until learning is fairly close to equilibrium. All of these expectations are confirmed, with some qualifications.

Learning by members does not simply complicate the adjustment of coordination, it often causes it to fail completely. Typically what happens is that at some point an extremely misleading inference is made, and the adaptation process is unable to recover. This catastrophe occurs when a small change in coordination precedes, but does not cause, a large change in performance. The adaptation rule for the coordinator treats the small previous change as having had a large direct effect and makes the next change orders of magnitude larger. Such catastrophes suggest a need to avoid making changes in coordination that are orders of magnitude larger than normal change. A natural mechanism for avoiding abnormal changes is to impose a constraint on the current change that reflects the magnitude of the previous change. Various ways of implementing such scaling were explored and a rule that compares the change suggested by the basic hill-climbing rule (9.11),

$$\Delta h_t = \frac{W_t^0 - W_{t-1}^0}{c_t - c_{t-1}} \qquad (9.12)$$

to the previous change Δc_{t-1} is:[14]

$$\Delta c_t = \frac{\bar{\theta}}{|\Delta h_t / \Delta c_{t-1}| + \bar{\theta} - 1} \Delta h_t \qquad (9.13)$$

where $\bar{\theta}$ is a parameter that controls the maximum relative magnitude of change. The next value for the coordination is then determined by:

$$c_{t+1} = c_t + \Delta c_t \qquad (9.14)$$

Adding this scaling heuristic changes adaptation in coordination from an unstable process to one that discovers the theoretical optimum fairly rapidly. The value of $\bar{\theta}$ can be varied over a range from 2 to 20 without significantly affecting performance.

However, even with this scaling heuristic, adaptation by the coordinator can still be misled by the learning by members. Subsequent outcomes are associated with antecedent changes in coordination even when they have been only marginally affected by them. If, for example, outcomes are strongly affected by exogenous factors that produce long periods of improving performance, a coordinator would be likely to experience a long series of signals reinforcing the changes made the previous time, thus whatever was being done when the series began. The contribution of the coordinator to performance, however, would not be improved, except fortuitously. Within the present model, the same kind of superstitious learning can be produced endogenously. This occurs most conspicuously as a team moves from an initial position of substantial ignorance and poor performance to a better position. The usual initial impact of learning by members is to cause a steady improvement in performance. As a result, adapting the control variable in any direction will be associated with improvement in overall performance, as long as the change in control variable is not too large. This effect leads a coordinator to impute the improvement to the change in coordination (rather than to the changes in members' beliefs). It results in further adjustments of coordination in the initial direction, thereby complicating both the learning by members and organizational performance.

A simple rule that ameliorates the problem in this situation is to allow the control variable to change only if performance is decreasing. In effect, such a rule treats performance improvements as confounded but treats performance decrements as containing information. A case where this heuristic dramatically reduces the time needed to achieve optimal final performance is shown in figure 9.2. In this case the bias is high, 100 percent, the learning rate is low, 0.1, and the strength of interactions is high, 1.0. Waiting until an upward trend has disappeared allows the process to reach the optimum directly and rapidly. The likelihood of having the estimate of interaction strength overshoot is greatly reduced. Thus, in systems where there are strong periodic upward trends, whether produced exogenously or endogenously, this kind of heuristic might be useful. It may be viewed as a form of the "fighting fires" rule for managerial attention allocation (Winter, 1981).[15] Such a heuristic will, of course, not work in the face of strong downward trends.[16]

The obvious speculation from these observations is that relatively efficient rules for learning in multilevel organizations involve simplifying the "experimental design" of natural experience by inhibiting learning in one part of the organization in order to facilitate learning in another, changing learning in different parts of the team from a parallel to a sequential process. It should be observed that this speculation is based on the case where learning has most impact, namely when measuring average performance over the whole simulation and when the learning rate is low. Final performance is optimal when using the scaling heuristic, regardless of the learning rate. Similarly, average performance is close to optimal for

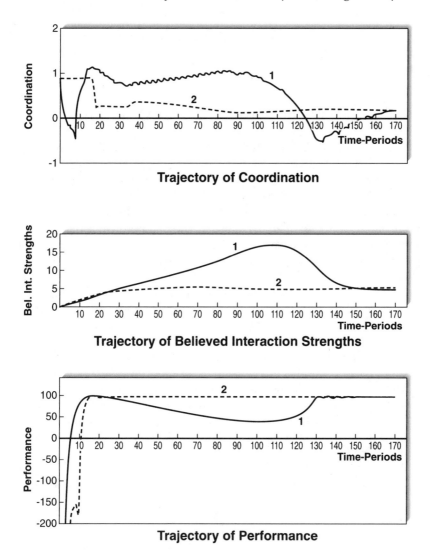

Figure 9.2 Impact of using the "change coordination factor only if performance is decreasing" heuristic. The curves are labeled as follows: (1) change every period; (2) use heuristic.

learning rates above 0.1. When environmental signals are unambiguous, another method for achieving sequential, instead of parallel, learning, is to increase the speed of learning of one part of the organization; but the sequencing has to be specified correctly. For instance, if learning by members is inhibited or the adaptation of coordination speeded up, the team performs poorly.

INTERACTIVE LEARNING WITH NOISY OBSERVATIONS

When noise is introduced in (9.8), this process of interactive learning and adaptation fails. Since the noise has a greater impact on performance than any single change in the control variable, the search for a good value for the coordination factor becomes a random, highly unstable, process with an outcome worse than any reasonable fixed level of coordination. This result stems from two related problems. The first problem is that the observations are based on just one time period. The resulting estimate of the performance is unreliable. Everything else being equal, learning could be made more effective if it were possible to increase the number of observations taken before changing the control variable. Second, changes in the control variable are sometimes too small, relative to the noise, for their effects to be detected. Everything else being equal, learning could be improved if it were possible to assure that any changes made in the control variable would be large enough to have a reasonable chance of being detected.

Thus, for the coordination factor to adapt effectively to noisy performance observations, two additional heuristics must be added. The first slows up adaptation in order to assure a larger number of observations. This is done by specifying K, the minimum number of performance observations required before making a change in coordination. Instead of using W_t^0 in (9.11), an average of K previous performance signals is used.[17] The new hill-climbing increment is based on the averages calculated at time t and t', the previous time that c_t was changed:

$$\Delta h_t = \frac{\bar{W}_t - \bar{W}_{t'}}{c_t - c_{t'}} \qquad (9.15)$$

An appropriate choice of the value for the new parameter K is critical for good performance. If K is too small, adaptation is close to a random process; and if K is too large, it slows down adaptation too much. Because a large value for K causes slow but accurate adaptation, a larger K is generally better for final performance than for average performance. This suggests that the maximum final performance would be achieved if there were enough time to allow a relatively large value for K and still have a suitably large number of changes in the control variable.[18]

In general, longer time horizons (simulation lengths) allow both averaging over longer periods and more changes in coordination, thus leading to better performance. There is, however, an important qualification. Making K larger ignores the consequences of learning of beliefs by the members. In particular, if bias is relatively high and no adjustment is made of the level of coordination for an extended period, the members can come to believe that mutual action is impossible, because q_t grows toward infinity if $c_t b > 1$. In that case, by the time action is taken on the coordination factor, the system will be impervious to it. Thus, increasing the simulation horizon is not alone sufficient to achieve optimal final performance.[19]

To meet this problem, a second heuristic can be introduced. In the previous section we suggested the need for a scaling rule that limited the magnitude of a change in the coordination variable relative to the previous change. The primary intent was to keep the change from being inappropriately large. Now we require a scaling rule that keeps changes from being too small. Using this heuristic, (9.15) becomes:

$$c_{t+1} = c_t + \text{sign}\,(\Delta c_t)\,\max\,(|\Delta c_t|,\,\underline{\theta}|c_t|) \qquad (9.16)$$

where $\underline{\theta}$ denotes the minimum fractional amount that the control variable has to change.[20] In the simulations reported here, the value 0.2 was used for $\underline{\theta}$, which means that the magnitude of change had to be at least 20 percent of the control variable's current magnitude. Smaller values did not have sufficient effect and larger values made the search erratic with a tendency to drive the control variable to zero.

The joint effects of $\underline{\theta}$ and $\bar{\theta}$ are shown in figure 9.3, where the result is an average of 100 trials each for the learning rates 0.1, 0.55 and 1.0 with high bias ($b = 1$) and high strength of interactions ($q = 1$). When K is low (0–4), a higher $\underline{\theta}$ is better, because it increases the signal to noise ratio, but a lower $\bar{\theta}$ is better, because it avoids spurious adaptation. When K is high, a higher $\underline{\theta}$ and a higher $\bar{\theta}$ are better, because both result in a larger step size, compensating for the time lost while sampling. Increasing $\bar{\theta}$ increases the optimal value of K, both because a higher K avoids spurious learning and because a higher $\bar{\theta}$ compensates for the time lost. Increasing $\underline{\theta}$ increases the change in coordination. The increase has two effects: It increases the signal to noise ratio and thus makes a lower K possible; at the same time it compensates for the time lost during the formation of the average and thus makes a higher K possible. The net effect is that increasing $\underline{\theta}$ has little or no effect on the optimal K. The overall conclusion from the 100 period simulations is that $\underline{\theta}$ increases the robustness of the adaptation but does not improve the final performance achieved with a high $\bar{\theta}$ (= 10) and medium K (= 7). When we extend the simulations to a larger number of time periods, it is possible to improve performance by using

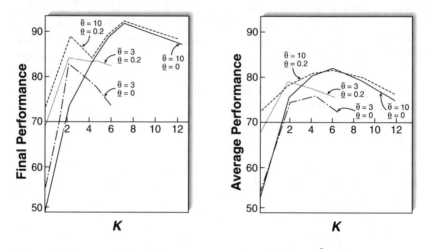

Figure 9.3 Impact of increasing maximum allowed change $\bar{\theta}$, and minimum required change $\underline{\theta}$, on final and average performance.

larger values of K, thus gaining more information about changes, provided $\underline{\theta}$ is large enough to prevent losing control over the process.

The effect of varying learning rates is shown in figure 9.4, where $\underline{\theta} = 0$, $\bar{\theta} = 10$, $b = 1$ and $q = 1$. The figure shows the average of 100 trials and the final performance for each learning rate. When learning by members is relatively slow, final performance increases as K increases. However, when learning by members is relatively rapid, final performance decreases rapidly with increase in K. Rapidly learning members drive the system to a point beyond effective control if the coordinator delays long enough to have a reliable sample of observations. As a result, the conclusion drawn from the fixed coordination case that medium learning rates produce the best average performance needs to be qualified. The conclusion holds for low values of K, but not for higher K. With higher K, the performance of medium learning rates deteriorates. A lower learning rate on the part of members allows for a slower, more precise, controller which in turn leads to better average performance. The general conclusion to be drawn from the analysis of simultaneously learning by members of a team and adaptive control by a coordinator is that, under conditions of noise, and in the absence of methods for slowing both the rate of learning by members and the rate of adaptation by the coordinator, the process is subject to instabilities that threaten effective joint learning. Thus, in contrast to the case of noise-free learning, noisy observations of performance put fast learning organizations at a disadvantage.

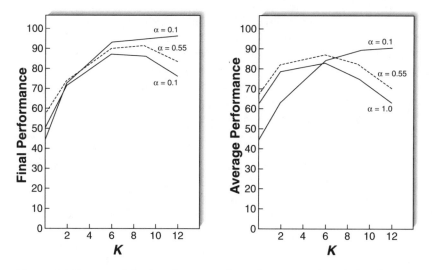

Figure 9.4 Impact of the learning rate of members a, on the relation between minimum number of performance observations, K, before changing coordination and performance.

CONCLUSION

A central dilemma in modern organization theory and operations research is the mismatch between the analytical capabilities of human institutions and the complexity of the environment in which they function. Although large bureaucratic institutions are impressive extensions of the already impressive intelligence of individual humans, they seem persistently to be imperfect instruments for solving the problems they face. Contemporary response to this mismatch has involved three broad strategies. The first strategy has been to improve the analytical capabilities of the institutions through training and by introducing various forms of simplifications of the analytical problem. This is the approach of much of operations research and decision theory (Raiffa, 1968). The second strategy has been to refine competition and selection mechanisms so that rules of behavior leading to better solutions survive and reproduce more reliably than do inferior rules. This is the approach of various evolutionary theories of human institutions, including substantial elements of market economics (Nelson and Winter, 1982). The third strategy has been to rely on incremental learning from experience as a way to discover good solutions to complex problems. This is the approach of substantial parts of the behavioral literature on organizations (Cyert and March, 1963).

This chapter is in the third of these traditions. It explores the possible intelligence of simple experiential learning in a situation in which different parts of an organization are learning simultaneously, and the actions each takes affect the others. The implications to be drawn from the analysis depend on some features of the model (most notably the absence of conflict among the members and the fact that one type of learning impacts the stability of another type of learning) that limit their generality. Nevertheless, they may cast some light on the possibilities and limitations of incremental experiential learning as an instrument of organizational intelligence.[21] Although learning clearly is a powerful mechanism with considerable relevance to improving organizational performance, the most general conclusion to be drawn from this model is that these simple forms of learning and adaptation require relatively careful calibration in order to be successful in moderately complex situations. In the absence of calibrating heuristics, experience becomes a poor teacher, and learning fails. Experience becomes a poor teacher primarily because the relation between the actions of individuals in the organization and overall organizational performance is confounded by the simultaneous learning of other actors and by errors in perceiving performance.

In contrast to recommendations that call for making organizations able to respond more quickly and to learn more rapidly, the model suggests some different rules for using organizational learning to improve organizational performance:

Slow the rate of adaptation. One conspicuous way in which the model fails is by being impatient when environmental signals are ambiguous. This is true with respect both to learning by members and to adaptation by the coordinator. If adjustments in coordination are made too frequently, they are based on observations that are too unreliable. The observations are unreliable because of the twin effects of noise and multiple simultaneous changes. Initiating changes less frequently counteracts the noise by providing a larger sample size and reduces the effect of simultaneous changes. The difficulty is that the system may move out of control while it is still being studied. By the time a reliable understanding of the structure can be developed, the dynamics may have brought the system to catastrophe. Although it is clear that change must normally be introduced before everything is known, the major conclusion is that it is unwise to be making continuous adjustments. Similarly, it is not true that fast learning of beliefs by members assures the best outcomes, either in the short or the long run. The basic problem with fast learning rates is that false lessons are learned rapidly as well as true lessons. The result is a system that tends to track misleading signals produced by noise and the simultaneous learning by others, and to produce confusing signals. Slow learning is less efficient in noise-free, simple worlds; but when there is significant error in the observation of outcomes, it is better to be changing beliefs relatively slowly.

Reduce the simultaneity of changes. Learning is confused by trying to associate an outcome with any one of several simultaneous changes. Under many circumstances, it is better to allow only part of the system to react at any one time. Thus, we have seen that a strategy of keeping coordination fixed is a reasonably effective procedure in the present case. Similarly, changing only when outcomes are declining is a procedure that allows one part of the system to learn while another part is held constant. In noise-free worlds, simultaneity can also be reduced by increasing the speed of learning in one part of the organization while keeping the other part's rate of adjustment relatively slow.

Scale the size of changes. We have shown how it is necessary both to avoid changes that are orders of magnitude greater than the changes made briefly before, and to make changes that are substantial enough to make a detectable difference. The latter requirement is sometimes overlooked in discussions of incremental adjustments, where very small changes might be assumed to be better. The problem with small changes is that they are likely to be lost in the noise. Substantial, even arbitrary, changes are important also in noise-free environments. They allow the organization to escape vicious circles and other traps in the dynamics of interactive learning.

These heuristics are not surprising. They square with some relatively standard folklore about management. They appear, however, to be counter to the spirit of some discussions of organizational learning. Insofar as those discussions argue that accelerating the rate of learning is desirable in organizations, this model provides a few cautions. Those cautions indicate that in an ambiguous world, slow learning may be more effective than fast learning, that quick adjustments within an organization are likely to be both unjustified and confusing to other parts of the organization. At the same time, they speak for supplementing patience with decisiveness, for making relatively sharp changes when changes are made.

Acknowledgment

This research has been supported by grants from the Spencer Foundation, the Stanford Graduate School of Business and the Hoover Institution. We are grateful for the assistance of Ann Bush and Stephen Mezias and for the comments of Scott Herriott, Daniel Levinthal, and Edison Tse.

Notes

1. That is, she believes that the intercept of the linear margin curve is higher for large cars than for small.
2. The model is defined in such a way that the anomaly of (9.6) giving a $d_t < 0$ practically never takes place. If $d_t < 0$, (9.5) drives $d_{it}(p)$ to infinity. In the simulations, we set $d_t = 1$ if this rare event occurs.
3. Errors in expectation are scaled by d_t^2 to obtain the right order of magnitude for q_t. To avoid numerical problems, q_t is updated only if $d_t \geq 0.05$.
4. In all figures, performance is shown as a percentage of optimum performance, achieved with (9.3).
5. For negative bias, the optimal level of coordination is above one and goes to infinity when b approaches $-q/(2 + 2q)$ from above. This suggests that the model should be reformulated if negative biases are to be examined, or for negative values of q.
6. The simulations were executed within the Lounamaa and Tse (1986) simulation environment. All simulations discussed in this chapter are 100 time-periods long unless specified otherwise. The term "final performance" refers to the performance in period 100. The term "average performance" refers to the average of the performance of the last 98 periods. The first two periods' performance is so low that these would dominate the average.
7. For the case of zero bias the optimal coordination value is 1.0.
8. The noise specifications used in all simulations are the same. They assume a uniformly distributed noise between -0.5 and 0.5, that is, a maximum of 50 percent error in the observation of performance.
9. As opposed to multiple candidate algorithms such as learning automata (Narendra and Thathachar, 1974) or genetic algorithms (Holland, 1975).
10. Usually one uses information about the first- and second-order derivatives in hill-climbing. The formation of derivatives is inconsistent with our basic objective to model an adaptive mechanism close to what is feasible for human subjects. This is true in at least two respects. First, such a process requires centralized estimates by the coordinator of the performance function parameters, which is inconsistent with the assumption of decentralized information in teams. Second, the second derivative estimates tend to be unstable when other factors influence their values. In the present model changes in beliefs of the members often affect performance as much or more than changes in the control variable. Thus, even in the deterministic case, using second-order differences degrades the effectiveness of adaptation.
11. We assume that the same observation is used both for learning by members and for adaptation by the coordinator. Under unusual circumstances, a change in coordination fails to change performance. This takes place when c_t would cause a negative d_t according to (9.6). If performance is unchanged, $c_{t+1} = c_t - 2\Delta c_{t-1}$ is used instead of (9.11) to avoid a "death" of the adaptive search process. This is a relatively crude heuristic that might in principle cause oscillations. However, in the present case it did not.
12. Because experimentation with alternative levels of coordination tends to it-

erate the value of c_t back and forth over the same interval, thus canceling the effects of the initial direction, this initial direction of movement rarely has an appreciable effect on the dynamics. A special case, where the initial direction does have a substantial impact, is discussed in the next section.

13. For coordination changes to have any effect the agents have to believe that there are some interaction effects. For this purpose the value 3.0 was used to q_0.

14. The form $\Delta c_t = \text{sign} (\Delta h_t) \min (\bar{\theta} |\Delta c_{t-1}|, |\Delta h_t|)$ was found similar in performance but the more smooth nature of (9.13) was thought to be both more plausible as a description of behavior and to result in a mechanism of more general applicability.

15. An additional scaling heuristic discussed later, the minimum-change requirement may avoid the poor performance, but in a qualitatively different way. Whereas using the "fighting fires" heuristic avoids getting trapped by the trends, the minimum-change heuristic does get trapped but is able to escape the trap rapidly.

16. A more sophisticated approach than simply not doing anything when substantial learning is going on is to try to estimate the trends in performance attributable to learning by others and subtract these trends when estimating the impact of control variable changes on performance. Various trend estimation heuristics have been explored (Lounamaa, 1985) but none was found to improve performance in this particular problem. The reason for failure of trend estimation heuristics lies in the nonlinear nature of the objective function and dynamics. This was confirmed by testing some trend heuristics with simpler systems, where they were found to improve performance dramatically.

17. Exponential averaging was also explored but resulted in slightly lower performance.

18. It would be possible to make K an increasing function of organizational age and examine the optimal rate and pattern of change in K. Since larger values of K can be described as producing more cautious behavior, such an investigation might cast light on sources of advantage stemming from increasing conservatism of organizations with age. We have not attempted such an investigation.

19. In this particular model, this result can be overcome by setting the initial coordination at zero instead of one, in which case the second heuristic below is not needed. But the more general proposition would remain: there is a classical trade-off involved in delay, a trade-off between gaining precision in control by collecting more information and losing control by failing to exercise it.

20. Thus, change in coordination is bounded above by $\bar{\theta} |\Delta c_t|$ and below by $\underline{\theta} |c_t|$.

21. For other explorations in a similar spirit, see Levinthal and March (1981) and Herriott et al. (1985).

References

Cyert, Richard M. and James G. March, *A Behavioral Theory of the Firm*, Prentice-Hall, Englewood Cliffs, NJ, 1963.

Elster, Jon, *Ulysses and the Sirens*, Cambridge University Press, Cambridge, UK, 1979.

Elster, Jon, *Sour Grapes*, Cambridge University Press, Cambridge, UK, 1983.

Herriott, Scott R., Daniel Levinthal and James March, "Learning from Experience in Organizations," *Amer. Economic Rev.*, 75 (1985), 298–302.

Holland, John H., *Adaptation in Natural and Artificial Systems: An Introductory Analysis with Applications to Biology, Control and Artificial Intelligence*, University of Michigan Press, Ann Arbor, 1975.

Jones, Edward E., and Richard E. Nisbett, "The Actor and the Observer: Divergent Perceptions of the Causes of Behavior," in Edward E. Jones, et al. (eds), *Attribution: Perceiving the Causes of Behavior*, General Learning Press, Morristown, NJ, 1972.

Kay, Neil M., *The Innovating Firm*, St. Martin's, New York, 1979.

Kiesler, Sara and Lee S. Sproull, "Managerial Response to Changing Environments: Perspectives on Problem Sensing from Social Cognition," *Admin. Sci. Quart.*, 27 (1982), 548–70.

Levinthal, Daniel and James March, "A Model of Adaptive Organizational Search," *J. Economic Behavior and Organization*, 2 (1981), 307–33.

Lindblom, Charles E., "The Science of Muddling Through," *Public Admin. Rev.*, 19 (1959), 79–88.

Lindblom, Charles E., *The Intelligence of Democracy*, Free Press, New York, 1965.

Lounamaa, Pertti H., *Models of Multi-Agent Behavior: A Simulation and Expert Environment Approach*, Department of Engineering-Economic Systems, Stanford University, Stanford, CA, 1985.

Lounamaa, Pertti and Edison Tse, "The Simulation and Expert Environment," in Janusz S. Kowalik (ed.), *Coupling Symbolic and Numerical Computing in Expert Systems*, North Holland, Amsterdam, 1986.

March, James G., "Bounded Rationality, Ambiguity, and the Engineering of Choice," *Bell J. Economics*, 9 (1978), 587–608.

March, James G. and Johan P. Olsen, *Ambiguity and Choice in Organizations*, Universitetsforlaget, Bergen, Norway, 1976.

March, James, G. and Herbert A. Simon, *Organizations*, Wiley, New York, 1958, 237–81.

Marschak, J. and R. Radner. *The Running Theory of Teams*, Yale University Press, New Haven, CT, 1972.

Narendra, Kumpati and M. Thathachar, "Learning Automata – A Survey," *IEEE Trans. Systems, Man, Cybernet.*, 4, 4 (1974).

Nelson, Richard R. and Sidney G. Winter, *An Evolutionary Theory of Economic Change*, Harvard University Press, Cambridge, MA, 1982.

Nisbett, Richard and Lee Ross, *Human Inference: Strategies and Shortcomings of Social Judgement*, Prentice-Hall, Englewood Cliffs, NJ, 1980.

Raiffa, Howard, *Decision Analysis*, Addison-Wesley, Reading, MA, 1968.

Winter, Sidney, "Attention Allocation and Input Proportions," *J. Economic Behavior and Organizations*, 2 (1981), 31–46.

CHAPTER TEN

The Future, Disposable Organizations, and the Rigidities of Imagination

Predictions of the future of organizations are variations on a theme of fantasy: reliably incorrect and usefully seductive. To illustrate a few general points about the role of imagination in human existence, some predictions about the future of organizations are developed from an interpretation of the environments that will shape organizational survival. The predictions emphasize the adaptiveness of populations of rigid, disposable organizations as well as some of the problems of sustaining rigidity. Imaginations of the future are portrayed as instruments of the organizational obstinacy required by such an adaptive system. Mention is made of one or two of the consequences of robbing fantasy of its innocence in this way.

Imaginations of the future, like imaginations of the past, are devices for living in the present. Eva Luna, the narrator in Isabel Allende's novel by the same name, recalls the imaginations of her mother, Consuelo:

> She manufactured the substance of her own dreams, and from those materials constructed a world for me. Words are free, she used to say, and she appropriated them; they were all hers. She sowed in my mind the idea that reality is not only what we see on the surface; it has a magical dimension as well and, if we so desire, it is legitimate to enhance it and color it to make our journey through life less trying. (Allende, 1988, p. 21)

This chapter considers some ways in which the telling of stories about possible futures of organizations serves to "make our journey through life less trying".

ENVIRONMENTAL VOLATILITY AND UNCERTAINTY

The most conventional story of contemporary futurology is a story that observes and predicts dramatic changes in the environments of organizations. Most observers agree that organizations of the future will confront higher levels of environmental volatility than their earlier antecedents did. Although the metric on which such assessments are based is sometimes elusive, the rate of change in economic, social, technological and political worlds seems to have accelerated, and the magnitude of changes produced by human agency seems to have multiplied. Since these changes have been simultaneous with a marked increase in the durability of human beings and their organizations, there has been a substantial increase in the amount of environmental change that occurs within the lifetime of the typical human and human organization.

Technologies are changing at unprecedented speeds, replacing technologies that developed over centuries with new ones that themselves have short life expectancies. Time pieces, vehicles for long-distance travel, instruments for communication, and hundreds of other technologies are being transformed repeatedly. Economic conditions and economic systems are changing. The flow of goods and services and the organization of their production and distribution are changing very rapidly. Social structures and cultural norms are changing. Communities, social networks and social conventions are changing within a single generation. Standards of morality and normal practice are changing so precipitously that parents and children are likely to find themselves unable to engage in meaningful dialogue about moral concerns, everyday living and musical taste.

Global linkages

The networks of associations and causal effects that describe contemporary organizational life spread easily across national political boundaries. Political control and identities are routinely transcended. There is surprisingly easy movement of people and material goods across national boundaries. And the movement of ideas and cultural products is routinely global. Only a few very large countries can maintain any substantial economic, political or social autonomy without making extraordinary sacrifices. These global interdependencies complicate traditional democratic political philosophy with its emphasis on political geography as a determinate of citizenship and politics (March and Olsen, 1995).

They also complicate thinking about organizations. Although most organizations are still basically local and exist with only minor direct global connexions, globalism is an increasing factor in contemporary organizational life. Changes in the organization of global connexions are conspicuous in transnational financial networks and transnational communication and transportation networks. They are becoming increasingly conspicuous in the form of transnational political and social networks. These developments are institutionalized in the form of international business firms and governmental and non-governmental international associations.

Information technology

The proposition that modern information technology has the capability of making radical differences to organizational structure and practice is a cliché, and, like other clichés, it is true. Despite the exaggerations of science fiction forecasts made by enthusiasts, information technology built around the capabilities of the modern computer and its components has produced a substantial transformation in the technological context of modern organizations (Kiesler and Sproull, 1991; Malone and Rockart, 1991).

By affecting the ways organizations monitor actions, keep records and determine accountability, information technology affects the capabilities for coordination and control. By affecting organizational access to information about the world, capabilities for analyzing such information to make decisions, and processes for storing and retrieving the lessons of history, information technology affects capabilities for organizational learning. By affecting the ease and nature of networks coordinating action, information technology changes the costs and benefits of alternative organizational structures (Lewin and Stephens, 1993).

Knowledge-based competition

Survival among organizations depends less than previously on access to material resources or markets and more on access to knowledge. The so-called knowledge explosion makes the ability to gain and use knowledge a primary source of competitive advantage (Corno, 1988; Winter, 1987). And the centrality of knowledge has stimulated new ideas about the international knowledge order, conceptions that tend to abandon the traditions of science (with its trappings of free exchange) in favor of the traditions of private property (with its trappings of exclusive property rights and restricted exchange).

As recognition of the importance of knowledge as a factor in competitive advantage has grown, students of organizational strategy have placed increasing emphasis on the ways in which the knowledge in one organization is shared with or appropriated by another organization (Starbuck, 1992). The sharing of knowledge is vital to modern joint ventures and has often proved difficult. The appropriation of knowledge involves awareness of the existence of relevant knowledge, access to the knowledge and the capability to use it. None of these is assured. Using new knowledge, for example, is likely to require considerable prior knowledge, and organizations that fall behind in competence will find it difficult to appropriate the knowledge of others, even if they have access to it (Cohen and Levinthal, 1989). Access is typically made difficult by the incentives organizations have to prevent appropriation of their own knowledge.

The changing nature and importance of knowledge makes investments in knowledge critical and at the same time poses problems for making such investments intelligently. Since the acquisition of knowledge requires time, and the relevance of possible knowledge is often difficult to know long in advance of when it is needed, organizations cannot ordinarily delay decisions about knowledge accumulation until it is needed. They invest in knowledge inventories (Feldman, 1989; Levinthal and March, 1993). Optimal knowledge inventory policy is, however, difficult to specify and implement. Knowledge acquisition policy is plagued by difficulties of trade-offs between distant returns and nearby costs and by the difficulties of balancing the mistakes of securing knowledge that is not used with the mistakes of not securing information that could have been used.

As rates of change have accelerated, processes of knowledge acquisition that emphasize direct experience within a particular organization have probably become less important to competitive advantage than those processes that emphasize more analytical and broader knowledge. Research and education have become more important; individual and organizational experience have become less relevant. As a result, the comparative advantage of the individual organization as a sustained accumulator of idiosyncratic experiential knowledge has declined.

Political uncertainty

Modern organizations exist in and are sustained by political systems that are under stress (March and Olsen, 1995). The phenomenon is too general and too consistent to be easily given a unique national interpretation or to be easily attributed to conspicuous failures of the political system. Recent western political history is, on the whole, not a period of abject failure and despair but a period of notable success. Nevertheless, the standing of public bureaucracies and political institutions seems to have declined very generally and remarkably consistently.

Western democracies seem to be having difficulty coping with simultaneous demands for more public services and lower taxes. They are commonly criticized as having insatiable urges to increase bureaucracy and the costs of government. There is discontent with the nation-state and there are some symptoms that it may be declining in importance (Wendt, 1994). On the one hand, the nation-state has lost its autonomy. There has been a general loss of control over boundaries. Communications flow freely among nations and, increasingly, so also do people. There has been a gradual yielding of authority to international organs – the European Union being the most conspicuous example. At the same time, there have been claims to "nationhood" within existing nation-states. Ethnic and religious groups have proclaimed their autonomous standing.

The organizational effects of these changes are accentuated by the weakening of traditional buffers that protected organizations from volatility. In part, this is a result of the internal pressure to eliminate inventories in manufacturing and distribution, but the elimination of buffers to volatility extends well beyond "just-in-time" movements. Globalism has reduced traditional buffers of distance, making organizations more interdependent across space. Rapid obsolescence in knowledge has reduced traditional buffers of time, leaving organizations with less room for temporal errors – less response time. The tightening of competition and modern enthusiasms for free markets have reduced market and political protections from competitors. Political uncertainties make institutional and political buffers of organization less easily taken for granted.

ORGANIZATIONAL ADAPTATION

Almost every theory of organizations presumes a tendency for environmental change to be reflected in organizational change. Environments and history shape organizational forms and practices, although they do so inefficiently (Carroll and Harrison, 1994; March and Olsen, 1989) and often jerkily (Mezias and Glynn, 1992; Tushman and Anderson, 1986; Tyre and Orlikowski, 1994). As a result, specific changes in the world are seen as being likely to lead to specific changes in organizations as they seek to survive and are selected by their competitive environments. For example, increases in global connectedness and uses of modern information technology are often seen as likely to lead to increased uses of nonhierarchical networks in coordinating activities, and increases in the importance of knowledge and in the rate of change in its content are often seen as likely to lead to a decreased emphasis on learning by doing and an increased emphasis on access to external sources of knowledge.

At a more general level, however, stories of rapid environmental change invite a prediction that future environments will favor organizations that are able to be flexible and to adapt quickly to change. Organizations that fail to adapt seem destined to expire as the world around them changes. This has led to considerable enthusiasm for designing organizations that are capable of learning, of adapting to the changes they face (Argyris and Schön, 1978; Hedberg et al., 1976; Senge, 1990).

Adaptiveness involves both the exploitation of what is known and the exploration of what might come to be known (March, 1991, 1994b). *Exploitation* refers to the short-term improvement, refinement, routinizing and elaboration of existing ideas, paradigms, technologies, strategies and knowledge. It thrives on focused attention, precision, repetition, analysis, sanity, discipline and control. Exploitation is served by knowledge, forms and practices that facilitate an organization's well-being in the short run. It emphasizes improving existing capabilities and technologies. It profits from close attention, systematic reason, risk aversion, sharp focus, hard work, training and refined detail. It includes locating and developing competencies and tying those competencies together to produce joint products. It includes managing the capabilities of an organization, facilitating communication and coordination, tightening slack. It includes defining and measuring performance and linking activities powerfully to performance measures.

Exploitation is also served by a pursuit of legitimacy. People in organizations and people with whom they deal are driven by understandings of appropriate behavior. They try to act appropriately and they expect others to do so too. Exhibiting proper organization forms and acting in an appropriate manner generate support and thereby aid survival (DiMaggio and Powell, 1983; Meyer and Rowan, 1977). As organizations seek technical efficiency and legitimacy, they focus energy on relatively short-run concerns. They refine capabilities, reduce costs and adopt standard procedures. They mobilize efforts to achieve clearly defined, short-term objectives. Some modern terms are reengineering, down-sizing and total quality management.

Exploration refers to experimentation with new ideas, paradigms, technologies, strategies and knowledge in the hope of finding alternatives that improve on old ones. It thrives on serendipity, risk-taking, novelty, free association, madness, loose discipline and relaxed control. The characteristic feature of exploration is that it is risky. Success is not assured – indeed it is often not achieved. Even when exploration is successful, its rewards are often slow in coming and not necessarily realized by the parts of the organization that have paid the costs. Exploratory risk-taking appears to be more likely when an organization is falling somewhat behind its target aspirations than when it is achieving them. It is stimulated by failure. It is sometimes also stimulated, largely unintentionally, by organizational slack and by illusions that organizational actors have about their abilities to overcome risks (March and Shapira, 1987, 1992).

Adaptiveness requires both exploitation and exploration. A system that specializes in exploitation will discover itself becoming better and better at an increasingly obsolescent technology. A system that specializes in exploration will never realize the advantages of its discoveries. The problem of balancing exploration and exploitation is well known to students of rational choice (where it is represented by the problem of balancing search and action), to students of evolution (where it is represented by the problem of balancing variation and selection) and to students of institutional change (where it is represented by the problem of balancing change and stability).

The dynamics of learning tend to destroy the balance (Levinthal and March, 1993; March, 1991). In general, returns to the exploitation of existing knowledge are systematically closer in time and space than are returns to the explorations of possible new knowledge. This produces two well-known "traps" of adaptive systems. The first is the "failure" trap. In the failure trap, an organization fails, tries a new direction, fails again, tries still another direction, and so on. The process leads to an endless cycle of failure and exploration. The cycle is sustained by the fact that most new directions are bad ideas and that most new ideas that are good ideas usually require practice and time in order to realize their capabilities. In the short run, even good ideas fail and are rejected. The failure trap leads to impatience with a new course of action as well as an excess of exploration.

The second trap is a "success" trap. When an organization succeeds, it repeats actions that appear to have produced the success. As a result of repeating actions, it becomes more proficient at the technology involved. As a result of the greater proficiency, it is likely to be successful again, and so on. The process leads to an endless cycle of success, increased competence and local efficiency. A new good idea or technology is not tried, or if tried does not do as well as the existing technology (because of the disparity in competence between the two). The success trap leads to a failure to experiment adequately (Arthur, 1989; Herriot et al., 1985).

Within this short story of organizational change can be seen a fundamental dilemma of organizations. Exploitation and exploration are linked in an enduring symbiosis. Each requires the other in order to contribute effectively to an organization's survival and prosperity. At the same time, however, each interferes with the other. Exploitation undermines exploration. It discourages the experimentation and variation that are essential to long-term survival. It results in sticking to one (currently effective) capability to such an extent that there is little exploration of others, or in failing to stick to one (currently ineffective) capability long enough to determine its true value. In a similar fashion, exploration undermines exploitation. Efforts to promote experimentation encourage impatience with new ideas, technologies and strategies. They are likely to be abandoned before enough time has been devoted to developing the competence that would make them useful. The impatience of exploration results in unrealized dreams and unelaborated discoveries. As a result of the ways in which exploitation and exploration tend to extinguish each other, organizations persistently fail to maintain an effective balance between the two.

DISPOSABLE ORGANIZATIONS

At first blush, the standard organizational response to modern contexts of environmental volatility and uncertainty appears to be inconsistent with contextual demands. The primary demand of the environment is for greater flexibility and change. It invites exploration, variation, experimentation and a long-run, systemic perspective. However, the primary current responses of organizations seem to be increase efficient exploitation. Those responses seem to be emphasize reliability, limited experimentation and a short-run, local perspective.

As students of organizational evolution have often noted, the apparent inconsistency between organizational pursuits of immediate efficiency and environmental pressures for longer-run adaptiveness can be resolved by extending the perspective beyond individual organizations to the social system of which they are a part. Exploration can be seen less as a property of individual organizations than as a property of populations of organizations (Baum and Singh, 1994; Hannan and Freeman, 1989). Populations of organizations adapt through selection among non-adaptive, efficient and legitimate organizations, retaining those that match the current environment and discarding those that do not.

A vision of system-wide adaptation through selection and recombination among efficient, non-adaptive units is a vision that captures some elements of contemporary trends and matches some elements of a plausible future. The conception is one of a system of disposable (throw-away) organizations of considerable short-run efficiency at exploiting and refining current capabilities but only modest adaptive durability. In this imagined world, organizational variety is maintained at the population level (Carroll, 1993). Each organization is driven to be highly efficient in its particular situation: slack is eliminated; skills are sharpened; coordination is made more precise. When this organizational strategy of exploitation becomes, as it must, dysfunctional in a new situation, one rigid organization is discarded and replaced with a new rigid one. Adaptive combinations of efficient components are familiar to the modern world. Throw-away technologies, where design maximizes short-run efficiency rather than flexibility or reparability, are common in modern engineering. Throw-away personnel policies, where emphasis is placed on selection and turnover rather than on training and learning, have become common in modern business, politics and marriage.

In such a throw-away world, organizations lose important elements of permanence. For various legal and other institutional reasons, they may preserve a semblance of continuity – a corporate name and skeleton, for example. But they become notably more temporary, as reflected in the *ad hoc* construction of project groups or collaborations linked together by constantly changing non-hierarchical networks (Håkansson, 1992; Powell and Smith-Doerr, 1994). These cobweb-like "virtual" organizations are not yet a dominant component of current organizational life, but they appear to be becoming more important.

A transition to more efficiently specialized, more rigid and more temporary organizations may very well not occur. If it does, it may well not occur in anything like the form that has been sketched here. The fantasies of organizational prophets have some pragmatic barriers to overcome. The forecasts need to be qualified by some clear complications – complications that have shaped organizations as we know them and been shaped by them. In particular, there are complications in fitting such a system into the existing social context, in achieving adequate exploitation within individual organizations, and in maintaining adequate exploration in systems of organizations.

The largest social context problem associated with a system of disposable organizations lies in a potential inconsistency with social, political and moral systems that have grown up around existing systems. In particular, relatively stable, enduring organizations composed of relatively stable, enduring workforces are vital components of most social systems that have evolved in the industrialized world. They represent key elements in the ways individuals and social systems create order and establish expectations and entitlements. Since organizations are embedded in political orders and require their tolerance, individuals who are disoriented or disadvantaged by changes can be expected to seek political redress. Moreover, organizations are embedded in a moral order that has aspirations for human existence and community that have to be reconciled in some way with a vision of disposability.

The largest problem in achieving efficiency within disposable organizations is that of focusing attention on the refinement of existing capabilities in the face of signs of the potential negative long-run consequences of such a focus. Although efforts spent on exploration of new possibilities detract from maximizing short-run efficiency and specialization, existing organizations sometimes try (usually unsuccessfully and with adverse consequences for their short-run efficiency) to escape the specialization/

exploitation rigidities that are an essential part of the disposable organization vision.

The largest problem in maintaining adequate exploration within a population of disposable organizations is that of assuring a renewing supply of mutant organizations. Selection fails as an instrument of development if there is inadequate variation. Thus, a system of disposable organizations works as an adaptive system only if there is a reliable process for generating new organizations that differ from existing ones. In order to be able to replace efficiently obsolescent organizations with alternatively specialized organizations when environments change, such alternatives have to be created. They also have to be sustained through their infancies and protected from pressure to mimic existing successful organizations while they develop their distinctive competencies.

Without a steady stream of exploratory efforts, adaptation fails. And it fails particularly when the environmental context is changing rapidly. Imagination contributes to exploration in two ways. First, the imagination of possible futures is a source of new experiments and different possible ways of thinking and acting. It stimulates playfulness and foolishness. Playfulness is not enough, however, because it does not support persistence. Play is transitory, and population-level adaptation requires perseverance at the organizational level, particularly among new organizations. Exploration becomes useful only if it can be sustained long enough to expose its true value. Thus, the second contribution of imagination is essential. Imagination insulates exploratory ideas from a hostile environment.

Revolutions require tenacity more than awareness. New ideologies, forms and practices need to be buffered from learning what is technically efficient and normatively legitimate long enough to explore alternative efficiencies and legitimacies and to transform understandings of what works. Organizational responsiveness to feedback from the environment often interferes with this development of new specialized efficiencies. If strategies, technologies and behavior are modified rapidly in response to feedback, the modifications confound the accumulation of information that would allow an informed separation of signal from noise (Lounamaa and March, 1987) and of new possibilities from old customs. At the same time, rapid modifications of technology or strategy interfere with the development of competence, thus leading to changing courses before their true potentials can be assessed (Levinthal and March, 1993).

In many ways, therefore, the problematic element in adaptation through disposable organizations is not organizational flexibility, but stability. The incentives for such rigidity are modest. Most heretics are burned, not sanctified; most inventions prove worthless, not priceless. Most deviant organizations perish. As a result, persistence in a deviant course of action normally requires, in addition to the more mundane rewards anticipated from patents and copyrights, illusions (Kahneman and Lovallo, 1993; Taylor and Brown, 1988), conservation of belief in the face of failure (March, 1994a), communities of irrational commitment (Festinger et al., 1956), and adequate social and economic capital to endure through adolescence (Levinthal, 1991).

How do organizations achieve sufficient rigidity in forms, strategies and technologies to make the process work well? The primary answer is that the natural dynamics of learning lead organizations into refining and exploiting existing patterns rather than exploring alternatives (Levinthal and March, 1993; March, 1991). The relative certainty of rewards from exploitation and their nearness in time and space give them a learning advantage over the rewards from exploration, and lead organizations into increasingly specialized competence and an emphasis on the refinement of existing procedures.

The rigidities produced by learning are reinforced by the rigidities of imagination. The tales that organizations develop to describe or invent the past and to describe and invent the future stabilize organizational understandings and expectations. In the business world, for example, imagination (sometimes cloaked in the drab garments of business plans) protects investors, workers, managers, customers and bankers from information that might lead them to abandon an experiment. Information is filtered through fantasy to confirm beliefs.

The Perils and Glories of Imagination

Enthusiasts for foretelling the future face a grim reality. Predictions about the future of organizations are predictably bad. Well-informed, careful analysts do not have a much better record than do consultants of tea leaves. This is not because tea-leaf consultation has a good record, but because analysis has a poor one. Even Marx, who was considerably smarter than most of us, didn't get it entirely right. Organizational futurology is a profession in which reputations are crafted from the excitements of novelty, fear and hope. They are destroyed by the unfolding of experience.

Imaginations of possible organizations are justified by their potential not for predicting the future (which is almost certainly small) but for nurturing the uncritical commitment and persevering madness required for sustained organizational and individual rigidity in a selective environment. Many observers have noted the role of imagination in stimulating discoveries, but from this point of view its primary role is less in creating new ideas than in protecting them from disconfirmation. Imagination is unlikely to be more correct than convention, but it is more lucid, more autonomous and more compelling.

Clarity of vision protects deviant imaginations from the disconfirmations of experience and knowledge. Attachment to a fantasy converts the ambiguities of history into confirmations of belief and a willingness to persist in a course of action. This self-sustaining character of imagination protects commitment from the importunities of reality. Soothsayers create sheltered worlds of ignorance, ideology and faith. Within the shell that they provide, craziness is protected long enough to elaborate its challenge to orthodoxy.

> I began to wonder whether anything truly existed, whether reality wasn't an unformed and gelatinous substance only half-captured by my senses . . . I was consoled by the idea that I could take the gelatin and mold it to create anything I wanted . . . a world of my own populated with living people, a world where I imposed the rules and could change them at will. In the motionless sands where my stories germinated, every birth, death, and happening depended on me. I could plant anything I wanted in those sands; I had only to speak the right word to give it life. At times I felt that the universe fabricated from the power of the imagination had stronger and more lasting contours than the blurred realm of the flesh-and-blood creatures around me. (Allende, 1988, pp. 187–8)

The modern word is "vision", and its overtones of dreams are appropriate. Imaginations of the future are stronger and more lasting than the blurred realm of the flesh and blood creatures around us, and that power protects exploration from its enemies.

The persistence of fantasy is, in the end, destructive for the individual organization; but it makes organizations and the individuals in them obdurate enough to serve the needs of effective selection. There is, of course, much that can be viewed as unjust in a system that sustains imaginative madness at the individual organization level in order to allow a larger system to choose among alternative insanities. In such a world, most of the consequences of fantastical imaginations for individual organizations are disastrous. The benefits accrue to the system as a whole and to the occasional madness that is judged (briefly) to represent genius (Shaw, 1946).

There is also much that is cruel in a rationalization of fantasy in the name of selection. As Eva Luna reminds us, intellectual passions for reasoned intelligence and constrained imagination have never entirely extinguished a human aesthetic based on fantasy. A commitment to arbitrarily imagined worlds has elements of simple beauty in it, and to relegate that commitment to the service of efficient selection among disposable organizations is to rob imagination of the irrelevance that is central to its beauty and its humanity. From this perspective, the occasional argument between those who imagine individual organizations as changing and enduring and those who imagine them as rigid and disposable is an argument not only about the truth but also about the beauty and justice of possible fantasies of human existence, thus perhaps worth taking seriously.

References

Allende, Isabel (1988) *Eva Luna*. New York: Alfred A. Knopf.

Argyris, C. and Schön, D. (1978) *Organizational Learning*. Reading, MA: Addison-Wesley.

Arthur, W. Brian (1989) "Competing Technologies, Increasing Returns, and Lock-in by Historical Events", *Economic Journal* 99: 116–31.

Baum, Joel and Singh, Jitendra, eds (1994) *The Evolutionary Dynamics of Organizations*. New York: Oxford University Press.

Carroll, Glenn R. (1993) "A Sociological View of Why Firms Differ," *Strategic Management Journal* 14: 237–49.

Carroll, Glenn R. and Harrison, J. Richard (1994) "On the Historical Efficiency of Competition between Organizational Populations," *American Journal of Sociology* 100: 720–49.

Cohen, Wesley M. and Levinthal, Daniel A. (1989) "Innovation and Learning: The Two Faces of R&D," *Economic Journal* 99: 569–90.

Corno, Fabio (1988) "Managing Knowledge as a Strategic Variable," *Economia Aziendale Review* 7: 193–224.

DiMaggio, Paul J. and Powell, Walter W. (1983) "The Iron Cage Revisited: Institutional Isomorphism and Collective Rationality in Organizational Fields," *American Sociological Review* 48: 147–60.

Feldman, Martha S. (1989) *Order without Design: Information Production and Policy Making*. Stanford, CA: Stanford University Press.

Festinger, Leon, Riecken, Henry W. and Schachter, Stanley (1956) *When Prophecy Fails*. Minneapolis: University of Minnesota Press.

Håkansson, Håkan (1992) "Evolution Processes in Industrial Networks," in B. Axelsson and G. Easton (eds) *Industrial Networks: A New View of Reality*, pp. 129–43. London: Routledge.

Hannan, Michael, T. and Freeman, John (1989) *Organizational Ecology*. Cambridge, MA: Harvard University Press.

Hedberg, B. L. T., Nystrom, P. C. and Starbuck, W. H. (1976) "Camping on Seesaws: Prescriptions for a Self-designing Organization," *Administrative Science Quarterly* 21: 41–65.

Herriott, Scott R., Levinthal, Daniel A. and March, James G. (1985) "Learning From Experience in Organizations," *American Economic Review* 75: 298–302.

Kahneman, Daniel and Lovallo, D. (1993) "Timid Choices and Bold Forecasts: A Cognitive Perspective on Risk Taking," *Management Science* 39: 17–31.

Kiesler, Sara B. and Sproull, Lee S. (1991) *Connections*. Cambridge, MA: MIT Press.

Levinthal, Daniel A. (1991) "Random Walks and Organizational Mortality," *Administrative Science Quarterly* 36: 397–420.

Levinthal, Daniel A. and March, James G. (1993) "The Myopia of Learning," *Strategic Management Journal* 14: 95–112.

Lewin, Arie Y. and Stephens, Carroll

U. (1993) "Designing Postindustrial Organizations: Combining Theory and Practice," in George P. Huber and William H. Glick (eds) *Organizational Change and Redesign*, pp. 393–409. New York: Oxford University Press.

Lounamaa, Pertti H. and March, James G. (1987) "Adaptive Coordination of a Learning Team," *Management Science* 33: 107–23.

Malone, Thomas M. and Rockart, J.F. (1991) "Computer, Networks, and the Corporation," *Scientific American* September: 111–17.

March, James G. (1991) "Exploration and Exploitation in Organizational Learning," *Organization Science* 2: 71–87.

March, James G. (1994a) *A Primer on Decision Making*. New York: Free Press.

March, James G. (1994b) *Three Lectures on Efficiency and Adaptiveness*. Helsinki: Swedish School of Economics and Business Administration.

March, James G. and Olsen, Johan P. (1989) *Rediscovering Institutions: The Organizational Basis of Politics*. New York: Free Press.

March, James G. and Olsen, Johan P. (1995) *Democratic Governance*. New York: Free Press.

March, James G. and Shapira, Zur (1987) "Managerial Perspectives on Risk and Risk Taking," *Management Science* 33: 1404–18.

March, James G. and Shapira, Zur (1992) "Variable Risk Preferences and the Focus of Attention," *Psychological Review* 99: 172–83.

Meyer, John and Rowan, Brian (1977) "Institutionalized Organizations: Formal Structure as Myth and Ceremony," *American Journal of Sociology* 83: 340–63.

Mezias, Stephen and Glynn, Mary Ann (1992) "The Three Faces of Corporate Renewal: Institution, Revolution, and Evolution," *Strategic Management Journal* 14: 77–101.

Powell, Walter W. and Smith-Doerr, Laurel (1994) "Networks and Economic Life," in Neil J. Smelser and Richard Swedberg (eds) *The Handbook of Economic Sociology*, pp. 368–402. Princeton, NJ: Princeton University Press.

Senge, P. M. (1990) *The Fifth Discipline: The Art and Practice of the Learning Organization*. New York: Doubleday.

Shaw, Bernard (1946) *Saint Joan*. Harmondsworth: Penguin.

Starbuck, William H. (1992) "Learning by Knowledge-intensive Firms," *Journal of Management Studies* 29: 713–40.

Taylor, Shelley E. and Brown, J. D. (1988) "Illusions and Well-being: A Social Psychological Perspective on Mental Health," *Psychological Bulletin* 103: 193–210.

Tushman, Michael L. and Anderson, Philip (1986) "Technological Discontinuities and Organizational Environments," *Administrative Science Quarterly* 31: 439–65.

Tyre, M. J. and Orlikowski, Wanda J. (1994) "Windows of Opportunity: Temporal Patterns of Technological Adaptation in Organizations," *Organization Science* 5: 98–118.

Wendt, A. (1994) "Collective Identity Formation and the International State," *American Political Science Review* 88: 384–96.

Winter, Sidney G. (1987) "Knowledge and Competence as Strategic Assets," in David J. Teece (ed.) *The Competitive Challenge: Strategies for Industrial Innovation and Renewal*, pp. 159–84. New York: Harper & Row.

CHAPTER ELEVEN

The Myopia of Learning
with Daniel A. Levinthal

Organizational learning has many virtues, virtues which recent writings in strategic management have highlighted. Learning processes, however, are subject to some important limitations. As is well-known, learning has to cope with confusing experience and the complicated problem of balancing the competing goals of developing new knowledge (i.e., exploring) and exploiting current competencies in the face of dynamic tendencies to emphasize one or the other. We examine the ways organizations approach these problems through simplification and specialization and how those approaches contribute to three forms of learning myopia, the tendency to overlook distant times, distant places, and failures, and we identify some ways in which organizations sustain exploration in the face of a tendency to overinvest in exploitation. We conclude that the imperfections of learning are not so great as to require abandoning attempts to improve the learning capabilities of organizations, but that those imperfections suggest a certain conservatism in expectations.

In this chapter, we examine processes of experiential learning as instruments of organizational intelligence. Learning processes are powerful aids to intelligence, and the modern vision of learning capabilities as a basis for strategic advantage is an important insight. However, there are limits to learning. Designing organizations to learn without attention to those limits is no more sensible than designing organizations to be rational without attention to the limits of rationality.

THE SEARCH FOR ORGANIZATIONAL INTELLIGENCE

Strategic management is built on a search for organizational intelligence, an attempt to make actions lead to outcomes that are consistent with desires or conceptions of appropriateness. The objective is one that is both ambiguously defined and imperfectly achieved.

The vision of rationality

Earlier visions of strategic management focused on the use (or lack of use) of analytically rational decision procedures and pictured the task of intelligent management as that of facilitating rational action (Lorange, 1980). Organizational intelligence was associated with the specification of well-defined objectives and the pursuit of those objectives by gathering information to assess alternatives in terms of their expected future consequences and choosing actions expected to fulfill objectives. The structure of tasks, assignments of individuals to those tasks, incentives, and relationships were seen as dictated by requirements for gathering information relevant to making allocative decisions, assuring that the best possible future-oriented actions were chosen, and controlling their implementation. Strategies for exploiting comparative advantage and competitive opportunities were built on a conception of calculated rationality.

This vision of calculative rationality as the basis of strategic management continues to be the dominant vision, though it has been modified on the basis of various criticisms of its assumptions, particularly those associated with the availability of information, the information processing capabilities of organizations, and the preference axioms of rationality. Because strategic anticipatory rationality seems to demand both greater cognitive and calculative capabilities and more consistency and stability in preferences than can be reliably assumed, considerable effort has been directed to improving the informational and analytical basis for organizational action and to developing consistent, stable organizational objectives. Modern decision-oriented information systems and procedures for defining (or negotiating) goals reflect this spirit (Keen and Morton, 1978; Jones and MacLeod, 1986).

The discovery of learning

At the same time as ideas of strategic calculative rationality have been modified and refined, learning has been "discovered" by the world of practice and the academic field of strategic management. As researchers have considered the stability of differences in firm performance in the face of changing business environments, many have come to view the ability to learn as an important, indeed in some accounts a unique, source of sustainable competitive advantage (Burgelman, 1990; Senge, 1990). This is reflected both in the attention to learning and learning organizations in management circles (Senge, 1990; Stalk et al., 1992) and in the exploration of learning models of adaptation by economists (Cross, 1983) and students of organizations (Argyris and Schön, 1978; Levitt and March, 1988).

Learning from experience

Organizations and the individuals in them often improve their performance over repetitions of the same task. Repetition-based improvements in manufacturing performance have been documented in some detail in numerous studies of learning curves (Yelle, 1979). The costs of producing manufactured items decrease with the cumulative number of items produced. It is natural to attribute the improvements documented in studies of manufacturing to knowledge gained from experience. The lessons of experience are transferable from one operating unit to another (Argote et al., 1990). They may also spillover from one activity to another (Udayagiri and Balakrishnan, 1993).

Such experiential-based knowledge can be an important basis of competitive advantage for a firm, and for some students of organizations and strategy, learning has become a plausible mechanism substituting for, or augmenting, calculative rationality in the pursuit of intelligent organizational action. The (re)discovery of learning has been stimulated by the current interest among students of strategic management in organizational capabilities and knowledge (Prahalad and Hamel, 1990). Successful organizations are described as having capabilities for learning – for responding to experience by modifying their technologies, forms, and practices (Stalk et al., 1992). Executives are enjoined to monitor their experience in order to learn from it and to organize to stimulate learning and the utilization of knowledge gained from the experience of others as well as their own (Senge, 1990). These enthusiasms supplement – and to some extent replace – earlier enthusiasms for long-term planning and rational calculation as bases for organizational prosperity and survival.

Confusions of experience

Studies of reductions in the cost of production associated with the number of units produced do not, in general, provide direct confirmation of the processes by which those improvements have occurred, nor do they demonstrate that experiential learning processes inexorably lead to optimal practices. The limitations of experience as an instrument of intelligence are not esoteric. They stem from relatively generic problems of adaptive intelligence.

Experience is often a poor teacher, being typically quite meager relative to the complex and changing nature of the world in which learning is taking place. Many of the same cognitive limits that constrain rationality also constrain learning. Learning from experience involves inferences from information. It involves memory. It involves pooling personal experience with knowledge gained from the experiences of others. The difficulties in learning effectively in the face of confusing experience are legendary. Even highly capable individuals and organizations are confused by the difficulties of using small samples of ambiguous experience to interpret complex worlds (Brehmer, 1980; Fischhoff, 1980).

The cognitive and inferential limitations of individuals are accentuated by organizational limitations. The interpretations of history are political, reflecting efforts to assign and evade responsibility and to establish favorable historical stories (Sagan, 1993). Organizations record the lessons of histories in the modification of rules and the elaboration of stories, but neither is a perfect instrument. Problems of memory, conflict, turnover, and decentralization make it difficult to extract lessons from experience and to retain them (March et al., 1991).

Self-limiting properties of learning

Recent examinations of learning as an adaptive process have raised questions not only about the confusions of experience but also about the ways in which learning is self-limiting. The effectiveness of learning in the short-run and in the near neighborhood of current experience interferes with learning in the long run and at a distance. Knowledge and the development of capabilities improve immediate performance, but they often simultaneously reduce incentives for and competence with new technologies or paradigms. Learning has its own traps.

In the next three sections, we consider the major mechanisms organizations use to reduce experimental confusion, the problems of myopia they face, and the dynamic complications of balancing exploration and exploitation in learning.

TWO MECHANISMS OF LEARNING

Organizations use two major mechanisms to facilitate learning from experience. The first is *simplification*. Learning processes seek to simplify experience, to minimize interactions and restrict effects to the spatial and temporal neighborhood of actions. The second mechanism is *specialization*. Learning processes tend to focus attention and narrow competence. Neither simplification nor specialization is unique to learning processes. They are, however, particularly salient to discussions of the design of learning organizations.

Simplification and the construction of buffers

Learning presumes interpretation of experience. Organizations code outcomes into successes and failures and develop ideas about causes for them. Experience is clouded by the interactive complexity of history, particularly by the way experience is shaped by many actors simultaneously learning. If one's own actions are embedded in an ecology of the actions of many others (who are also simultaneously learning and changing), it is not easy to understand what is going on. The relationship between the actions of individuals in the organization and overall organizational performance is confounded by simultaneous learning of other actors. Particularly in environments in which performance is a noisy reflection of organizational decisions, highly interactive learning is likely to be unrewarding. For example, while isolated subunits can often learn quite effectively (Cyert and March, 1992; Lave and March, 1993), simultaneous learning by several interacting subunits in a noisy environment can be quite difficult (Lounamaa and March, 1987).

Organizations that want to disentangle the interactions introduced by multiple simultaneous learners have two general options: They can seek to generate enough experience so that they can fit relatively complicated models to the data. In practice, this is often not feasible. Alternatively, organizations can seek to control the effects of interactions by preventing multiple simultaneous adjustments. One means of increasing the effectiveness of learning is to simplify natural experience by inhibiting learning in one part of an organization in order to make learning more effective in another part (Lounamaa and March, 1987). Organizations seek to transform confusing, interactive environments into less confusing, less interactive ones by decomposing domains and treating the resulting subdomains as autonomous. They create buffers. They enact environments.

Decomposition and organizational structures

Departmentalization is, perhaps, the most basic mechanism to mitigate interaction effects in learning within a complex organization. Although the transformation from functional to product organizations has usually been justified as a means to enhance control and coordination (Chandler, 1962), it also is a way of segregating experience. Less prominent in the normative literature on strategy and organizations, but prominent in more descriptive accounts (Cyert and March, 1992) is the sequential allocation of attention to divergent goals. While the sequential allocation of attention is generally viewed as an outcome of goal conflict and bounded rationality, it also results in a simplification of experiments in organizational change.

The conception of buffers as enhancing organizational effectiveness has a long tradition in the organizations literature (Thompson, 1967), and resource or other buffers between units can achieve substantial simplifications of the learning environment. Buffers between units (departmentalization) and between goals (sequential attention) allow local consequences to be examined. Marketing departments experiment with alternative marketing strategies and production departments experiment with alternative production strategies, each evaluated in such a way that their effects on each other are ignored. Depending on an organization's structure, global problems of poor performance are viewed as local problems of cost reduction or as local problems of revenue enhancement.

It is noteworthy, however, that many contemporary academics and practitioners advocate the tight coupling of organizations (Bower and Hout, 1988). Perhaps the most prominent application of ideas of tight coupling is the notion of lean production systems and just-in-time inventory systems. The ideas extend beyond manufacturing, however. In some cases, the idea of making organizations tightly coupled is tied to ideas about the importance of linkages to customers and has produced popular organizational slogans about the desirability of being "customer driven." In other cases, the ideas have been extended to linkages within the organization (Schonberger, 1990).

Advocates of these various mechanisms of tight coupling suggest that an important virtue of such structures is that they enhance learning. Learning is enhanced because the problems that arise through ongoing operations in one part of the system become observable, and hence an occasion for learning, in other elements of the system. Customer complaints are not merely absorbed by boundary spanning personnel but become more broadly known. Problems in production are not masked by a buffer inventory of partially assembled units or by postproduction inspection and repair.

The apparent discrepancy between the two perspectives on buffers can, in part, be resolved by considering the simultaneous difficulties of oversight produced by the way buffers conceal signals of problems and difficulties of misinterpretation of signals produced by trying to understand complex, interactive systems. The former difficulties suggest tight coupling in order to facilitate detection of signals; the latter difficulties suggest loose coupling in order to facilitate their interpretation. The basic argument of those who advocate tight coupling is that many organizations have gone too far in attempting to segregate the problems they face. The arguments are twofold. On the one hand, they are assertions that modern markets and technologies link things together more than earlier ones did. On the other hand, they are also assertions that modern analytical and coordination techniques – perhaps due to new developments in information technology – reduce the costs of centralized problem solving.

Tightly coupled systems are relatively good for system-wide error detection, but they are relatively poor for error diagnostics. Loosely coupled systems make diagnostics easier (assuming that the system is, in fact, decomposable) but localize error detection, thereby making more general awareness of problems difficult. The appropriate balance between investments in error detection and in diagnostics presumably depends on the frequency of errors and the difficulty of diagnosis.

Decomposition and enactment

The conditions under which the buffers of departmentalization or sequential attention lead to effective local learning are usually described in terms of the extent to which the problems that are faced are decomposable, so that relatively few interactions occur across departmental boundaries or across goals (Gulick and Urwick, 1937). Decomposability is usually treated as an inherent property of a problem. Insofar as decomposability is invariant, simplifications produced by departmentalization or sequential attention will work (or not work) depending on the nature of the problem. Part of the appeal of the so-called horizontal organization (Ostroff and Smith, 1992) is that it forces formerly buffered units of the organization to learn more about end-customer preferences. The argument is that standard organizational structures make an inappropriate decomposition of the problems of the organization.

Decomposability may, however, be imposed rather than given. The problems an organization faces are not only exogenous technical ones but also social and political problems whose existence and character are affected by the character of organizational attention structures. Organizations enact their own environments. By treating problems as separable, they make them separable (Weick, 1979). Problems that are not seen do not exist. Or at least, their manifestations are delayed, and being delayed are likely to be transformed over time – possibly becoming more severe and unavoidable but also possibly becoming irrelevant or minor.

Many forms of enactment involve the realization and elaboration of an imposed social structure. The drawing of national boundaries or the departmentalization of organizations or the definition of markets creates self-confirming political, economic, technological, and social processes that convert relatively arbitrary units into real ones (March and Olsen, 1989). Consider, for example, the construction of attention barriers between subunits of an organization. Restricting the flow of information restricts knowledge of opportunities and activities. The reduction in knowledge leads to a reduction in salience. Ideas change about what is relevant and what is not. Solutions to problems are localized to the domains of the problems as defined organizationally. A classic form of the enactment of an environment is the development of mental models of the world, such as those institutionalized into scientific disciplines, each of which creates a relatively autonomous system. Similarly, as organizations find or construct "niches" for themselves, they simultaneously construct private comprehensible worlds.

Organizations and the individuals in them are notoriously reluctant to give up such mental models (Kuhn, 1970). Rigidity results not only from the institutionalization of specialized capabilities, but also from the institutionalization of an organization's political structure (Boeker, 1989). Success tends to launch managers associated with it into positions of power within the organization. Organizational power associated with past successes tends to linger.

Specialization and the principle of learning substitution

A learning system can adapt through several different mechanisms at several different points with approximately the same overall effect. Consequently, different learning locales or mechanisms are substitutes for each other. Assuming that the system avoids becoming unstable with simultaneous, interactive adaptations that confound all learning, the success of adaptation by one part of a system has two major effects: On the one hand, it relieves pressure for adaptation in another part. Insofar as equivalent effects can be achieved in several different ways, adjustment in one way tends to inhibit adjustment in another. At the same time, the adapting part of the system develops greater and greater adaptive competence relative to the part of the system that is not used. The two effects combine to produce specialization of learning competence.

Multiple actors: Fast learners and slow learners

Rapid adaptation by one party reduces the need for, and likelihood of, adaptation by another. The proposition is well-known in theories of bargaining, where conscious efforts are made to force opponents to adjust first (Schelling, 1960). Thus, a hard bargainer might introduce various devices to demonstrate the impossibility of changing positions, for example irrevocable decisions. In the world of mutual adaptation, strategic calculation is less central, but the proposition remains the same. In this case, the fast learning collaborator moves more than the slower partner (Lave and March, 1993).

The classic situation is one involving two drivers on a collision course. The first driver to understand the situation and react to it relieves the other driver of the necessity of response. (In this case, of course, there is the possibility that a sequence of independent adaptations will not avoid a collision.) Similarly, parents who are particularly fast in adapting to their children's needs reduce the pressure on the latter to be adaptive, resulting in a lack of socialization (manners) in children of highly adaptive parents. Or, political/legal systems that meet special or changing circumstances through adaptation by law enforcement agencies or by courts reduce the pressure on legislatures for changes in the statutes.

Multiple mechanisms: Targets, search, and slack

In bounded rationality search models, an organization is seen as responding to success or failure by varying the intensity of search, the level of organizational slack, and the target (aspiration level) for performance (Cyert and March, 1992). Success decreases search and increases slack and targets, while failure increases search and decreases slack and targets. Changes in search, slack, and targets function effectively as substitutes for each other. Adjustments in search substitute for adjustments in slack or aspirations, and vice versa. The different responses have equivalent effects from the point of view of restoring the aspiration/performance equilibrium, but they are not necessarily equivalent from the point of view of the organization and its learning.

In particular, there may be substantial differences in the long run between a system that adjusts aspirations slowly and slack rapidly and slack slowly. For example, the standard pygmalion story is one in which aspiration adjustments to unsatisfactory performance are slowed by means of rosy interpretations of that performance. The classic pygmalion complication is that rosy interpretations of performance inhibit a downward adjustment of aspirations, but they also inhibit reduction of slack and an increase in search (by underestimating the discrepancy between aspirations and performance).

Preferences also adapt in response to experience (March, 1988). Tastes for opera, ballet, and baseball are developed at the same times as competencies at those activities, and they are considerably affected by those competencies. Similarly, preferences for particular technologies develop in tandem with competencies at them. Since propensities to reevaluate the wisdom of engaging in particular activities are reduced by gains in competence at them, preference change is an adaptive substitute for search or change in an activity.

Multiple responses: Exit, voice, and loyalty

The substitution principle has been used by Hirschman (1970) to account for some features of the development of rail transport in Nigeria, public school systems, and other systems that have dissatisfied participants. In

Hirschman's framework, participants who experience a decline in quality of organizational services or products have two possible responses: The first alternative is to exit from the unsatisfactory relationship and seek another. The second alternative is to try to fix the existing relationship. The two are substitutes in the adaptive story of correcting declines in quality. From the vantage point of the dissatisfied participant, either of the alternatives is satisfactory in the sense that each has a reasonable prospect of removing the difficulty. Exit can substitute for voice, and vice versa.

From the point of view of the organization, however, the two alternative responses have quite different implications. If dissatisfied participants exit, they abandon the organization to less demanding participants, thus condemning it to a gradual degradation of capabilities. On the other hand, if dissatisfied participants exercise voice, they encourage the organization to improve quality. The organizational problem is to slow the exit of quality-conscious participants long enough to use their influence in improvement. One solution is found through the encouragement of loyalty, a form of friction on exit. The Hirschman loyalty mechanism can be seen as a way of slowing search and adjustment of aspiration levels in order to increase pressure on slack.

Multiple, nested options

Learning experience is nested. That is, learning occurs at several different but interrelated levels at the same time. An organization simultaneously learns *which* strategy to follow and *how* to operate within various alternative strategies (Herriott et al., 1985). An individual simultaneously learns *whether* to think like an economist and *how* to think like an economist. An army learns *which* technology to use and *how* to use several alternative technologies. A business firm learns *which* market to enter and *how* to function effectively in several alternative markets.

When learning is nested, learning at one level is effectively a substitute for learning at another. Refining an existing technology substitutes for recognizing a better one, and vice versa. Strengthening abilities within an existing paradigm substitutes for finding a new one that is better, and vice versa. Learning the nuances of an existing relationship substitutes for finding an alternative that is better, and vice versa.

The same thing happens within an organizational structure. Fast adaptation at one level in an organization leads to slow adaptation at other levels. Insofar as operating levels in an organization make adjustments in implementing policies as conditions change, the pressure for changes in policies is relieved. The operating managers of a firm in a changing competitive environment may adjust by discovering new markets for the firm's existing products. For instance, a defense manufacturer could respond to the decline in the US military budget by pursuing foreign military markets for its wares.

Such adaptation, however, masks a higher level problem that the firm faces. Learning at the operating level of an organization substitutes for learning at higher levels. Insofar as customers adapt to the inadequacies of the products they use, manufacturers are less likely to do so. Insofar as subordinates respond to individual customer complaints, bosses are less pressed to do so. Lower-level adaptation is a sensible activity that tends to enhance an organization's position in its present environment. In the long run, however, such first-order learning can not substitute for second-order learning of new routines and strategies.

PROBLEMS OF MYOPIA

By simplifying experience and specializing adaptive responses, learning improves organizational performance, on average. However, the same mechanisms of learning that lead to the improvements also lead to limits to those improvements. In particular, we will note three forms of learning myopia: The first form of myopia is the tendency to ignore the long run. The short run is privileged by organizational learning. As a result, long-run survival is sometimes endangered. The second form of myopia is the tendency to ignore the larger picture. The near neighborhood is privileged by organizational learning. As a result, survival of more encompassing systems is sometimes endangered. The third form of myopia is the tendency to overlook failures. The lessons gained from success are privileged by organizational learning. As a result, the risks of failure are likely to be underestimated.

Overlooking distant times

There is no guarantee that short-run and long-run survival are consistent. It is easy to imagine situations in which the only strategies that permit survival in the short run assure failure in the long run and vice versa. Thus, it is fairly easy to make an argument that any consideration of the future must accept survival in the short run as a constraint. Simplification and specialization, however, seem exceptionally myopic with respect to the future. We can illustrate this by looking at the erosion of enactment with time, at the second order effects of learning substitution, and at some problems associated with knowledge inventories.

Erosion of enactment

Learning processes tend to enact environments that are sufficiently simple to permit inferences and incremental gains. There is, however, a limit to enactment. The classic tension between social construction of reality and the interventions of other reality processes (for example, of nature) is well-known. Learning creates a simplified world and specializes an organization to it. Such models are more likely to capture the central elements of past environments than the contingencies of current circumstances. Only the most enthusiastic observers of enactment deny that the world of nature constrains social enactment and sometimes forces reconsideration. Inexorably, at some point a mental model becomes unsustainable, and the organization's competencies become irrelevant. The process is as familiar to modern firms as it was to ancient systems of magic, religion, warfare, and trade.

Second-order effects of specialization

Substitutions of learning in one part of an organization for learning in another part are normally sensible forms of specialized adaptation. They do, however, produce some dysfunctional second-order effects in the form of disparities in the development of adaptive capabilities. These effects typically take longer than do the immediate effects of local learning, involving as they do the development or decay of skills, procedures, and technologies of learning. A strategic problem is created by the fact that the learning that yields a comparative advantage in one domain is likely to be rewarding in the short run, but it leads to a longer-run potential decay of adaptive capability in other domains.

Traps of distinctive competence

An organization develops better skills in some parts of the organization, in some markets, in some technologies, and in some strategies than in others. The mechanism is one of mutual positive feedback between experience and competence. Organizations engage in activities at which they are more competent with greater frequency than they engage in activities at which they are less competent. The differences in the frequency with which different activities are pursued translate into differences in the amount of experience at the various potential activities, which in turn translate into differences in competence. These distinctive competencies invite utilization, which furthers their additional development. The self-reinforcing nature of learning makes it attractive for an individual or organization to sustain current focus. The result is that distinctive competence is accentuated, and organizations become specialized to niches in which their competencies yield immediate advantage.

Learners become increasingly removed from other bases of experience and knowledge and more vulnerable to change in their environments (David, 1985). Since the degree to which firms or individuals learn about alternative opportunities is a function of their level of involvement in them (Cohen and Levinthal, 1994), knowledge about and use of old competencies inhibit efforts to change capabilities. Abernathy and Wayne (1974) provide a classic illustration of this pathology when they describe Ford's pursuit of efficient production of the Model T. While the company was able to drive down the cost of the Model T, the transition to the Model A was extraordinarily difficult and required shutting down the manufacturing facility for a considerable period of time.

Traps of power

Organizational power is a short-run asset but potentially a long-run liability. Power allows an organization to change its environments rather than adapt to them. Thus, firms with strong market positions impose their policies, products, and strategies on others, rather than learn to adapt to an exogenous environment. This capability to define an environment – such as a firm's capability to set industry standards – provides an advantage to the organization since it can organize around a specific plan without concern about contingencies. This advantage is exploited and improved upon by refining the skills of power.

In the long run, however, the use of power to impose environments is likely to result in atrophy of capabilities to respond to change. An organization becomes skilled at influencing its environment, but not at responding to the environment (Deutsch, 1966, p. 111). Should its ability to influence the environment be overwhelmed by economic, political, or demographic forces beyond its control, the underdevelopment of adaptive skills will be exposed, and there may not be enough time to overcome the resulting disadvantage.

Knowledge inventories and the problem of timing

The complications in balancing the long- and short run are also illustrated by the management of knowledge inventories. Organizations sometimes act by solving problems after they arrive. They discover problems, diagnose their causes, experiment with solutions to them, and then implement solutions that appear likely to yield favorable outcomes. Such a procedure is implied in many theories of decision making and by the design of many decision support systems. Often, however, organizational action is better seen as a programmed exercise of prior capabilities (Starbuck,

1983), or as the result of monitoring environments and drawing appropriate responses from a prior repertoire (March and Simon, 1993).

The surveillance/response mode is particularly likely when response times are short. The time between the anticipation of a problem and its arrival may not be adequate for an organization to identify and develop the knowledge, or accumulate the experience, required to respond effectively. As Dierickx and Cool (1989) suggest, there are time compression diseconomies in building organizational capabilities. As a result, organizations build inventories of competencies (Feldman, 1989). The inventories are represented by storehouses of information and experience both within the organization and outside it. Organizations develop contingency plans. They stockpile knowledge about products, technologies, markets, and social and political contexts. They develop networks of contacts with consultants and colleagues.

In a world in which there are only a few possible situations and the appropriate responses are stable, maintaining appropriate knowledge inventories is relatively uncomplicated. Normally, those inventories are represented by a small number of specialized competencies maintained by the individuals and groups that make up the organization. Where situations or proper responses are numerous and shifting, it is harder to specify and realize optimal inventories of knowledge. By the time knowledge is needed, it is too late to gain it; before knowledge is needed, it is hard to specify precisely what knowledge might be required or useful. It is necessary to create inventories of competencies that might be used later without knowing precisely what future demands will be.

Determining the variety and depth of knowledge to be added to the inventory is filled with potential pitfalls. Knowledge that has clear, immediate uses is specialized to current technologies and markets. It is easily specified and has relatively early and local returns. Broader or deeper knowledge is less likely to have immediate pay-off but results in a greater ability to adapt to changes. Moreover, knowledge facilitates the use of other knowledge. Organizations that have some competence in an emerging technological domain are better able to assess the potential importance of that domain and to evaluate possible investments in new knowledge in that domain (Cohen and Levinthal, 1990, 1994).

Overlooking distant places

As has been observed often in the study of the evolution of nested systems, it is relatively unusual for a strategy that maximizes the prospects for survival of the components of a system to be the same as a strategy that maximizes the prospects for the survival of the system as a whole (March, 1994). Strategies of survival for organizations may be optimal neither for survival of the economies or social systems of which they are a part, nor for the individuals and groups that form the organization.

Selection among learners

As we have argued earlier, learning gives advantage to results in the spatial neighborhood of current action. Organizations that learn effectively become well-adapted to their environments, even as their environments become well-adapted to them. When the world changes exogenously, as inevitably it does, the matches between organizations well-adapted to their previous environments and the new environments are at risk. Existing organizations are likely to die and be replaced by new organizations which will, in turn, become specialized to the new environment.

This threat to organizational survival is substantial, but the resulting cycle of specialization and replacement may well be an efficient system for the system as a whole, combining as it does the advantages of learning at the organization level and the advantages of selection at the system level. Thus, the "self-destructive" properties of learning are properties that make the replacement of obsolescent organizations easier. Rigidities in one individual or organization serve to exploit current knowledge and simultaneously make old markets vulnerable to new entities with new capabilities (Hannan and Freeman, 1984). Systematic advantages stemming from component vulnerability have, of course, long been favorite topics of evolutionary theorists, and it should be no surprise that they arise here.

Learning is, however, not entirely benign in its consequences for systems of organizations. The fruits of successful exploration, whether new technologies, product ideas, or modes of management, tend to diffuse over populations of organizations. They are public goods. In contrast, the risks and costs of exploration are private goods; they tend to be borne by organizations carrying out such initiatives. The result is that the best strategy for any individual organization is often to emphasize the exploitation of successful explorations of others. Such a strategy, if followed by all, produces no innovations to imitate and a downward spiral of refining existing technologies and strategies. The system as a whole underinvests in exploration.

Knowledge diffusion

Not only do the returns to refinement and imitation depend on the degree to which others engage in exploration, so also do the returns to knowledge. Cohen and Levinthal (1989, 1990) make this argument in the context of research activities in business firms. Research performs the dual role of both generating new knowledge and enhancing a firm's ability to absorb new knowledge generated by others. With respect to this latter incentive to invest in research, the returns to research activity depend on the richness of the pool of external knowledge and the research activity of other firms. As a result, there may be multiple equilibria. If others engage in a high level of exploration activity, the pool of new knowledge into which an organization taps will be quite rich. As a result, it is attractive for the organization to invest at high levels as well. Alternatively, there may be low-level equilibria in which the pool of new knowledge is sufficiently modest so that individual organizations are not motivated to invest.

Such arguments suggest that, at the population level, there are increasing returns to investing in learning. A more knowledge-intensive environment tends to beget more investment in knowledge development. Similar arguments have appeared in recent years in the literature on economic development (Romer, 1986; Lucas, 1988). A puzzle for development economists has been why, with capital mobility, rates of productivity have not converged across countries. The answer that Romer (1986) and others provide is that the return to investment is a function of the existing infrastructure and human capital within a country.

Analogous arguments can made at the organization level. The returns to knowledge to a particular actor or subunit will depend on the level of knowledge developed by others in the organization. As a result, organizations may find themselves in self-reinforcing spirals of knowledge-generating activity leading to high levels of organizational renewal and growth. Alternatively, the self-reinforcing cycle can be a downward spiral in which individuals and subunits within the organization find the enhanced learning capability that results from knowledge of lesser and less value, leading to a reduction in their own knowledge-seeking activity, which in turn contributes toward a reduction in knowledge throughout the organization.

Overlooking failures

Learning is likely to be misleading if the experiential record on which it draws is a biased representation of past reality, and thus of future likelihoods. Organizational learning produces such a biased history. Learning generates successes rather than failures. In every domain of learning, the likelihood of success tends to increase with competence (even allowing for aspiration level adjustments). As learners settle into those domains in which they have competence and accumulate experience in them, they experience fewer and fewer failures. Insofar as they generalize that experience to other domains, they are likely to exaggerate considerably the likelihood of success.

As successes are translated into knowledge and knowledge into successes, not only do capabilities increase but also self-assurance. Organizations and the individuals in them become more confident that they have the skills to deal with problems that lie within their domains. Confidence in control over outcomes leads to learning from expectations of consequences before the consequences are observed, and it leads to reinterpretation of results to make them more favorable (Björkman, 1989; March et al., 1991). In these ways, confidence finds confirmation in its own imagination. Since lack of confidence is similarly self-confirming for unsuccessful individuals, learning is less self-correcting than might be expected. Confidence grows slowly in the early stages of refining competence, when there are relatively frequent failures. Confidence grows rapidly as learning produces increasing numbers of successes.

Confidence is likely to become excessive when the experiential record of successes is a poor predictor of future success. Consider, for example, using experiential learning to learn how to avoid or produce an extremely rare event – for example, a major nuclear disaster or a major scientific discovery. Experience rarely generates a rare event. As a result, most people involved in nuclear safety are likely to come to believe they are more capable of producing a safe environment than they actually are, and most people involved in scientific discovery are likely to come to believe they are less likely to produce a major scientific discovery than they actually are. Experience probably makes nuclear safety engineers over-confident and scientific researchers under-confident.

Research on individual attributions of causality to events indicates that individuals are more likely to attribute their successes to ability and their failures to luck than they are to attribute their successes to luck and their failures to ability (Miller and Ross, 1975). Biases in the perception of the relative contributions of ability and luck to outcomes translate into biases in the estimation of risk. Any inclination to over attribute outcomes to luck will be associated with overestimating risk, thus with decreasing risk taking. Similarly, any inclination to overattribute outcomes to ability will be associated with underestimating risk, thus with increasing risk taking. As a result, persistent failure leads to a tendency to overestimate the risks of actions, and persistent success leads to a tendency to underestimate those risks. Successful people have confidence in their ability to beat the apparent odds. They tend to underestimate the risks of their actions and overestimate their expected returns (March and Shapira, 1987; Kahneman and Lovallo, 1993). Since organizations promote successful people to positions of power and authority, rather than unsuccessful ones, it is the biases of success that are particularly relevant to decision making.

THE EXPLOITATION/EXPLORATION BALANCE

The elements of myopia detailed above are embedded in a broader problem for adaptive intelligence. Organizations divide attention and other resources between two broad kinds of activities (March, 1991). They engage in exploration – the pursuit of new knowledge, of things that might come to be known. And they engage in exploitation – the use and development of things already known. An organization that engages exclusively in exploration will ordinarily suffer from the fact that it never gains the returns of its knowledge. An organization that engages exclusively in exploitation will ordinarily suffer from obsolescence. The basic problem confronting an organization is to engage in sufficient exploitation to ensure its current viability and, at the same time, to devote enough energy to exploration to ensure its future viability. Survival requires a balance, and the precise mix of exploitation and exploration that is optimal is hard to specify.

Problems in maintaining a balance

Maintaining a balance between exploitation and exploration is complicated not only by the difficulty of determining what the appropriate balance should be, but also by several ways in which learning itself contributes to imbalances. Learning leads organizations into dynamics of accelerating exploitation or exploration, and learning makes negative as well as positive contributions to competitive position.

The traps of learning

Organizations become trapped in one or more of several dynamics of learning that self-destructively lead to excessive exploration or excessive exploitation. These dynamic distortions of the exploitation/exploration balance are not perverse. They stem from the same processes of adaptation that lead to effective matching of organizational behavior with environmental conditions (Hedberg et al., 1976). They are processes that involve short-term positive feedback on either exploration or exploitation and thus upset a balanced attention to both.

The failure trap

Sometimes exploration drives out exploitation. Organizations are turned into frenzies of experimentation, change, and innovation by a dynamic of failure. Failure leads to search and change which leads to failure which leads to more search, and so on. New ideas and technologies fail and are replaced by other new ideas and technologies, which fail in turn. This pathology is driven by three pervasive features of organizational life:

1. Most new ideas are bad ones, so most innovations are unrewarding.
2. The return from any particular innovation, technology, or reform is partly a function of an organization's experience with the new idea. Even successful innovations, when first introduced, are likely to perform poorly until experience has been accumulated in using them.
3. Aspirations adjust downward more slowly than they adjust upward and exhibit a consistent optimistic bias. (Lant, 1992)

These three features can trap an organization in an endless cycle of failure and unrewarding change. The cycle of exploration and the failure trap can be broken by the introduction of an exceptionally good alternative or the relatively rapid downward adjustment of aspirations, as might occur in a situation in which all organizations experience similar histories of failure.

The success trap

Sometimes exploitation drives out exploration. The returns to exploitation are ordinarily more certain, closer in time, and closer in space than are the returns to exploration (March, 1991). Exploratory experiments with new procedures or forms are likely to lead to poorer results in the short run, and the returns to exploration are likely to be greater for the organization, or a population of organizations, than for an individual.

Particularly with rapid rates of turnover of decision makers, the uncertain and distant returns associated with exploration are likely to have a high discount rate associated with them. Furthermore, past exploitation in a given domain makes future exploitation in the same domain even more efficient. As a result, organizations discover the short-term virtue of local refinement and the folly of exploration (Levinthal and March, 1981). As they develop greater and greater competence at a particular activity, they engage in that activity more, thus further increasing competence and the opportunity cost of exploration. This competency trap is a standard, potentially self-destructive product of learning. The trap can be broken by rapid upward adjustment of aspirations or by false feedback as to the high value of exploration, but it forms a powerful consequence of learning processes.

Learning and competitive advantage

There are two characteristic features of learning that are important to competitive advantage. The first is that learning generally increases average performance. More experienced and more extensively trained individuals or groups will generally do better than less experienced or less trained ones. The second feature of learning is that it generally increases reliability. More experienced and more extensively trained individuals and groups produce fewer surprises. Moreover, organizations accumulate experience across individuals. They use rules, procedures, and standard practices to ensure that the experiences of earlier individuals are transferred to newer members of the organization. This process of routinization is a powerful factor in converting collective experience into improved average performance. It is also a powerful influence on reliability and reduces the average amount of deviation from normative behavior as an individual or organization ages. Learning reduces variability.

Competitive advantage is clearly helped by the improved average performance that learning ordinarily offers. Indeed, this feature of learning makes it a prime contributor to competitive advantage. Improved reliability, on the other hand, is a mixed blessing from the point of view of competitive advantage. By increasing the reliability of individuals and organizations, learning tends to reduce exploratory deviation. When we ask whether individuals and organizations that learn will be selected by a competitive environment, we find that the answer is complicated. Competition can make reliability (and therefore learning) a disadvantage.

Consider the following simple model (March, 1991): Assume that survival is based on comparative performance within a group of competitors. Each single performance is a draw from a performance distribution specific to a particular individual or organization. The mean of the distribution reflects the individual's or organization's ability level and the variance reflects the individual's or organization's reliability. If position is based on a sample of performances that is very large, the relative positions of the competitors, and therefore their survival, are determined by relative abilities.

However, performance samples are often rather small. For small performance samples, relative position no longer depends exclusively on ability but is a joint consequence of ability and reliability. If the survival criterion is severe (i.e., only the very best survive), survival is heavily dependent on having a performance draw that is extreme. Thus, in such a case, improving average ability through learning helps relatively little, and increasing reliability (reducing variability) through learning hurts survival. If learning increases reliability substantially and a mean performance only a little (e.g., standardization, simplification) it is not good for competitive advantage when the number of competitors is large. Finishing first in a large field requires not just doing things well but doing something different and being lucky enough to have that particular deviation pay off.

It may be no accident that while experience (as reflected in years of prior work) and knowledge of standard beliefs (as reflected by success in school) are fair predictors of individual success in organizations on average, very conspicuous success in highly competitive situations is not closely related to either experience or knowledge as conventionally defined. Establishing preeminence involves exploration. Exploration is, on average, unfruitful, but it is the only way to finish first. Once a position of primacy is established by good fortune, it can be solidified and maintained for a reasonable period through exploitation. As learning exploits the gains that lucky ignorance produces, however, the advantage is very likely to be lost to some new fortunate exploratory behavior on the part of others.

Sustaining exploration

Although there are clear occasions on which organizations need to stimulate exploitation and restrain exploration, the more common situation is one in which exploitation tends to drive out exploration. This phenomenon has sometimes been explained as stemming from established firms not wishing to make their own products obsolete (Reinganum, 1989). The explanation suggested here is somewhat different. Learning processes are driven by experience. Exploitation generates clearer, earlier, and closer feedback than exploration. It corrects itself sooner and yields more positive returns in the near term. As a result, the primary challenge to sustaining an optimal mix of exploration and exploitation is the tendency of rapid learners and successful organizations to reduce the resources allocated to exploration. Proposed solutions to the problem of sustaining exploration ordinarily operate on either incentives, organizational structure, individual beliefs, or selection processes.

The role of incentives

The classic economic response to sustaining exploration is one of incentives (Reinganum, 1989). In particular, the assignment of property rights to successful search activity is a prime focus of economic analysis of innovative activity. The presumption is that monopoly rights to successful innovations provide an incentive for bearing the risks of innovative activity. Thus, organizations and societies encourage exploration by bestowing enormous rewards on those few individuals associated with successful explorations and by providing safety-nets for exploratory failures.

Instruments such as patents change the actual return associated with exploration and are assumed to encourage exploration. Bankruptcy laws and the use of "other people's money" in conjunction with the large rewards of a successful public offering, have been credited with fostering entrepreneurial activity in the United States. Organizations can offer similar incentive schemes. In general, however, organizational arrange-ments seem to be more effective in removing downside risks than in pro-viding extremely rich rewards for great success.

The role of organizational structure

Organizational structure can be used to strengthen exploration by under-mining the effectiveness of exploitation (Hedberg et al., 1976; Hedberg and Jönsson, 1978). Failures to recall past lessons, to implement past so-lutions, to communicate about current problems, or to exchange feed-back all contribute to inefficiency in refining current practice, thus to the development of experiments – all of them foolish, most of them distinctly unrewarding, but an occasional one or two containing the seeds of a new direction (March, 1988).

It should be observed, of course, that the distinction between exploita-tion and exploration becomes somewhat confounded by variations in per-spective. Effectively segregated exploitation, for example in new venture subunits (Burgelman, 1988), results in activities that contain considerable variation and exploration from the point of view of a higher organiza-tional level. The dangers of such a procedure are obvious. The expected return is modest, and the most likely outcome is not exploratory behavior but a variety of uncoordinated exploitation.

Organizations may also try to design structures that avoid excessive socialization of new members. In a socialization process, two things are happening at the same time: (1) The code of received knowledge is learning from the beliefs and practices of individuals. (2) Individuals are learning the code. In such a system of mutual adaptation, individuals "get ahead" by learning the code as rapidly as possible. The code, on the other hand, devel-ops by learning from individuals who deviate from the code in a useful way. Thus, there is a system-level, long-term advantage in slowing socialization to the code (so that the code can learn), but an individual-level, short-run advantage in speeding socialization (March, 1991). Organizational struc-tures that encourage rapid acculturation and socialization reduce the capa-bilities of the organization to learn from individual deviance.

The role of beliefs

Studies of risk taking suggest there are two major ways in which beliefs affect risk taking. The first is by influencing *risk preference*, the propen-sity to engage in apparently risky behavior. The second is by influencing *perceived risk*, the estimates that decision makers make about the riski-ness of the alternatives they consider. Organizations affect risk prefer-ences by influencing aspirations. They influence perceived risks by selecting and promoting individuals with particular experiences.

Influencing risk preference

Numerous studies of risk-taking behavior have indicated that risk taking is affected by the relation between current (or expected) outcomes and aspirations for them. Individuals who find themselves in the neighborhood of their aspiration levels tend to act in a more risk averse manner when they are above their aspiration levels than when they are below them. When operating below the aspiration level, individuals seem to increase risk taking as they fall further below the target until they approach (and focus on) a survival point, when they become distinctly risk averse. Above the aspiration level, risk taking seems to rise slowly with success. In general, therefore, exploratory behavior is associated with failure (until survival is in question) and with substantial success. Modest success is associated with risk aversion (MacCrimmon and Wehrung, 1986; March and Shapira, 1987).

Most of the time, learning keeps performance and aspirations fairly close together. Performance adjusts to aspirations; aspirations adjust to performance (March and Simon, 1993). This tendency to keep performance and aspirations close tends to keep a focus on exploitation, rather than exploration. Where aspirations are strictly self-referential (that is, where current aspirations are a mix between immediate past performance and immediate past aspiration), greater risk taking is associated with slower adaptation of aspiration levels and with slower improvement in performance. Slowly adjusting aspirations and performance allow performance and targets to diverge, tending on average to increase the taking of risky actions. On the other hand, where aspirations are tied to the performance of superior performers in a population, aspiration adjustment tends to make most actors fail and to take risks. In such a case, higher levels of risk taking are associated with those who learn slowly how to improve performance and learn rapidly to aspire for the performance of superior others (Lopes, 1987; March and Shapira, 1992).

Influencing perceived risk

One way of producing more exploratory behavior is through ignorance, through misperception of its risks. Successful organizations build a "can do" attitude. This "can do" attitude is likely to be especially prevalent in young, high growth organizations where the experience of managers leads them to believe they know the secrets of beating the odds. Successful managers (and the journalists and folk-story artists who record their stories) tend to underestimate the risk they have experienced and the risk they currently face, and intentionally risk-averse decision makers may actually be risk seeking in behavior.

This inducement of risk underestimation may, of course, be useful for the organization or for the population of organizations. On the one hand, it is a way of compensating for the negative effects of success on risk taking. On the other hand, it is a way of inducing the individually self-sacrificing risk taking that serves the organization and the larger society. In situations in which risks must be taken in order to be successful, most overconfident individuals and organizations will undoubtedly perish to the risks they unwittingly face. But only the overconfident will ever be heroes. Actors in high performance, quick decision, high risk professions all share a common professional stereotype of being unusually confident. Overconfidence often leads to disaster, but in some situations organizations or populations of organizations profit from the individual foolishness that unwarranted self-confidence provides.

The role of internal selection

Organizations promote individuals with experiences that make them confident of their own abilities and of the relevance of those abilities to organizational outcomes. Suppose every outcome that is experienced is a joint consequence of something that might be called "capability" and something that might be called "luck." Across a population of learners whom luck neither favors nor disfavors, there will be no systematic bias in the experience of good fortune. However, if we partition the population into two groups on the basis of relative success, the sample of relatively unsuccessful people will have drawn a set of past experiences that was, on average, less favorable than they should expect in the future. Conversely, the sample of relatively successful people will have drawn a set of experiences that was, on average, more favorable than they should expect in the future.

The selection practices of organizations typically over-sample successful people. That is, indeed, their intention. People who have been successful in the past are retained and promoted to greater influence. People who have been unsuccessful in the past are removed or demoted to positions of lesser influence. The learning consequence is that organizations systematically under-sample failure. High level managers are likely to anticipate a better world than they will experience, to assume that they are running fewer risks than they actually are, and to expect that they can control their destinies more than they actually can.

In short, their past successes give executives an illusion of control (Langer, 1975). Their experience makes them confident in their ability to handle future events, leads them to believe strongly in their wisdom and insight (Einhorn and Hogarth, 1978). They have difficulty in recognizing the role of luck in their achievements. These illusions are furthered by organizational folklore. In addition to promoting successful people, organizations actively foster beliefs in the control exercised by managers. There is sample selection bias in the stories told of past exploration efforts. Efforts associated with successful outcomes tend to be more popular stories. Those stories focus on the successful outcome as if it were an inevitable outcome of individual and organizational actions, ignoring many likely (but not experienced) paths toward failure.

LEARNING AND STRATEGIC MANAGEMENT

Strategic management is the art of dealing intelligently with three grand problems of decision making:

1. The problem of *ignorance* – uncertainty about the future and the past and the causal structure of the world.
2. The problem of *conflict* – multiple-nested actors confronting multiple-nested time perspectives with preferences and identities that are inconsistent across individuals and across time.
3. The problem of *ambiguity* – lack of clarity, instability, and endogeneity in preference and identitities.

Human imagination seems capable of providing only rather restricted, incomplete "solutions" to any of these problems. Each succeeding metaphor for strategic management has been found to have flaws.

Organizational learning is no exception. Designing organizations to learn from experience and to exploit the knowledge of others is possible, and such designs are major contributions to organizational intelligence. But closer examination of learning as a route to intelligence suggests that learning is less than a panacea for organizations. The contributions of learning to intelligence are constrained by three major problems of myopia:

1. *Temporal myopia.* Learning tends to sacrifice the long run to the short run. Effective learning requires exploration, but the difficulty of sustaining exploratory behavior is a problem that is accentuated, rather then relieved, by learning. As learning develops distinctive competencies and niches, it simultaneously compromises capabilities outside those competencies and niches. When conditions change, the learned skills become impediments. There is, of course, no assurance that the organizational problem is solvable. An organization cannot survive in the long run unless it survives in each of the short runs along the way, and strategies that permit short-run survival tend to increase long-run vulnerability. A possible option for individuals or sources of capital is to move in and out of organizations as entrepreneurs, leaving others to experience their decline, but this may be scant comfort to those who suffer the fate of the specific organization.

2. *Spatial myopia.* Learning tends to favor effects that occur near to the learner. The "social welfare" aspects of the distribution of the effects of learning over space make strategic management itself problematic. In particular, the contribution of component self-destruction to system endurance poses a problem. Most students of strategic management have little difficulty in subordinating the interests of individuals and subunits in an organization to the interests of the organization. The focus their attention on maintaining the survival of the firm or other organization and recommend policies of reorganization and restructuring that seriously compromise the prosperity and survival of components of the organization. By extension, we might anticipate that students of strategic management would similarly favor survival of the firm over the interests of larger systems of which the firm is a component (at least until hired by the larger system). The conflict is illustrated in contemporary politics by the contrast between advocates of free competitive markets and advocates of current businesses. The latter (like students of strategic management) seek to support existing firms in their struggle for survival; the former seek to strengthen the selective pressures of the environment.

3. *Failure myopia.* Organizational learning oversamples successes and undersamples failures. Any learning process tends to eliminate failures, and this tendency is accentuated by the way learning produces confidence and confidence produces favorable anticipations and interpretations of outcomes. The undersampling of failures is also a consequence of organizational selection processes. Organizations promote successful people. On average, successful people have drawn experiences that have been more favorable than they should expect to continue, and unsuccessful people have drawn experiences that have been less favorable than they should expect in the future. Learning does not easily correct for these biases in experience. Since these elements of over-confidence may be necessary to overcome the learning pressures toward exploitation, they may actually be useful in sustaining exploration.

All of these elements of myopia compromise the effectiveness of learning. In particular, they complicate the problem of maintaining an appropriate balance between exploitation and exploration. For the most part, they lead learning organizations to have difficulty in sustaining adequate exploration. The imperfections of learning are not bases for abandoning attempts to improve the learning capabilities of organizations, but they suggest a certain conservatism in expectations. Conservative expectations, of course, will not always enhance the selling of learning procedures to strategic managers, but they may provide a constructive basis for a realistic evaluation and elaboration of the role of learning in organizational intelligence. Magic would be nice, but it is not easy to find.

Acknowledgments

The research has been supported by the Spencer Foundation, the Scandinavian Consortium for Organizational Research, the Stanford Graduate School of Business, and the Sol C. Snider Entrepreneurial Center at the Wharton School, University of Pennsylvania

References

Abernathy, W. J. and K. Wayne (1974). "Limits of the learning curve," *Harvard Business Review*, 52, pp. 109–19.

Argote, L., S. L. Beckman and D. Epple (1990). "The persistence and transfer of learning in industrial settings," *Management Science*, 36, pp. 140–54.

Argyris, C. and D. Schön (1978). *Organizational Learning*. Addison-Wesley, Reading, MA.

Björkman, I. (1989). *Foreign Direct Investments: An Empirical Analysis of Decision Making in Seven Finnish Firms*. Svenska Handelhögskolan, Helsinki.

Boeker, W. (1989). "The development and institutionalization of subunit power in organizations," *Administrative Science Quarterly*, 34, pp. 388–410.

Bower, J. L. and T. M. Hout (1988). "Fast-cycle capability for competitive power," *Harvard Business Review*, 66, pp. 110–18.

Brehmer, B. (1980). "In one word: Not from experience," *Acta Psychologica*, 45, pp. 223–41.

Burgelman, R. A. (1988). "Strategy-making as a social learning process: The case of internal corporate venturing," *Interfaces*, 18, pp. 74–85.

Burgelman, R. A. (1990). "Strategy-making and organizational ecology: A conceptual framework." In J. V. Singh (ed.), *Organizational Evolution*. Sage Publications, Newbury Park, CA, pp. 164–81.

Chandler, A. (1962). *Strategy and Structure*. MIT Press, Cambridge, MA.

Cohen, W. M. and D. A. Levinthal (1989). "Innovation and learning: The two faces of R&D," *Economic Journal*, 99, pp. 569–90.

Cohen, W. M. and D. A. Levinthal (1990). "Absorptive capacity: A new perspective on learning and innovation," *Administrative Science Quarterly*, 35, pp. 128–52.

Cohen, W. M. and D. A. Levinthal (1994). "Fortune favors the prepared firm," *Management Science*, 40, pp. 227–51.

Cross, J. G. (1983). *A Theory of Adaptive Economic Behavior*. Cambridge University Press, New York.

Cyert, R. M. and J. G. March (1992). *A Behavioral Theory of the Firm* (2nd edn). Blackwell, Oxford.

David, P. A. (1985). "Clio and the economics of QWERTY," *American Economic Review*, 75, pp. 332–7.

Deutsch, K. W. (1966). *Nerves of Government*. Free Press, New York.

Dierickx, I. and K. Cool (1989). "Asset stock accumulation and sustainability of competitive advantage," *Manage-*

ment Science, 35, pp. 1504–11.

Einhorn, H. and R. Hogarth (1978). "Confidence in judgment: Persistence in the illusion of validity," *Psychological Review*, 85, pp. 395–416.

Feldman, M. S. (1989). *Order without Design: Information Production and Policy Making*. Stanford University Press, Stanford, CA.

Fischhoff, B. (1980). "For those condemned to study the past: Reflections on historical judgment." In R. A. Shweder and D. W. Fiske (eds), *New Directions for Methodology of Behavioral Science*. Jossey-Bass, San Francisco, CA, pp. 79–93.

Gulick, L. H. and L. Urwick (eds) (1937). *Papers on the Science of Administration*. Columbia University Institute of Public Administration, New York.

Hannan, M. T. and J. Freeman (1984). "Structural inertia and organizational change," *American Sociological Review*, 49, pp. 149–64.

Hedberg, B. L. T., P. C. Nystrom and W. H. Starbuck (1976). "Camping on seesaws: Prescriptions for a self-designing organization," *Administrative Science Quarterly*, 21, pp. 41–65.

Hedberg, B. L. T. and S. Jönsson (1978). "Designing semi-confusing information systems for organizations in changing environments," *Accounting, Organizations and Society*, 3, pp. 47–64.

Herriott, S. R., D. A. Levinthal and J. G. March (1985). "Learning from experience in organizations," *American Economic Review*, 75, pp. 298–302.

Hirschman, A. O. (1970). *Exit, Voice and Loyalty*. Harvard University Press, Cambridge, MA.

Jones, J. W. and R. McLeod, Jr (1986). "The structure of executive information systems: An exploratory analy-

sis," *Decision Sciences*, 17, pp. 220–49.

Kahneman, D. and D. Lovallo (1993). "Timid choices and bold forecasts: A cognitive perspective on risk taking," *Management Science*, 39, pp. 17–31.

Keen, P. and M. S. Morton (1978). *Decision Support Systems: An Organizational Perspective*. Addison-Wesley, Reading, MA.

Kuhn, T. S. (1970). *The Structure of Scientific Revolutions*. University of Chicago Press, Chicago, IL.

Langer, E. J. (1975). "The illusion of control," *Journal of Personality and Social Psychology*, 32, pp. 311–28.

Lant, T. K. (1992). "Aspiration level adaptation: An empirical exploration," *Management Science*, 38, pp. 623–44.

Lave, C. A. and J. G. March (1993). *An Introduction to Models in the Social Sciences* (2nd edn). University Press of America, Lanham, MD.

Levinthal, D. A. and J. G. March (1981). "A model of adaptive organizational search," *Journal of Economic Behavior and Organization*, 2, pp. 307–33.

Levitt, B. and J. G. March (1988). "Organizational learning," *Annual Review of Sociology*, 14, pp. 319–40.

Lopes, L. L. (1987). "Between hope and fear: The psychology of risk," *Advances in Social Psychology*, 20, pp. 255–95.

Lorange, P. (1980). *Corporate Planning*. Prentice Hall, Englewood Cliffs, N.J.

Lounamaa, P. and J. G. March (1987). "Adaptive coordination of a learning team," *Management Science*, 33, pp. 107–23.

Lucas, R. E. (1988). "On the mechanics of economic development," *Journal of Political Economy*, 22, pp. 3–42.

MacCrimmon, K. R. and D. A. Wehrung (1986). *Taking Risks: The Management of Uncertainty.* Free Press, New York.

March, J. G. (1988). *Decisions and Organizations.* Blackwell, Oxford.

March, J. G. (1991). "Exploration and exploitation in organizational learning," *Organization Science*, 2, pp. 71–87.

March, J. G. (1994). "The evolution of evolution." In. J. Baum and J. V. Singh (eds), *The Evolutionary Dynamics of Organizations.* Oxford University Press, New York, pp. 39–49.

March, J. G. and J. P. Olsen (1989). *Rediscovering Institutions: The Organizational Basis of Politics.* Free Press, New York.

March, J. G. and Z. Shapira (1987). "Managerial perspectives on risk and risk taking," *Management Science*, 33, pp. 1404–18.

March, J. G. and Z. Shapira (1992). "Variable risk preferences and the focus of attention," *Psychological Review*, 99, pp. 172–83.

March, J. G. and H. A. Simon (1993). *Organizations.* Blackwell, Oxford.

March, J. G., L. S. Sproull and M. Tamuz (1991). "Learning from samples of one or fewer," *Organization Science*, 2, pp. 1–13.

Miller, D. T. and M. Ross (1975). "Self-serving biases in the attribution of causality," *Psychological Bulletin*, 82, pp. 213–25.

Ostroff, F. and D. Smith (1992). "The horizontal organization," *McKinsey Quarterly*, 1, pp. 148–68.

Prahalad, C. K. and G. Hamel (1990). "The core competence of corporation," *Harvard Business Review*, 68, pp. 79–91.

Reinganum, J. J. (1989). "The timing of innovation: Research, development, and diffusion." In R. Schmalensee and R. D. Willig (eds), *Handbook of Industrial Organization.* North-Holland, New York, pp. 849–908.

Romer, P. M. (1986). "Increasing returns and long-run growth," *Journal of Political Economy*, 94, pp. 1002–36.

Sagan, S. D. (1993). *The Limits of Safety: Organizations, Accidents, and Nuclear Weapons.* Princeton University Press, Princeton, NJ.

Schelling, T. C. (1960). *The Strategy of Conflict.* Oxford University Press, New York.

Schonberger, R. J. (1990). *Building a Chain of Customers.* Free Press, New York.

Senge, P. M. (1990). *The Fifth Discipline: The Art and Practice of the Learning Organization.* Doubleday, New York.

Stalk, G., P. Evans and L. E. Shulman (1992). "Competing on capabilities: The new rules of corporate strategy," *Harvard Business Review*, 70, pp. 57–69.

Starbuck, W. H. (1983). "Organizations as action generators," *American Sociological Review*, 48, pp. 91–102.

Thompson, J. D. (1967). *Organizations in Action.* McGraw-Hill, New York.

Udayagiri, N. D. and S. Balakrishnan (1993). "Learning curves and knowledge spillovers: The case of semiconductor memories." Jones Center Working Paper, Wharton School, University of Pennsylvania.

Weick, K. (1979). *The Social Psychology of Organizing* (2nd edn). Addison-Wesley, Reading, MA.

Yelle, L. E. (1979). "The learning curve: Historical review and comprehensive survey," *Decision Sciences*, 10, pp 302–28.

PART THREE

Risk Taking in Organizations

CHAPTER TWELVE

Wild Ideas: The Catechism of Heresy

Most dramatically heretical imaginations are wrong, and it is impossible to distinguish the many novel wild ideas that are wrong from the few that are the bases of genius except through subsequent judgments of history. As a result, it generally makes sense for any one individual to avoid wild ideas until they are tested by others; but the individual imperative to avoid wild ideas flies in the face of the collective imperative to stimulate them. Society sustains the altruistic pursuit of crazy ideas by individuals through incentives, illusions of efficacy, and obligations associated with personal identities.

George Bernard Shaw wrote that a genius is "a person who, seeing farther and probing deeper than other people, has a different set of ethical valuations from theirs, and has energy enough to give effect to this extra vision and its valuations."

Great historical leaders – Gandhi, Bismarck, Elizabeth I, Napoleon, Alexander the Great, Mao Tse-tung, Luther – are such people. We honor them as visionaries, as people who had a special talent for seeing beyond the self-evident.

Great writers, great artists, and great scientists are similar individuals of vision. Baudelaire, Van Gogh, and Darwin saw farther and probed deeper than others. They challenged established beliefs with new ideas that transformed our understandings.

Great visionary leaders of modern business organizations – Carnegie, Ford, Sloan, Hewlett, Packard – likewise saw farther and probed deeper. Their questioning of received organizational and business doctrine led to new forms of business organization and manufacturing procedures.

Memories of such giants induce us to seek similar genius in contemporary leaders. We look for people who have something special – some kind of vision, new ideas, new dreams – to offer. But we usually don't find it: Most current leaders seem to be competent and analytical rather than imaginative and visionary. They seek to refine the establishment rather than challenge it or transform it.

Our disappointment in the blandness and reliability of modern leaders is understandable, but it may also be misleading. If it were easy to identify visionary genius, we would embrace it without hesitation. Unfortunately, the difference between visionary genius and delusional madness is much clearer in history books than in experience.

Without the advantages of retrospection, what we see are deviants – heretics, fools, and eccentrics. We cannot reliably identify the geniuses among them until that quality of genius emerges in the unfolding of history.

If crazy ideas often turned out to be good ones, we would have little problem. We could bear the few mistakes as a minor cost. The elementary dilemma is that although new, deviant ideas are essential to improvement, most of the dramatically imaginative ideas turn out to be bad ones. We recognize this in our children. When a child, noticing the visual beauty of fire, tries to experience how fire feels to the touch, or how it tastes, the idea is unquestionably imaginative – but unambiguously unwise.

Likewise, the wild ideas of political crackpots, religious heretics, crazy artists, mad scientists, and organizational dreamers are overwhelmingly foolish, rather than brilliant. Only a tiny fraction of our heretics will ever be canonized, and we cannot identify the saints ahead of time.

Society cannot support unbridled foolishness; without considerable talent for conventional thinking, leadership fails. At the same time, society needs processes that induce and sustain the craziness of wild ideas. It needs to stimulate and protect heresy. Although the overwhelming majority of heretical leaders are not geniuses, we need substantial numbers of crazy leaders in order to have an occasional leader who does turn out to be a visionary genius.

Since most new ideas will not pay off, it is, on average, unwise to have wild ideas. Most of the time their expected costs far exceed their expected benefits. Thus, a sensible person avoids them, and society relies on foolishness to generate them.

So, we have a catechism of visionary leadership:

- Most heretical leaders are fools or worse, but it is impossible to distinguish (a priori) between foolish heretics and visionary ones.
- It is ordinarily more sensible to adopt new ideas through imitation of successful heresies rather than through experimentation with new ones, but if everyone adopts such a strategy, there is no testing of possible visions.

- The ways new visions are evaluated and implemented tend to inhibit heretics, and the ways visionaries are encouraged tend to inhibit effective evaluation.

How, then, do we encourage foolish visionaries? The standard answer is that we should provide incentives for heresy and genius. The most obvious way is to reward *successful* foolishness richly. This is the intent of patent laws and of other systems that offer exceptional compensation for those few wild ideas that turn out to be right.

But if we reward only the successes, relatively few people will ever be rewarded. So most efforts to provide incentives for heresy should supplement rewards for success with rewards for interesting failures.

For example, I once had a student who was an apprentice teacher in a middle school. She reported hearing a teacher tell her class, "To add two fractions, you add the numerator of the first fraction to the numerator of the second; that becomes the numerator of the sum. Then you add the two denominators to get the denominator of the sum."

The error is certainly egregious, but the teacher was not just acting randomly. She was trying to imagine a solution to a problem for which she did not have an answer. Her imagination failed her, but perhaps she should be rewarded for the quality of her failure.

One of the errors we often make as parents, teachers, or managers is failing to see the imagination involved in a mistake, and thus failing to reward interesting failures. We don't want to reward mistakes, but we should reward the imagination that sometimes leads to them.

A second way to encourage visionary foolishness is through illusions of efficacy, that is, by creating the myth that being a visionary pays off. How do we do this? We tell stories of heretics who turned out to be right, thus encouraging a biased estimate of the likelihood of that outcome. We promote successful deviants to higher positions and elaborate stories of their successes to suggest that they were geniuses (rather than somewhat lucky fools). We surround leaders with people who reassure them that they are doing the right thing, that they have great ideas, that their heresies have been, and will continue to be, brilliant. We invite only the successful visionaries to speak to our business students, thus exaggerating the likelihood of their own successes.

Illusions of efficacy can motivate heresy, but creating illusions is risky business. They tend to evaporate in the real world, and disillusionment quickly becomes cynicism.

A third way heresy is facilitated is through seeing our behavior as driven by obligations rather than by the likelihood of great consequences. What I do is not what I want to do, not what will lead to particular consequences – but what I must do.

The rules of obligation are different from the rules of consequence. In a consequential logic, a person is "in touch with reality" and asks, What are my alternatives? What are the probable consequences of those alternatives? What are the values to me of those probable consequences? Then the person selects the alternative whose consequences he or she values the most.

In an obligatory logic, a person is "in touch with self" and asks, What kind of situation is this? What kind of person am I? What does a person such as I do in a situation such as this?

Even in a society as captivated by consequential logic as our own, obligatory logics are common. Parents do what parents should do. Accountants do what accountants should do. Managers do what managers should do. A new employee in an organization is substantially more likely to ask questions about appropriate behavior than about optimal behavior.

A visionary leader who follows an obligatory logic is not affected by evidence that his actions are foolish or ineffective. Don Quixote saw himself as a knight-errant; as a knight-errant, he had to do all the things that knight-errants are expected to do: defend maidens, contest giants, protect the weak. Because the consequences of his actions were not relevant to him in the same way they might be to most of us, Don Quixote sustained his vision against the "realism" of others around him until they came to see the genius in it.

These three sources of foolishness – rewards for wild ideas, illusions of efficacy, and a sense of obligation – sustain a visionary greatness and leadership. If we reward wild ideas, we will have wild ideas; but most of those ideas will be foolish, and some will be dangerous. If we create illusions of efficacy, we will sustain great actions; but most of those actions will be unsuccessful, and some will be disastrous. If we encourage obligatory logics of action, many of the things people do will be misguided, and some will be horrendous.

The dilemma is real. Society needs visionaries; it does not need maniacs. But it cannot have the former without the latter. It is not a new problem. It is not one that will be solved. It is, however, ameliorated by a consciousness that leadership demands a continual dialectic between vision and reality, between foolishness and reason. And among educated, intelligent, experienced people – the people who run the world and read this book – sustaining that dialectic usually means strengthening the protections for craziness against the powerful demands of sanity.

CHAPTER THIRTEEN

Variable Risk Preferences and Adaptive Aspirations*

Observations of human decision making indicate that risk prefer-ences depend on the values of possible outcomes relative to levels of aspiration. A model of such variable risk preferences is specified. It suggests that some risk averse behavior may result from a human tendency to focus on targets and from the adaptation of those targets to experience rather than from a fixed trait of risk aversion. In addi-tion, the model shows how risk preferences varying around adaptive aspirations produce both a greater long-run likelihood of survival and a higher average return for survivors than do fixed risk prefer-ences.

OBSERVATIONS OF RISK PREFERENCES

In modern treatments of rational choice, it is usually imagined that pref-erences among alternatives (at any level of expected return) vary with riskiness. Risk aversion is generally assumed in the formal literature on decision theory (Friedman and Savage, 1948; Arrow, 1971), where it is typically defined as a concavity in the utility for monetary (or other) re-turn, and in analyses of organizational decision making (Cyert and March, 1963), where it is sometimes called uncertainty avoidance. Most studies indicate, however, that risk preference is not fixed, but depends on the context of a choice. This point is recognized in formal theories of risk by attention to the interdependence of asset level and the degree of risk aver-sion (Pratt, 1964; Arrow, 1965), but its implications for the intuitive idea of risk preference are often overlooked. The empirical data are generally consistent. Given a choice between two alternatives of equal expected return in an experimental setting, human subjects are more likely to select the riskier alternative if the outcomes involve losses (or are below some target or aspiration level) than they are if the outcomes involve gains or are above some target or aspiration level (Tversky and Kahneman, 1974; Kuhl, 1978; Kahneman and Tversky, 1979). The strict reflection around zero has been questioned, but primarily in the name of more complicated contextual factors or in the name of reflections defined around an aspiration level (Hershey and Schoemaker, 1980; Schneider and Lopes, 1986). The general result has been confirmed using a wide variety of experimental subjects, including business executives (Laughhann et al., 1980, Payne et al., 1981), and in somewhat different form in experimental studies of portfolio decisions (Gordon et al., 1972).

Similar empirical results are obtained from observations in non-experimental settings. Friend and Blume (1975) found well-to-do households to be particularly risk-averse. Swalm (1966) studied the revealed utilities of 13 decision makers in business enterprises. Most of them appear to be risk averse with gains above zero and risk seeking below. Fishburn (1977) reports studies by Halter and Dean and Grayson that give a generally similar picture, but include some contrary data. Using aggregate stock market data, Mezias (1988) has inferred individual investor preference functions that are concave above a reference point defined in terms of expectations and convex below. Studies of race track betting (Snyder, 1978) show a negative correlation between risk and return, a result that has sometimes been attributed to a risk-seeking trait, but also to "the common phenomenon that bettors, when losing, tend to bet more and more on longer odds horses" (Hausch et al., 1981, p. 1438). Bowman (1980, 1982) found that risk and return were negatively correlated across industries and argued that firms in danger of failing are more likely to enter risky ventures. MacCrimmon and Wehrung (1986) and March and Shapira (1987) found that managers believe fewer risks will be taken when things are going well. Santalainen and Tainio (1985) and Singh (1986) report that poorly performing firms make riskier choices than do firms performing well, and Mayhew (1979) found a similar phenomenon among colleges. Firms in industries with a prior history of low profitability appear to be more likely to engage in behavior that is illegal than are firms in more profitable industries (Lane, 1953; Staw and Szwajkowski, 1975; Asch and Seneca, 1976). Ethnographic studies of fishermen (Acheson, 1981) and farmers (Johnson, 1971; Bartlett, 1980) describe a relation between risk-taking and success that is similar. Since most of these studies are cross-sectional in design, they do not decisively reject the possibility that the variation in risk taking across organizations stems from stable differences among the organizations (e.g., in their ability to assess risk) that also produce differences in their successes, but the studies support a general view that risk taking is related to the context of adversity.

The results from observations of human decision makers have parallels in observations of insects and birds. Risk averse behavior is commonly reported (Real, 1981; Waddington et al., 1981); but when energy needs are manipulated, variable risk preferences are observed, at least among the small, granivorous birds with whom such experiments have been run. Situations in which the mean rate of food available is below energy expenditures lead to risk prone behavior, while risk averse behavior is observed where there is a positive energy balance (Caracao and Lima, 1985). Kamil and Roitblat (1985) suggest that a similar argument might explain the observations (Leventhal et al., 1959) of variations in risk proneness as a function of mean number of food pellets offered to rats in a standard learning experiment. However, Battalio et al. (1985) did not find risk aversion varying with energy needs (among the six rats they studied) given a choice between eight pellets with certainty and a lottery offering one pellet with probability 0.75 and 29 pellets with probability 0.25.

Such empirical reports of variation in risk preference fit naturally into three related traditions in the behavioral study of decision making. The first tradition emphasizes survival as a criterion for decision making by individuals and organizations, thus tends either to define the objective function for rational action as maximizing the likelihood of survival or maximizing expected value subject to a survival constraint (Maynard Smith, 1978; Gordon, 1985; Karni and Schmeidler, 1986), to consider issues of "safety" as central to organizational decision making (Roy, 1952; Day et al., 1971), or to see variation and selection as modifying the distribution of decision structures or rules through differential survival of those that are comparatively well-adapted (Hannan and Freeman, 1977; Aldrich, 1979; Nelson and Winter, 1982).

The second tradition focuses on the importance of targets in directing attention, thus the significance of the level of subjective success (or expected success) for search behavior (Simon, 1955; March and Simon, 1958; Radner, 1975a, 1975b) and learning (Day, 1967; Levinthal and March, 1981; Herriot et al., 1985). The ideas are an amalgam of the notion that levels of attention and search are affected by a subjective sense of how well the decision maker is doing, and the notion that decision makers partition outcomes into a small number of classes, at the limit into two – "success" and "failure." Such a perspective has typified explorations of organizational slack as a factor in decision making (Cyert and March, 1963; Singh, 1986), the development of semi-variance models of risk in financial decision making (Hogan and Warren, 1974; Fishburn, 1977; Holthausen, 1981), some discussions of risk taking in the psychological literature (Lopes, 1984, 1987), and studies of managerial perspectives on risk (MacCrimmon and Wehrung, 1986; March and Shapira, 1987). The ideas are closely related to considerations of framing in decision making, particularly of the "mental accounting" by which decision makers define subjective success.

The third tradition sees the definition of "success" as changing over time (Leventhal et al., 1959; Kuhl and Blankenship, 1979), in particular in response to experience. The idea that aspiration levels are responsive to the results of search or performance is an important feature of theories of organizational decision making, as are the dynamics of the interrelation between changing aspirations and changing outcomes (March and Simon, 1958; Cyert and March, 1963); and such adaptive aspirations have long been recognized as significant to understanding subjective utility and choice behavior (Siegel, 1957). These ideas suggest that an understanding of variable risk preferences will require not only making preferences for risk dependent on a target, but also making the target itself a function of experience.

A Model of Variable Risk Preferences

As a model of variable risk preferences, consider a simple random walk in which risk preference is a function of the current resources (e.g., wealth, reputation, earnings) of a decision maker relative to an aspiration level. In such a formulation, we imagine that each decision maker begins with a stake, that accumulated resources are increased or decreased as a result of the outcomes of choices among alternatives of equal expected value but varying risk, that the greater the accumulated resources relative to an aspiration level, the more favorable the decision context (and thus the more risk averse the choice), that negative position constitutes ruin and is absorbing, and that aspirations adapt in the direction of the realized position.

Specifically, we assume:

1. *Sequential sampling random walk.* Each decision maker begins with an initial stake, W^*, that is the same for all decision makers. Each decision maker makes a series of decisions, choosing at each of T steps from among a set of alternatives, each characterized in terms of a known probability distribution over returns. The realized gains or losses at each step are accumulated over time to produce cumulated wealth W_{it}, up to each step, t, where $W_{i0} = W^*$, for each individual i.
2. An *absorbing barrier.* If the cumulated wealth of a decision maker reaches zero during the course of the process (i.e., if the initial stake is exhausted), that decision maker is eliminated. Thus, the process has an absorbing barrier at 0, and is equivalent to a game played with a stake of W^* against an opponent with infinite resources (Feller, 1968).
3. *Replacement.* Whenever a decision maker is eliminated from the proc-

ess, another decision maker enters the process with an initial stake equal to W^*.

4. *Equal expected return.* The expected returns of the alternatives available to a decision maker at any particular step are all equal, thus there is no expected return basis for choice. This assumption can be viewed as an assumption that the expected return to be realized from an alternative is captured by its price.

5. *Variable risk preference.* A decision maker's preferred risk varies inversely with that decision maker's cumulated resources, or wealth, W_{it}. The larger the resources relative to a target, A_{it}, the smaller the most preferred risk.

6. *Risk availability.* An alternative with a risk equal to a decision maker's most preferred risk is available and is selected at each step.

7. *Adaptive aspirations.* A_{it} is initially equal to the initial stake, W^*. Over time it increases when W_{it} increases, declines when W_{it} declines.

The process requires that we specify an explicit function for the relation between cumulated resources and preferred risk, and for changes in aspirations. Among the large number of possible preferred risk functions that might be considered, a simple family of functions that has the desired properties is

$$R_{it} = \beta(A_{it}/W_{it}) \tag{13.1}$$

where R_{it} is some measure of variation in the probability distribution over returns for decision maker i at time t, thus the risk. In one interpretation, R_{it} can be seen as the "bet size" in a fair game with unit variance, or as the standard deviation of the chosen alternative from a collection of alternatives with equal expected values but varying risk. The intention, however, is to allow R_{it} to be any measure of variation defined on the outcome distribution (e.g., Lopes, 1984). Note that (13.1) defines preferred risk as a function of current resource level, given an aspiration level. It is not a utility function. The parameter β can be seen as a scale factor for risk. Since variations in β produce variations in R_{it} and affect the outcomes due to risk taking that are discussed below, it would be possible to explore the relative effects of variations in β and variations in the other parameters of the model. In the present chapter, however, β is treated as a fixed feature of the risk environment. All of the analyses assume a given β.

The target, or aspiration, level for wealth is assumed to change over time, adapting to the level of wealth actually achieved. We assume that $A_{i,1} = W^*$, the initial stake, for all i. Thereafter,

$$A_{i,t+1} = aW_{it} + (1 - a)A_{it} \tag{13.2}$$
$$0 < a < 1.$$

This function is a standard one (Levinthal and March, 1981; Lant, 1987) and makes the aspiration level an exponentially weighted moving average of experienced wealth. The analysis below focuses primarily on the effects of variations in a, which can be viewed as susceptible to change either through strategic control or long term learning.

The model includes two special cases of particular interest. The first case is the case of fixed aspiration level. If $a = 0$, then the initial stake remains the aspiration level over time. This is the case normally considered in semi-variance models of risk in financial decisions (Hogan and Warren, 1974; Fishburn, 1977), in some interpretations of cross-sectional variations in risk taking behavior (Kunreuther and Wright, 1979; Lopes, 1984), and in other models in which targets are seen as stable exogenous properties of decision makers. The second case is the case of fixed risk preferences. If $a = 1$, then aspirations adapt immediately to experience and preferred risk is fixed at β. This is the case considered in classical analyses of ruin (Feller, 1968).

GENERAL PROPERTIES OF THE PROCESS

For the fixed aspiration level case ($a = 0$), the process can be described in terms of a sequence of entering cohorts. The size of an entering cohort is determined by the number of vacancies in the population, thus by the number of exits from previous cohorts. Each entering cohort consists of a group of individual decision makers, each with the same stake, and the same preferred risk, β. As a result of the sequential realizations of the process, each individual within a cohort gains or loses. The joint distribution of accumulated wealth and aspirations for wealth in the cohort determines the distribution of preferred risks and the ruin rate in a particular time period. Those who accumulate losses become more risk prone; those who accumulate gains become more risk averse. Those with losses equal to or exceeding the initial stake are ruined and leave. Gradually, the distribution of accumulated wealth in the cohort becomes narrower and the average becomes higher. Losers are eliminated; winners become more and more risk averse; the ruin rate approaches zero. If the only source of turnover is ruin, a cohort approaches a stable size as time continues on indefinitely.

The population at any point is a collection of cohorts of varying ages. The expected distribution of wealth for a cohort at any particular cohort age (i.e., time since entry) is the same for each cohort and depends on the initial stake and the aspiration adaptation rate, as well as the scale (β) of risk taking. The sum over those cohort distributions produces the population distribution of wealth. With a fixed population size and exit produced only through ruin, the time eventually comes when all positions in the population are occupied by members of cohorts who are unlikely to experience ruin and who have a nearly stable distribution of wealth. The system as a whole becomes stable, with entries and exits approaching zero and with only modest changes in wealth. If exit is also produced by a death rate unrelated to current wealth (e.g., a maximum life), the system finds an equilibrium that maintains the population, and that keeps both the distribution of wealth and the ruin rate constant. An equilibrium ruin rate is achieved when the size of each entering cohort is equal to the combined ruin and death rates generated by a population of cohorts of that size ranging in ages from 1 to the maximum life. At that point, both the ruin rate and the wealth distribution are stable.

Because of these properties of the process, along with its relative slowness, any analysis must involve an exploration both of the equilibrium properties of the process and of the time paths by which equilibrium is achieved. As a result, the discussions below sometimes consider the shorter-run time paths, sometimes the long-run equilibria. Shorter-run analyses seem most appropriate for investigating the behavioral implications of the model, as in the next two sections. Longer-run outcomes become more appropriate for evaluating various risk taking strategies, as in the section following these.

BEHAVIORAL IMPLICATIONS OF VARIABLE RISK PREFERENCES

Variable risk preferences associated with deviations from a (possibly adaptive) performance target lead to choice behavior different from that produced by fixed risk preferences. In this section, a few implications of variable risk preferences with fixed aspirations are examined. In the following section, the consequences of adaptive aspirations are considered.

Risk and return

Some studies of the aggregate relation between risk and return indicate that risk and return are positively correlated in the stock market (Jensen, 1972; Fama and MacBeth, 1973), though the result seems to hold more strongly within an industry than across industries. Since (at least within decision theory) risk averse decision makers will choose relatively high risk alternatives only if they also offer relatively high expected values, the positive correlation between risk and return has been taken as evidence that risk aversion is, on average, a trait of human decision makers. Risk aversion is assumed to increase the demand for low risk alternatives, thus to raise their price.

A substantial demand for low risk alternatives is, however, also consistent with variable risk preferences of the sort assumed here. The model makes preferred risk vary inversely with accumulated resources. Relatively wealthy decision makers will seek alternatives that have relatively low risks associated with them; less wealthy decision makers will seek higher risk alternatives. As the population distribution of wealth changes, so also will the average risk preference. In the model, the relatively high demand for safe alternatives comes not from an unexplained generic risk aversion, but from the high levels of individual resources produced by a process that eliminates losers. Moreover, the model suggests occasions on which there might be a greater demand for higher risk alternatives even though average return is relatively high.

One such situation is where the initial stake, W^*, is large. The larger their initial stakes, the slower the elimination of decision makers with losses and thus with preferences for relatively high risks. At any given stake level, average wealth increases and average preferred risk decreases with time; but compared to smaller stakes, larger stakes result in more risk taking as well as greater average increases in wealth. A second situation leading to greater demand for high risk alternatives is one in which there are negative cumulative effects on expected returns. The classic example is where a decision maker begins with a stake and faces a series of choices among alternatives, each having a negative expected value. Preferred risk is affected sharply by the expected values of the alternatives.

As an example of a situation in which negative expected values accumulate over the course of experience, consider a day of parimutuel betting at a race track offering a number of races sequentially over the day. The key features of parimutuel betting from the present point of view are (a) that it is, on average, a losing bet because of the deduction from the betting pool of the track and state share, and (b) that the odds that are paid are determined by the amounts bet. Since the odds are determined by the willingness of bettors to make bets, they depend on the (possibly erroneous) estimates bettors make of the true odds and on their preferences for risk. If individual bettors are not perverse estimators of the true odds and risk preference is constant, the likelihood of a horse winning will be monotone decreasing with the length of the odds (Griffith, 1949; McGlothin, 1956; Snyder, 1978), and the function relating track odds to likelihood of victory will be invariant across races.

However, the fact that track betting is, on average, a losing bet means that, on average, bettors will experience losses over the day. Suppose a bettor treats the initial stake as given and has a target of "breaking even" by the end of the day. If risk preference varies in the way suggested by the model, a bettor will, on average, become increasingly risk prone as the day goes on. This will lead to some combination of larger bets and more bets being placed on long shots. Since the size of bets is constrained by the initial stake depleted by losses, there is a tendency for increased betting on long shots, thus driving their odds down and the odds of short shots up, relative to their true odds. If we plot the likelihood of winning as a function of the track odds, we should observe a monotone decreasing function; and we should observe that the function has a steeper slope for the early races than for the later ones, that the demand for risk varies over the course of the day. Such a prediction is confirmed by studies of parimutuel betting (Snyder, 1978; Hausch et al., 1981; Hausch and Ziemba, 1985).

Thus a variable risk model makes some predictions about the relation between risk and return. If we examine empirical studies of risk and return, we should discover that the correlation between risk and return varies with such factors as (a) the age of the industry, (b) the capitalization at entry, and (c) the business cycle. The younger the industry, or the greater the capitalization, or the lower the average return across industries, the less the demand for safe alternatives, thus making the intra-industry correlation between risk and return less positive, or even negative.

Reputation and mobility

As has often been noted in studying mobility, the likelihood of leaving most jobs increases for a brief time after an individual enters the job, then declines steadily (Bartholomew, 1973). The decline of exit rates with job duration (after an initial rise) is usually discussed in the economics literature as being due to "firm-specific human capital." In the sociological literature, it has been variously attributed to mutual adaptation over time (Tuma, 1976), i.e., non-stationarity, to the elimination of poorer matches over time (McFarland, 1970; Singer and Spilerman, 1975), i.e., heterogeneity, or to reduced sampling variation in performance evaluation over time (March and March, 1978; Romanow, 1984; Romanow and Sellke, 1985), i.e., performance sampling. The variable risk model provides yet another possible explanation for the decline of exit rates with duration in the job if we interpret the cumulated resources in the model not as monetary wealth but as reputation on the job. Like the performance sampling model, but unlike the others, it also predicts relatively low initial departure rates. Exit occurs through ruin. What we observe is that, for a brief time after entry into the system, the likelihood of ruin is an increasing function of time since entry; but rather early in the process, the likelihood of ruin becomes a decreasing function of duration and continues to decrease indefinitely.[1]

The variable risk preference interpretation of decreasing likelihood of departure from a job over time is quite different from the standard alternative explanations of mutual adaptation or reduced heterogeneity. The decreasing chance of exit from a job with increasing duration in it comes not from an improvement of the average match between jobs and jobholders, but simply by a form of optional stopping. Persons who are successful in building reputations, in the model, reduce their willingness to risk that reputation, thus inhibiting regression to the mean. Successful people continue to be viewed as successful on the basis of their early substantial successes, but they are unlikely either to repeat those triumphs or to fail significantly.

Risk and the death rate of organizations

A similar analysis of organizational birth and death processes as affected by variable risk taking suggests that after a brief initial period, during which the likelihood of death should increase with the age of the organization, death rates should decline with length of survival. Empirical reports on death rates in organizations generally describe organizational mortality as declining with age, when age is measured in years (Carroll and Delacroix, 1982; Carroll, 1983; Freeman et al., 1983). It seems plausible to suggest that if age were measured in finer units (e.g., weeks), the data would exhibit a short initial period of rising death rates, followed by a long period of declining rates. Tucker et al. (1984) found such a pattern in aggregate organizational death rates as a function of organizational age among voluntary organizations in Toronto (see also Singh, House, and Tucker (1986), Singh, Tucker, and House (1986)). As in the case of individual mobility, there are alternative models consistent with such a pattern; but variable risk taking seems likely to be involved and to provide an interpretation of the result that is consistent with a variety of other risk-related phenomena.

BEHAVIORAL IMPLICATIONS OF ADAPTIVE ASPIRATIONS

In general, the model predicts that success (relative to aspiration) leads to a preference for smaller risks, that failure leads to a preference for larger risks. The discussion in the previous section focused on the effects of changing cumulative resources on risk taking. In this section, we consider the effect of changing aspirations. Decreases in aspirations produce increases in the subjective sense of wealth and consequent decreases in the demand for higher risk alternatives. Such aspirations may be affected by exogenous pressures. For example, if a decision maker has maintenance requirements for resources and those requirements increase because of some outside threat or internal condition, the resulting increase in aspiration level will, according to the model, produce a preference for riskier alternatives. The primary source of aspiration change within the present model, however, is from direct experience, from changes in targets as a consequence of realized successes.

Risk and the adaptation of aspirations to experience

If wealth is evaluated in terms of an aspiration for wealth, and the subjective sense of wealth affects the choice of risk, the adaptation of aspiration levels makes a difference. Aspiration levels, or targets, are essentially ways of indexing performance. Insofar as they adapt to past performance, they lead to a form of behavior smoothing. That is, they make behavior less sensitive to variations in performance outcomes than it would otherwise be. Rapid learning of aspiration levels tends to produce risk preferences that are independent of wealth. In the model, if aspiration adapts instantly to performance (i.e., $a = 1$), preferred risk is constant at β, and the process is equivalent to a game played with a stake of W^* against an opponent with infinite resources.

Slower adaptation of aspirations makes risk taking sensitive to a decision maker's performance history. For example, consider the relation between conservatism and success. The model associates risk aversion with success and risk seeking with failure. Thus, it associates conservative, risk-avoiding behavior with any attribute associated with success. But through the adaptation of aspiration levels, it also associates preferred risk with the past history of performance. In particular, if we compare the risk preferences of two decision makers with identical current wealth but different histories, we will see different risk preferences. A prior history of greater wealth will tend to produce higher aspirations and therefore a preference for greater risk than will a history of less wealth.

The relationship may provide some insight into the relation between age and risk taking. In a world in which age is positively correlated with accumulated resources, older decision makers will tend to be more conservative than their younger brethren. Within the present model, this is not because of a loss of desire for risk through aging, but because older decision makers have greater resources, on average. If we control for current level of resources, the histories of older actors are likely to show greater past successes than younger decision makers, thus leading to higher aspiration levels. As a result, controlling for current wealth, older decision makers are likely to be less conservative than younger decision makers. Similarly, position and status should lead to conservatism; but at any position or status which is the highest yet achieved by the people in it, the longer a person has held the position (and thus the more the aspiration level has adjusted to that success), the less conservative that person will be. As a general rule, we would expect holders of inherited wealth (or reputation) to be systematically less risk averse than self-made individuals with the same resources.

Extending the argument to societies is risky; but if we assume that the average behavior of organizational leaders in different societies reflects the results of adaptive aspirations for wealth and the achievements of wealth, risk taking should vary systematically from culture to culture less as a function of current wealth than as a function of the rate of positive change in wealth, with the greatest propensity to risk taking being found in cultures that are doing less well than they have in the past, and the greatest risk aversion being found in societies that are doing substantially better than they traditionally have done. Cross national data on risk taking (Hofstede, 1980; Tainio and Santalainen, 1984) suggests that the picture is probably not quite so simple, but that the speculation is not entirely without merit. The idea is familiar to students of revolution (Brinton, 1938; Tilly, 1978; Goldstone, 1982) in the form of the hypothesis that revolutionary action is produced not by prolonged despair but by rising aspirations stimulated by improved conditions and the availability of resources.

Risk and the diffusion of aspirations

The model for aspiration adaptation can easily be extended to consider changes resulting from the diffusion of experience from others in a population of decision makers (Herriott et al., 1985). If the aspiration level of one decision maker is affected by the experienced wealth of other decision makers, then wealthier decision makers will be persistently above their own aspirations and less wealthy decision makers will be persistently below their own aspirations. Indeed, at the limit where all decision makers share a common (changing) aspiration because of the pooling of their experience in determining targets, variation in risk preference among individuals at a given time depends only upon variation in wealth.

This effect of the diffusion of aspirations is reflected in the pattern of risk-taking in a population over time. The tendency for the median wealth of surviving decision makers to increase over time causes each cohort of newly entering decision makers to face a more demanding target, thus to prefer riskier alternatives than preceding cohorts. As a result, early death rates of new entries increase with the age of the system. Since variations in initial stakes can be used to compensate for variations in initial aspirations, the model can also be used to estimate the increases in initial stakes required to maintain equivalent survival rates over a series of entering cohorts as the system ages.

The dynamics within a population of decision makers with aspirations that adapt to the median wealth in a population involve cycles of risk taking and success. Success relative to others in the population produces a preference for relatively low risk alternatives, thus relative stability in wealth. Failure relative to others leads to a preference for risky alternatives, thus relative stability in wealth. The failing, high risk-taking decision makers tend to be driven either to ruin or to substantial success. If they are ruined, they are replaced with decision makers who are also relatively risk prone. Most of these risk seeking decision makers are ruined, but a fraction of each cohort is successful enough to drive the originally successful (and risk averse) decision makers into a less favorable position, where they become more risk seeking.

PRESCRIPTIVE IMPLICATIONS FOR RISK PREFERENCE STRATEGIES

Although decision theory anticipates that different individuals will have different risk preferences and thus will make different choices, there is no immediate reason, within that theory, either for selecting a particular risk preference or for making it variable. The present model permits us to treat risk preference strategies as being chosen deliberately, or as having evolved, by some criteria of effectiveness. A risk preference strategy is a choice of a value for a, given β and W^*, recalling that the case of $a = 1$ is equivalent to a fixed risk preference and the case of $a = 0$ is equivalent to variable risk preferences with an unchanging target. In this section, the consequences of alternative risk strategies are explored for the case in which the risk measure, R_{it}, is interpreted as the standard deviation of a normal distribution of outcomes.

Related models have been developed for considering investment problems of security investors or the capital structure decisions of firms where the objective is to maximize the probability of long-run survival (Gordon, 1985), and for analyzing the behavior of animals with limited foraging time, some energy requirements, and a set of alternative foraging behaviors characterized in terms of the means and variances of their yields (Caracao, 1980; Stephens, 1981; Houston and McNamara, 1982). In such models, survival is assumed to be the objective; the main strategic problem is assuring a flow of resources adequate to survive, given that the outcome of any particular behavior yields a draw from a distribution of known properties.

The present model is in the same spirit. It has several minor and three major differences from then. First, it treats the decision maker as, in effect, having two reference points rather than one – a ruin point (survival) and a success point (aspiration level). Second, it treats the aspiration level, and thus risk preference, as adapting with experience (and possibly the experience of others). Third, it considers the overall performance of a renewable population of decision makers, as well as the expectations of a single actor. The models in animal ecology, like some of the discussions in the literature on human decision making, have emphasized optimizing on risk preference at each decision point, thinking of surviving decision makers as selecting, not necessarily through calculation, alternatives that maximize their individual chances of survival.

Two criteria for evaluating outcomes over the first T periods of an initially undifferentiated population are considered: Average wealth, defined as the mean cumulative resources (in excess of the stake) among decision makers surviving at period T; and ruin rate, defined as the ratio of the number of ruined decision makers over the first T periods to the population size. It might plausibly be argued that an attractive risk preference strategy would be one that exhibited a relatively large average wealth and a relatively small ruin rate. The obvious problem is, of course, that risk strategies that produce low ruin rates tend also to produce low levels of wealth for survivors. Since it is not immediately obvious that a risk preference strategy good for the short run is necessarily also good for the long run, we allow for the possibility that a preferred strategy may depend on the time horizon, T. For any particular initial stake, we ask for the effect of various aspiration adaptation rates on the T-period outcomes.

Most discussions of variable risk preferences suggest they are particularly useful for keeping an individual decision maker from ruin. The usual intuitive argument is that some level of performance or resources is required for survival, that a low risk alternative keeps a healthy decision maker safe, but does nothing for an ailing one, and thus that intelligence requires making risk preferences a function of current condition. Such discussions, however, generally fail to consider the possibility that, while protecting survival, variable risk strategies may sacrifice possible gains in the average wealth of survivors, thus may be suboptimal for the society of decision makers. It is not clear that a society of decision makers would want to choose, or would evolve, a strategy that minimized the ruin rate without regard for the consequences for average accumulated resources.

Decision situations with expected values of zero

Consider a "game" in which each trial has an expectation of zero. Holding β constant, there is no risk preference strategy that dominates others on both criteria. The ruin rate is minimized by $\alpha = 0$. Thus, a variable risk preference with a fixed target produces the lowest number of ruined decision makers. Average wealth, on the other hand, is maximized by some value of α that is greater than zero and less than one. Figure 13.1 shows

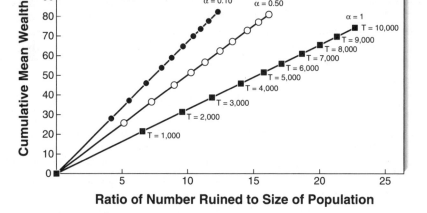

Figure 13.1 The relation between ruin rate among decision makers and mean cumulated wealth among survivors over 10,000 time periods for various values of α ($\beta = 1$, $W^* = 3$), estimated from simulations using 500 decision makers.

the relation between ruin rate and mean accumulated wealth for various values of α, as a function of T, where $\beta = 1$ and $W^* = 3$.

The positive relation between ruin rate and average wealth can be understood most easily against the background of a slightly modified model. The process specified in the model, by making the expected value of a risky choice independent of the wealth of the decision maker, is a losing proposition for "the house." The cumulative value of the game increases at a rate that exceeds the additions provided by the stakes of new entries. A process that avoided this "excess" increase would make the expected value at each trial dependent on the chance that the particular decision maker involved would be ruined on that trial and unable to absorb the full magnitude of the loss. The modification required is well-specified by the preferred risk and the wealth and can be viewed as the premium required to protect the "house" from uncovered losses. If we make such an adjustment in the process, the total wealth in the system (and therefore the mean wealth, since the number of decision makers is constant) remains constant. With conservation of wealth, therefore, the only basis for choice among strategies is their effect on survival. In that case, the results are unambiguous. For any fixed scale of risk (β), variable risk preferences with fixed aspiration levels dominate either fixed risk preferences or adaptive aspirations.

Where wealth is not conserved, as in the present process, the connection between ruin rate and average wealth is also linear but the slope of the relation is, as shown in figure 13.1, greater than the stake. The figure indicates a reason for preferring adaptive aspiration levels. For any value of T, variable risk strategies (i.e., $\alpha < 1$) exist that result in both higher average wealth and a lower ruin rate than does a fixed risk preference (i.e., $\alpha = 1$). This result is a joint consequence of the effect of α on the ruin rate and the effect of α on the relation between ruin rate and average wealth.

Decision situations with non-zero expected values

The observations above can be extended to situations in which expectations are not zero. Many standard situations of interest in decision making involve negative expectations for the outcome distribution. The most obvious examples are situations in which resource demands on the decision maker deplete accumulated resources continuously (as in many animal ecology situations). Other standard situations involve games with positive expectations. A conspicuous example involves decision making by favored individuals or groups in a society.

With some qualifications, the results obtained in the case of zero expectations can be extended to the positive and negative expectation cases. Where expectations are positive, the ruin rate is less and the accumulated wealth is greater than in the zero case. If the positive expectations are modest (i.e., on the order of $\beta/10$), a variable risk strategy with appropriately adaptive aspirations dominates a fixed risk strategy with respect to both the likelihood of ruin and average wealth, though the differences with respect to the latter are modest. If the expectations are substantially positive (i.e., on the order of β), ruin becomes unlikely and the returns to a fixed risk strategy and any variable risk strategy become virtually indistinguishable.

Where expectations are negative, the ruin rate is greater and the accumulated wealth is less than in the zero case. With small negative expectations (i.e., on the order of $-\beta/10$), the pattern recorded in figure 13.1 is observed again. Variable risk preferences with adaptive aspirations are superior to fixed risk preferences both with respect to the ruin rate and with respect to average wealth. With large negative expectations (i.e., on the order of $-\beta$), all variable risk strategies, including the case without adaptive aspirations, dominate a fixed risk strategy.

CONCLUSION

Nothing in the behavioral literature denies decisively the existence of some trait elements in risk preference. If behavioral studies of human risk preferences are to be given credence, however, propositions about fixed risk preferences arising from exogenous forces need to be supplemented with context-dependent considerations, particularly considerations of the success level at which choices occur. The model outlined above describes one possible direction for elaborating received doctrine. Modeling variable risk preferences may contribute to understanding a variety of familiar decision phenomena. These include the relation between risk and return, the relation between duration and mobility within organizations, and the relation between the age of an organization and its likelihood of death.

If we assume that aspirations change on the basis of experience or imitation of others, variable risk preferences make risk taking dependent on the historical and reference group context within which the decision maker acts. If we compare the risk preferences of two decision makers with identical current wealth but different histories, we should observe different risk preferences. Prior histories of greater wealth produce higher aspirations and therefore a preference for greater risk than do histories of less wealth. In the long run, the adaptation of aspiration levels to a decision maker's own experience tends to make risk taking independent of that person's wealth; adaptation of aspirations to the wealth of others tends to make risk taking dependent on the decision maker's current wealth relative to that of others.

The model leads in a relatively natural way to understanding why decision rules based on variable risk preferences and adaptive aspirations might come to dominate rules based either on fixed risk preferences or on variable risk preferences around a fixed target. Discussions of risk taking behavior generally associate variable risk preferences with a survival strategy and do not always consider how a strategy that maximizes individual survival might adversely affect the average performance of survivors. When total wealth is not conserved, a strategy of variable risk preferences with risk seeking for losses contributes to the chances of survival for the individual decision maker; but increases in the chances of individual survival reduce the average wealth of survivors, thus is not clearly optimal for a renewable society of decision makers. This might suggest that it would be better to have fixed risk preferences than to have variable risk preferences of the same scale. However, when the reference point for distinguishing gains from losses is an adaptive aspiration level, variable risk preferences generate *both* higher survival rates *and* higher average wealth for survivors than do fixed preferences. Thus, a combination of adaptive aspirations and variable risk preferences is likely to be a better strategy than either is alone.

Acknowledgment

*I am grateful for the assistance of Gary C. March and Michal Tamuz, and for the comments of Farid Aitsahlia, Amihai Glazer, Pertti Lounamaa, Allyn Romanow, Jitendra Singh, Risto Tainio, and Richard H. Thaler.

The research has been supported by the Hoover Institution, the Spencer Foundation and the Stanford Graduate School of Business.

Note

1. It should be noted that this result of the model does not depend on the variability of the risks, but stems from the relation between the stake and the risk in a ruin process. It is also obtained where $a = 1$, though in weaker form.

References

Acheson James M., 1981, Anthropology of fishing, *Annual Review of Anthropology* 10, 275–316.

Aldrich, Howard A., 1979, *Organizations and environments* (Prentice-Hall, Englewood Cliffs, NJ).

Arrow, Kenneth J., 1965, *Aspects of the theory of risk-bearing* (Yrjö Jahnssonin Säätiö, Helsinki).

Arrow, Kenneth J., 1971, *Essays in the theory of risk bearing* (Markham, Chicago, Il.).

Asch, P. and J. J. Seneca, 1976, Is collusion profitable?, *Journal of Law and Economics* 58, 1–12.

Bartholomew, David J., 1973, *Stochastic models for social processes* (Wiley, London).

Bartlett, Peggy F., 1980, Adaptive strategies in peasant agricultural production, *Annual Review of Anthropology* 9, 545–73.

Battalio, R. C., J. H. Kagel and N. MacDonald, 1985, Animal choices over uncertain outcomes – Some initial experimental results, *American Economic Review* 75, 597–613.

Bowman, Edward H., 1980, A risk-return paradox for strategic management, *Sloan Management Review* 21, 17–31.

Bowman, Edward H., 1982, Risk seeking by troubled firms, *Sloan Management Review* 23, 33–42.

Brinton, Crane, 1938, *Anatomy of revolution* (Norton, New York).

Caracao, T., 1980, On foraging time allocation in a stochastic environment, *Ecology* 61, 119–28.

Caracao, T. and S. L. Lima, 1985, Survivorship, energy budgets, and foraging risk, in: M. Commons, S. J. Shettleworth and J. Nevin, eds, *Quantitative analyses of behavior*, vol. 6 (Ballinger, Cambridge, MA).

Carroll, Glenn R., 1983, A stochastic model of organizational mortality: Review and reanalysis, *Social Science Research* 12, 303–29.

Carroll, Glenn R. and Jacques Delacroix, 1982, Organizational mortality in the newspaper industries of Argentina and Ireland: An ecological approach, *Administrative Science Quarterly* 27, 169–98.

Cyert, Richard M. and James G. March, 1963, *A behavioral theory of the firm* (Prentice-Hall, Englewood Cliffs, NJ).

Day, Richard H., 1967, Profits, learning, and the convergence of satisficing to marginalism, *Quarterly Journal of Economics* 81, 302–11.

Day, Richard H., Dennis J. Aigner and Kenneth R. Smith, 1971, Safety margins and profit maximization in the theory of the firm, *Journal of Political Economy* 79, 1293–1301.

Fama, E. F. and J. D. MacBeth, 1973, Risk, return and equilibrium: Empirical tests, *Journal of Political Economy*

81, 607–36.

Feller, William, 1968, *An introduction to probability theory and its applications*, 3rd edn. (Wiley, New York).

Fishburn, Peter C., 1977, Mean-risk analysis with risk associated with below-target returns, *American Economic Review* 67, 116–26.

Freeman, John, Glenn R. Carroll and Michael T. Hannan, 1983, The liability of newness: Age dependence in organizational death rates, *American Sociological Review* 48, 692–710.

Friedman, Milton and L. J. Savage, 1948, The utility analysis of choices involving risk, *Journal of Political Economy* 56, 279–304.

Friend, Irwin and M. E. Blume, 1975, The demand for risky assets, *American Economic Review* 65, 900–22.

Goldstone, Jack A., 1982, The comparative and historical study of revolutions, *Annual Review of Sociology* 8, 187–207.

Gordon, Myron J., 1985, The portfolio policy that maximizes the probability of long-run survival, unpublished ms., University of Toronto, Toronto.

Gordon, Myron J., G. E. Paradis and C. H. Rorke, 1972, Experimental evidence on alternative portfolio decision rules, *American Economic Review* 62, 107–18.

Griffith, R. M., 1949, Odds adjustments by American horse race bettors, *American Journal of Psychology* 62, 290–4.

Hannan, Michael T. and John Freeman, 1977, The population ecology of organizations, *American Journal of Sociology* 82, 929–96.

Hausch, Donald B. and William T. Ziemba, 1985, Transactions costs, extent of inefficiencies, entries and multiple wagers in a racetrack betting model, *Management Science* 31, 381–94.

Hausch, Donald B., William T. Ziemba and Mark Rubenstein, 1981, Efficiency of the market for racetrack betting, *Management Science* 27, 1435–52.

Herriott, Scott, Daniel Levinthal and James G. March, 1985, Learning from experience in organizations, *American Economic Review* 75, 298–302.

Hershey, J. C. and Paul J. H. Schoemaker, 1980, Prospect theory's reflection hypothesis: A critical examination, *Organizational Behavior and Human Performance* 25, 395–418.

Hofstede, Geert, 1980, Motivation, leadership, and organization: Do American theories apply abroad?, *Organizational Dynamics*, Summer, 42–63.

Hogan, William W. and James M. Warren, 1974, Toward the development of an equilibrium capital-market model based on semivariance, *Journal of Financial and Quantitative Analysis* 9, 1–11.

Holthausen, Duncan M., 1981, A risk-return model with risk and return measured as deviations from a target return, *American Economic Review* 71, 182–8.

Houston, A. I. and J. McNamara, 1982, A sequential approach to risk-taking, *Animal Behavior* 30, 1260–1.

Jensen, M. C., ed., 1972, *Studies in the theory of capital market* (Praeger, New York).

Johnson, A. W., 1971, Security and risk taking among poor peasants, in: George Dalton, ed., *Studies in economic anthropology* (American Anthropological Association, Washington, DC), 144–51.

Kahneman, Daniel and Amos Tversky, 1979, Prospect theory: An analysis of decision under risk, *Econometrica* 47,

263–91.

Kamil, Alan C. and Herbert L. Roitblat, 1985, The ecology of foraging behavior: Implications for animal learning and memory, *Annual Review of Psychology* 36, 141–69.

Karni, Edi and David Schmeidler, 1986, Self-preservation as a foundation of rational behavior under risk, *Journal of Economic Behavior and Organization* 7, 71–81.

Kuhl, J., 1978, Standard setting and risk preference: An elaboration of the theory of achievement motivation and an empirical test, *Psychological Review* 85, 239–48.

Kuhl, J. and V. Blankenship, 1979, Behavioral change in a constant environment: Shift to more difficult tasks with constant probability of success, *Journal of Personality and Social Psychology* 37, 549–61.

Kunreuther, Howard and G. Wright, 1979, Safety-first, gambling and the subsistence farmer, in: J. A. Roumasset, J.-M. Boussard and I. Singh, eds, *Risk, uncertainty and agricultural development* (Agricultural Development Council, New York), 213–30.

Lane, Robert E., 1953, Why businessmen violate the law, *Journal of Criminal Law, Criminology, and Police Science* 44, 151–65.

Lant, Theresa K., 1987, Goals, search, and risk taking in strategic decision making. Unpublished PhD dissertation (Stanford University, Stanford, CA).

Laughhann, Dan J., John W. Payne and Roy L. Crumm, 1980, Managerial risk preferences for below-target returns, *Management Science* 26, 1238–49.

Leventhal, A. M., R. F. Morrell, E. Morgan, F. J. Perkins and C. C. Perkins, Jr, 1959, The relation between mean reward and mean reinforcement, *Journal of Experimental Psychology* 57, 284–7.

Levinthal, Daniel and James G. March, 1981, A model of adaptive organizational search, *Journal of Economic Behavior and Organization* 2, 307–33.

Lopes, Lola L., 1984, Risk and distributional inequality, *Journal of Experimental Psychology: Human Perception and Performance* 10, 465–85.

Lopes, Lola L., 1987, Between hope and fear: The psychology of risk, *Advances in Experimental Social Psychology* 20, 255–95.

MacCrimmon, Kenneth R. and Donald A. Wehrung, 1986, *Taking risks: The management of uncertainty* (Free Press, New York).

McFarland, David D., 1970, Intergenerational mobility as a markovian process: Including a time stationary markovian model that explains declines in mobility rates over time, *American Sociological Review* 35, 463–76.

McGlothlin, W. H., 1956, Stability of choices among uncertain alternatives, *American Journal of Psychology* 69, 604–15.

March, James C. and James G. March, 1978 Performance sampling in social matches, *Administrative Science Quarterly* 23, 434–53.

March, James G. and Zur Shapira, 1987, Managerial perspectives on risk and risk taking, *Management Science* 33, 1404–18.

March, James G. and Herbert A. Simon, 1958, *Organizations* (Wiley, New York).

Mayhew, Lewis B., 1979, *Surviving the eighties* (Jossey-Bass, San Francisco, CA).

Maynard Smith, J., 1978, Optimization

theory in evolution, *Annual Review of Ecology and Systematics* 9, 31–56.

Mezias, Stephen J., 1988, Aspiration level effects, *Journal of Economic Behavior and Organization.*

Nelson, Richard R. and Sidney G. Winter, 1982, *An evolutionary theory of economic change* (Harvard University, Cambridge, MA).

Payne, John W., Dan J. Laughhunn and Roy. L. Crum, 1981, Further tests of aspiration level effects in risky choice behavior, *Management Science* 27, 953–8.

Pratt, J., 1964, Risk aversion in the small and in the large, *Econometrica* 32, 122–36.

Radner, Roy, 1975a, A behavioral model of cost reduction, *Bell Journal of Economics* 6, 196–215.

Radner, Roy, 1975b, Satisficing, *Journal of Mathematical Economics* 2, 253–62.

Real, L. A., 1981, Uncertainty and pollinator-plant interactions: The foraging behavior of bees and wasps on artificial flowers, *Ecology* 62, 20–6.

Romanow, Allyn L., 1984, A brownian motion model for decision making, *Journal of Mathematical Sociology* 10, 1–28.

Romanow, Allyn L. and Thomas Sellke, 1985, Performance sampling and multiple choices: Brownian motion models, *Journal of Mathematical Sociology* 11, 223–44.

Roy, A. D., 1952, Safety first and the holding of assets, *Econometrica* 20, 431–49.

Santalainen, Timo and Risto Tainio, 1985, Managerial work and business performance of banks, unpublished ms. (Finnish School of Economics, Helsinki).

Schneider, Sandra L. and Lola L. Lopes, 1986, Reflection in preferences under risk: Who and when may suggest

why, *Journal of Experimental Psychology: Human Perceptions and Performance* 12, 535–48.

Siegel, Sidney, 1957, Level of aspiration and decision making, *Psychological Review* 64, 253–62.

Simon, Herbert A., 1955, A behavioral model of rational choice, *Quarterly Journal of Economics* 69, 99–118.

Singer, Burton and Seymour Spilerman, 1975, Social mobility models for heterogeneous populations, in: Herbert L. Costner, ed., *Sociological methodology, 1973–1974* (Jossey-Bass, San Francisco, CA) 356–401.

Singh, Jitendra, 1986, Performance, slack, and risk taking in organizational decision making, *Academy of Management Journal* 29, 562–85.

Singh, Jitendra, Robert J. House and David J. Tucker, 1986, Organizational change and organizational mortality, *Administrative Science Quarterly* 31, 587–611.

Singh, Jitendra, David J. Tucker and Robert J. House, 1986, Organizational legitimacy and the liability of newness, *Administrative Science Quarterly* 31, 171–193.

Snyder, Wayne W., 1978, Horse racing: Testing the efficient markets model, *Journal of Finance* 33, 1109–18.

Staw, Barry M. and Eugene Szwajkowski, 1975, The scarcity-munificence component of organizational environments and the commission of illegal acts, *Administrative Science Quarterly* 20, 345–54.

Stephens, D. W., 1981, The logic of risk-sensitive foraging preferences, *Animal Behavior* 29, 628–9.

Swalm, Ralph O., 1966, Utility theory – insights into risk taking, *Harvard Business Review* 47, 123–36.

Tainio, Risto and Timo Santalainen, 1984, Some evidence for the cultural relativity of organizational development programs, *Journal of Applied Behavioral Science* 20, 93–111.

Tilly, Charles, 1978, *From mobilization to revolution* (Addision-Wesley, Reading, MA).

Tucker, David J., Jitendra V. Singh, and Robert J. House, 1984, The liability of newness in a population of voluntary service organizations, unpublished ms., University of Toronto, Toronto.

Tuma, Nancy B., 1976, Rewards, resources, and the rate of mobility: A nonstationary multivariate stochastic model, *American Sociological Review* 41, 338–60.

Tversky, Amos and Daniel Kahneman, 1974, Judgment under uncertainly: Heuristics and biases, *Science* 185, 1124–31.

Waddington, K. D., T. Allen and B. Heinrich, 1981, Floral preferences of bumblebees (*Bombus edwardsii*) in relation to intermittent versus continuous rewards, *Animal Behavior* 29, 779–84.

CHAPTER FOURTEEN

Variable Risk Preferences and the Focus of Attention

with Zur Shapira

Empirical investigations of decision making indicate that the level of individual or organizational risk taking is responsive to a risk taker's changing fortune. Several nonstationary random-walk models of risk taking are developed to describe this phenomenon. The models portray a risk taker's history as the cumulated realizations of a series of independent draws from a normal probability distribution of possible outcomes. This performance distribution is assumed to have an unchanging mean and a variance (risk) that changes. The changes are seen as determined by (a) a focus of attention on one of two reference points (an adaptive aspiration for resources and the survival point) and (b) the relation between current resources and the focal point. The models are elaborated by examining the impact of adaptive aspirations and attention focus on risk taking over time in a cohort of risk takers and in a renewing population of risk takers.

Theories of decision making under uncertainty most commonly assume that returns to decisions are draws from a probability distribution that is conditional on the choice made. Decision makers are generally assumed to prefer alternatives with higher expected values to those with lower ones, but they also are assumed to consider the riskiness of an alternative. Riskiness is associated with lack of certainty about the precise outcome of a choice and thus with variation in the probability distribution. Psychological studies of risk preference and risk taking emphasize the ways in which such variability affects choice.

Empirical investigations of choices by individuals and organizations indicate that preferences for variability are not constant but are responsive to changing fortune. The mechanisms of response are familiar to students of the psychology of decision making, but they yield a somewhat complicated picture:

1. *Risk taking and danger.* Risk taking appears to be affected by threats to survival. The reported effects, however, appear to be contradictory. On the one hand, it had been observed that increasing threats to survival stimulate greater and greater risk taking, presumably in an effort to escape the threats (Bowman, 1982; Bromiley and Wiseman, 1989; Mayhew, 1979). On the other hand, danger has been portrayed as leading to rigidity and to extreme forms of risk aversion (Greenhalgh, 1983; Staw, 1976; Staw et al., 1981; Roy, 1952; Stone, 1973).

2. *Risk taking and slack.* Risk taking appears to be affected by slack, that is, by resources in excess of current aspirations. Where slack is plentiful, it is pictured as leading to relaxation of controls, reduced fears of failure, institutionalized innovation, increased experimentation, and thus to relatively high levels of risk taking (Antonelli, 1989; MacCrimmon and Wehrung, 1986; March, 1981; Wehrung, 1989). Where slack is small (or negative), tight controls and efforts to improve productivity using known technologies and procedures are seen as producing relatively low levels of risk taking (Burns and Stalker, 1961; Czarniawska and Hedberg, 1985; Libby and Fishburn, 1977; Wehrung, 1989).

3. *Risk taking in the neighborhood of an aspiration level.* The idea of an aspiration-level reference point is central to modern theories of individual and organizational choice (March, 1988a; Tversky and Kahneman, 1991). When they orient to a target and are close to it, individuals appear to be risk seeking below the target and risk averse above it (Hausch et al. 1981; Payne et al., 1980, 1981; Tversky and Kahneman, 1974). A similar result has been observed in organizations (Bromiley, 1991; MacCrimmon and Wehrung, 1986; March and Shapira, 1987) and in societies (Brenner, 1983; Olson, 1963). The result is robust across a variety of circumstances involving fairly symmetric probability distributions of outcomes, but it appears to be sensitive to skewness in those distributions (Hershey and Schoemaker, 1980; Schneider and Lopes, 1986). It is consistent with a long history of observations in organizational studies that relate search activity to failure (Antonelli, 1989; March and Simon, 1958; Singh, 1986).

4. *Risk taking and the assimilation of resources.* Risk-taking behavior seems to be sensitive to risk takers' perceptions of whose resources are being risked. Greater risks are taken with new resources than with resources held for a longer time (Samuelson and Zeckhauser,

1988). Among successful managers, those who are older and have longer tenure take fewer risks than do those who are younger and have shorter tenure (MacCrimmon and Wehrung, 1990). Managers appear to be more inclined to take risks with an organization's resources than with their own (March and Shapira, 1987). Experimental subjects appear to be more inclined to take risks with the "house's" money than with their own (Battalio et al., 1990; Thaler and Johnson, 1990).

5. *Risk taking and self-confidence.* Successful risk takers seem to feel that their past successes in risky situations are a result of their skills or their environment's munificence rather than their good fortune (Keyes, 1985; March and Shapira, 1987). That is, they accept some mixture of the following beliefs: that their past successes are attributable to their special abilities, that nature is favorable to them, and that they can beat the odds. This tendency to attribute favorable outcomes to enduring features of the situation rather than to good luck has been observed in experimental subjects (Langer, 1975), in athletes (Gilovich et al., 1985), and in organizations (Boisjoly, 1988; Roll, 1986) and leads to a positive bias in anticipations.

In this chapter we use some relatively simple random-walk conceptions of performance, aspirations, and risk preferences to model this pattern of risk taking. The models build on earlier random-walk perspectives for variable risk preferences (March, 1988b; March and Shapira, 1987) and on more general application of random walks to modeling adaptation (Levinthal, 1990, 1991). They emphasize focus-of-attention factors as critical to understanding human choice (Shapira and Venezia, 1992; Tversky and Kahneman, 1991).

RANDOM-WALK MODELS OF RISK TAKING

In a random walk, an individual or organization begins with an initial supply of resources and accumulates (or depletes) resources over time by a sequence of independent draws from a distribution of possibilities (Dubins and Savage, 1965; Feller, 1968). In standard applications of random walks to adaptation, the usual focus is on changes in resources over time up to the point at which they reach a level that can be treated as absorbing. The absorbing state of interest is typically zero, but there are other possibilities (March and March, 1978; Romanow and Sellke, 1985).

Such models have a certain amount of appeal by virtue of their parsimony, their straightforward characterization of the process of engagement between a risk taker and the environment over time, and the ease with which they produce key observed features of survival experience. They yield distributions of exits (e.g., deaths, departure from jobs, endings of marriages, exhaustion of capital) over time that are qualitatively consistent with many empirical observations. As a result, they often provide plausible baseline interpretations of the distributions of exits within a cohort (Bartholomew, 1973; Levinthal, 1991).

The initial supply of resources in a random walk can be interpreted as a capital endowment. The mean can be interpreted as the capability or efficiency of the risk taker or, more generally, as the fit of the individual or organization to the environment (Levinthal, 1991). The variance can be interpreted as unreliability or risk taking. *Unreliability* is normally used to refer to variability that is relatively involuntary and *risk* to refer to variability that is relatively voluntary, but the distinctions are not always easy to maintain. We are interested in behavior that is neither strictly voluntary nor strictly involuntary but a mixture of the two. By pursuing a particular strategy, technology, market, control procedure, or product in a particular way, an individual or organization determines (within some constraints) the variability of possible experience. Thus, we may describe individuals or organizations that pursue actions with small variability in outcomes as either "reliable" or "risk averse" depending on the context. Those that pursue actions with large variability in outcomes can similarly be described either as "unreliable" or "risk seeking."

We consider a population of risk takers each of whom experiences history as the realizations of a sequence of independent draws from a normal performance distribution of possible outcomes. The population is initially homogeneous with respect to the mean and variance parameters of the performance distribution. Although we provide a few comments on nonstationary means, for the most part, we assume the mean of the distribution to be stationary and equal to zero. The variance parameter changes over time by a process that is common to all risk takers, but it produces a heterogeneous, nonstationary population as a result of differences in specific realized histories.

The variance depends both on the amount of current resources and on the history of reaching that amount. We assume that risk taking is controlled by two simple "decision" rules. The first rule applies whenever cumulated resources are above the focal reference point: Variability is set so that the risk taken increases monotonically with distance above the reference point. This rule, or a close proxy, is a common interpretation of risk aversion in the positive near-neighborhood of an aspiration level or threat of death. A specific version might make the probability of landing below the reference point equal to some fixed (and presumably relatively low) number; that is, it might make the relation between distance from the reference point and risk linear.

Such rules have been examined in the literature on organizations (Singh, 1986), individuals (Kahneman and Tversky, 1979), and animals (Kamil and Roitblat, 1985). Presumably they reflect a combination of resistance to falling below the focal point and a limitation imposed on risk taking by the amount of available resources. Under this first rule, as a risk taker's resources (above a target) increase, the unreliability in outcomes that is tolerated becomes greater and greater. The rule is different in this respect from the function assumed in an earlier model of variable risk taking (March, 1988b). In that model, preferred risk was assumed to decline monotonically with the ratio of resources to aspiration. The differences between the models reflect an unresolved conflict in the research on variable risk taking – the impact of excess resources on reliability and risk taking (Bromiley, 1991; Bromiley and Miller, 1990).

The second decision rule applies whenever cumulated resources are *below* the focal reference point: Variability is set so that the risk taken increases monotonically with (negative) distance from the focal point. A specific linear version might make the probability of landing some fixed distance above the reference point equal to some fixed (and presumably relatively high) number. This rule provides an interpretation of risk seeking for losses. The further current resources are below the reference point, the greater the risk required to make recovery likely.

Risk can be varied in two ways – by choosing among alternatives with varying odds or by altering the scale of the investment in the chosen one, that is, by changing the "bet size." Because the availability of the latter alternative depends on the resources available, there is a constraint on risk taking that can be quite severe as a risk taker exhausts resources. This resource constraint is not reflected explicitly in the present model. In effect, we assume that alternatives with any desired variance within a very wide range are available.

In keeping with earlier work on the psychology of risk taking (Atkinson, 1957; Lopes, 1987), we consider two target reference points: An aspiration level for resources that adapts to experience (Kuhl, 1978; Lewin et al., 1944) and a fixed survival point at which resources are exhausted. Thus, the present models differ from a strict aspiration-level conception of targets by introducing a second critical reference point, the survival point, and by assuming a shifting focus of attention between these two reference points (Lopes, 1987; March and Shapira, 1987). The two rules make risk-taking behavior sensitive to (a) where a risk taker is (or expects to be) relative to an aspiration level and a survival point, and (b) whether the risk taker focuses on the survival reference point or the aspiration-level reference point. Consequently, aggregate risk-taking behavior in a population is attributable partly to the way the process affects the accumulation of resources, partly to the way it distributes risk takers to success and failure (in terms of their own aspiration levels), and partly to the way it allocates attention between the two reference points.

Rules such as these are commonly cited by risk takers (Bowman and Kunreuther, 1988; MacCrimmon and Wehrung, 1986; March and Shapira, 1987) and have a certain amount of theoretical appeal, but they make it easy to confuse two quite different versions of the meanings of "risk." In the first meaning, risk is associated with variability in the probability distribution conditional on a choice. In the second meaning, risk is associated with the danger of landing below, or the chance of landing above, a focal target. The behavioral rules specified earlier keep "danger" or "opportunity" constant under changing conditions. In a sense, therefore, they are "fixed-danger" and "fixed-opportunity" rules. As will become clear later in this chapter, however, any rule that keeps danger fixed as cumulated resources vary will produce variability in risk taking. And any rule that keeps risk taking (in the sense of variability) fixed will make danger variable.

THE SPECIFIC MODELS

We assume that each risk taker begins with a certain level of initial resources that is common to all. The process for each risk taker continues through a sequence of draws from that risk taker's changing performance distribution until resources are exhausted. The term *resources* is intentionally general. It might include the capital assets of an entrepreneur or a business firm, the political support of a politician or a public agency, the reputation of a professional or a professional association. The history of any particular risk taker consists in a series of independent draws from a performance distribution. The realized draws are added sequentially to the resources to produce a history of cumulated resources, or wealth.

Each of the basic models we consider assumes that the performance distribution from which draws are made by a particular risk taker is normal, with a mean of 0. The standard deviation of the distribution for any particular risk taker at time t is assumed to be a function of the cumulated resources of that risk taker at time t. Thus, all of the models are expressions for s_t, the standard deviation of the normal distribution from which a draw is made at time t. We assume that s_t is bounded by unavoidable risk (here assumed to be 10^{-1}) and by maximum possible risk (here assumed to be 10^9).

Model 0: Fixed risk

In this model, we assume that the $s_t = s^*$ for all t. This is the standard, homogeneous, stationary random walk.

In all subsequent models, we introduce an experience-based estimation of the mean of the distribution. We assume that each risk taker estimates the mean of possible realizations in the next time period to be equal to the mean of that risk taker's experience over previous time periods. That is, if E_t is the estimated return for period t, R_t is the accumulated resources at t, and k is the initial stake, then,

$$E_{t+1} = (R_t - k)/t \qquad (14.1)$$

If the estimated mean is low enough to make estimated resources at the end of the period less than zero, the estimated mean is assumed to be zero.

Model 1: Survival reference point

In this model, we assume that the risk taker has one reference focus, the survival point, and the level of risk taken depends on the distance from that point. It also depends on a (possibly erroneous) estimate by the risk taker of the mean of the distribution. Specifically,

$$S_t = (R_{t-1} + E_t)/D(p_d^*) \qquad (14.2)$$

where $D(p_d^*)$ is the standard deviate of the normal distribution associated with p_d^*, the probability that the draw in this period will wipe out the cumulated resources up to this point – that is, the probability of death. The model makes the estimated probability of death constant over all levels of cumulated resources, thus over time. By virtue of the assumption of a symmetric (normal) performance distribution. p_d^* is constrained to be less than 0.5.

Model 2: Aspiration reference point

In this model, we assume that the focus is always on an aspiration level ($L > 0$) for cumulated resources. The effect of the focus depends on whether resources are above or below the aspiration for them. Specifically,

$$s_t = \begin{cases} (R_{t-1} + E_t)/D(p_f^*), & \text{if } R_{t-1} \geq L_{t-1'} \\ (R_{t-1} + E_t + q)/D(p_s^*), & \text{if } R_{t-1} < L_{t-1'} \end{cases} \qquad (14.3)$$

where L_t is the aspiration level at t, q is the distance above the aspiration level that is deemed "safe," p_f^* is the probability that a draw in this period will bring cumulated resources below the aspiration level, and p_s^* is the probability that a draw in this period will bring cumulated resources to a position at least q above the aspiration level. By virtue of the assumption of a symmetric (normal) performance distribution, p_f and p_s are each constrained to be less than 0.5, but they have no necessary relation to each other. The psychological basis for q ($q > 0$) lies in the frequent observation that there is a positive bias in aspirations (Revelle and Michaels, 1976), although its precise form is slightly different from that suggested by others (Lant, 1992). When cumulated resources exceed the aspiration level, s_t is set so that the estimated probability (depending partly on the possibly erroneously estimated mean of the distribution) of landing below the aspiration level is constant. When cumulated resources are less than the aspiration level, the model assumes that risk is set so that the (possibly erroneously) estimated probability of "safe success," that is, of being above the aspiration level by some fixed amount, is constant over cumulated wealth.

Model 3: Shifting focus

This model is a combination of the two single-reference-point models (Models 1 and 2). The risk taker attends either to the aspiration level or to the survival point, but not to both. When attention is given to the survival point, the model is equivalent to the survival reference-point model (Model 1). When attention is given to the aspiration level, the model is equivalent to the aspiration reference-point model (Model 2). Attention can shift according to a number of different possible rules, and we introduce two more complicated rules in later sections. Initially, we consider only a simple probabilistic attention rule: Each risk taker attends to the survival point with probability u ($0 \leq u \leq 1$). The two single-reference-point models (Models 1 and 2) are then special cases of the shifting reference-point model (Model 3), with $u = 1$ and $u = 0$, respectively.

Risk-taking functions

The two basic risk-taking functions specified in the models are shown in figure 14.1. Each function shows the risk taken at any level of cumulated resources. The aspiration level is assumed to be fixed. The functions plotted in figure 14.1 are not utility functions. They show risk taking directly as the standard deviation of the performance distribution, rather than as a nonlinearity in the utility for money. The two specific functions reflect particular parameter values for each model; thus they should be viewed as representing a class of models. By varying the parameters, it is possible to vary the scale of risk taking arbitrarily – thus the relative position of the several plots on the y-axis. However, the qualitative pattern of relative risk taking as a function of cumulated resources for any one model remains as pictured.

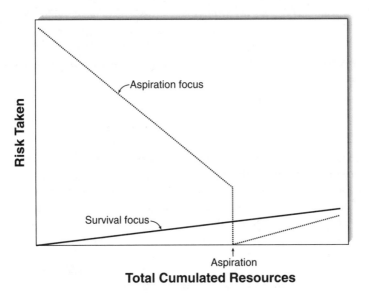

Figure 14.1 Risk taken as a function of cumulated resources for fixed-focus models of variable risk ($p_d = 0.0001$, $p_f = 0.05$, $p_s = 0.3$, $L = 30$, and $q = 10$)

Parameters of the models

Each risk taker is assumed to have a performance distribution that is normal with an unchanging mean, x, and a changing variance. Each risk taker begins with an initial stake, k, and an initial aspiration level equal to that stake plus or minus a small amount. In addition to x and k, the following parameters are involved:

p_d^*, the probability of death, that is, the probability of moving from the present resource position to a position below the survival reference point as a result of the draw this period (Models 1 and 3; $0 < p_d^* < 0.5$);

p_f^*, the probability of failure, that is, the probability of moving from the present resource position above the aspiration level to a position below the aspiration level as a result of the draw this period (Models 2 and 3; $0 < p_f^* < 0.5$);

p_s^*, the probability of success, that is, the probability of moving from the present resource position below the aspiration level to a "safe" position above the aspiration level as a result of a draw this period (Models 2 and 3; $0 < p_s^* < 0.5$);

q, the increment about the aspiration level that defines a "safe" success (Models 2 and 3; $q > 0$);

a, the learning parameter for adjusting the aspiration level, where R_t is the cumulated resources at t, L_t is the aspiration level for resources at t, and $L_t = aR_{t-1} + (1-a)L_{t-1}$ (Models 2 and 3; $0 \leq a \leq 1$);

u, the probability of attending to the survival reference point (Model 3; $0 \leq u \leq 1$).

CONSISTENCY WITH EMPIRICAL DATA

Because the models can lead, through probabilistic variation, to a variety of outcomes in any particular case, it is necessary to consider the distribution of possible outcomes stemming from any particular set of parameters. To derive distributions, we use Monte Carlo simulations. Except where indicated, all of the simulations set $p_d^* = 0.0001$, $p_f^* = 0.05$, $p_s^* = 0.3$, $q = 2$, $k = 3$, and $u = 0.5$; thus they do not provide information on the sensitivity of the results to variations in those parameters. The emphasis is on comparing the models and on considering the effects of variations in the value of the aspiration adjustment parameter, *a*.

The three variable-risk models produce distinctly different patterns of risk taking, which lead to differences in the extent to which the several models fit the stylized empirical observations listed earlier.

Risk taking and danger

The survival reference-point model (Model 1) exhibits decreasing risk taking as survival is increasingly threatened. The aspiration reference-point model (Model 2) exhibits increasing risk taking as survival is threatened. In the neighborhood of the survival reference point, the shifting-focus model (Model 3) exhibits oscillation between relatively small risks and relatively large ones as the focus of attention shifts. The effects in the cases of the two models that include aspiration reference points (Models 2 and 3) depend on the speed of aspiration adjustment.

Risk taking and slack

All of the models exhibit increasing risk taking as slack (resources in excess of aspirations) increases. Because the amount of slack is a joint function of accumulated resources and aspirations for them, it is sensitive to the rate at which aspirations adjust to experience.

Risk taking in the neighborhood of an aspiration level

In the neighborhood of current aspirations, the models using aspiration-level reference points (Models 2 and 3) exhibit higher risk taking when expectations are below the aspiration level than when they are above it. Thus, in the neighborhood of the target, they are risk seeking for "losses" and risk avoiding for "gains." Risk avoidance for gains is, however, less and less characteristic in these two models as the distance between the gains and the aspiration level increases. The survival reference-point model (Model 1) is insensitive to aspirations.

Risk taking and the assimilation of resources

Through aspiration-level adjustment, the two models with aspiration-level reference points (Models 2 and 3) make the effect of current resources on risk taking dependent on the length of time resources are held. Because risk taking depends on the relation between aspirations and current resources, and aspirations depend on the history of accumulation, there is a period of time after acquiring (or losing) resources when those accumulations are not fully discounted by adjustment in aspirations. The slower the adjustment of aspirations, the longer the period of time before resources are assimilated. The survival reference-point model (Model 1) is insensitive to aspirations and thus to assimilation of resources.

Risk taking and self-confidence

Even though all risk takers draw from distributions with the same mean, their realizations from those distributions vary. Some have cumulative experience that exceeds the true expected value and consequently overestimate the mean; others have less favorable cumulative experience and consequently underestimate the mean. Because the process differentially eliminates those with negative experience, it generates a positive bias in expectations. Risk takers following the rules in the three variable-risk models (Models 1, 2, and 3) generally take greater risks than they would if their estimates were correct. The only exception occurs when they are focused on the aspiration-level reference point and their biased expectations place them above the aspiration, whereas a correct estimation would place them below.

Table 14.1 summarizes the results. The fixed-risk model (Model 0) clearly does not predict human risk taking as it has been observed. The survival reference-point model (Model 1) has some of the qualitative features desired, but it fits the data less well than the others. Moreover, that model has a strong property that appears to be inconsistent with empirical observations. When focus is strictly on the survival point, individual histories vary, but they tend to converge to the survival point. As a result, most risk takers spend most of their histories barely surviving and taking very little risk.

Table 14.1
Empirical observations and models compared

Observations	Models
1. Low risk taking near survival point	1, 3
High risk taking near survival point	2, 3
2. High risk taking when well above aspiration level	2, 3
3. Risk seeking just below aspiration, risk avoiding just above	2, 3
4. Effect of one-time increase in resources is short-term increase in risk taking followed by decline	2, 3
5. Underestimate of risk	1, 2, 3

The aspiration reference-point model (Model 2) and the shifting reference-point model (Model 3) come closest to reflecting the observed qualitative results. Because a shifting focus generates variability among individuals having the same resource level, the outcomes in Model 3 provide a possible interpretation of some of the puzzles in the empirical data. Risk takers who find themselves below their aspiration level are divided into two (unstable) groups, the first of which is focused on the dangers of death and the second of which is focused on the opportunities for being safely above the aspiration level. The two different foci lead to different levels of risk taking. Similarly, risk takers who find themselves above their aspiration level are divided into two (unstable) groups, the first of which is focused on the (distant) dangers of death and the second of which is focused on the (nearer) dangers of failure. Again, these two different foci lead to different levels of risk taking.

RESOURCE ACCUMULATION AND ADAPTIVE ASPIRATIONS

The variable risk taking portrayed in these models is dependent on three things. First are the changing resources of the risk takers; the risk taken by a particular risk taker changes as a result of the realizations of the random walk. Second are the changing aspirations of risk takers for resources. Aspirations adjust to experience (Lant, 1992; Revelle and Michaels, 1976). Insofar as attention is directed to the aspiration focal point, such adjustments affect the risk taken. Third is the focus of attention. The level of risk taken depends on whether attention is directed to the survival point or the aspiration level. In this section, we consider resource accumulation by survivors, its effect on aspirations for resources, and their joint effect on risk taking. In the next section, we examine the effects of the focus of attention.

Resource accumulation by survivors

Suppose risk takers all have the same, stationary performance distribution means, the same initial stakes, the same decision parameters, and the same learning parameter. Except where indicated, we assume $x = 0$, $k = 3$, $q = 2$, $u = 0.5$, $p_d^* = 0.0001$, $p_f^* = 0.05$, and $p_s^* = 0.3$. In the absence of involuntary risk, Model 1 (survival reference point) tends to trap most risk takers in a near neighborhood of the survival point. With nonnegative expectations, Models 2 (aspiration reference point) and 3 (shifting reference point) tend to generate increases in average gains of survivors over time. These increases, in turn, produce three major effects on risk taking: The first effect is the direct one from the tendency for cumulated resources to increase. Within the models, risk taking is high if a risk taker is relatively far above a reference point. In cohorts in which performance distributions have nonnegative expectations that are stable, the average level of risk taking among survivors is more likely to be determined by a history of being above the reference point than being below it, and increasingly so as the cohort ages. Thus, risk taking tends to increase.

The second effect of increasing assets on risk taking stems from a systematic bias in the expectations of survivors. Cumulation of resources over time (in a process in which the average accumulation is zero) leads survivors to overestimate the expected mean of the process in which they are involved. This leads them generally to expect to have greater resources at the end of each time period than they will in fact have. As a result, except when they are in the near neighborhood of, and below, their aspirations, they take greater risks than they would have taken if they had correctly predicted their resources.

The third effect of increasing resources for survivors is to increase aspiration levels. As long as aspirations are below realizations, increasing aspiration levels will tend to reduce risk taking. At the limit, the changes in aspiration level negate the effects of increasing resources on risk taking because increases in resources are discounted by rising aspirations for them.

If we relax the assumption of homogeneous and stationary means, these effects on resource accumulation and risk taking are affected in relatively straightforward ways. Suppose that individual means (x_i) are distributed normally with mean = 0 and variance = 1. Such heterogeneity has substantial effects. Because losers are eliminated, there is a strong tendency to eliminate those risk takers with performance distributions having negative means. As a result of the differential survival and the consequent shifting composition of the population, heterogeneity in means generates much higher levels of average risk taking and cumulated resources among survivors than is found in homogeneous populations with means equal to the average of the heterogeneous population at Period 0. Those risk takers having advantages of fit do better and survive longer. As they do better, they take greater risks.

Suppose the means, x_i, are initially homogeneous but are not stationary. For example, we might imagine that the mean increases with experience in the manner of standard learning curves. Or we might imagine that the mean is related positively to cumulated wealth. Such changes in the mean lead to increases in the accumulation of resources by survivors and thus (in general) to increases in risk taking. However, if increases in the mean come at a decreasing rate, upward adjustments in the aspiration level reduce the level of risk taking.

Alternatively, we might imagine that variations in the mean of a performance distribution are linked to variations in the variance. The literature provides two, quite different, stories on the relation between risk and expected value. In one story, relatively standard in the literature on financial markets, risk and expected value are positively related (Feigenbaum and Thomas, 1986; Gibbons, 1982). In a second story, relatively standard in research on organizational search and change, risk and expected value are negatively related (Bowman, 1982; Bromiley, 1991; Bromiley and Miller, 1990). Within the present models, a positive correlation between risk and return increases, and a negative correlation decreases, the accumulation of resources by survivors and the average risk taken.

Effects of the rate of aspiration adjustment

Unlike the survival reference point, which is insensitive to endogenous change, aspiration reference points adjust to reflect realized experience. The history-dependence of aspirations combines with the importance of aspiration levels for risk taking to make the rate and character of these aspiration adjustments a key feature of models using aspiration-level reference points (Models 2 and 3). Self-referential aspiration adjustment leads to the aspiration level's being closer to current position than it would otherwise be. This, in turn, tends to constrain the risk taken by any risk taker focusing on the aspiration level, because risk taking is relatively low in the neighborhood of the aspiration level (see figure 14.1). As a result, in both models using an aspiration-level reference point (Models 2 and 3), slower adaptation of aspirations leads to taking greater risks. For example, figure 14.2 shows, for $a = 0.1$ and $a = 0.9$, the average risk taken by survivors over time for Model 2 (aspiration reference point only). When $a = 0.1$, the average risk taken by survivors by Period 100 is more than three times that taken when $a = 0.9$.

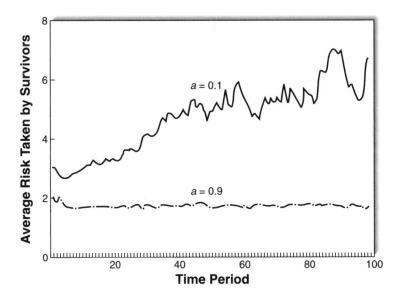

Figure 14.2 Average risk taken by survivors over 100 time periods for model ($a = 0.1, 0.9$: $N = 5,000$ [nonrenewed], $p_d = 0.0001$, $p_f = 0.05$, $p_s = 0.3$, $x = 0$, $q = 2$, and $k = 3$).

In a population of risk takers, the aspiration level of each risk taker may depend not only on that risk taker's achieved resources but also on the resource level reached by others – in particular, others who do better (Brenner, 1983; Bromiley, 1991). If j is the rank of a risk taker in terms of accumulated resources (where the risk taker with the greatest amount of resources in the population is ranked 1), and e ($0 < e < 1$) is a positive fraction, then the rank of a superior comparison target is equal to the nearest integer value of ej. The lower the value of e, the higher the relative standing of the comparison target. (If the nearest integer value of e_j is 0, then the rank of the comparison risk taker is assumed to be 1.) The aspiration updating function becomes

$$L_t = acR'_{t-1} + a(1 - c)R_{t-1} + (1 - a)\,L_{t-1} \qquad (14.4)$$

where R'_t is the accumulated resources of the comparison risk taker at t, and c is the fraction of the weight assigned to R'_t (rather than R_t). The conspicuous consequence of having aspirations depend partly on the achievements of superior performers is to increase average aspirations and the frequency with which cumulated resources fall well below the aspiration level. This tends to increase risk taking, a tendency somewhat ameliorated (in the shifting-focus-of-attention models) by the focus on survival. Moreover, insofar as aspiration adaptation is related to the performance of superior others, rapid aspiration adjustment leads to higher levels of risk than does slow aspiration adjustment.

These effects of *a* on risk taking in situations involving homogeneous values for *a* suggest that *a* might be selected within a population of risk takers that was heterogeneous with respect to the adaptation rate. This speculation is true. Figure 14.3 shows the Period 100 distribution of the population across nine values of *a*, given a uniform distribution at Period 1, for the situation in which aspirations are entirely self-referential in the two aspiration reference-point models (Models 2 and 3). Risk takers with low values for *a* represent a substantially smaller fraction of the cohort of survivors at Period 100 than they did in the original cohort.

FOCUS-OF-ATTENTION EFFECTS

At some levels of resources, the risk taking specified by the functions portrayed in figure 14.1 is relatively insensitive to changes in focus from one reference point to the other. In other cases, the differences are large. For

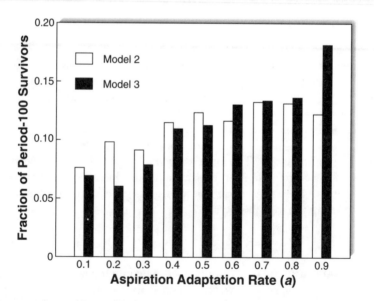

Figure 14.3 Period 100 distribution of *a* among survivors for heterogeneous *a* (*M* = 0.5) in models 2 and 3 (*N* = 5,000 [nonrenewed], p_d = 0.0001, p_f = 0.05, p_s = 0.3, *x* = 0, *q* = 2, *k* = 3, and *u* = 0.5).

example, if the aspiration level is substantially above the survival point and the risk taker is close to the latter, a focus on the survival point will lead to taking very little risk, whereas a focus on the aspiration level will lead to taking a substantial risk. Conversely, if the risk taker is well above the survival point but barely above the aspiration level, a focus on the survival point will lead to substantially greater risk taking than a focus on the aspiration level. The precise effects of increasing (or decreasing) the likelihood of focus on the survival point, relative to the focus on the aspiration level, depend on the decision rules and parameters, but a few general implications can be drawn.

Effects of varying probabilistic attention to survival

Model 3, with its changing focus of attention, tends to generate patterns of risk taking that are different from those produced by the fixed-focus models. By varying the value of u, the probability of attending to the survival reference point in Model 3, we can examine how a fixed likelihood of attending to one reference point or the other affects risk taking. Because risk taking also depends on the rate of aspiration adjustment, we

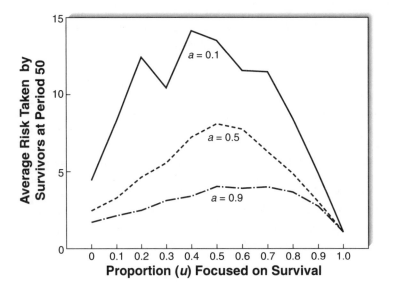

Figure 14.4 Average risk taken by survivors (Model 3) at Period 50 as a function of u and a (N = 5,000 [nonrenewed], p_d = 0.0001, p_f = 0.05, p_s = 0.3, x = 0, q = 2, and k = 3).

plot in figure 14.4 the average risk taken in Period 50 as a function of u for three different values of a, where aspiration adjustment is self-referential. The observation (see figure 14.2) that slower adjustment of aspirations leads to higher risk taking when $u = 0.5$ is confirmed as a general property for all values of $u < 1$. By narrowing the gap between realizations and aspirations, rapid adjustment of aspirations has a negative effect on average risk taking in situations such as this (in which assets tend to grow over time).

The plotted results with respect to u are sensitive to the specific parameters chosen, but the nonmonotone dependence of risk taking on u is quite general. Very high values of u, including $u = 1$, which is equivalent to the survival reference point model (Model 1), lead to low levels of risk taking. This risk aversion leads to relatively low levels of accumulated resources, which reinforce the relatively low levels of risk taking. Very low levels of u, including $u = 0$, which is equivalent to the aspiration-level reference point model (Model 2), link risk taking to aspiration levels – which tend to adapt to accumulated resources, thus constraining risk taking. By producing fairly frequent attention to the aspiration-level reference point, moderate levels of u provide relatively high levels of risk taking when accumulated resources are low. Subsequently, when accumulated resources are relatively high, moderate levels of u direct attention to the survival point often enough to keep risk taking relatively high. The joint consequence is to make risk taking higher, on average, for intermediate values of u than for values that are either close to 0 or close to 1.

Effects of alternative attention-allocation rules

The analysis of Model 3, in which attention to the two reference points is allocated in a strictly probabilistic way, indicates some reasons why fixed-focus models – Model 1 ($u = 1$) and Model 2 ($u = 0$) – generally generate less risk taking than a shifting-focus model ($0 < u < 1$). But the assumption of a constant probability of attending to survival seems too limiting as a description of behavior. It seems possible that attention shifts according to some features of experience rather than strictly as a probabilistic process. Consider the following two different ways by which attention might be allocated to one or the other focal point.

Model 3, variant A: relative distance

The probabilities of attending to the survival reference point and the aspiration reference point are inversely proportional to their relative distances from the current resource position of the risk taker. The closer cumulated resources are to zero, the greater the probability of focusing on the survival point; the closer they are to the aspiration level, the greater the probability of focusing on the aspiration level.

Model 3, variant B: learning from experience

The probability of attention to the survival reference point, rather than the aspiration-level reference point, changes as a result of simple trial and error learning. Trial-by-trial experience associated with a focus on one point or the other leads to modifications in the likelihood of maintaining or changing a focus. Success (defined as cumulated resources being above the aspiration level) decreases the chance of a change in focus, whereas failure (resources below the aspiration level) increases the chance of a change. To simplify the variation, we assume that whenever current cumulated resources fail to achieve the current aspiration, the focus of attention shifts, and that whenever the cumulated resources exceed the aspiration level, the focus of attention remains the same.

These variants on the shifting-focus model result in risk-taking patterns that differ from each other as well as from the previous models. Because both resources and aspirations tend to rise over time, the (stable) survival reference point becomes more distant over time, and the (adaptive)

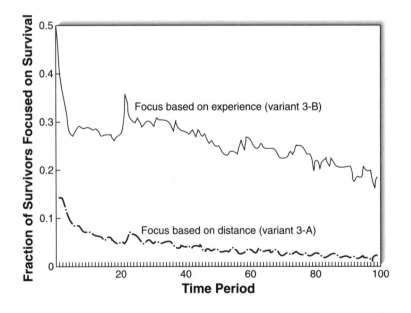

Figure 14.5 Fraction of survivors focused on survival reference point over 100 time periods for variant 3-A and variant 3-B ($N = 5,000$ [nonrenewed], $p_d = 0.0001$, $p_f = 0.05$, $p_s = 0.3$, $x = 0$, $q = 2$, $k = 3$, and $a = 0.5$).

aspiration-level reference point comes closer. Moreover, resources tend to exceed aspirations as long as the latter do not adapt too rapidly to the former. Where the focus of attention is tied to the relative distances between current cumulated resources and the two reference points (Variant A), the changing distances lead to increased attention on the aspiration level over time. When the risk taker learns which focus to adopt as a result of experience (Variant B), the frequency with which focus is shifted depends on the frequency with which cumulated resources fall below aspirations and thus on the speed with which aspirations adjust to experience.

As a result of these differences, an experience-based focus (Variant B) generally leads to more frequent attention to the survival point than does a distance-based focus (Variant A). The differences are shown in figure 14.5 over 100 time periods. If expectations are nonnegative, higher rates of focusing on survival are associated with higher levels of risk taking. Clearly, that effect arises not from focusing on survival when it is most threatened, but from focusing on a nonthreatening survival point when resources are plentiful. Differences in risk taking, in turn, lead to differences both in the fraction of a cohort surviving up to any particular period (greater when relative distance matters, i.e., Variant A) and in the average cumulated gains of survivors up to any particular period (greater when experience matters, i.e., Variant B).

The effects of the rate of aspiration adjustment in the two variants are also different in important ways from what they are in the purely probabilistic version of a shifting-focus model (Model 3). As in the probabilistic version, higher values for a lead to lower levels of risk taking at Period 50. However, in contrast to the probabilistic version, which tends to eliminate high risk takers, Variants A and B lead to the elimination of low risk takers. Risk takers with higher values for a are less likely to survive (as long as aspirations are self-referential). This seemingly contradictory result is produced by the fact that in the rule-based models (Variants A and B), slow adaptation of aspirations leads to relatively low risk taking early (when most deaths occur) and relatively large risk taking later.

RISK TAKING AND SURVIVAL IN RENEWING POPULATIONS

Random-walk models do not ordinarily treat the effects of competition directly. The game of life is portrayed as a game against nature rather than a game against other actors. Nevertheless, it is possible to exercise the present models to explore a few aspects of competitive effects and to use those analyses as a basis for some discussion of the survival advantages (and disadvantages) of particular risk-taking rules. In this section, we explore the trade-off between cumulated resources and survival by considering the changing character of a renewing population that is heterogeneous with respect to the risk-taking rules followed.

Differential survival over time

Suppose we have a population that consists of individual risk takers, each of whom follows the rules of one of the variable-risk models. Thus, each risk taker is of a particular model type, and the model type for each risk taker is invariant as long as that risk taker endures. We exclude Model 0 because comparisons would depend on an arbitrarily chosen value for s^*. We focus on the five other models and use identical values for p_d, p_f, and p_s (i.e., $p_d = 0.0001$, $p_f = 0.05$, and $p_s = 0.3$). We assume that every risk taker who fails is replaced by a new risk taker with a stake, k, the same as that provided to risk takers in the original cohort. Note that this specifies an expanding resource base because each departing risk taker leaves with a negative cumulated resource level and is replaced by a new risk taker with a new positive stake.

The five different sets of rules produce different patterns of risk taking in the five subgroups of risk takers. The different patterns of risk taking lead to different survival rates and different accumulation of resources among survivors. Changes in the distribution of types in a renewing population depend, however, not only on death rates among the types but also on their birth rates. As risk takers are eliminated, they are replaced by new risk takers. We assume that the probability of a replacement's being of a particular type is some mix of the current proportion of the population found in that type and the current share of population resources held by that type.

By these assumptions, we describe a simple birth and death process that captures (in a very specific way) the trade-off·between protecting survival by reducing risk and strengthening reproductive capability by taking risks successfully. Insofar as the probability of a replacement's being of a particular type is proportional to the current number of survivors of that type, high reproduction rates tend to be associated with low risk taking. Insofar as the probability of a replacement's being of a particular type is proportional to the total resources held by survivors of that type, high reproduction rates tend to be associated with high risk taking.

The process can be illustrated in purest form by considering a population in which all risk takers follow the fixed-risk model (Model 0) but vary in the level of risk they take. Suppose there are four types of fixed risk takers: In Type 1, $s^* = 1$; in Type 2, $s^* = 2$; in Type 3, $s^* = 3$; and in Type 4, $s^* = 4$. If each of the types initially includes 25 percent of the population, the changing distribution over time depends sharply on whether replacements are

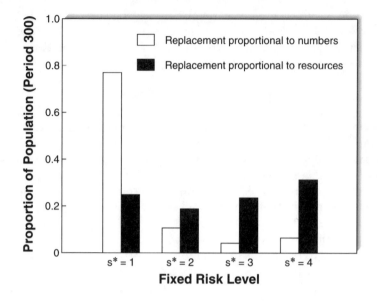

Figure 14.6 Proportion of population with s* = 1, 2, 3 and 4 at Period 300 for two different replacement rules ($N = 200$ [renewed], $p_d = 0.0001$, $p_f = 0.05$, $p_s = 0.3$, $x = 0$, $q = 2$, $k = 3$, and $v = 100$).

proportional to the numbers of survivors of each type or the total amount of resources held by survivors of each type. As figure 14.6 shows, types that are relatively risk averse are significantly more favored by a numbers-dependent reproductive process than by a resources-dependent reproductive process.

In the same spirit, we examine the distribution of rules in the population over time from an initial distribution in which each of the five variable-risk models (Models 1, 2, 3, 3-A, and 3-B) represents one fifth of the population. The distribution depends on the specific parameter values chosen for p_d, p_f and p_s, but there are three general things that can be said. First, the relative positions of the various types change over time, so that superiority depends on the time horizon involved. Second, the long-term proportion of the population represented by risk takers who focus only on survival (Model 1) is highly dependent on the replacement process and the rate at which aspirations adjust (among other risk takers). To the extent that replacement depends on the numbers of survivors rather than on their resources, risk takers focusing on survival only (Model 1) are favored, particularly when aspirations adjust slowly. To the extent that replacement depends on resources, risk takers focusing on survival only (Model 1) tend to be eliminated.

Third, aspiration levels that are upwardly other-referential, rather than self-referential (i.e., $e < 1$, $c > 0$), tend to increase risk taking, resource accumulation by survivors, and the rate of failure of risk takers following the aspiration-level models (Models 2 and 3). As a result, the consequence of emphasizing other- rather than self-referential aspirations depends on the replacement rules. Where replacement depends on numbers, a survival focus rule (Model 1) is strengthened by having aspirations (of others) attend to the performances of others. Where replacement depends on resources, other-referential aspirations tend to strengthen the position of two-reference-point risk-taking types at the expense of those having an unconditional focus on one reference point or the other.

Differential survival when relative resource position matters

In the preceding discussion, the birth rate of a type depends on the relative position of the type, but the survival of individual risk takers does not depend on the performance of others in the population. Suppose that survival requires that a risk taker's cumulated resources not only be greater

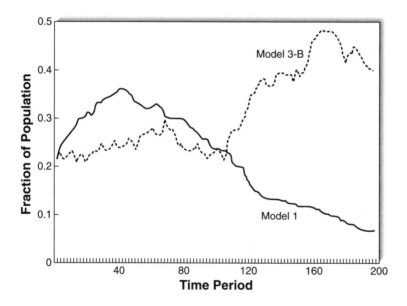

Figure 14.7 Fraction of population in models 1 and 3-B over 200 time periods where relative position matters and replacement is governed by resources ($N = 200$ [renewed]. $p_d = 0.0001$, $p_f = 0.05$, $p_s = 0.3$, $x = 0$, $q = 2$, $k = 3$, $a = 0.5$, and $v = 90$).

than zero but also be large enough to place that risk taker within the top v percent of the population. Such a requirement makes the absorbing barrier at zero irrelevant unless more than $(100 - v)$ percent of the population falls below zero in a particular time period.

Not surprisingly, where the zero point is (almost) irrelevant to survival, a focus on it does not help in the long run. For example, consider a renewing population consisting of risk takers following each of the five variable-risk models (Models 1, 2, 3, 3-A, and 3-B). Suppose that each of the five types initially represents 20 percent of the population, replacement is proportional to cumulated resources, aspirations are other-referential, and relative position matters ($v = 90$). Figure 14.7 shows the proportion of the population represented by two of the types (those following Models 1 and 3-B) over time. In the short run, the survival reference-point model (Model 1) dominates the experience-based, shifting-focus model (Variant B of Model 3), as well as other types. In the longer run, it is dominated by Variant B, as well as by the others.

The broad general implication is that insofar as relative position with respect to resources matters to survival, a focus on an adaptive aspiration level is strongly favored over a focus on survival. This is true even when replacement rules emphasize numbers rather than resources. The only partial exception is when aspirations are other-referential, rather than self-referential. Generally, though not universally, the two determinate variants of a two-reference-point strategy (Models 3-A and 3-B) are more successful than is a strictly probabilistic shift in focus (Model 3).

Concluding Remarks

Random-walk models of variable risk taking are stylized representations of relatively complicated processes of attention, choice, rules, procedures, and habit. The notions underlying the present models are an amalgam of ideas portraying individuals and organizations as more or less consciously choosing a level of risk (or unreliability) and of ideas portraying the level of risk (or unreliability) as being a largely unintended consequence of variation in experience, conflict, and control. In both perspectives, one core idea is that the implicit trade-off between the downside dangers and the upside possibilities of variability is organized less by explicit calculation of their net attractiveness than by attending primarily to one or the other and relating the dangers (or possibilities) to a specific target. From this point of view, for example, slack resources can be seen as focusing attention on the advantages of greater variability and experimentation rather than the dangers.

The models have some claim to usefulness as descriptions of risk-taking behavior. They seem to capture important empirical regularities. Specifically, they can show unstable risk-taking behavior in the neighborhood of death, relatively high levels of risk taking when slack resources are large, risk seeking for losses and risk aversion for gains in the neighborhood of a target, a tendency to change risk preference over time with the same resources, and a tendency to underestimate risks as a result of favorable experience with them.

Exercising the models suggests the following three additional descriptive attributes of variable risk taking. First, in most cases as time goes on, the survivors in a cohort of risk takers will tend to have resources that are fairly substantial, relatively high aspirations for resources, and positive biases in their estimates of the means of their own performance distributions. Second, the rate at which a risk taker's aspirations adjust to that risk taker's own experience is a significant factor in determining risk preference. When aspirations are self-referential, slow adaptation of aspirations to a risk taker's own experience generally leads to greater risk being taken than does fast adaptation. On the other hand, when aspirations are tied to the performance of superior others, fast adaptation tends to lead to greater risk taking than does slow adaptation. Third, the way in which attention is shifted from one reference point to another makes a difference. For example, where attention is allocated to the two reference points by a fixed-probability process, the level of risk taking depends nonmonotonically on the likelihood of attending to the survival point.

The analysis here also confirms previous suggestions that there may be broad survival advantages to variable risk taking oriented to an adaptive aspiration level (March, 1988b). The precise nature of those advantages depends, however, on interactions among the rate of aspiration adjustment (Levitt and March, 1988), the extent to which aspirations attend to one's own achievements compared to attention to others (Herriott et al 1985), the extent to which the focus of attention shifts between a survival point and an aspiration level and the rules governing such shifts (Lopes, 1987), and other specifications of the situation (e.g., the correlation between risk and return, the level of competition, and the "birth process" by which eliminated risk takers are replaced). Thus, although it is possible to see how rules such as those described here might come to dominate risk strategies, it is not possible to rationalize them unconditionally within the present framework.

Acknowledgments

The research was supported by grants from the Recanati Foundation, the Russell Sage Foundation, the Spencer Foundation, and the Stanford Graduate School of Business.

We are grateful for the comments of Howard Kunreuther and Lola Lopes.

References

Antonelli, C. (1989). A failure-induced model of research and development expenditure: Italian evidence from the early 1980s. *Journal of Economic Behavior and Organization, 12*, 159–80.

Atkinson, J. (1957). Motivational determinants of risk taking behavior. *Psychological Review, 64*, 359–72.

Bartholomew, D. J. (1973). *Stochastic models for social processes* (2nd edn). New York: Wiley.

Battalio, R. C., Kagel, J. H., and Jiranyakul, K. (1990). Testing between alternative models of choice under uncertainty: Some initial results. *Journal of Risk and Uncertainty, 3*, 25–50.

Boisjoly, R. (1988). Ethical decisions – Morton Thiokol and the space shuttle Challenger disaster. *American Society of Mechanical Engineers Journal, 87-WA/TS-4*, 1–13.

Bowman, E. H. (1982). Risk seeking by troubled firms. *Sloan Management Review, 23*, 33–42.

Bowman, E. H., and Kunreuther, H. (1988). Post-Bhopal behaviour at a chemical company. *Journal of Management Studies, 25*, 387–402.

Brenner, R. (1983). *History – the human gamble.* Chicago: University of Chicago Press.

Bromiley, P. (1991). Testing a causal model of corporate risk-taking and performance. *Academy of Management Journal, 34*, 37–59.

Bromiley, P., and Miller, K. D. (1990). Strategic risk and corporate performance: An analysis of alternative risk measures. *Academy of Management Journal, 33*, 756–79.

Bromiley, P., and Wiseman, R. (1989). *Risk taking by declining organizations.* Unpublished manuscript, Carlson School of Management, University of Minnesota.

Burns, T., and Stalker, G. M. (1961). *The management of innovation.* London: Tavistock.

Czarniawska, B., and Hedberg, B. (1985). Control cycle response to decline. *Scandinavian Journal of Management Studies, 2*, 19–39.

Dubins, L. E., and Savage, L. J. (1965). *How to gamble if you must: Inequalities for stochastic processes.* New York: McGraw-Hill.

Feigenbaum, A., and Thomas, H. (1986). Dynamic and risk measurement perspectives on Bowman's risk-return paradox for strategic management: An empirical study. *Strategic Management Journal, 7*, 395–408.

Feller, W. (1968). *An introduction to probability theory and its applications* (vol. 1, 3rd edn). New York: Wiley.

Gibbons, M. R. (1982). Multivariate tests of financial models: A new approach. *Journal of Financial Economics, 10*, 3–27.

Gilovich, T., Vallone, R., and Tversky, A. (1985). The hot hand in basketball: On the misperception of random sequences. *Cognitive Psychology, 17*, 295–314.

Greenhalgh, L. (1983). Organizational decline. *Research in the Sociology of Organizations, 2*, 231–76.

Hausch, D. B., Ziemba, W. T., and

Rubenstein, M. (1981). Efficiency of the market for racetrack betting. *Management Science, 27,* 1435–52.

Hershey, J. C., and Schoemaker, P. J. (1980). Prospect theory's reflection hypothesis: A critical examination. *Organizational Behavior and Human Performance, 25,* 395–418.

Herriott, S. R., Levinthal, D., and March, J. G. (1985). Learning from experience in organizations. *American Economic Review, 75,* 298–302.

Kahneman, D., and Tversky, A. (1979). Prospect theory: An analysis of decision under risk. *Econometrica, 47,* 263–91.

Kamil, A. C., and Roitblat, H. L. (1985). The ecology of foraging behavior: Implications for animal learning and memory. *Annual Review of Psychology, 36,* 141–69.

Keyes, R. (1985). *Chancing it.* Boston: Little, Brown.

Kuhl, J. (1978). Standard setting and risk preference: An elaboration of the theory of achievement motivation and an empirical test. *Psychological Review, 85,* 239–48.

Langer, E. J. (1975). The illusion of control. *Journal of Personality and Social Psychology, 32,* 311–28.

Lant, T. (1992). Aspiration level adaptation: An empirical exploration. *Management Science, 38,* 623–44.

Levinthal, D. A. (1990). Organizational adaptation, environmental selection, and random walks. In J. Singh (ed.), *Organizational evolution: New directions* (pp. 201–23). Newbury Park. CA: Sage.

Levinthal, D. A. (1991). Random walks and organizational mortality, *Administrative Science Quarterly, 36,* 397–420.

Levitt, B., and March, J. G. (1988). Organizational learning. *Annual Review of Sociology, 14,* 319–40.

Lewin, K., Dembo, T., Festinger, L., and Sears, P. (1944). Level of aspiration. In J. M. Hunt (ed.), *Personality and the behavior disorders* (vol. 1, pp. 333–78). New York: Ronald.

Libby, R., and Fishburn, P. C. (1977). Behavioral models of risk taking in business decisions: A survey and evaluation. *Journal of Accounting Research, 15,* 272–92.

Lopes, L. L. (1987). Between hope and fear: The psychology of risk. *Advances in Experimental Social Psychology, 20,* 255–95.

MacCrimmon, K. R., and Wehrung, D. A. (1986). *Taking risks: The management of uncertainty.* New York: Free Press.

MacCrimmon, K. R., and Wehrung, D. A. (1990). Characteristics of risk taking executives. *Management Science, 36,* 422–35.

March, J. C., and March, J. G. (1978). Performance sampling in social matches. *Administrative Science Quarterly, 23,* 434–53.

March, J. G. (1981). Footnotes to organizational change. *Administrative Science Quarterly, 26,* 563–77.

March, J. G. (1988a). *Decisions and organizations.* Oxford: Basil Blackwell.

March, J. G. (1988b). Variable risk preferences and adaptive aspirations. *Journal of Economic Behavior and Organization, 9,* 5–24.

March, J. G., and Shapira, Z. (1987). Managerial perspectives on risk and risk taking. *Management Science, 33,* 1404–18.

March, J. G., and Simon, H. A. (1958). *Organizations.* New York: Wiley.

Mayhew, L. B. (1979). *Surviving the eighties.* San Francisco: Jossey-Bass.

Olson, M. (1963). Rapid growth as a destabilizing force. *Journal of Economic History, 23,* 529–52.

Payne, J. W., Laughhann, D. J., and Crum, R. L. (1980). Translation of gambles and aspiration effects in risky choice behavior. *Management Science, 26*, 1039–60.

Payne, J. W., Laughhann, D. J., and Crum, R. L. (1981). Further tests of aspiration level effects in risky choice behavior. *Management Science, 27*, 953–8.

Revelle, W., and Michaels, E. (1976). The theory of achievement motivation revisited: The implications of inertial tendencies. *Psychological Review, 83*, 394–404.

Roll, R. (1986). The hubris hypothesis of corporate takeovers. *Journal of Business, 59*, 197–216.

Romanow, A. L., and Sellke, T. (1985). Performance sampling and multiple choices: Brownian motion models. *Journal of Mathematical Sociology, 11*, 223–44.

Roy, A. D. (1952). Safety first and the holding of assets. *Econometrica, 20*, 431–49.

Samuelson, W., and Zeckhauser, R. (1988). Status quo bias in decision making. *Journal of Risk and Uncertainty, 1*, 7–59.

Schneider, S. L., and Lopes, L. L. (1986). Reflection in preferences under risk: Who and when may suggest why. *Journal of Experimental Psychology: Human Perception and Performance, 12*, 535–48.

Shapira, Z., and Venezia, I. (1992). Size and frequency of prizes as determinants of the demand for lotteries. *Organizational Behavior and Human Decision Processes, 52*, 307–19.

Singh, J. V. (1986). Performance, slack, and risk taking in organizational decision making. *Academy of Management Journal, 29*, 562–85.

Staw, B. M. (1976). Knee-deep in the big muddy: A study of escalating commitment to a chosen course of action. *Organizational Behavior and Human Performance, 16*, 27–44.

Staw, B. M., Sandelands, L. E., and Dutton, J. E. (1981). Threat-rigidity effects in organizational behavior: A multilevel analysis. *Administrative Science Quarterly, 26*. 501–24.

Stone, J. M. (1973). The theory of capacity and the insurance of catastrophic risks *Journal of Risk and Insurance, 40*, 231–43, 339–55.

Thaler, R. H., and Johnson, E. J. (1990). Gambling with the house money and trying to break even: The effects of prior outcomes on risky choice. *Management Science, 36*, 643–60.

Tversky, A., and Kahneman, D. (1974). Judgment under uncertainty: Heuristics and biases. *Science, 185*, 1124–31.

Tversky, A., and Kahneman, D. (1991). Loss aversion in riskless choice: A reference dependent model. *Quarterly Journal of Economics, 106*, 1039–61.

Wehrung, D. A. (1989). Risk taking over gains and losses: A study of oil executives. *Annals of Operations Research, 19*, 115–39.

CHAPTER FIFTEEN

Learning to Be Risk Averse

Experimental learning that conforms to standard learning models is shown to lead learners to favor less risky alternatives when possible outcomes are positive. This learning disadvantage for risky alternatives is likely to be quite substantial and persistent, particularly among relatively fast learners. Learning to choose among alternatives whose outcomes lie in the negative domain, on the other hand, leads to favoring more risky alternatives in the short run but tends to become risk neutral in the long run. Thus, the fact that human beings exhibit greater risk aversion for gains than for losses in a wide variety of situations may reflect accumulated learning rather than inexplicable human traits or utility functions. Some implications of an experiential learning interpretation of risk preferences are discussed.

Two of the grandest theoretical traditions for understanding human choices are found in theories of rational choice and theories of experiential learning. For the most part, the two theoretical traditions remain largely separate, though there are occasional efforts to relate the two primarily by noting some conditions under which they appear to predict different behavior. This chapter explores the possibility that risk aversion, a key concept of many theories of rational choice, may be produced by learning from experience. In particular, experiential learning processes of a standard kind produce systematic effects on choice behavior that can be characterized as showing greater risk aversion for gains than for losses.

EXPLAINING RISK-TAKING BEHAVIOR

A canonical situation for the study of individual behavior is one in which repetitive choices are made between two alternatives under conditions in which information about the consequences of the alternatives can be secured only by choosing them. In theories of rational choice, this situation is commonly called the "two-armed bandit" problem. In theories of learning, it is commonly called a *T-maze* problem. Decision makers begin with some prior beliefs and propensities and accumulate experience with the two alternatives by making choices. A central question about such situations concerns the ways in which individuals respond to choices involving consequences that are subject to probabilistic variation. Of particular interest is the issue of risk, the possibility that choices depend on some features of the riskiness of alternatives, as well as their expected values, and questions of the extent to which reactions to risk are generic human traits, individual-specific traits, or dependent on situational factors and framing (Lopes, 1987; Schoemaker, 1982; Shapira, 1995; Yaari, 1987.)

Risk taking with gains and risk taking with losses

Consider the following experiment: A participant is offered a choice between two options. The first option pays k (with certainty). The second option pays k/r with probability r ($0 < r < 1$) and otherwise nothing. Because the two options are equal in monetary expected value, any consistent pattern of choosing one alternative rather than the other can be interpreted as reflecting risk preference. Participants who choose the second (more risky) alternative rather than a certainty of the same monetary expected value are characteristically described as *risk seeking*. Participants who choose the first alternative are characteristically described as *risk averse*.

Behavior in such experiments, as well as in situations that occur naturally in the real world, depends on whether k is positive or negative. Generally, less risky choices are likely to be made when k is positive than when k is negative. Greater risk aversion for gains than for losses has been observed in studies of a wide range of human (and animal) participants and a wide range of experimental and real-world situations (Bromiley, 1991; Caracao, 1980; Johnson, 1971; Kahneman and Tversky, 1979; Payne et al., 1981.) Business executives, students drawn from many disciplines and countries, gamblers, and small graniverous birds all have exhibited behavior consistent with the experimental results.

For the most part, studies in this tradition have treated returns that are greater than zero as *positive* or *gains* and returns that are less than zero as *negative* or *losses*. It is recognized, however, that the relevant reference point is, in general, not literally zero but some value that reflects aspirations, expectations, or targets. From this point of view, a gain is a return that falls above a reference point, and a loss is a return that falls below. Most discussions presume stable reference points, but some analyses of risk taking have emphasized the significance of reference points that change, particularly those that change endogenously (March, 1988; March and Shapira, 1992).

Theories of choice and risk taking

The most common explanation of risk aversion in choices involving positive monetary outcomes is one that assumes that choices exhibit decreasing marginal utility for money. In revealed preference versions of choice theory, risk aversion and decreasing marginal utility for money in the positive domain are equivalent (Arrow, 1971). In other versions, decreasing marginal utility for money is treated as a fundamental primitive of behavior, and risk aversion is derived from it. Such an assumption in its usual form fails, however, to account for the observed differences in risk taking between situations involving gains and situations involving losses.

One possible solution to this difficulty maintains the tradition of revealed risk preferences. By making a relatively modest modification in the decreasing marginal utility argument, risk preferences in the negative domain can also be interpreted as reflecting nonlinearities in the utility for money. Suppose we assume that individuals view both losses and gains from the vantage point of the zero point. Then, an assumption of decreasing marginal disutility for money losses is a natural correlate of an assumption of decreasing marginal utility for money gains. But a decreasing marginal disutility for money losses is equivalent to an increasing marginal utility for money. Thus, the utility function for losses is convex, whereas the utility function for gains is concave (Kahneman and Tversky, 1979). The joint consequence is to make risk preferences more risk averse for gains than for losses.

There are several other explanations of the tendency toward greater risk aversion in the positive domain (for a discussion, see Lopes, 1994). For the most part, they retain the idea that choices in the face of risk are related to beliefs about possible consequences and subjective values associated with those consequences. However, they suggest that choices may depend on various features of the probability distributions over outcomes other than their expected values and variances and on other ways that individuals have of thinking about their preferences and expectations of consequences (Bell et al., 1988; Kleindorfer et al., 1993; Lopes, 1994). For example, in an aspiration-level explanation, decision makers are pictured as having targets for performance. They are imagined to respond to situations involving gains (i.e., alternatives whose distributions lie mostly above the target) in a relatively risk averse manner so as to keep the chance of falling below the target small. And they are imagined to respond to situations involving losses in a relatively risk-seeking manner so as to make the probability of falling above the target relatively large (March and Shapira, 1992). Such a rule results in greater risk aversion above a target than below it.

Learning and risk taking

In an alternative explanation of choice behavior, selection among alternatives is seen not as a calculated, consequential choice but as a response learned from experience. The traditions of such a conception are ancient, but its modern development probably can be dated from Thorndike (1898) and the "law of effect." Proponents of reinforcement learning theories in this tradition suppose that decision makers have propensities to choose one alternative or another and modify those propensities on the basis of experienced outcomes. Favorable experiences are assumed to lead to increases in the propensity to choose an alternative associated historically with those experiences; unfavorable experiences are assumed to lead to decreases in that propensity. Models of experiential learning of this type have been explored extensively and applied to a variety of learning situations involving animals and humans (Estes, 1959). They are distinguishable from, but also overlap considerably with, ideas about learning that emphasize thought and cognition as mediating processes, on the one hand (Johnson-Laird, 1983), and ideas that emphasize response strength as a function of the amount and timing of rewards in a free response situation, on the other (Skinner, 1938; Williams, 1988).

Risk preference does not enter directly into such ideas about learning from experience. Experiential learning involves incremental adjustment to the results of action. Propensities to pursue one alternative or another determine behavior and are themselves determined by realized results, but there is no explicit consideration of the riskiness of alternatives as a factor in choice. Suppose individuals learn how to respond to situations involving risk the same way they learn other things, by experiencing the apparent consequences of their behavior and modifying their rules of behavior as a result of accumulated experience. In this sense, a learning process (rather than a learner) can be implicitly risk seeking or risk averse. The proposition explored here is that observed patterns of risk taking can be explained as a result of simple trial-and-error learning without any assumption of trait-based preferences for risk, nonlinear utility functions for money, target-related satisficing, biases in risk estimation, or poorly designed incentives.

MODELS OF EXPERIENTIAL LEARNING

The strategy in the remainder of this chapter is (a) to define several simple stochastic models of experiential learning that have some claim to representing human trial-by-trial learning; (b) to show what takes place within such models when a learner is confronted with alternatives of varying risk; and (c) to examine the possible implications of considering risk taking as a propensity that is, in part, learned.

I consider a broad class of models of experiential learning. Each model in this class is characterized by the following:

1. *A set of alternatives.* Each alternative is described by a probability distribution over returns, conditional on its choice.
2. *A learner.* Each learner is described by an initial probability vector over alternatives and, subsequently, after each learning trial by a revised probability vector.
3. *A decision rule.* In each of a sequence of trials, the learner chooses an alternative. The choice is probabilistically determined by the probability vector of that learner.
4. *An outcome rule.* The return from a choice of a particular alternative is a draw from the probability distribution of returns for that alternative.
5. *A learning rule.* After each trial, the learner modifies the probability vector. If $p_{i,t}$ is a specific learner's probability of choosing alternative i on trial t, a learning rule specifies how $p_{i,t}$ is transformed to $p_{i,t+1}$.

Several learning models fit such a description. They differ only in the learning rules they assume.

Three learning rules are considered here: The first defines a *fractional* adjustment model. It is a variation on standard Bush-Mosteller-Estes stochastic learning models (Bush and Mosteller, 1955; Estes, 1959). The second learning rule defines an *average return* model. It is a variation on standard Herrnstein matching models (Herrnstein, 1961, 1970; Staddon, 1977). The third learning rule defines a *weighted return* model. It is a variation on exponential updating. Each of the learning rules is linked to rules in the literature, but each simplifies the rules. They are intended to capture the basic spirit, but not all the rich detail, of several standard models.

Fractional adjustment model

In the fractional adjustment model, $p_{i,t}$ changes as a result of the action taken and the outcomes observed at $t-1$. If outcomes are favorable, then the probability associated with the action taken increases. If outcomes are unfavorable, then the probability associated with the action taken decreases. In cases involving more than two alternatives, the entire vector has to be renormalized when one probability is adjusted, but a simple form is available in the two alternative situations. In the case of a reward after choosing the ith alternative $(0 \le a \le 1)$,

$$p_{i,t+1} = p_{i,t} + a(1 - p_{i,t}) \qquad (15.1)$$

If the ith alternative is chosen but not rewarded $(0 \le a \le 1)$,

$$p_{i,t+1} = (1 - a)\, p_{i,t} \qquad (15.2)$$

The greater the value of a, the faster the adaptation. To allow for variable rewards, the learning rule is modified to allow the increment to depend on the magnitude of the reward. If alternative i is chosen at t and a positive return of k is realized $(0 \le a \le 1)$, then $p_{i,t+1}$ is increased by applying the reward operator k times to $p_{i,t}$. Thus,

$$p_{i,t+1} = 1 - [(1 - a)^k\,(1 - p_{i,t})] \qquad (15.3)$$

If a negative reward of $-k$ is realized, then $p_{i,t+1}$ is decreased by applying the nonreward operator k times to $p_{i,t}$ $(0 \le a \le 1)$. Thus,

$$p_{i,t+1} = p_{i,t}\,(1 - a)^k \qquad (15.4)$$

Initial probabilities can assume any values that satisfy the requirements that they lie between 0 and 1 and sum to 1 over all i, but each of the $p_{i,0}$ might normally be set equal to $1/n$, where n is the number of alternatives. In the present case, with two alternatives, $p_{2,t} = 1 - p_{1,t}$ and $p_{1,0} = 0.5$.

The fractional adjustment model used here is clearly drawn from the Bush-Mosteller-Estes tradition, but it by no means captures all of the variations in that tradition. Treating the learning parameter for reward as the same as the learning parameter for nonreward is a simplification, as is setting the implicit learning limits in the model to 1 and 0. The method for dealing with varying amounts of reward is only one among several possibilities.

Average return model

In the average return model, $p_{i,t}$ changes on the basis of the history of returns that have been gained from the various alternatives. A learner is seen as maintaining a memory of the average return from each alternative. Thus, if $S_{i,t}$ is the sum of rewards received when alternative i was chosen in any period prior to t, and $m_{i,t}$ is the total number of times alternative i was chosen prior to t, then

$$A_{i,t} = S_{i,t}/m_{i,t} \qquad (15.5)$$

In order to avoid cases that are ambiguous within the average returns and weighted returns models, we consider only cases in which possible outcomes for all alternatives are restricted to either the positive or the negative domain, thus where all values of $A_{i,t}$ have the same sign.

The probability of choosing alternative i in period t is proportional to past average results. Where the memory traces are all positive ($j = 1$ to n),

$$p_{i,t} = A_{i,t}/\Sigma A_{j,t} \qquad (15.6)$$

Thus, where there are two alternatives, the ratio of the two probabilities is equal to the ratio of their average returns-to-date. Where the memory traces are all negative ($j = 1$ to n),

$$1 - p_{i,t} = A_{i,t}/\Sigma A_{j,t} \qquad (15.7)$$

Initial values for the $S_{i,0}$ and $m_{i,0}$ can be set to any values, but the simplest assumption is that $m_{i,0} = 1$ and that $S_{i,0}$ = the expected value of the ith alternative, thus that $p_{i,0} = 1/n$ for all n alternatives if the alternatives have equal expected values.

The spirit of the average return model was drawn from various learning models that can be grouped under the general heading of "matching models" (Herrnstein, 1961). The present model is at least a simplification and in some respects a fundamental modification of such models, however. Most matching models, for example, do not assume an indefinitely long memory of results, normally assuming a memory of some fixed length of experience. The biggest deviation here, however, is in relating the model to trial-based sequential choices among alternatives with differing probabilities of reward rather than to response rates in the face of differing amounts and delays of reinforcement, which are central to most models in the matching tradition (Williams, 1988). The relationship is basically that between a discrete time probabilistic model and a continuous time duration model.

Weighted return model

In the weighted return model, as in the average return model, $p_{i,t}$ changes on the basis of the history of returns that have been gained from the various alternatives. A learner is seen as updating the memory of returns after each choice of alternative i by computing a weighted average of the previous memory and the most recent experience. Thus, $A_{i,t}$ is unchanged in any period in which alternative i is not chosen. If the ith alternative is chosen at t, $A_{i,t+1}$ is a mix between $A_{i,t}$ and the outcome realized in period t, $O_{i,t}$, with the weight assigned to the two being $(1 - \beta)$ and β respectively $(0 \le \beta \le 1)$. Thus,

$$A_{i,t+1} = \beta\, O_{i,t} + (1 - \beta)\, A_{i,t} \qquad (15.8)$$

More recent experiences on any particular alternative are weighted more than more remote experiences on that alternative, with the relative rate of learning or forgetting being indexed by β. The value of $p_{i,t}$ is derived from the $A_{i,t}$ in the same way as in the average return model (Equations 15.6 and 15.7).

The weighted return model can be seen as capturing some elements of a limited memory version of the average return model. It is equivalent to maintaining a memory of the exponentially weighted moving average of returns from the choice of each alternative. The impact of more recent experiences is greater than that of earlier ones. This approach to limitations in memory differs from an assumption of some arbitrary memory horizon, but either assumption produces the same qualitative results for the analyses below. The weighted return model can also be seen as a model of rational estimation, thus linked to theories of experiential smoothing. Exponentially weighted moving averages are plausible ways of balancing the need for large samples with the possibilities that more recent observations contain more relevant information for estimating current conditions.

Exercising the Models

To confirm that they have standard learning properties, the three models can be exercised in situations involving choosing between two alternatives, each characterized by a fixed magnitude and probability of reward. As would be expected, each model exhibits distributions of $p_{i,t}$ over a series of learning trials that are consistent with human and animal learning in standard situations. For example, in a probability learning situation in which Alternative 1 (if chosen) is rewarded with probability r and Alternative 2 (if chosen) is rewarded with probability $(1 - r)$, each of the models approaches asymptotic values for the probability, p, of choosing Alternative 1. In the case of the fractional adjustment and average return models, the asymptote appears to be (and indeed can be proven to be) equal to r. In the case of the weighted return model, the asymptote appears to be somewhat greater than r for $0.5 < r < 1$. Except for the special cases of $r = 0$, $r = 0.5$, and $r = 1$, a prediction that p will approach r through learning is (as is frequently noted) different from conventional predictions of optimal rational choice, but such probability matching is often observed in human and animal learning.

To consider learning behavior within the models in situations involving differences in risk, suppose r_i is the probability that a choice of the ith alternative will be rewarded and k_i is the magnitude of the reward if it is received. In the classic experiments, which are simulated here, there are two alternatives with $r_1 = 1$, $r_2 = 0.01$, $k_1 = 1$ (or -1), and $k_2 = 100$ (or -100). I asked two basic questions: (a) To what extent and in what ways does the distribution of $p_{i,t}$ over a series of learning trials depend on the values of r_i and k_i (and thus on the expected values and risks of the two alternatives)? and (b) to what extent and in what ways does the distribution of $p_{i,t}$ over a series of learning trials depend on the learning rates (represented by the values of a, m, and β in the various models)?

In order to explore such questions, each of the models has been used to simulate learning under the assumptions specified. In each case reported, the simulations involved 1,000 simulated learners.

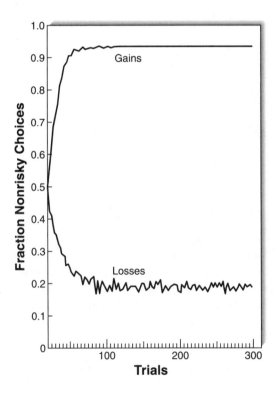

Figure 15.1 Comparing risk preference for gains and losses, fractional adjustment model ($k_1 = 1$ or -1, $k_2 = 100$ or -100, $r_1 = 1$, $r_2 = 0.01$, $a = 0.1$).

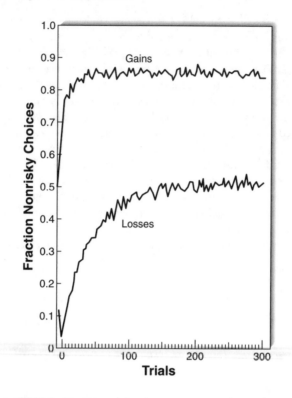

Figure 15.2 Comparing risk preference for gains and losses, average return model (k_1 = 1 or −1, k_2 = 100 or −100, r_1 = 1, r_2 = .01, m = 1 $S_{i,0}$ = 1).

Dependence on r_i and k_i

The central issue here is whether learning generates risk-taking biases. In particular, does simple experiential learning give a more privileged position to risky alternatives in a domain of losses than in a domain of gains? To examine this question, I simulate the standard experimental situations, described earlier, in which Alternative 1 (if chosen) has a certain return of k and Alternative 2 (if chosen) has a return of k/r with probability r and otherwise a return of 0.

Greater risk aversion for gains than for losses

The simulations confirm the speculation that learning affects risk taking. When simulated learners face two alternatives, one offering a certain re-

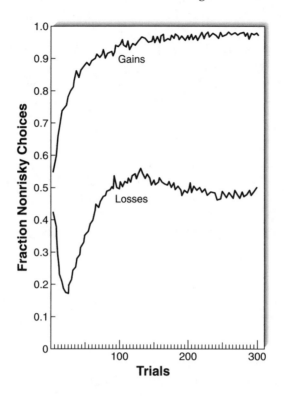

Figure 15.3 Comparing risk preference for gains and losses, weighted return model ($k_1 = 1$ or -1, $k_2 = 100$ or -100, $r_1 = 1$, $r_2 = .01$, $\beta = 0.2$).

turn of k and the other offering k/r with probability r, they are more likely to choose the risky alternative when k is negative than when k is positive. (Note that if $k = 0$, then $k/r = 0$, the two alternatives are indistinguishable, and there is no issue of risk taking or avoiding. Similarly, if $r = 1$, the two alternatives are indistinguishable.) Figures 15.1, 15.2, and 15.3 show the results over the first 300 trials for the fractional adjustment, average return, and weighted return models, respectively, in the experimental setting described earlier. The simulations assume that $r = 0.01$, $a = 0.1$, $m = 1$, $S_{i,0} = 1$, and $\beta = 0.2$, and the figures compare (a) a case of positive outcomes in which $k = 1$ with (b) a case of negative outcomes in which $k = -1$. As the figures indicate, choosing the less risky alternative (risk aversion) is much more likely when possible outcomes lie in the positive domain than when they are negative when $r = 0.01$.

The tendency for learners (on average) to exhibit greater risk aversion for gains persists indefinitely in the fractional adjustment and weighted return models. The average return model ultimately comes to have an equal number of learners choosing each alternative, but the amount of experience required to reach such a result when $r = 0.01$ is quite substantial – about 50,000 trials with the present parameters.[1]

Ordinary experimential learning as found in these models results in greater risk aversion for gains than for losses, particularly when r is small, but it would not be correct to portray learning as reliably producing risk seeking (in the sense of making $p_{i,t} < 0.5$ as t becomes large) when returns lie in the negative domain. Such a result is found in the short run for all of the models. In the longer run, however, only the fractional adjustment model maintains risk seeking for losses (see figures 15.1, 15.2, and 15.3). Learning that conforms to the average return and weighted return models ultimately results in risk neutrality for losses (in combination with risk aversion for gains). The short run is, however, sometimes rather long, particularly if r is small.

Risk premiums

Because it favors lower risk over higher risk, learning in the positive domain exhibits a tendency to choose alternatives with lower expected monetary value if they also offer reduced risk. To calibrate the risk premium imposed by learning to be risk averse in the positive domain, I estimate the approximate reward for success on the risky alternative (k_2/r_2), and therefore the expected value (k_2) required to produce an equal number of choices for each of the two alternatives on the 300th learning trial when the nonrisky alternative has a certain return of 1 (i.e., $k_1 = 1$, $r_1 = 1$) and the risky alternative has a probability of reward equal to 0.01 (i.e., $r_2 = 0.01$). The results are shown in table 15.1. Given the indicated parameters, the least biased model requires an expected value for the risky alternative that is four times that of the nonrisky alternative in order to have the two alternatives be equally attractive (on average) after 300 learning trials.

Effect of a, m, and β

The learning parameters a, m, and β all affect the rate at which learning took place. High values of a and β and low values of m are associated with fast learning. As might be expected, fast learning accentuates the tendency toward risk aversion in the positive domain, slow learning reduces it – provided the initial probabilities of choosing the various alternatives are (as in this case) equal. Slow learners are more likely than fast learners to make enough risky choices to realize an occasional very favorable consequence. Figure 15.4 illustrates the learning rate effect us-

Table 15.1 Risk premiums

Model	Reward (k_2/r_2)	Expected value (k_2)
Fractional adjustment	1,900	19
Average return	400	4
Weighted return	1,300	13

Note Approximate reward (k_2/r_2) for success on the risky alternative and expected value (k_2) required to produce an equal number of choices for each of the two alternatives on the 300th learning trial when the nonrisky alternative has a certain return of 1 (i.e., $k_1 = 1$, $r_1 = 1$) and the risky alternative has a probability of reward equal to 0.01 (i.e. $r_2 = 0.01$).

ing the fractional adjustment model. It shows the fraction of choices of the less risky alternative over 300 trials for three different values for the learning parameter, a, where $r_1 = 1$, $r_2 = 0.01$, $k_1 = 1$, and $k_2 = 100$. Similarly, figures 15.5 and 15.6 show the effect of variations in m and β in the average return and weighted return models, where $r_1 = 1$, $r_2 = 0.01$, $k_1 = 1$, and $k_2 = 100$.

Effects of skewness

As long as r is less than 0.5 (as in most experiments on choice of this genre), the risky alternative in the positive domain has a positively skewed outcome distribution; the mean is higher than the median. The risky alternative in the negative domain has a negatively skewed outcome distribution; the mean is lower than the median. The skewness of the distributions has an effect on the mix of outcomes that will be experienced, and a reasonable speculation would be that it is the skewed nature of the outcome distribution, rather than the positive or negative character of the choice, that produces greater risk aversion for gains in some situations than in others. In particular, it might be predicted that if the skewness were reversed, so also would be the effect of learning.

The speculation is plausible, but it is not true. As might be expected from the reduced difference in the riskiness associated with the two alternatives, the difference between learned risk preferences for gains and learned risk preferences for losses decreases as r increases. When r is close to 1, risk neutrality is common for both gains and losses, and the difference disappears; but for no value of r between 0 and 1 is average risk aversion greater for losses than for gains. The relations between r and the difference between gains and losses in the proportion of choices made of the nonrisky

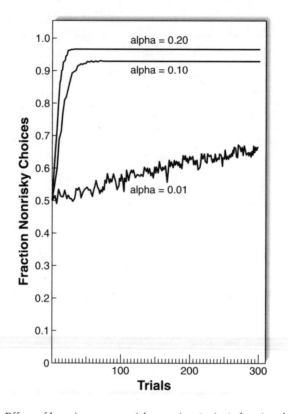

Figure 15.4 Effect of learning rate on risk aversion (gains), fractional adjustment model ($k_1 = 1$, $k_2 = 100$, $r_1 = 1$, $r_2 = 0.01$).

alternative over the first 30 trials for each of the three models are shown in figure 15.7. Over longer periods, the differences decline in the average return model, but there is no length of experience that produces greater risk aversion for losses than for gains for any value of r in any model. A brief elaboration of the sampling reasons for the speculation about skewness and the learning reasons for its failure can be found in the Appendix.

INTERPRETING THE RESULTS

The results implicate learning in risk-taking behavior. If learning from experience that is accurately modeled by the models examined here, it is not neutral with respect to risk taking. Learning in the domain of gains, that is, where expected returns of alternatives are positive, leads to behavior

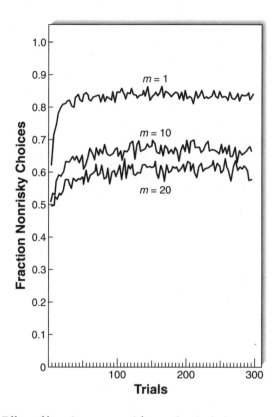

Figure 15.5 Effect of learning rate on risk aversion (gains), average return model ($k_1 = 1$, $k_2 = 100$, $r_1 = 1$, $r_2 = .01$, $S_{i,0} = 1$).

that is decidedly more risk averse than does learning in the domain of losses. Risk aversion in the positive domain can be understood as learned without any attribution of a risk-taking trait. At the same time, it should be noted that the models yield a distribution of risk-taking behavior, that the same process that produces greater risk aversion for gains than for losses for most individuals sometimes produces individuals who are prone to take risks for gains and avoid them for losses. I ask whether the results can be given a somewhat more general intuitive interpretation than as simply the output of three standard models of learning.

Learning as sequential sampling

Experiential learning modifies behavior in response to each small sample of information as it arrives. At the same time, experiential learning

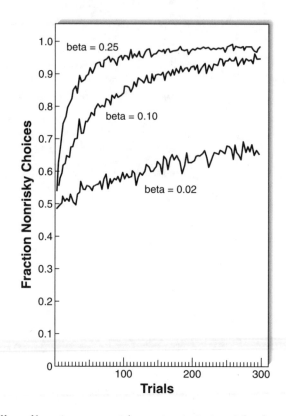

Figure 15.6 Effect of learning rate on risk aversion (gains), weighted return model ($k_1 = 1$, $k_2 = 100$, $r_1 = 1$, $r_2 = 0.01$).

modifies the sampling rate of the alternatives (by changing behavior). Much of the power of learning stems from these sequential sampling properties. By shifting sampling from apparently inferior alternatives to apparently superior ones, the process improves performance.

However, those same properties of sequential sampling complicate learning from experience. An experiential learning process reduces the rate of sampling of apparently inferior alternatives and thus reduces the chance to experience their value correctly, particularly those with high variance in returns. Correction in estimates of expected return from each alternative is a natural consequence of the unfolding of experience, but it is inhibited by any learning process that quickly focuses choice and thus reduces the sampling rate of one alternative. Whenever a large sample advantage of one alternative over another is paired with a small sample disadvantage, learning is likely to lead to an implicit miscoding of the relative value

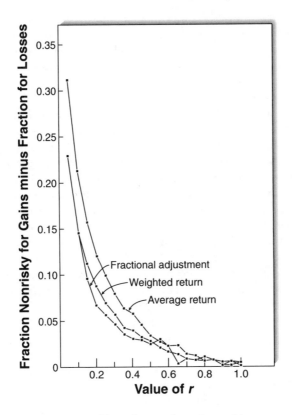

Figure 15.7 Difference between risk preference for gains and losses as a function of r_2, Trials 1–30, three models ($r_1 = 1$, $k_1 = 1$ or -1, $k_2 = k_1/r_2$ $a = 0.1$, $\beta = 0.2$, $m = 1$, $S_{i,0} = 1$).

of the alternatives. Small sample learning with respect to risky alternatives is quite likely to be misguided. Alternatives that are usually fairly poor but occasionally very good are likely to be interpreted as better than they really are. Implicit overestimation of the attractiveness of an alternative is likely to be self-correcting in an experiential learning process, as it increases sampling of that alternative, but implicit underestimation tends to persist.

The way in which a learning process favors risk aversion in the domain of gains when $r < 0.5$ is easiest to see intuitively in the case of a choice between a certain return of k and a return of k/r with a probability of r. The less risky (certain) choice is likely to be more rewarding, and that likelihood rather quickly translates into greater propensity to choose the less risky choice. The joint probability of choosing the risky choice and being rewarded for it becomes smaller and smaller. That joint probability does not become zero, so it can occur. Except in the case of the average return model, however, the very unlikely joint event is itself very unlikely to lead to a correction, inasmuch as subsequent experience simply reproduces the process of focus on the less risky alternative.

In the domain of losses, on the other hand, sampling tends to be self-correcting when $r < 0.5$. Each choice of the certain alternative results in a greater loss than most choices of the risky alternative, which translates into a reduction in the probability of making that choice. As a result, there is substantially more sampling of the risky alternative. Whenever the more risky option is taken and the unlikely event occurs, the large negative reward (k/r) results in a substantial increase in the probability of taking the less risky alternative. The less risky alternative also fails when it is chosen, thus leading to a tendency for the learner to sample the more risky alternative (until realizing the unlikely negative outcome). The result is that learners tend to oscillate between the two choices. This tendency to oscillate brings the average return and weighted return learners closer to risk neutrality as they sample the two alternatives equally and produce actions that implicitly mirror reality more accurately.[2]

Implications of a learning perspective on risk taking

Systematic risk-taking biases stemming from simple learning processes have been demonstrated for several common models of experiential learning. Those biases are consistent with common observations of risk-taking behavior, observations that have, for the most part, been given different interpretations. If the models are, indeed, correct representations of learning, the conclusions about the effect of learning on risk taking within the models may extend to risk-taking behavior. And if such a leap is imaginable, it may be useful to examine how a learning interpretation of risk aversion leads to different implications for understanding and influencing risk-taking behavior.

As long as risk taking is studied and interpreted only within a framework of expected value rationality of the standard kind, the understanding of risk aversion or risk seeking is couched in terms of features of utility functions. A learning perspective provides a different view of the sources of risk aversion and risk seeking. Risk preference can be interpreted as a learned response, rather than as an inexplicable personal trait, a consequence of prior nonlinear utilities or discounting, a result of a satisficing pursuit of targets, or a conscious factor in a rational choice. In choice situations in which a decision maker makes repeated choices in the face of the same alternatives and the same outcome distributions, direct learning in the situation should produce decision rules that produce greater risk aversion for gains than for losses. The greater the risk and the faster the learning, the more profound the effect.

Implications for interpreting risk aversion

A link between learning and risk taking, in particular the idea that effective learning both requires risk taking in the long run and reduces it in the short run, is familiar to students of innovation and creativity (March, 1991). The usual arguments are twofold. First, it is argued that knowledge has two effects on performance distributions. On the one hand, increased knowledge is reflected in an increased mean performance. Knowledgeable people do better on average. On the other hand, knowledge also increases reliability. Knowledgeable people exhibit less variability. Reductions in ignorance are, by this argument, reductions in involuntary risk taking.

Second, it is argued that local experience gives an advantage to familiar, safe alternatives. Returns to such alternatives are normally clearer, closer in time, and closer in social or physical distance to the actions that are taken than are the returns to less familiar, riskier ones. As learning processes respond to experience, those clearer and closer returns come to dominate returns that are more distant. These clear, neighborhood returns can easily come to eliminate behavior that might, at a greater distance in time or space or over a larger sample, result in more rewarding experience.

The present analysis provides a possible grounding of these arguments. It shows that risk aversion can be linked in a systematic way to experiential learning. If the models of learning that are simulated here capture the essentials of experiential learning and learning often takes place in situations that resemble the simple choice situation specified here, then ordinary learning will affect risk taking in a systematic way. The decision rules and preferences that learners develop from their experience are more likely to be neutral with respect to risk that is encountered in the domain of losses than to risk encountered in the domain of gains. Insofar as greater risk aversion for gains than for losses is a learned propensity, it should be correlated with other learned propensities. In particular, it should be correlated with propensities to make correct choices, thus with knowledge and intelligence. The same process that teaches an individual to add sums correctly also teaches risk aversion for gains; and individuals who learn one lesson relatively quickly are also likely to learn the other.

Generally, of course, direct experience by any one individual with any one situation will be limited, so extensive learning effects on individual behavior require some mechanisms by which learning is accumulated across situations and across individuals. One possible mechanism of such accumulation is the development of rules or heuristics for dealing with risky situations. Alternative rules accumulate the lessons of experience across a variety of situations by noticing similarities among the situations and generalizing the rules. Rules accumulate experience across individuals and nonrepetitive situations in the same basic way as do individuals across repetitive situations. Rules of risk aversion in the positive domain, if widely shared, will produce behavior that can be described in terms of revealed decreasing marginal utilities for money. The description in terms of nonlinear utilities for money, however, is – under this interpretation – simply a conventional label and rationalization for behavior, not an explanation of it. The behavior stems from rules, and the rules stem from a history of ordinary experiential learning that yields risk propensities as a side effect.

Implications for influencing risk taking

Experiential learning leads to risk aversion in the positive domain. It is possible that such risk aversion is socially or individually valuable, but there is no guarantee that the risk behavior learned from experience will reliably be optimal. In effect, risk aversion is a learned response in the classic two-armed-bandit problem of rational choice (Chernoff, 1972, pp. 102–8). In the two-armed-bandit problem, a decision maker must decide how to allocate a series of investments between two alternatives. The problem is to determine which alternative is better without wasting too much money on the inferior one. Solving the problem for an optimal solution requires an assortment of assumptions that are normally not provided explicitly to participants in a learning situation: assumptions about the number of trials, the independence and stability of the outcome distributions associated with the arms, the nature of the unknown outcome distributions, and the extent to which future returns are discounted to the present. Optimal strategies, when they can be identified, depend critically on such assumptions.

The result here indicates that the learning solution to this problem will generally be to learn to choose less risky alternatives over more risky alternatives of equal expected value in the positive domain, and will often be to learn to choose alternatives of lower expected value if they are less risky. If there are reasons to believe that such risk aversion is not a good idea, there may be interest in how experience or experiential learning can be modified to reduce or eliminate learned tendencies toward risk aversion. Insofar as risk aversion in the positive domain is a result of learning, encouraging risk seeking for gains involves slowing the rate of learning. There is a trade-off between learning rate and differences in riskiness (i.e., for any degree of riskiness there exists some rate of learning slow enough to allow the learning process to find the true values of alternatives). Slow learning can result from an individual being given powerful indoctrination outside the realm of experience, from limited learning experience, or from noise in the learning experience (e.g., from parents intervening to protect a child from the real odds of life's gambles). Thus, learning of risk aversion by an individual can be slowed by introducing noise in feedback (in effect, by obscuring true differences in variability among alternatives), by embedding a learning process in a set of strong prior beliefs in favor of risk seeking, or by limiting experience. All of these, of course, have the consequence not only of slowing learning of risk aversion but also of slowing the learning of other, possibly useful, things.

Implications for adaptiveness

One of the more reliable of empirical results in the study of risk taking (more risk aversion for gains than for losses) is shown to be implicit in one of the more reliable portrayals of human behavior (experiential learning). The argument is not that learning will account for all risk-taking behavior. It seems likely that various forms of human heuristics, calculative rationality, target-based action, and errors in estimation may also be involved. But the fact that ordinary learning, if it follows some conventional models of trial-and-error learning, leads to systematic biases in risk taking may not be entirely irrelevant for understanding adaptiveness by learning systems. In particular, the fact that fast learning (i.e., in which behavior is modified rapidly in response to feedback) or precise learning (i.e., in which the returns from choice are reliable and free from noise) is especially likely to produce risk aversion may give pause to the easy assumption that fast, precise learning is a sure route to adaptiveness.

Some cautions

The basic result that experiential learning leads to greater risk aversion for gains than for losses appears to be fairly robust. There is, however, no direct empirical test here of the effects of learning on risk taking. The claim is a weaker one: Because the models examined here are consistent with key empirical patterns of learning, they can be portrayed as representations of learning processes. The processes they portray have been shown to lead to risk aversion under standard situations. Thus, existing interpretations of risk-taking behavior, interpretations that are tied to ideas of choice and nonlinearities in the utility for money or to satisficing search, may overlook ways in which simple trial-and-error learning of a kind well-documented in humans may explain greater risk aversion for gains than for losses.

Generalizations to more outcome distributions, more models of learning processes, more alternatives, and more adaptive reference points have not been undertaken. Although the present analysis deals explicitly with only one kind of outcome distribution, similar results seem likely with a wide variety of distributions, particularly those in which the means and medians are different. The discussion above of sequential sampling and deviant experience suggests, however, the importance of finding somewhat richer distributions to study the effects of positive and negative skewness in the outcome distributions. Distributions that include both positive and negative possible outcomes can easily be explored within the fractional adjustment model but would require a respecification of the other two models. Matching theories of learning have developed within an experimental frame that considers either rewards of varying magnitudes and delays or penalties of varying magnitudes and delays but rarely mixes the two.

Although the present analysis deals explicitly with only three models of experiential learning, it seems likely (but is not conclusively demonstrated here) that the learning effects described here will be generated by any learning process in which information about alternatives can only be gained from choosing them and in which choice depends on experience with alternatives. This is a very large class of processes but excludes situations in which information is freely available about alternatives that have not been chosen. The present analysis deals explicitly only with two-alternative situations. Generally, the qualitative characteristics observed in two-alternative models of experiential learning have been found to hold for multiple alternatives, but the extent to which generalization beyond the two-alternative case is possible without surprises in this case has not been investigated.

Adaptive aspirations present a more complicated problem. Experimental studies of risk taking normally assume a reference or zero point that divides results into gains and losses. The present analysis is limited to the case in which the reference point does not change. The assumption of stable reference points is a reasonable assumption for many situations, particularly those in which the focus is on adaptation to broad social expectations. In many cases, however, reference points are not stable. Several analyses have suggested that the way an aspiration level separating gains and losses changes may be a significant long-run factor in risk taking (March, 1988; March and Shapira, 1992). For example, if current gains or losses are indexed by past gains or losses (as occurs when aspirations are self-referential), objective gains or losses become relatively unimportant. Consideration of adaptive reference points would be relatively easy within the framework of the fractional adjustment model. As has been noted above, it is less obvious to see how either the average return or weighted return model could be modified sensibly to accommodate the possibility of the mixed positive and negative returns, which would ordinarily be generated by adaptive reference points.

Acknowledgment

This research has been supported by the Spencer Foundation and the Stanford Graduate School of Business. I am grateful for comments by Michael Cohen, J. Michael Harrison, Scott Herriott, Terje Lensberg, Lola Lopes, and R. Duncan Luce.

Notes

1. The predicted distributions of $p_{i,300}$ among individual learners are quite similar for the average return and weighted return models, with relatively symmetric distributions around the means shown in figures 15.1 to 15.3. The fractional adjustment model, on the other hand, yields a bimodal distribution with $p_{i,300}$ being close to either 1 or 0 for almost all learners. The differences in distributions are transparently due to the differences in learning rules.
2. For a discussion of why sampling does not produce greater risk aversion for losses than for gains when $r > 0.5$, see the Appendix.

References

Arrow, K. J. (1971). *Essays in the theory of risk bearing*. Chicago: Markham.

Bell, D. E., Raiffa, H., and Tversky, A. (eds). (1988). *Decision making: Descriptive, normative, and prescriptive interactions*. New York: Cambridge University Press.

Bromiley, P. (1991). Testing a causal model of corporate risk-taking and performance. *Academy of Management Journal, 34*, 37–59.

Bush, R. R., and Mosteller, F. (1955). *Stochastic models for learning*. New York: Wiley.

Caracao, T. (1980). On foraging time allocation in a stochastic environment. *Ecology, 61*. 119–28.

Chernoff, H. (1972). *Sequential analysis and optimal design*. Philadephia:

Society for Industrial and Applied Mathematics.

Estes, W. K. (1959). The statistical approach to learning. In S. Koch (ed.), *Psychology: A study of a science* (vol. 2, pp. 380–491). New York: McGraw-Hill.

Herrnstein, R. J. (1961). Relative and absolute strength of response as a function of frequency of reinforcement. *Journal of the Experimental Analysis of Behavior, 4*. 267–72.

Herrnstein, R. J. (1970). On the law of effect. *Journal of the Experimental Analysis of Behavior, 13*, 244–266.

Johnson, A. W. (1971). Security and risk taking among poor peasants. In G. Dalton (ed.), *Studies in economic anthropology* (pp. 144–51). Washington, DC: American Anthropological Association.

Johnson-Laird, P. N. (1983). *Mental models: Toward a cognitive science of language, inference, and consciousness*. Cambridge, MA: Harvard University, Press.

Kahneman, D., and Tversky, A. (1979). Prospect theory: An analysis of decision under risk. *Econometrica*. 47, 263–91.

Kleindorfer, P. R., Kunreuther, H., and Schoemaker, P. J. H. (1993). *Decision sciences: An integrative perspective*. New York: Cambridge University Press.

Lopes, L. L. (1987). Between hope and fear: The psychology of risk. *Advances in Experimental Social Psychology, 20*, 255–95.

Lopes, L. L. (1994). Psychology and economics: Perspectives on risk, cooperation, and the marketplace. *Annual Review of Psychology, 45*, 197–227.

March, J. G. (1988). Variable risk preferences and adaptive aspirations. *Journal of Economic Behavior and Organization, 9*, 5–24.

March, J. G. (1991). Exploration and exploitation in organizational learning. *Organization Science, 2*, 71–87.

March, J. G., and Shapira, Z. (1992). Variable risk preferences and the focus of attention. *Psychological Review*; 99, 172–83.

Payne, J. W., Laughhann, D. J., and Crumm, R. L. (1981). Further tests of aspiration level effects in risky choice behavior. *Management Science, 27*, 953–8.

Schoemaker, P. J. H. (1982). The expected utility model: Its variants, purposes, evidence and limitations. *Journal of Economic Literature, 20*, 529–63.

Shapira, Z. (1995). *Risk taking: A managerial perspective*. New York: Russell Sage Foundation.

Skinner, B. F. (1938). *The behavior of organisms*. New York: Appleton-Century-Crofts.

Staddon, J. E. R. (1977). On Herrnstein's equation and related forms. *Journal of the Experimental Analysis of Behavior, 28*, 163–70.

Thorndike, E. L. (1898). Animal intelligence: An experimental study of the associative processes in animals. *Psychological Review Monographs Supplement, 2*, (8).

Williams, B. A. (1988). Reinforcement, choice, and response strength. In R. C. Atkinson, R. J. Herrnstein, G. Lindzey, and R. D. Luce (eds), *Stevens' handbook of experimental psychology* (vol. 2, pp. 167–244). New York: Wiley.

Yaari, M. E. (1987). The dual theory of choice under risk. *Econometrica, 55*, 95–115.

Appendix

The effects of skewness

The text discussion of the effects of skewness in the outcome distributions of the risky alternative is brief. This appendix elaborates that discussion slightly with respect to two things. The first is the sampling basis for speculating that a positively skewed outcome distribution for the risky alternative in the negative domain combined with a negatively skewed distribution for the risky alternative in the positive domain might lead to a reversal of the basic result. The second is the learning explanation of why the speculation is false.

The speculation stems from a simple feature of the sampling situation and thus is most directly relevant to the average return model, but the broad principles are similar for the other models as well. A sample of n experiences with a risky alternative having a probability r of a return of k/r and otherwise nothing has $n + 1$ different possible sample means corresponding to whether the outcome that results in a k/r outcome occurs $i = 0,1 \ldots, n$ times. The likelihoods of occurrence are given by $\{n!/[i!(n - i)!]\} \, r^i \, (1 - r)^{(n - i)}$. When $r < 0.5$ (i.e., in cases involving positively skewed distributions for the risky alternative in the positive domain and negatively skewed distributions for the risky alternative in the negative domain), most sampling errors involve underestimating the positive risky alternative and overestimating the negative risky alternative (i.e., underestimating its expected losses). On the other hand, when $r > 0.5$ (i.e., in cases involving negatively skewed distributions for the risky alternative in the positive domain and positively skewed distributions for the risky alternative in the negative domain), most sampling errors involve overestimating the positive risky alternative and underestimating the negative risky one (i.e., overestimating its expected losses). This suggests that one should expect greater risk aversion for losses than for gains when the gain distribution is negatively skewed and the loss distribution is positively skewed.

Understanding why greater risk aversion for losses than for gains actually does not occur (see figure 15.7) even when gains are negatively skewed and losses are positively skewed ($r > 0.5$) requires recognizing that the skewness of the outcome distribution for the risky alternative affects not only the relative likelihoods of over-and underestimating that alternative but also the magnitudes of such errors in estimation and their learning effects and thus the possibility of realizing a high probability of choosing the nonrisky alternative through learning. Consider, for example, the average return model: By equations 15.6 and 15.7, if A is the average return experienced with the nonrisky alternative and B is the average return experienced with the risky alternative, the probability of choosing the nonrisky alternative (p) is equal to $A/(A + B)$, in the domain of gains, and to $1 - [A/(A + B)] = B/(A + B)$, in the domain of losses. $A = k$, for all trials. B changes whenever the risky alternative is chosen, but is constrained to lie between 0 and k/r. Thus, p is constrained to be between $r/(r + k)$ and 1 in the domain of gains, and between 0 and $k/(r + k)$ in the domain of losses. As long as r is relatively small, these constraints are not particularly significant. As r approaches 1, however, the maximum possible p in the domain of losses becomes small enough (e.g., at $r = 0.9$, the maximum possible p is 0.526) to assure frequent sampling of the risky alternative. Though most experience indicates that the risky alternative is inferior (in the domain of losses), the differences and their effects are small enough that the risky alternative continues to be chosen almost as frequently as the nonrisky one; and the error is corrected relatively quickly. As r approaches 1 in the domain of gains, on the other hand, the maximum possible p approaches 1. Although underestimation of the risky alternative is unlikely, when it occurs, the resulting increase in the probability of choosing the nonrisky alternative is large enough to keep a learner risk neutral or risk averse.

PART IV

The Giving and Taking of Advice

CHAPTER SIXTEEN

Model Bias in Social Action

The speculations that underlie policy analysis introduce systematic biases into social action. In particular, the fundamental assumptions of rational theories of choice introduce presumptions: that purpose antedates action; that preferences should be consistent; and that action should be taken by considering its consequences. Such assumptions and theories have undoubtedly been important and productive, but they need to be moderated by a recognition that goals are constructed through action as well as guide action. Such a recognition leads to valuing the roles of imitation, coercion, rationalization, and playfulness in social choice. The technology of reason needs to be complemented by a technology of foolishness.

EVALUATING SPECULATIONS ABOUT THE WORLD

The basis for social action is speculation. By speculation I mean nothing more profound than models of social structure and behavior. Whether such models are viewed as ideology, art, or wisdom, they consist in imaginations about the world. Social policy builds on those imaginations. The major claim to legitimacy by a social scientist is the claim that his procedures systematically evaluate the quality of his models and, thus, that his speculations are good ones. For the most part, I think the claim is reasonable; but we need occasionally to examine the problems of evaluating our imaginations and the biases that confound our efforts to produce good speculations.

A speculation is good if it is true, beautiful, and just. A speculation is true to the extent to which it correctly predicts observable behavior. A speculation is beautiful to the extent to which its contemplation produces aesthetic pleasure. A speculation is just to the extent to which a belief in it and action based on it produce better people and better worlds.

There are important biases in the selection of models that reduce their average truth value. Such problems sustain a major share of our standard efforts in methodology. They are far from trivial. Consider, for example, the persistent problems we have with various forms of specification bias. Despite their importance, I do not intend to devote attention to such biases. Similarly, there are biases that systematically reduce the aesthetic value of our models. I believe that most treatises on social science methodology underestimate the significance of beauty as an evaluative criterion for speculations. My intention here, however, is to ignore beauty also. My concern is with justice, the extent to which belief in our speculations (however true or beautiful) produces attractive behavior.

We should like to be just. We should like to be able to say that our models contribute to making better, rather than poorer, worlds. The idea is a quaint one, and a complicated one. A major consideration of the concept of justice is beyond the scope of both this commentary and this writer. Wiser people have said wiser things on the subject already. My limited purpose is to remind you of the importance of justice in the construction of social science theory and to identify some possible domains in which our current instincts may be biased in significant ways.

Like truth and beauty, justice is an ideal rather than a state of existence. We do not achieve it; we pursue it. In that pursuit we accept responsibility for social myths by which we live. As critics of modern social science have easily demonstrated, models are not neutral. I will not attempt to reproduce those critiques. I believe that they often underestimate the possibilities for introducing considerations of justice into modern social science methodology. Though social scientists need to be appropriately humble about the prospects for justice and their contributions to it, they need not be shy about trying.

The point is simple. Independent of its truth value, a model has a justice value. Different models suggest different actions, and the attractiveness of the social and moral consequences of those actions do not depend entirely on the degree to which the models are correct. Nor is this problem solved in any significant way by producing a more correct model. Since two equally correct models may have radically different action implications and radically different moral force, we can easily imagine a circumstance in which we would be willing to forego some truth in order to achieve some justice.

SOCIAL SCIENCE AND THE CRITERION OF JUSTICE

The complications of justice in models of social science can be illustrated by some familiar speculations about individual human behavior. These speculations are the myths by which we deal with other people; they are the myths by which we deal with ourselves. Insofar as our speculations impute unattractive features to people, so will we in our ordinary life. Consider, for example, the following speculations about interpersonal behavior:

> Human beings aspire for power and direct their behavior primarily toward gaining a favorable power balance with respect to other people. Power is secured by offering resources, or promises of resources (e.g., support, money, respect) in exchange for acquiescence.

Such a model has some attractive features. It predicts some important aspects of behavior. It is simple. But it makes a series of predictions about human behavior that are unattractive as a basis for dealing with other people. For example, it predicts that most favorable statements made in an interpersonal situation are probably lies. This is particularly true of statements reporting supportive behavioral intentions or positive feelings with respect to other people. The probable truthfulness of an insult is higher than the probable truthfulness of praise. Insofar as we come to believe such a series of assertions, we almost certainly make our daily life less pleasant and ourselves less attractive as human beings.

Consider similarly the following assertion common to a rather large number of models of individual behavior:

> Adult human behavior is understandable in its basic forms as stemming primarily from experience of early childhood.

Such an assertion seems plausible. Yet, if believed, it has at least two dubious side-effects. First, it leads parents and children both to believe that parents should accept primary credit (and blame) for a child's beliefs, character, and general intellectual and moral performance. School report cards become more important to the parent's self-respect than to the child's; parents are valued in terms of their children's behavior. As a consequence, parent–child relations combine the worst features of juvenile blackmail (children threatening to behave in such a way that parents will lose respect) and parental repression (parents determined to manage their children).

Second, belief in the model seems likely to create a static bias in personal self-analysis. Individuals who believe the "formative years" hypothesis seem quite likely to consider the problem of personal identity to be a problem of "discovering" a pre-existing "real" self rather than one of "creating" an "interesting" self. The notion of discovery is biased against adult change. A person who believes his basic character has been formed at an early age can have but modest expectation of being able to modify his style of life as an adult. He is inhibited by his model of personality development from the dangers and pleasure of continuous personal change.

Consider finally the following assertions, which form a part of a relatively large number of familiar models of individual behavior:

> Things are not what they seem. Human beings are guided by a number of unconscious motives that affect their behavior in subtle ways.

Such assertions seem reasonable. They may indeed often be true. What makes them unattractive from the point of view of justice is the basic ambiguity a belief in them introduces with respect to human action. We are led to ask: What does he *really* mean? Indeed, we are led to ask: What do *I* really mean? By introducing substantial elements of affective ambiguity into interpersonal communications, we undermine trust as a basis for dealing with people. We each become a little more paranoid.

These elementary ideas of common social science illustrate the basic point that some of our most easily accepted truths are dubious guides to the ordinary encounters of everyday life. If the analysis is correct, social science is culpable in some significant corruptions of our culture. The illustrations are intended, however, as a prologue, not a conclusion. They are a prologue to an examination of a basic model bias in our analysis of social policy. It is a bias that has some significant implications for accountability, performance measurement, social responsiveness, and evaluation in social policy, as well as for efforts to improve resource allocation decisions in areas such as education, welfare, transportation, urban life, environment, and energy. As in the case of the simple examples, we can identify a set of assumptions that appear self-evidently correct in our models but which lead to policy implications that can legitimately be questioned.

BIASES IN POLICY ANALYSIS

Just as interpersonal interactions depend on models of human behavior, policy analysis depends on a model of social policy making. The ideas for that model are probably taken from, and are certainly consistent with, the views found in most current social science thinking. I refer particularly to economic theories of markets, social welfare, and the firm; to political science theories of democratic politics; to sociological and political theories of power; to managerial theories of bureaucracy and administration; and to a miscellany of theories of individual and social choice.

Consider, for example, the standard social welfare theories in economics and political science. In these theories, we typically assume that the individual members of a society have preferences with respect to alternative social actions. The social welfare problem is to find a social preference that is, in some sense, appropriate given the individual preferences. The classic solutions lean toward rules of Pareto optimality, and the literature is filled with complications – both technical and philosophical – associated with Pareto optimality as a criterion.

Or, consider the standard theories of political democracy. In these theories we assume that each citizen has preferences defined over possible social policies. He casts his vote for one of a set of candidates. The candidate receiving the largest number of votes is elected and assumes power (until the next election). In order to be elected, candidates make various promises to voters; voters seek to obtain promises by threatening to withhold votes. The literature abounds with discussions of the complications – particularly those associated with assuring that all potentially winning coalitions of voters and policies are considered.

Or, consider the standard theories of social power. In these theories we assume that each individual has a preference function defined over available social options. In addition, the social system, in conjunction with attributes of the individual or the role he occupies, assigns to each individual a certain amount of power. The social action adopted by the society is presumed to be a weighted average of the individual preferences, where the power of an individual is the weight assigned to his preferences. The literature is focused to a considerable extent on the problems of finding a set of measurements of power and an elaboration of the model that are jointly consistent with reality.

Or, consider standard theories of public interest, or bureaucratic–managerial behavior. In these theories we assume that a social welfare function defining social preferences exists. We postulate a criterion function: provide for the common defense, maximize discounted long-run expected profit; minimize educational disparities. The technical and theoretical problem is that of designing a system to make decisions that meet the criterion. The ideas form the base for much of modern management (e.g., the development of modern accounting) and management science (e.g., the development of statistical decision theory).

The differences among these theories are important; but they share a common normative view of the process of choice. In that view, individuals or groups can be seen as having some set of objectives that they pursue through action. The problems of policy making are seen as first discovering a set of acceptable social objectives, second finding a set of procedures for achieving those objectives, and third evaluating the achievement of those prior objectives in order to modify future actions to make them more efficacious for the objectives.

Such a view has at least two major biases that need to be questioned in terms of their policy implications. The first is a *relativist* bias, the belief that preferences need to be treated as exogenous primitives, not susceptible to normative evaluation. Each of the models of social policy making presumes prior preferences. The second bias is a *rationalist* bias, the belief that, from a normative point of view, purpose antedates action. Each of the models of social policy accepts choice as appropriately consequent upon purpose.

PRESUMPTIONS OF THEORIES OF CHOICE

In order to examine these biases, we need to consider the fundamental dogma of theories of choice. The concept of choice as a focus for interpreting and guiding human behavior has rarely had an easy time in the realm of ideas. It is beset by theological disputations over free will, by the dilemmas of absurdism, by the doubts of psychological behaviorism, by the claims of historical, economic, social, and demographic determinism. Nevertheless, the idea that humans make choices has proven robust enough to become a major matter of faith in important segments of contemporary western civilization. It is a faith that is professed by virtually all theories of social policy making.

The major tenets of this faith run something like this:

> Human beings make choices. If done properly, choices are made by evaluating alternatives in terms of goals on the basis of information currently available. The alternative that is most attractive in terms of the goals is chosen. The process of making choices can be improved by using the technology of choice. Through the paraphernalia of modern techniques, we can improve the quality of the search for alternatives, the quality of information, and the quality of the analysis used to evaluate alternatives. Although actual choice may fall short of this ideal in various ways, it is an attractive model of how choices should be made by individuals, organizations, and social systems.

These articles of faith have been built upon, and have stimulated, some scripture. It is the scripture of theories of decision making. The scripture is partly a codification of received doctrine and partly a source for that doctrine. As a result, our cultural ideas of intelligence and our theories of choice bear some substantial resemblance. In particular, they share three conspicuous interrelated ideas:

The first idea is the *pre-existence of purpose*. We find it natural to base an interpretation of human choice behavior on a presumption of human purpose. We have, in fact, invented one of the most elaborate terminologies in the professional literature: "values," "needs," "wants," "goods," "tastes," "preferences," "utility," "objectives," "goals," "aspirations," "drives." All of these reflect a strong tendency to believe that a useful interpretation of human behavior involves defining a set of objectives that (a) are prior attributes of the system, and (b) make the observed behavior in some sense intelligent *vis-à-vis* those objectives.

Whether we are talking about individuals or about organizations, purpose is an obvious presumption of the discussion. An organization is often defined in terms of its purpose. It is seen by some as the largest collectivity directed by a purpose. Action within an organization is justified (or criticized) in terms of the purpose. Individuals explain their own behavior, as well as the behavior of others, in terms of a set of value premises that are presumed to be antecedent to the behavior. Normative theories of choice begin with an assumption of a pre-existent preference ordering defined over the possible outcomes of a choice.

The second idea is the *necessity of consistency*. We have come to recognize consistency both as an important property of human behavior and as a prerequisite for normative models of choice. Dissonance theory, balance theory, theories of congruency in attitudes, statuses, and performances have all served to remind us of the possibilities for interpreting human behavior in terms of the consistency requirements of a limited capacity information-processing system.

At the same time, consistency is a cultural and theoretical virtue. Action should be made consistent with belief. Actions taken by different parts of an organization should be consistent with each other. Individual and organizational activities are seen as connected with each other in terms of their consequences for some consistent set of purposes. In an organization, the structural manifestation of the dictum of consistency is the hierarchy with its obligations of coordination and control. In the individual, the structural manifestation is a set of values that generates a consistent preference ordering.

The third idea is the *primacy of rationality*. By rationality I mean a procedure for deciding what is correct behavior by relating consequences systematically to objectives. By placing primary emphasis on rational techniques, we implicitly have rejected – or seriously impaired – two other procedures for choice: (a) The processes of intuition, by means of which people may do things without fully understanding why; (b) The processes of tradition and faith, through which people do things because that is the way they are done.

Both within the theory and within the culture we insist on the ethic of rationality. We justify individual and organizational action in terms of an analysis of means and ends. Impulse, intuition, faith, and tradition are outside that system and viewed as antithetical to it. Faith may be seen as a possible source of values. Intuition may be seen as a possible source of ideas about alternatives. But the analysis and justification of action lie within the context of reason.

These ideas are obviously deeply imbedded in the culture. Their roots extend into ideas that have conditioned much of modern western history and interpretations of that history. Their general acceptance is probably highly correlated with the permeation of rationalism and individualism into the style of thinking within the culture. The ideas are even more obviously imbedded in modern theories of choice. It is fundamental to those theories that thinking should precede action; that action should serve a purpose; that purpose should be defined in terms of a consistent set of pre-existent goals; and that choice should be based on a consistent theory of the relation between action and its consequences.

Every tool of management decision that is currently a part of management science, operations research, or decision theory assumes the prior existence of a set of consistent goals. Almost the entire structure of microeconomic theory builds on the assumption that there exists a well-defined, stable, and consistent preference ordering. Most theories of individual or organizational choice behavior accept the idea that goals exist and that (in some sense) an individual or organization acts on those goals, choosing from among some alternatives on the basis of available information. Discussions of educational policy, for example, with the emphasis on goal setting, evaluation, and accountability, are directly in this tradition.

From the perspective of all of man's history, the ideas of purpose, consistency, and rationality are relatively new. Much of the technology currently available to implement them is extremely new. Over the past few centuries, and conspicuously over the past few decades, we have substantially improved man's capability for acting purposively, consistently, and rationally. We have substantially increased his propensity to think of himself as doing so. It is an impressive victory, won – where it has been won – by a happy combination of timing, performance, ideology, and persistence. It is a battle yet to be concluded, or even engaged, in many cultures of the world; but within most of the western world, individuals and organizations see themselves as making choices.

CONSTRUCTION OF GOALS AND THE TAKING OF ACTION

The tools of intelligence as they are fashioned in modern theories of choice are necessary to any reasonable behavior in contemporary society. It is difficult to see how we could, and inconceivable that we would, fail to continue their development, refinement, and extension. As might be expected, however, a theory and ideology of choice built on the ideas outlined above is deficient in some obvious, elementary ways, most conspicuously in the treatment of human goals.

Goals are thrust upon the intelligent man. We ask that he act in the name of goals. We ask that he keep his goals consistent. We ask that his actions be oriented to his goals. We ask that a social system amalgamate individual goals into a collective goal. But we do not concern ourselves with the origin of goals. Theories of individual organizational and social choice assume actors with pre-existent values.

Since it is obvious that goals change over time and that the character of those changes affects both the richness of personal and social development and the outcome of choice behavior, a theory of choice must somehow justify ignoring the phenomena. Although it is unreasonable to ask a theory of choice to solve all of the problems of man and his development, it is reasonable to ask how something as conspicuous as the fluidity and ambiguity of objectives can plausibly be ignored in a theory that is offered as a guide to human choice behavior.

There are three classic justifications. The first is that goal development and choice are independent processes, conceptually and behaviorally. The second is that the model of choice is never satisfied in fact and that deviations from the model accommodate the problems of introducing change. The third is that the idea of changing goals is so intractable in a normative theory of choice that nothing can be said about it. Since I am unpersuaded of the first and second justifications, my optimism with respect to the third is somewhat greater than most of my fellows.

The argument that goal development and choice are independent behaviorally seems clearly false. It seems to me perfectly obvious that a description that assumes goals come first and action comes later is frequently radically wrong. Human choice behavior is at least as much a process for discovering goals as for acting on them. Although it is true enough that goals and decisions are "conceptually" distinct, that is simply a statement of the theory. It is not a defense of it. They are conceptually distinct if we choose to make them so.

The argument that the model is incomplete is more persuasive. There do appear to be some critical "holes" in the system of intelligence as described by standard theories of choice. There is incomplete information, incomplete goal consistency, and a variety of external processes impinging on goal development – including intuition and tradition. What is somewhat disconcerting about the argument, however, is that it makes the efficacy of the concepts of intelligent choice dependent on their inadequacy. As we become more competent in the techniques of the model, and more committed to it, the "holes" become smaller. As the model becomes more accepted, our obligation to modify it increases.

The final argument seems to me sensible as a general principle, but misleading here. Why are we more reluctant to ask how human beings might find "good" goals than we are to ask how they might make "good" decisions? The second question appears to be a relatively technical problem. The first seems more pretentious. It claims to say something about alternative virtues. The appearance of pretense, however, stems directly from the theory and the ideology associated with it.

In fact, the conscious introduction of goal discovery as a consideration in theories of human choice is not unknown to modern man. For example, we have two kinds of theories of choice behavior in human beings. One is a theory of children. The other is a theory of adults. In the theory of childhood, we emphasize choices as leading to experiences that develop the child's scope, his complexity, his awareness of the world. As parents, or psychologists, we try to lead the child to do things that are inconsistent with his present goals because we know (or believe) that he can only develop into an interesting person by coming to appreciate aspects of experience that he initially rejects.

In the theory of adulthood, we emphasize choices as a consequence of our intentions. As adults, or economists, we try to take actions that (within the limits of scarce resources) come as close as possible to achieving our goals. We try to find improved ways of making decisions consistent with our perceptions of what is valuable in the world.

The asymmetry in these models is conspicuous. Adults have constructed a model world in which adults know what is good for themselves, but children do not. It is hard to react positively to the conceit. The asymmetry has, in fact, stimulated a rather large number of ideologies and reforms designed to allow children the same moral prerogative granted to adults – the right to imagine that they know what they want. The efforts have cut deeply into traditional child-rearing, traditional educational policies, traditional politics, and traditional consumer economics.

In my judgment, the asymmetry between models of choice for adults and models of choice for children is awkward; but the solution we have adopted is precisely wrong-headed. Instead of trying to adapt the model of adults to children, we might better adapt the model of children to adults. For many purposes, our model of children is better. Of course, children know what they want. Everyone does. The critical question is whether they are encouraged to develop more interesting "wants." Values change. People become more interesting as those values and the interconnections made among them change.

One of the most obvious things in the world turns out to be hard for us to accommodate in our theory of choice: A child of two will almost always have a less interesting set of values (yes, indeed, a *worse* set of values) than a child of 12. The same is true of adults. Values develop through experience. Although one of the main natural arenas for the modification of human values is the area of choice, our theories of adult and organizational decision making ignore the phenomenon entirely.

Introducing ambiguity and fluidity to the interpretation of individual, organizational, and societal goals, obviously has implications for behavioral theories of decision making. The main point here, however, is not to consider how we might describe the behavior of systems that are discovering goals as they act. Rather it is to examine how we might improve the quality of that behavior, how we might aid the development of interesting goals.

We know how to advise a society, an organization, or an individual if we are first given a consistent set of preferences. Under some conditions, we can suggest how to make decisions if the preferences are only consistent up to the point of specifying a series of independent constraints on the choice. But what about a normative theory of goal-finding behavior? What do we say when our client tells us that he is not sure his present set of values is the set of values in terms of which he wants to act?

It is a question familiar to many aspects of ordinary life. It is a question that friends, associates, students, college presidents, business managers, voters, and children ask at least as frequently as they ask how they should act within a set of consistent and stable values.

Within the context of the normative theory of choice as it exists, the answer we give is: First determine the values, then act. The advice is frequently useful. Moreover, we have developed ways in which we can use conventional techniques for decision analysis to help discover value premises and to expose value inconsistencies. These techniques involve testing the decision implications of some successive approximations to a set of preferences. The object is to find a consistent set of preferences with implications that are acceptable to the person or organization making the decisions. Variations on such techniques are used routinely in operations research, as well as in personal counseling and analysis.

The utility of such techniques, however, apparently depends on the assumption that a primary problem is the amalgamation or excavation of preexistent values. The metaphors – "finding oneself," "goal clarification," "self-discovery," "social welfare function," "revealed preference" – are metaphors of search. If our value premises are to be "constructed" rather than "discovered," our standard procedures may be useful; but we have no *a priori* reason for assuming they will.

Perhaps we should explore a somewhat different approach to the normative question of how we ought to behave when our value premises are not yet (and never will be) fully determined. Suppose we treat action as a way of creating interesting goals at the same time as we treat goals as a way of justifying action. It is an intuitively plausible and simple idea, but one that is not immediately within the domain of standard normative theories of intelligent choice.

Interesting people and interesting organizations construct complicated theories of themselves. In order to do this, they need to supplement the technology of reason with a technology of foolishness. Individuals and organizations need ways of doing things for which they have no good reason. Not always. Not usually. But sometimes. They need to act before they think.

IMITATION, COERCION, AND RATIONALIZATION

In order to use the act of intelligent choice as a planned occasion for discovering new goals, we apparently require some idea of sensible foolishness. Which of the many foolish things that we might do now will lead to attractive value consequences? The question is almost inconceivable. Not only does it ask us to predict the value consequences of action, it asks us to evaluate them. In what terms can we talk about "good" changes in goals?

In effect, we are asked either to specify a set of super-goals in terms of which alternative goals are evaluated, or to choose among alternatives *now* in terms of the unknown set of values we will have at some future time (or the distribution over time of that unknown set of future values). The former alternative moves us back to the original situation of a fixed set of values – now called "super-goals" – and hardly seems an important step in the direction of inventing procedures for discovering new goals. The latter alternative seems fundamental enough, but it violates severely our sense of temporal order. To say that we make decisions now in terms of goals that will only be knowable later is nonsensical – as long as we accept the basic framework of the theory of choice and its presumptions of pre-existent goals.

I do not know in detail what is required, but I think it will be substantial. As we challenge the dogma of pre-existent goals, we will be forced to reexamine some of our most precious prejudices: the strictures against imitation, coercion, and rationalization. Each of those honorable prohibitions depends on the view of man and human choice imposed on us by conventional theories of choice.

Imitation is not necessarily a sign of moral weakness. It is a prediction. It is a prediction that if we duplicate the behavior or attitudes of someone else, the chances of our discovering attractive new goals for ourselves are relatively high. In order for imitation to be normatively attractive we need a better theory of who should be imitated. Such a theory seems to be eminently feasible. For example, what are the conditions for effectiveness of a rule that you should imitate another person whose values are in a close neighborhood of yours? How do the chances of discovering interesting goals through imitation change as the number of other people exhibiting the behavior to be imitated increases?

Coercion is not necessarily an assault on individual autonomy. It can be a device for stimulating individuality. We recognize this when we talk about parents and children (at least sometimes). What has always been difficult with coercion is the possibility for perversion that it involves, not its obvious capability for stimulating change. What we require is a theory of the circumstances under which entry into a coercive system produces behavior that leads to the discovery of interesting goals. We are all familiar with the tactic. We use it in imposing deadlines, entering contracts, making commitments. What are the conditions for its effective use? In particular, what are the conditions for coercion in social systems?

Rationalization is not necessarily a way of evading morality. It can be a test for the feasibility of a goal change. When deciding among alternative actions for which we have no good reason, it may be sensible to develop some definition of how "near" to intelligence alternative "unintelligent" actions lie. Effective rationalization permits this kind of incremental approach to changes in values. To use it effectively, however, we require a better idea of the kinds of metrics that might be possible in measuring value distances. At the same time, rationalization is the major procedure for integrating newly discovered goals into an existing structure of values. It provides the organization of complexity without which complexity itself becomes indistinguishable from randomness.

There are dangers in imitation, coercion, and rationalization. The risks are too familiar to elaborate. We should, indeed, be able to develop better techniques. Whatever those techniques may be, however, they will almost certainly undermine the superstructure of biases erected on purpose, consistency, and rationality. They will involve some way of thinking about action now as occurring in terms of a set of unknown future values.

PLAYFULNESS AND INCONSISTENCY

A second requirement for a technology of foolishness is some strategy for suspending rational imperatives toward consistency. Even if we know which of several foolish things we want to do, we still need a mechanism for allowing us to do it. How do we escape the logic of our reason?

Here, I think, we are closer to understanding what we need. It is playfulness. Playfulness is the deliberate, temporary relaxation of rules in order to explore the possibilities of alternative rules. When we are playful, we challenge the necessity of consistency. In effect, we announce – in advance – our rejection of the usual objections to behavior that does not fit the standard model of intelligence.

Playfulness allows experimentation. At the same time, it acknowledges reason. It accepts an obligation that at some point either the playful behavior will be stopped or it will be integrated into the structure of intelligence in some way that makes sense. The suspension of the rules is temporary.

The idea of play may suggest three things that are, in my mind, quite erroneous in the present context. First, play may be seen as a kind of Mardi Gras for reason, a release of emotional tensions of virtue. Although it is possible that play performs some such function, that is not the function with which I am concerned. Second, play may be seen as part of some mystical balance of spiritual principles: Fire and water, hot and cold, weak and strong. The intention here is much narrower than a general mystique of balance. Third, play may be seen as an antithesis of intelligence, so that the emphasis on the importance of play becomes a support for simple self-indulgence. My present intent is to propose play as an instrument of intelligence, not a substitute.

Playfulness is a natural outgrowth of our standard view of reason. A strict insistence on purpose, consistency, and rationality limits our ability to find new purposes. Play relaxes that insistence to allow us to act "unintelligently" or "irrationally," or "foolishly" to explore alternative ideas of possible purposes and alternative concepts of behavioral consistency. And it does this while maintaining our basic commitment to the necessity of intelligence.

Although play and reason are in this way functional complements, they are often behavioral competitors. They are alternative styles and alternative orientations to the same situation. There is no guarantee that the styles will be equally well-developed. There is no guarantee that all individuals, all organizations, or all societies will be equally adept in both styles. There is no guarantee that all cultures will be equally encouraging to both. Our design problem is either to specify the best mix of styles or, failing that, to assure that most people and most organizations most of the time use an alternation of strategies rather than persevere in either one. It is a difficult problem. The optimization problem looks extremely difficult on the face of it, and the learning situations that will produce alternation in behavior appear to be somewhat less common than those that produce perseveration.

Consider, for example, the difficulty of sustaining playfulness as a style within contemporary American society. Individuals who are good at consistent rationality are rewarded early and heavily. We define it as intelligence, and the educational rewards of society are associated strongly with it. Social norms press in the same direction, particularly for men. Many of the demands of modern organizational life reinforce the same abilities and style preferences.

The result is that many of the most influential, best educated, and best placed citizens have experienced a powerful overlearning with respect to rationality. They are exceptionally good at maintaining consistent pictures of themselves, of relating action to purposes. They are exceptionally poor at a playful attitude toward their own beliefs, toward the logic of consistency, or toward the way they see things as being connected in the world. The dictates of manliness, forcefulness, independence, and intelligence are intolerant of playful urges if they arise. The playful urges that arise are weak ones.

The picture is probably overdrawn, but not, I believe, the implications. For societies, for organizations, and for individuals reason and intelligence have had the unnecessary consequence of inhibiting the development of purpose into more complicated forms of consistency. In order to move away from that position, we need to find some ways of helping individuals and organizations to experiment with doing things for which they have no good reason, to be playful with their conception of themselves. It is a facility that requires more careful attention than I can give it, but I would suggest five things as a small beginning:

First, we can *treat goals as hypotheses*. Conventional decision theory allows us to entertain doubts about almost everything except the thing about which we frequently have the greatest doubt – our objectives. Suppose we define the decision process as a time for the sequential testing of hypotheses about goals. If we can experiment with alternative goals, we stand some chance of discovering complicated and interesting combinations of good values that none of use previously imagined.

Second, we can *treat intuition as real*. I do not know what intuition is, or even if it is any one thing. Perhaps it is simply an excuse for doing something we cannot justify in terms of present values or for refusing to follow the logic of our own beliefs. Perhaps it is an inexplicable way of consulting that part of our intelligence that is not organized in a way anticipated by standard theories of choice. In either case, intuition permits us to see some possible actions that are outside our present scheme for justifying behavior.

Third, we can *treat hypocrisy as a transition*. Hypocrisy is an inconsistency between expressed values and behavior. Negative attitudes about hypocrisy stem from two major things. The first is a general onus against inconsistency. The second is a sentiment against combining the pleasures of vice with the appearance of virtue. Apparently, that is an unfair way of allowing evil to escape temporal punishment. Whatever the merits of such a position as ethics, it seems to me distinctly inhibiting toward change. A bad man with good intentions may be a man experimenting with the possibility of becoming good. Somehow it seems to me more sensible to encourage the experimentation than to insult it.

Fourth, we can *treat memory as an enemy*. The rules of consistency and rationality require a technology of memory. For most purposes, good memories make good choices. But the ability to forget, or overlook, is also useful. If I do not know what I did yesterday or what other people in the organization are doing today, I can act within the system of reason and still do things that are foolish.

Fifth, we can *treat experience as a theory*. Learning can be viewed as a series of conclusions based on concepts of action and consequences that we have invented. Experience can be changed retrospectively. By changing our interpretive concepts now, we modify what we learned earlier. Thus, we expose the possibility of experimenting with alternative histories. The usual strictures against "self-deception" in experience need occasionally to be tempered with an awareness of the extent to which all experience is an interpretation subject to conscious revision. Personal histories, and national histories, need to be rewritten rather continuously as a base for the retrospective learning of new self-conceptions.

Each of these procedures represents a way in which we temporarily suspend the operation of the system of reasoned intelligence. They are playful. They make greatest sense in situations in which there has been an overlearning of virtues of conventional rationality. They are possibly dangerous applications of powerful devices more familiar to the study of behavioral pathology than to the investigation of human development. But they offer a few techniques for introducing change within current concepts of choice.

The argument extends easily to the problems of social organization. If we knew more about the normative theory of acting before you think, we could say more intelligent things about the functions of management and leadership when organizations or societies do not know what they are doing. Consider, for example, the following general implications.

First, we need to reexamine the functions of management decision. One of the primary ways in which the goals of an organization are developed is by interpreting the decisions it makes, and one feature of good managerial decisions is that they lead to the development of more interesting value premises for the organization. As a result, decisions should not be seen as flowing directly or strictly from a pre-existent set of objectives. Managers who make decisions might well view that function somewhat less as a process of deduction or a process of political negotiation, and somewhat more as a process of gently upsetting preconceptions of what the organization is doing.

Second, we need a modified view of planning. Planning in organizations has many virtues, but a plan can often be more effective as an interpretation of past decisions than as a program for future ones. It can be used as a part of the efforts of the organization to develop a new consistent theory of itself that incorporates the mix of recent actions into a moderately comprehensive structure of goals. Procedures for interpreting the meaning of most past events are familiar to the memoirs of retired generals, prime ministers, business leaders, and movie stars. They suffer from the company they keep. In an organization that wants to continue to develop new objectives, a manager needs to be relatively tolerant of the idea that he will discover the meaning of yesterday's action in the experiences and interpretations of today.

Third, we need to reconsider evaluation. As nearly as I can determine, there is nothing in a formal theory of evaluation that requires that the criterion function for evaluation be specified in advance. In particular, the evaluation of social experiments need not be in terms of the degree to which they have fulfilled our *a priori* expectations. Rather we can examine what they did in terms of what we now believe to be important. The prior specification of criteria and the prior specification of evaluational procedures that depend on such criteria are common presumptions in contemporary social policy making. They are presumptions that inhibit the serendipitous discovery of new criteria. Experience should be used explicitly as an occasion for evaluating our values as well as our actions.

Fourth, we need a reconsideration of social accountability. Individual preferences and social action need to be consistent in some way. But the process of pursuing consistency is one in which both the preferences and the actions change over time. Imagination in social policy formation involves systematically adapting to and influencing preferences. It would be unfortunate if our theories of social action encouraged leaders to ignore their responsibilities for anticipating public preferences through action and for providing social experiences that modify individual expectations.

Fifth, we need to accept playfulness in social organizations. The design of organizations should attend to the problems of maintaining both playfulness and reason as aspects of intelligent choice. Since much of the literature on social design is concerned with strengthening the rationality of decision, managers are likely to overlook the importance of play. This is partly a matter of making the individuals within an organization more playful by encouraging the attitudes and skills of inconsistency. It is also a matter of making organizational structure and organizational procedures more playful. Organizations can be playful even when the participants in them are not. The managerial devices for maintaining consistency can be varied. We encourage organizational play by permitting (and insisting on) some temporary relief from control, coordination, and communication.

TECHNOLOGIES OF REASON AND FOOLISHNESS

Social action is built upon models of social choice. Contemporary theories of decision making and the technology of reason have considerably strengthened our capabilities for effective social action. The conversion of the simple ideas of choice into an extensive technology is a major achievement. It is, however, an achievement that has reinforced some biases in the underlying models of choice in individuals and groups. In particular, it has reinforced the uncritical acceptance of a static interpretation of human goals.

There is little magic in the world, and foolishness in people and organizations is one of the many things that fail to produce miracles. Under certain conditions, it is one of several ways in which some of the problems of our current theories of intelligence can be overcome. It may be a good way. It preserves the virtues of consistency while stimulating change. If we had a good technology of foolishness, it might (in combination with the technology of reason) help in a small way to develop the unusual combinations of attitudes and behaviors that describe the interesting people, interesting organizations, and interesting societies of the world.

Acknowledgments

The chapter borrows heavily from two books. The first is an introduction to analysis in social science, co-authored with Charles A. Lave (*An Introduction to Models in Social Sciences*, New York, Harper and Row, 1975). The second is a book on the American college presidency, co-authored with Michael D. Cohen *Leadership and Ambiguity*, New York, McGraw-Hill (1974) [2nd edn Boston, Harvand Business School Press, 1986]. I cheerfully attribute a part of the blame to them. In addition, the ideas have been the basis for extended conversations with a number of friends. I want to acknowledge particularly the help of Lance Bennett, Patricia Nelson Bennett, Michael Butler, Soren Christensen, Michel Crozier, Claude Faucheux, James R. Glenn, Jr, Gudmund Hernes, Helga Hernes, Jean Carter Lave, Harold J. Leavitt, Henry M. Levin, Leslie Lincoln, Andre Massart, John Miller, Johan Olsen, Richard C. Snyder, Alexander Szalai, Eugene J. Webb, and Gail Whitacre.

The Carnegie Commission on Higher Education and the Ford Foundation are financially responsible.

CHAPTER SEVENTEEN

Organizational Consultants and Organizational Research

Ever since Aristotle taught Alexander the Great, the relation between research on organizations and the giving of advice to organizational leaders has intrigued both scholars and consultants. In the modern world of organizations, consultants and researchers exist in different cultures, but they share a concern for understanding the ways organizations learn and improve. Experiential learning by organizations ordinarily produces a good deal of powerful context-specific knowledge, knowledge that is inaccessible to a usual consultant. As a result, a consultant who presumes to give specific advice to a specific organization is likely to be misguided. However, experiential learning is imperfect: it tends to exaggerate the importance of actual events relative to events that might have happened. It tends to close the door to experimentation. It tends to encourage the adoption of disconfirmable theories. Consultants help organizations escape these problems by two major mechanisms. First, they help pool experience across organizations, a practice that is clearly useful, though it has some well-known difficulties. Second, they provide alternative interpretations of history and possibilities, interpretations that are quite likely to be wrong by themselves but that combine with ordinary knowledge to provide improvements in understanding. From this perspective, good consulting is rather like good theory. It becomes useful less by being precisely correct than by being interesting in a way that is not redundant with ordinary knowledge.

INTRODUCTION

The earliest students of organizations made very little distinction between consulting and research, and their clients made very little distinction between theoretical and practical knowledge. When Aristotle taught

Alexander the Great, the terminology of the lesson was, we presume, as simultaneously profound and mundane as Aristotle writing about political institutions. Plato discussed organizational forms using the same style and intellectual apparatus that he used in discussing the details of physical education. And Thomas Aquinas was as comfortable advising the Duchess of Brabant about the pragmatics of treating wealthy Jews as he was in assessing the theological basis for hierarchy. Even Machiavelli, the patron saint of organizational consulting, spent as much time on philosophy as on designing incentive schemes and was not sure they were profoundly different.

Those were, of course, simpler times. We live on a different scale. If the Academy of Management had existed in ancient Greece and if its membership had included the same fraction of the total citizenry as the membership of the present Academy does of the citizens of the United States and Canada, the annual meetings could have been on a small park bench. The Academy involves a minority of North American students of management; yet it has a larger membership than either the American Political Science Association or the American Sociological Association had at the end of World War II. There are more of us now, and we are probably more intelligently informed about management than we used to be.

We are also more specialized. I am a student of organizational decision making, learning, change, leadership, and power. I am aware of and admire numerous specialists in other domains of organization and management studies; but I would not presume to speak on their behalf. I am an academic, ivory-tower student of organization theory, I am aware of and admire numerous others who are concerned with aspects of the study of people trying to survive in or with organizations; but I would not imagine that I am one of them. I do research, drink wine, and pontificate in an academic cloister, most of the time happily buffered from relevance.

Because my own life is so peacefully academic, filled with sabbatical leaves, thoughtful students, and the peculiar perquisites of professorial pretense, the excitements and problems of being useful are mostly denied me. But sometimes the real world intrudes gently, as it did recently when I was asked by a major periodical to comment (presumably negatively) on the research base of one recent best selling book dealing with organizations and management. The invitation recalled other best sellers of recent years and their claims to standing as scholarship, and it brought echoes of broader concerns about the pursuit of knowledge and the giving of advice.

Declining the invitation from the journal was easy, but it led to some conversations with friends about the relation between organizational consulting and organizational research in a world containing a fair amount of each rather than a single Aristotle or two. This chapter is an ethnographer's report on those conversations. It is an examination of how we might think about the intellectual relation between consulting and research. I talk about the "intellectual" relation, not because I think it can be separated finally from the many other relations that have been admirably delineated by writers on experts and expertise, such as Harold Wilensky, Marvin Sussman, and Guy Benveniste, but because I think it may be easy to lose track of the intellectual nature of the pursuit of knowledge in our enthusiasms for understanding its social and political aspects. The "new naivete" in social science is, after all, the subordination of idealism to realism. In small tribute to a "new sophistication," I will talk less about research and consulting as they actually exist than as they might be imagined to exist.

THE SINS OF CONSULTANTS

Consulting, as I use the term, includes any activity that has as its main apparent justification the giving of advice to organizational participants about how to improve the effectiveness of organizations or specific individuals in them. Within such a definition, I include not only individuals or groups who offer advice on a fee-for-service basis, but also, and perhaps preeminently, people who write books and people who teach. Research, as I use the term, is any activity that involves gathering systematic data about organizations or speculating about them in a systematic way, and reporting the results publicly in a form that relates them to other research in a cumulative and impersonal way. Within such a definition, one can include various kinds of theoretical and empirical studies familiar to the journals of organizational studies.

It is clear that there are many differences between consulting and research as we observe them. In particular and most conspicuously, they exist in different social structures. They have different incentive systems, different social norms, different bases of competition and survival. Although a few people live comfortably in both cultures and bring distinction to both most people are mostly one or the other. The talents involved may well be different; but even if they are not, socialization and experience conspire to differentiate the two groups and lead to a certain amount of mutual discomfort, even antagonism.

When I ask friends who identify with the research community to articulate their distaste for consultants, most of what they have to say can be summarized by the expression a friend of mine used: "Consultants talk funny and make money." Consultants do make money, or at least some of them do, Consulting is a substantial industry with substantial fees. The complaint, however, is probably less that they make money than that the payments they receive are not warranted by the knowledge they provide, They pander to their employers' prejudices and preferences, serve as window dressing for their atrocities, allow them to spend their personnel budgets without long-run commitments.

They also talk funny. They frequently violate reasonable research standards. They generalize on the basis of elusive observations made on ill-defined samples drawn from unspecified universes. They often seem to ignore – out of ignorance, laziness, or greed – relevant research literature. They simplify complex things, thereby misrepresenting them, and fail to provide adequate warnings of the restrictions that apply to their statements. They thrive on a diet of truisms, hyperbole, and gimmicks. Any ideas they may have are lost in a terminology of salesmanship and a format of overconfidence.

I recite the litany of complaint not to endorse it, though I think it has substantial elements of truth in it, nor to deny the obvious extent to which a very similar list could be complied for the perpetrators of research, but to suggest the magnitude of the cultural division. If you believe such statements, you might be excused if you concluded that not only do consultants talk funny but they also say nothing and are disconnected from organizational research; but there I think you would be mistaken. The language may be strange to the ear of an academic, and the attribution and citation procedure a bit alien; but the ideas are sometimes remarkably familiar and sometimes strikingly provocative. It was after all, Chester Barnard who started a lot of this.

In fact, many of the most important theoretical developments in the study of organizations, as in the rest of social science, have come from and are likely to continue to come from a logic somewhat different from the logic that fills our literature on research methodology and philosophy. The logic is that of engineering and problem solving. We seek to be able to specify *sufficient antecedent* conditions to produce a *particular subsequent* condition. The contrast is with an alternative vision of knowledge in which we seek to be able to specify the *necessary subsequent* conditions following any *arbitrary antecedent* conditions. The differences are important. We do not ask a bridge designer to tell us the probable consequences of all possible combinations of materials and their conformation. Rather, we ask for a solution to a problem, a bridge that meets certain specifications in an acceptable way. In a complex system, the former approach is normally several orders of magnitude easier than the latter. Indeed, the latter can easily become impossible.

Because I think such a logic is important to developing an understanding of organizations and management. I want to avoid asking the kinds of questions that will lead me inexorably to conclude that consultants are unacceptable researchers. Rather, I want to talk about consulting as it might be imagined to be, and perhaps sometimes is; and to draw some parallels with research as it might be imagined to be, and perhaps sometimes is. I want to imagine that among all the impressive realities of careers, power, intrigue, chicanery and self-interested cleverness that crowd the organizations we know, there are adaptive organizations, actually collections of interconnected adaptive subunits. And I want to imagine that research and consulting, in addition to satisfying the various powerful lusts of comfortable human actors, stabilizing a status quo endowed with the usual elements of corruption, and symbolizing important aspects of contemporary ideology and mythology, also make contributions to the way organizations learn from their experience.

It is a romantic story; and by imagining it, I do not intend to demean other, less romantic, stories we might also tell. The romanticism is not so much a worldview as a tactic. I want to examine some aspects of the contributions to organizational learning that research and consulting might make, in order to ask whether – without necessarily sacrificing significant income, glory, or cynicism – we might do better.

Learning From Experience in Organizations

Organizations learn from their experience. That is, organizational actions and beliefs change as a result of monitoring and interpreting the consequences of past actions. Such experiential learning is one form of history-dependent behavior in organizations and has been considered by decision engineers, students of business tactics and organizational design, and behavioral students of organizations.

Organizations learn concurrently along at least three dimensions. First, they learn what *strategies* to adopt, where to locate themselves, how to allocate resources. They learn to devote more (or less) time or money to making widgets than to baseballs. They learn to pursue battles of position more than battles of attrition. They learn to search for solutions in the neighborhood of past solutions more than in distant places. Although there are other factors involved, they respond to reinforcement. They come to allocate more resources to those activities that have, in the past, been associated with success and less resources to those activities that have been associated with failure.

Second, organizations learn (and forget) *competence*. They become more able at those things they do frequently, lose abilities that are not used. An organization produces widgets at lower cost after producing one million of them than it could after having produced only one thousand, but the value of production experience declines with distance from it. The battle efficiency of armies and the effectiveness of research and development activities improves with experience, but the value of experience declines with time. There are numerous organizational mechanisms by which an increased potential gained from experience may be captured by individuals or subunits in the form of organizational slack, but we generally expect both that organizations will become better at what they do the longer they continue doing it, and that experiential competence decays with disuse.

Third, organizations change their *aspirations*, or expectations, as a result of their experience. They learn what they can reasonably expect from their environment. They discover what a reasonable profit is, what an army should expect, what research and development can do. They modify their aspirations to reflect their experience. As a result, they change their subjective definitions of success (reward) and failure (punishment).

For the most part, discussions of organizational learning in the literature treat each of these three forms of learning separately and develop the implications of each without attention to parallel implications of the others, or to the ways in which they interact. Yet, it is clear that the three learning dimensions are not independent. Allocations affect organizational actions and thus effect the distribution of organizational actions and thus affect the distribution of organizational competence. Competencies, in turn, affect the likelihood of success with a particular allocation, and thus affect the learning of both allocations and aspirations. Aspirations, by defining success and failure, affect the learning of allocations and thus the development of competencies. The interrelations make it difficult to examine any of the three dimensions without attention to the others.

These interactions among the dimensions of learning are further complicated by the fact that an organization is a collection of subunits that are simultaneously changing their own allocations, competencies, and aspirations on the basis of their own experiences. These subunits are linked to the organization by their mutual consequences for outcomes and by efforts at hierarchical coordination. For example, the allocation decisions that lead to success on subunit goals do not necessarily lead to success on organizational goals. This familiar complication of rational theories of organizations and agency has a counterpart in ideas of learning under conflict of interest. Since the separate decisions made by the several subunits and the organization affect the outcomes for the others, their learning experiences are intertwined.

In addition, organizations that are learning allocations, competencies, and aspirations (while adapting to subunits that are simultaneously developing their own allocations, competencies, and aspirations) compete in an environment consisting of other organizations that also are learning (and also contain learning subunits). Widget manufacturers meet other widget manufacturers in a competition for customers. Armies meet other armies in a competition for military victory. Research and development organizations meet other research and development organizations in a competition for discoveries and new products. As a result of competition and imitation, the learning of one organization depends on the actions of the others.

Finally, recent work on organizational learning and decision making has emphasized the importance of uncertainty and ambiguity to an understanding of modern organizations. Organizational performance may not be precisely determined by organizational actions; environmental constraints may not be precisely specified; organizational goals may be ambiguous, as may be results or their causes. It is easy to show that prima facie sensible learning procedures may produce anomalous results under conditions in which learning is affected by these, and other, forms of "noise."

Although these complications are significant, organizational learning ordinarily works rather well. Organizations and the people in them come, through experience, to know how to do a lot of things. Simple learning from experience generates a substantial amount of specialized ordinary knowledge. Any organization that has endured for some time has accumulated a good deal of particularistic, context-specific knowledge. What to expect; when to expect it; how to deal with it; what works; what doesn't.

The role of consultants in advising organizations is constrained by the effectiveness of such experiential learning in organizations and the importance of context-specific knowledge. In most situations in most organizations the best source of intelligence for action is ordinary knowledge, Most of what matters is captured in the particularistic features of the organizations (including what is relevant that might be drawn from more general forms of intelligence). In most cases a manager who wants advice would find it better from himself or his associates than from a consultant or a research study.

Mostly, therefore, good advice giving assumes the existence of ordinary knowledge and tries to contribute something that is as little redundant with that knowledge as is possible. The obvious implication is possibly disquieting: Since ordinary context-specific knowledge is extensive and powerful, advice that tries to summarize as much "truth" as possible will tend to be redundant with what is already known, thus not very useful. Put in other terms, an advisor who provides knowledge that maximizes the "explained variance," or managerial judgement, will generally tell an organization too many things that are already known.

CONTRIBUTIONS ON THE MARGIN

Against this background of ordinary knowledge, research and consulting make their contributions on the margin. They attempt to complement, rather than duplicate, the contributions of experiential learning in specific organizations. Learning from experience is not perfect. It has its own traps. I will mention three that are important in the present context: First, experiential learning tends to exaggerate the importance of actual events relative to events that might have happened, thus to be quite sensitive to the rate of experience relative to the rate of change in the world.

Second, experiential learning tends to close the door on experimentation. It is fairly easy for a fast learner to become fixed on behavior that is rewarding but less than the best possible. This occurs particularly because of the ways in which strategies, competence, and aspirations adapt simultaneously.

Third, experiential learning is not a good way to learn theories of behavior. Assuming that confirmation of theory is rewarding and disconfirmation is not, simple learning will tend to drive organizational participants to discomfirmable theories.

Because of these problems, simple experiential learning by individual organizations is flawed. Research and consulting can supplement that learning, not by attempting to substitute for it but by helping to protect against the limitations of ordinary knowledge.

Pooling experience

Research and consulting are devices for pooling experience across organizations. Most organizational consulting, as well as most organizational research, involves describing current practice and spreading the benefits of experience. That is, what we, whether as consultants or as researchers, do most of the time is serve as part of an information network that shares experiences. We report what other people are doing these days.

Some of the early work on learning by doing in engineering economics, and particularly some of the policy recommendations derived from it, failed to consider the extent to which it is possible to learn from the experiences of others. The second widget manufacturer will often not require as much experience to reach a given level of costs as the first widget manufacturer. The process by which relevant experience is shared across organizations and codified into rules and procedures is a process in which consultancy and research are typically important.

Research and consulting in this genre tell stories of success and failure and report the antecedent organizational conditions that were associated with one or the other, The implicit objective is to spread technologies and procedures associated with the success and inhibit the spread of technologies and procedures associated with failures, thus the pooling of experience. It is a powerful device which if effective, produces an evolving system of organizations. The evolutionary system, however, is not one of invariant organizational forms but one in which the distribution of forms changes not only through differential survival and growth but also through shared experiences and imitation.

Solving a problem efficiently usually involves doing things you have previously done successfully, or copying someone else's successful solution. Whether we want to know how to produce shoes, how to fight wars, how to invest money, how to build bridges, or how to make love, the best way to improve our own capabilities normally is to imitate the technologies of others who have had successful experience doing the same thing. In the course of that process, there is a role for innovation carriers, people who identify a new organizational form or practice somewhat before it becomes standard practice and present it as a new solution to a problem, a solution with special advantages demonstrated elsewhere but not yet fully exploited. These new discoveries become the gimmicks, mousetraps, and innovations of organizational consultancy. "Quality circles," for example, or "small wins." Gradually, successful technologies are collected into norms of behavior in the form of standard practices, operating procedures, and rules of thumb and communicated through professional associations, educational institutions, consultants, and researchers.

This pooling of experience by communicating the experiences of others ameliorates some of the problems of ordinary knowledge. It extends experience, thus effectively increasing the rate of experience; and since there are several learners rather than a single one, pooled experience is likely to provide the variation in experience that reduces vulnerability to local optima.

However, these gains may prove to be less than we hope. The pooling of experience can be deceptive. On the one hand, if the experiences that are pooled are not independent, the advantages of multiple learners are attenuated. When Ford learns from General Motors and General Motors learns from Ford, some of what each learns from other is an echo of its own previous knowledge. Moreover, the inferences to be drawn from history are rarely obvious. Pooling is unlikely to be particularly helpful when history is obscure. Where ambiguous experience is pooled rapidly, we would expect consensus on organizational recommendations and beliefs to bear about as much relation to the maintenance of effective management as the fads of clothing bear to the maintenance of health. Finally, as was noted earlier, direct personal experience and the pooling of experience are not guaranteed to lead to improved theories of behavior, even when they lead to improved action. Nothing in the pooling of experience provides protection from the tendency toward adopting tautological theoretical interpretations of experience.

As a result, although the pooling of experience is unquestionably one of the more powerful devices available for organizations to learn from experience, it can lead to remarkably incomplete or flawed understandings of important domains of experience in management. Consider, for example, the relatively dismal record of organizational consulting (and research) on topics such as time management, executive compensation, and management information systems. In these areas, progress in understanding seems discouragingly slow despite considerable organizational concern, experience, and consulting help. If I am right, however, the problem stems not from a lack of competence on the part of the individuals involved but from the limitations of learning from ambiguous, echoed experiences.

These problems are, of course, not unique to organizations or other multiple actor systems. They are endemic to learning from accumulated experience. We learn from experience in order to modify our behavior; but every modification complicates learning. In the well-known "two-armed bandit" case, for example, there is a trade-off between acting on our current knowledge and improving that knowledge (by delaying a change in behavior). In a world in which our competencies are improved by practice, we may become so competent at some skills as to inhibit the development of others. In a world in which pooled experience is partly an echo of direct experience, we may substantially exaggerate the significance of that experience. The problems are not trivial, and they have no general solution that is sufficiently concrete to be translated into action easily.

Providing interpretations for experience

Not all consulting in research consists in expanding experience. Certain forms of research and consulting contribute counterpoints to the norms of history, thereby broadening the base for learning. A primary way of doing this is by providing new interpretations for experience. These are the ideas, metaphors, models, and words that impose order on a confusing world, thus reconstructing our appreciation of experience. When we talk about research, we refer to theoretical speculations. It is a familiar style. MacGregor, Barnard, Simon, Vickers. When Jeffrey Pfeffer writes about resource dependency and when Chris Argyris writes about learning, they are not so much reporting experience or empirical results as they are elaborating themes of interpretation.

Although speaking of theoretical speculation gives overtones of irrelevance that make the activity seem uniquely academic, such an orientation is also characteristic of several conspicuously successful contemporary consultants, notably Peters and Waterman and Deal and Kennedy. Perhaps, the classic modern consultant in this mode was Dale Carnegie. What Carnegie tried to do was to provide, in addition to a host of concrete suggestions for action, a theoretical interpretation of influence relations between people, especially sellers and buyers of commodities (including ideas).

Carnegie argued that the conventional model for selling pots and pans was wrong. Most people imagined that what was involved in selling pots and pans was providing information about the pots and pans that led a potential buyer to see them as advantageous from the point of view of possible uses to which they might be put. Carnegie suggested that there were several exchange relations involved, but the key exchange had very little to do with properties of the pots and pans. As he saw, there were two general kinds of goods in the world, self-esteem and substantive decisions (e.g., purchase decisions). Moreover, he observed a persistent disparity in the supply of these goods. At almost any time and place, self-esteem is in shorter supply than substance. So, he suggested that anyone who offered self-esteem could exchange that for substance at favorable rates of exchange. This insight, in fact, had considerable research support and parts of Carnegie's elaboration are related to the balance and consistency theories of academic social psychology, although he was probably unaware of the linkages between his speculations, that arose in the context of giving practical advice, and theories of social influence, balance theory, and cognitive dissonance theory, that arose in the context of more formal research.

Providing ideas to be used in interpreting experience is a major function of both consulting and research. Thus, much of consulting, like much of research is not primarily oriented to the transmission of empirical experience. It provides interpretative schema for experience. The main link between several recent popular books and the research literature is not a connection between best-sellers and empirical studies of management or organizations but a connection between those books and theoretical ideas. The impact of ideas drawn from theories of organizations is conspicuous in them. As a result, an appropriate evaluation of consulting, including popular books on management, is often more similar to the evaluation of theory (or art) than it is to the evaluation of empirical research.

A comprehensive discussion of how we might evaluate interpretive speculations is far beyond my intent, not to mention my competence. Characterizing the quality of alternative interpretations requires elements of literary and art criticism as well as positivist empirical methodology. It involves an assessment of a speculation's truth, beauty, and justice. Or more precisely, an assessment of a theory's contribution to truth, beauty, and justice at the margin. Interpretive knowledge, like external experiential knowledge, contributes at the margin. It is an interpretation of a world already comprehended by ordinary knowledge. Almost any reasonably experienced participant in an organization can do a better job of predicting and controlling organizational events than can be done using theoretical knowledge (interpretation) by itself.

Thus, good consulting, like good theory and good art, emphasizes aspects of events and interpretative schema that may be, by themselves, quite misleading or overstated, but that lead in combination with what is accessible to ordinary knowledge to improvements in understanding. From this perspective, the extent to which a speculation is non-redundant in an interesting way is likely to be as important as whether it is precisely true. Making an interpretation both non-redundant and interesting involves an awareness of what is known and of the possible ways in which good approximations to historical understanding may be inadequate. Thus, it calls for an appreciation of the role of surprise, evocativeness, and beauty in interpretation.

By such criteria, much consulting is undoubtedly inadequate; the ideas that are provided are either part of general knowledge or wrong in uninteresting ways. But the inadequacy is an inadequacy of ideas, not simply an inattention to the rules of empirical research. Since a similar assessment could be made of much of our research literature, it suggests that some deeper attention to the nature of interesting ideas about organizational behavior might contribute more usefully to our research literature and'to our airport reading than would an effort to make the latter more like the former.

A Concluding Note

I began with a romantic story, one in which we imagined that consulting and research have something to do with organizational adaptation – in addition to numerous less edifying things. In that romantic world, the intellectual problems of consulting are much the same as the intellectual problems of research. They include the complications of accumulating experience when events are not independent and history is ambiguous; the difficulty of providing non-redundant increments to a base of ordinary knowledge; the delicacies of learning from events that didn't actually occur; the art of generating interesting interpretative frames within which to learn from experience. Neither research nor consulting deals exceptionally well with these problems. They are, in fact, not easy.

If I were to continue the romantic fantasy of a collective concern with improving the ways in which organizations adapt to their worlds on the basis of their experience, I might suggest that the problems seem serious enough, even intriguing enough, for us to forego the pleasures of listing (or denying) the virtues of consultants or the sins of researchers. Rather, we might get on with the task of trying to figure out an idea or two worthy of a glass of wine and the other lesser perquisites of either trade, recognizing that good ideas are often wrong and always scarce and that neither Luther Gulick nor Dale Carnegie was entirely foolish.

Acknowledgment

This chapter is based on a talk delivered at the 1984 annual meeting of the Academy of Management. I am grateful for the support of grants from the Spencer Foundation, the Mellon Foundation, the Stanford Graduate School of Business, and the Hoover Institution.

CHAPTER EIGHTEEN

Organizational Performance as a Dependent Variable

with Robert I. Sutton

Most studies of organizational performance define performance as a dependent variable and seek to identify variables that produce variations in performance. Researchers who study organizational performance in this way typically devote little attention to the complications of using such a formulation to characterize the causal structure of performance phenomena. These complications include the ways in which performance advantage is competitively unstable, the causal complexity surrounding performance, and the limitations of using data based on retrospective recall of informants. Since these complications are well known and routinely taught, a pattern of acknowledging the difficulties but continuing the practice cannot be attributed exclusively to poor training, lack of intelligence, or low standards. Most researchers understand the difficulties of inferring causal order from the correlations generated by organizational histories, particularly when those correlations may be implicit in the measurement procedures used. We suggest that the persistence of this pattern is due, in part, to the context of organizational research. Organizational researchers live in two worlds. The first demands and rewards speculations about how to improve performance. The second demands and rewards adherence to rigorous standards of scholarship. In its efforts to satisfy these often conflicting demands, the organizational research community sometimes responds by saying that inferences about the causes of performance cannot be made from the data available, and simultaneously goes ahead to make such inferences. We conclude by considering a few virtues and hazards of such a solution to dilemmas involving compelling contradictory imperatives and the generality of the issues involved.

Organizations are commonly defined as instruments of purpose. They are seen as coordinated by intentions and goals. Such a formulation has often troubled students of organizations. It is not clear that organizational purpose can be portrayed as unitary or that the multiple purposes of an organization are reliably consistent. It is not clear that a single conception of purposes is shared among participants in an organization. It is not clear that purpose antedates activities. Nevertheless, talking about the purposes of organizations and evaluating comparative organizational success and failure in fulfilling those purposes are conspicuous parts of conventional discourse. Business firms are compared in terms of profits, sales, market share, productivity, debt ratios, and stock prices. Hospitals use cost recovery, mortality and morbidity rates, board certification of physicians, and occupancy rates. Universities use research productivity and prestige of faculties, test scores of students, rankings by popular magazines, and won/loss records of football teams. Such comparisons become a basis for evaluating executives, for making decisions about allocation of human and other resources, for writing history, and for stimulating arrogance and shame.

Explaining variation in performance or effectiveness is also one of the more enduring themes in the study of organizations.[1] It is manifested most distinctively in studies with a focus on "management" but extends to a wide range of research that seeks to understand competitive survival and to construct interpretations of organizational histories that emphasize the adaptation of organizations to feedback from their environments. Organizational performance can, of course, be considered at a disaggregated level, as for example in studies of the direct costs of producing a particular product using a specific technology or of efficiency in performing a particular task. Our interest here, however, is in more aggregate assessments of organizational performance, as for example in accounting, sales, or financial reports, in stories of organizational history, or in other socially constructed evaluations of overall organizational effectiveness.

PROBLEMS IN STUDIES OF PERFORMANCE

In studies of organizations, performance sometimes appears as an independent variable, but it is more likely to appear on the left-hand side of the equation as a dependent variable.[2] This emphasis is most explicit in the field of organizational strategy, which is often defined as having organizational performance as its primary focus, but the idea that performance is to be predicted, understood, and shaped is commonplace throughout the field. Such a posture is also embraced as a code of proper behavior.

The second sentence in the Academy of Management Code of Ethical Conduct is: "Our professional goals are to enhance the learning of students, colleagues, and others and to improve the effectiveness of organizations through our teaching, research, and practice of management" (Academy of Management, 1995, p. 573).

Efforts to fulfill the implicit promise of the code, the hopes of managers, the logic of performance improvement, and the ambitions of students of organizational adaptation encounter a fundamental complication, however: identifying the true causal structure of organizational performance phenomena on the basis of the incomplete information generated by historical experience is problematic. Students of organizational performance rarely exercise experimental control over predictor variables. They rely instead on analyses of observations made of naturally occurring events. As a result, they confront problems of finding adequate archival data and of soliciting and interpreting the accounts of informants. These records of naturally occurring histories of organizational performance are notoriously difficult to interpret. Any observation-based organizational history is rife with resolute ambiguities that can frustrate the efforts of statistical and interpretive imagination to identify causal links among historical events.

Without attempting to be comprehensive, we mention three of the more conspicuous problems involved in understanding variations in organizational performance: First, information about apparent determinants of differences in performance diffuses through a population of competitors and thereby tends to eliminate variation in both the determinants and their effects. Second, the theoretical ideas and analytical models that are normally used ignore a variety of feedback loops that are likely to be important. Third, the data that are used to record organizational histories often rely on retrospective recall of informants, recall that is likely to reconstruct the past to make it consistent with subsequent performance results, conventional story lines, and current beliefs. These problems are neither new nor difficult to recognize but they are not well accommodated in studies seeking to explain organizational performance.

Instabilities of performance advantage

Organizations compete with one another, consciously seeking advantage. A major feature of that competition is competitive imitation. Poor performance rankings are interpreted by potential competitors as indications that a practice does not work or a market does not exist, thus inhibit imitation and competition, thereby reducing the competitive pressure and improving relative performance. Good performance rankings, on the other hand, not only stimulate admiration; they also encourage imitation and competition that tend to erode a favorable position. Organizations seek to emulate the performance successes of others by emulating their organizational forms and practices. This practice is institutionalized through concepts of "best practice" and in the activities of managerial media and consultants.

The result is the progressive elimination of organizational factors that are clearly relevant to performance advantage or disadvantage. This complication has often been used, by itself, to explain the relatively poor record of organizational research in explaining variations in performance. The basic idea is that any feature of organizational practice that might provide major competitive advantage is ordinarily adopted by all competitors. This competitive shaping of practice and various forms of institutionalized diffusion (DiMaggio and Powell, 1983) reduce the variation in powerfully effective practices and obscure their effects, leaving any analysis the unenviable task of detecting weak signals in a performance world of substantial noise.

In this way, successes at understanding performance differences are self-destructive. As knowledge spreads, factors that previously distinguished high performers from low performers tend to disappear; and the more powerful the explanatory mechanism is believed to be, the faster the diffusion of knowledge about it. This imitative mechanism does not require that the performance advantage or disadvantage attributed to a particular factor necessarily be "real," only that it be generally accepted and acted upon, so as to reduce variation in the independent variables. The mechanism is obviously more enduring, however, if a true performance advantage or disadvantage has been identified, thus reducing variation in the dependent variable as well.

In order for knowledge to be imitatively self-destructive in this way, the relevant factors must be controllable so that an organization can be imagined to be able to adopt attributes and practices that are thought to give advantage and to reject those that are thought to give disadvantage. Although this requirement seems relatively unrestrictive with respect to many of the organizational forms, practices, and programs that are given credit for performance advantage, sources of advantage vary in their susceptibility to transfer (Barney, 1991). Characteristically, they are imperfectly or imaginatively implemented. Profound differences between organizational policies as formally adopted (e.g., total quality management, zero-based budgeting) and actual organizational practices have been observed, thus in principle assuring continued variation in organizations even in the face of widespread beliefs about effective practices. Unfortunately, normal procedures for recording organizational practices for research purposes tend either to accept the formal policies without assessing their implementation or to introduce considerable noise in measurement.

Simple models of complex worlds

Performance instabilities are a special case of a more general complication. Most interpretations of organizational performance are built on elementary causal conceptions, sometimes encased in multiple regression or analysis of variance models, at other times embedded in less formal historical speculations. Theories are characteristically specified in terms of a causally "dependent" variable to be predicted and several explanatory variables imagined to be causally antecedent. Particularly where the various variables are observed at the same time, it is often unclear what variable should be treated as causally dependent. The choice is made by the researcher. Neither the data nor the analytical frames are of much help in making such a decision. It is normally based on a prior judgment about the causal structure. This judgment may be valid, but it cannot be confirmed by the analysis, which can only assess the likely strength of the relationships on the assumption that the causal structure is correctly specified. In their specifications of causal relations, students of organizational performance tend to construct theories and models that ignore important mutual effects that are frequently noted in the literature on organizations. These effects cannot be described as established beyond doubt, in part because of the observational complications already noted, but they are sufficiently plausible to make simple causal models injudicious.

First, there are mechanisms by which performance in one time period is affected positively by performance in previous periods. Many of the cognitive and affective factors that seem likely to affect performance (for example, investor, customer, and worker confidence in the organization) are themselves likely to be affected by prior performance. Good performance rankings lead both to self-assurance and to being treated favorably by others; poor performance rankings lead both to loss of self-assurance and to being treated unfavorably by others. People who experience positive emotions as a result of being assessed as successful have been found to be more creative, more persistent, more likely to help others, and more likely to make decisions quickly (see Isen and Baron, 1991 for a review). As a result, it seems quite likely that positive experiences in organizations will contribute to future positive experiences. Poor performance assessments are likely to be similarly self-reinforcing (Sutton and Callahan, 1987). According to one interpretation at least, negative assessments create an emotional climate of failure, where interlocked cycles of declining performance and internal reactions lead to organizational demise (Greenhalgh, 1983; Masuch, 1985).

Moreover, there may well be a difference between the positive and negative assessment cases. Studies of the way individuals – including the leaders of organizations – make attributions with respect to their own performance, indicate that they typically take credit when their own performance is good and blame external causes when their own performance is poor (Jones and Wortman, 1973, Staw et al., 1983, Adams et al., 1985). The resulting self-confidence among successful individuals is likely to contribute positively to organizational performance, whereas the disassociation from failure restrains the loss of self-confidence among individuals who are not successful. As a result, the motivations generated by performance and its attributions are likely to accelerate success more than failure among current leaders.

Second, at the same time, there are also negative feedback effects by which success or failure in organizational performance creates countervailing tendencies. According to one common speculation, organizational performance below target or aspiration levels (failure) triggers increases in search, decreases in organizational slack, and decreases in aspirations (Cyert and March, 1963; March, 1988). Each of these effects of failure increases the likelihood of subsequent success. The idea of stimulating improvement by defining past performance as a failure is a familiar theme in the goal setting literature (Pritchard et al., 1988; Locke and Latham, 1990).

According to the same theories, performance that is above aspiration levels (success) triggers adjustments in the opposite direction, so that success stimulates subsequent failure either through an increase in aspirations or through a decrease in search and an increase in slack. Whether the cyclic process produced by these two negative feedbacks leads to an observed positive or negative serial correlation for performance depends on the speeds of the three adjustments to failure or success and the frequency of observation.

Third (as is suggested by the preceding example), the short-run effects of some mechanisms are likely to be different from their long-run effects. One of the more obvious is the contrast between the short-run (efficiency) and long-run (adaptiveness) effects of attention. According to standard theories of problemistic search, decreases in slack and increases in search in response to failure ordinarily improve organizational performance in the short run, but the improvements pose complications for longer-run performance (March, 1994). For example, the threat posed by poor performance causes decision makers to restrict experimentation, tighten controls, and place greater reliance on formal procedures which require less complex information processing (Staw et al., 1981; D'Aunno and Sutton, 1992). The long-run consequences are likely to be to be damaging to performance. Conversely, increases in slack and decreases in search in response to success tend to reduce organizational performance in the short run but facilitate experimentation and risk taking that can yield long-run returns (March, 1991).

The learning dynamics of success are similar. Success at using one technology, strategy, or behavior leads to increased use. Increased use leads to greater competency, thus to greater success, thus to greater use. The resulting local positive feedback produces a competency trap which is detrimental in the long run (Levitt and March, 1988; Arthur, 1989). Thus; the use of organizational power to impose an environment (for example by dominant firms or nations) erodes the capability to adjust to an environment externally imposed (Levinthal and March, 1993; Miller, 1993). The notion that short-term success leads to longer-term failure is also reflected in the idea that avoidance of potential disaster leads to an underestimation of danger and a degradation of safety (March and Shapira, 1987; Starbuck and Milliken, 1988).

This brief foray into the feedback dynamics of performance is not intended to be exhaustive or to present a parsimonious integration of the relevant complications. Rather the aim is merely to suggest why a simple unidirectional causal interpretation of organizational performance is likely to fail. Performance feeds back upon itself through numerous mechanisms. Despite this substantial, and distinctly not secret, literature, the effects of performance on organizational predictor variables (and thus ultimately on performance) are frequently forgotten in research that purports to identify factors in organizational performance. Many standard specifications do not deal effectively with causal relations involving mutual effects among the variables, particularly between the "dependent" variable and one or more "independent" variables. As a result, simple unidirectional interpretations of performance are common in a world in which effects are interrelated in a rich system of probable feedback loops. Although using prior performance as a control variable (which is common) meliorates these problems to some extent, it tends to obscure the mechanisms involved.

Retrospective recall

Research on organizational performance is further complicated by the difficulty of choosing measures for the explanatory variables of interest, particularly the difficulty of avoiding measures that are themselves causally connected independent of any links among the variables they measure. The problem is particularly characteristic of the extensive use of retrospective accounts as sources of data. Many of the key independent variables in organizational performance studies are not observed directly. Where they are observed directly, they normally are not observed over time. This is true not only of studies using field research methods and narrative analysis but also of those using more classical statistical techniques. Commonly, informants are asked to assess things like group cohesiveness, management style, goals, intentions, and power, as well as changes that might have taken place in such things. Variables used to explain performance are sometimes assessed considerably after the performance is well-known to the informants (Tosi and Gomez-Mejia, 1994).

The result is the probable introduction of significant retrospective bias (Fischhoff, 1975; Fischhoff and Beyth, 1975). Performance information itself colors subjective memories, perceptions, and weightings of possible causes of performance. Informants exist in a world in which organizational performance is important. That world is filled with widely believed conventional stories about the causes of good and poor performance, and those stories are evoked by knowledge of performance results. As a result, retrospective reports of independent variables may be less influenced by memory than by a reconstruction that connects standard story lines with contemporaneous awareness of performance results.

For example, students who were led to believe (falsely) that their groups had performed well in a financial puzzle game reported higher group cohesiveness, greater personal influence over the task solution, higher quality communication, more confrontation of ideas with teammates, and more openness of teammates than were students who were led to believe their group did poorly. Relative to students who were given negative feedback, they believed that they and their teammates had higher motivation and ability, that the task was more enjoyable, and that the instructions were clearer (Staw, 1975).

Given that many informants in studies of effectiveness and performance are themselves members or leaders of the groups about which they are making attributions, their reports are particularly prone to bias. As observers and the observed collaborate in developing an understanding of history, the past is likely to become a product fashioned from consciousness of the present and framed by currently conventional storylines. The resulting construction of history is likely to attribute organizational successes or failures to properties of organization and the wills of managers, but such interpretations probably provide more credible evidence for their legitimacy than their validity.

Storylines and personal interests are intertwined to produce a fable that fits expectations and, as much as possible, confirms a story teller's conceptions of self-worth and the worth of others. Because the stories of informants can be fitted into standard storylines, they are likely to be accepted by researchers and their audiences (Staw, 1975). For example, observed correlations between a firm's "quality" as reported in an annual survey of corporate reputations and that firm's financial performance are likely to be due more to the effect of performance on perceptions of quality than to the effect of quality on performance (McGuire et al., 1990)

Despite the hazards of using cross-sectional and retrospective data and informants' interpretations to identify the possible causes of organizational performance, much research that attempts to explain observed performance differences continues to rely on such evidence. Brown and Eisenhardt's (1995) recent review and integration of the product development literature indicates that the bulk of research on the performance of product development efforts involves cross-sectional and retrospective studies. For example, the most common method for studying how rational planning affects product development success entails asking informants to recall why products have succeeded or failed, often asking them to compare a successful product with an unsuccessful one (e.g., Zirger and Maidique, 1990). As Brown and Eisenhardt point out, this means that the findings are likely to have been shaped by a host of cognitive biases. These studies may actually tell us less about the determinants of performance than about the ways performance information affects memory, cognitive processing, and story telling.

The Emperor's Clothes

Most studies of organizational performance are incapable of identifying the true causal relations among performance variables and other variables correlated with them through the data and methods they normally use. Although there are studies that mitigate these shortcomings, the emperor of organizational performance studies is for the most part rather naked. New enthusiasms succeed old ones, but the process often appears to be less one of gradual accumulation of knowledge than of intellectual drift stimulated by competition for scholarly reputation.

The questionable status of studies in which organizational performance appears as a causally dependent variable is not a secret. The difficulties in identifying causes of performance differences are common knowledge, part of the most basic training in the field (Staw, 1975; Lenz, 1981). As a result, the more intriguing part of this history is not the fact that the performance emperor has no clothes, for that is hardly "news." Rather it is the impressive persistence in making inferences about organizational performance histories that are so conspicuously and so generally known to be suspect.

A standard response to these persistencies has been to assume a failure of intelligence, standards, or training. Remedies of better research recruitment and training, better reviewing of journals, better consciousness of the problems have been pursued. These efforts have had very little impact. A steady flow of studies making questionable interpretations of performance evidence continues. Even though almost everyone knows that the emperor has no clothes, few people talk about that fact, and many of the same people who note the emperor's nakedness nevertheless discuss the tailoring of his suits. Since the journals involved are serious, peer-reviewed journals and the researchers are serious, well-trained researchers, the pattern reflects the field and cannot be attributed exclusively to particularistic inadequacies of specific journals or individuals.

This suggests that properties of the research context, rather than individual ignorance or journal incompetence, may be primary contributors to this curiosity. For example, the research context, particularly in the USA, provides numerous barriers to the kind of richly detailed, multiple-site, long historical studies using in-depth scholarly analyses and complex models that might yield data more appropriate to the task. Such studies are inconsistent in important ways with short-term research funding practices, rules for reputation accumulation among researchers, and the normal expectations of professional journals and publishers. The kind of persistence, attention to complexity, and delayed gratification required for a thoroughly informed and theoretically sophisticated study of the historical development of an organization has to be seen as an unusual achievement (Padgett and Ansell, 1993).

Such contextual restrictions on the kind of research that is likely may provide partial explanations for the failure to improve organizational scholarship in directions that are well known to be needed. Those elements of context do not, however, explain the gap between accepted standards of inference and assertions about causes of variations in performance. To understand the latter inconsistency it is necessary to examine some features of the organizational and social context of organizations research.

Many organizational researchers, and particularly those prone to making assessments of the factors affecting performance, are employed by professional schools. Aspiring managers, engineers, and other professionals who attend these schools presume that they are being groomed to create conditions for organizations, and people and groups within them, to perform better than others and better than in the past. Researchers secure compensation and attention as consultants to organizations, as lecturers to organizational audiences, or as authors of books providing suggestions for improving organizational performance. These occasions and constituencies provide funding and legitimacy to organizational researchers. They encourage researchers to create and espouse speculations about predicting and controlling performance outcomes. And their enthusiasm for speculation about performance differences seems largely unaffected by a long history involving the continuous overturning of old enthusiasms with new ones. In such a climate, it is not overly surprising that organizational researchers become courtiers of a naked emperor.

At the same time, many organizational researchers are linked to academic institutions and professions, systems that are less immediately concerned with improving performance and more concerned with attention to standards of research and inference that mark research institutions of distinction. They produce and review papers for professional journals, talk to colleagues in the language of inferential method, and serve as judges of the adequacy of research. These occasions and constituencies also provide funding and legitimacy to organizational researchers, but their expectations are different. They encourage researchers to question simple causal stories of performance and retrospective accounts of history. Academic researchers become not only the courtiers of a naked emperor but also keepers of a sacred faith in the methods of scholarship, systematic inference, and defensible interpretations of history.

In the tradition of such dilemmas, conflicts between these two perspectives are often "solved" by separating the two contexts. In academic institutions, one can find a culture of advice givers who tell stories about the things that affect organizational performance to people involved in trying to produce improved performance. These advice givers are ordinarily quite disconnected from serious research on organizations and quite unconcerned about research standards, as are their patrons. One can also find a culture of research workers who tell stories to each other about why one cannot make inferences about causality from correlational and retrospective studies. These research workers are ordinarily quite disconnected from the immediate problems of management and quite unconcerned about organizational performance improvement, as are their patrons. In most American universities, the two cultures are protected from each other by the semi-permeable barrier that divides professional schools from schools of arts and sciences. The buffer allows the two cultures to avoid confronting the implications of their incompatibility.

In and around professional schools, however, and particularly in the USA this simple separation is made more difficult. The soldiers of organizational performance and the priests of research purity often occupy not only the same halls but also the same bodies. These students of organizations inhabit both cultures and cannot easily achieve the delicate pleasures of consistency that are granted to their more fortunate colleagues who reside exclusively in a world of performance concerns or exclusively in the core realms of academe. The two culture solution is supplemented by a more localized two-sidedness in which individuals and individual institutions announce that it is not possible to make valid inferences, yet simultaneously proclaim them; or adopt the paraphernalia of scholarship without much attention to their assumptions. In a schizophrenic tour de force, the demands of the roles of consultant and teacher are disassociated from the demands of the role of researcher.

WHAT'S A SCHOLAR TO DO?

It is easy to bemoan a state of affairs in which students of organizations are driven both to proclaim scholarly standards of inferential discourse and to collaborate in subverting them in practice. The result is, in many ways, unfortunate from the point of view of scholarly traditions. It certainly calls for renewed efforts to change the context of scholarship to make it either less demanding of performance implications or more consistent with scholarly research on performance. Journals can do a better job of enforcing standards; senior scholars can do a better job of escaping the short-run research horizons learned in the course of securing tenure; funding agencies can provide more sustained support for long historical studies.

Such a call to virtue is doubtless salutary, but it ignores the extent to which there is deep social truth in simultaneously identifying factors affecting organizational performance and admitting that the identification is quite probably false. It is a cliché of speculative discourse that ideas are not to be judged solely by their empirical truth as assessed by scholarly precepts. The classical admonition to embrace beauty and justice, as well as truth, has led to a long tradition of struggle among aspirations for scholarly truth, intellectual elegance, and ethical or ideological propriety. The struggle is captured poignantly in contemporary efforts to write about things such as human motivations and social power, where claims of veracity are juxtaposed with claims of human traditions and the demands of ideological correctness.

Since the earliest days of scholarship, the role of the scholar as researcher has been to pursue a vision of reality as lying outside social beliefs about that reality. The role of the scholar as part of the social establishment has been to support a social system that allows scholarship to flourish. The role of the scholar as educator has been to transform social beliefs about reality, encouraging beliefs that conform more to the understandings of scholars. The dilemma of scholarship is twofold: First, it involves finding a route between a course that is precipitous in destroying vital elements of community built on social myths and intuitive knowledge and a course that is precipitous in corrupting the integrity of scholarship. Second, it involves finding a conception of knowledge that does not discourage its pursuit, that holds out the possibility of augmenting knowledge through systematic scholarship in the face of a long history of scholarly recantations and a chronic vulnerability to nihilism.

The dilemma leads naturally to a course of collective and individual hypocrisy. Organizational researchers have often observed that organizations do not reliably connect their "talk" and their "action" (Edleman,

1964; Weick, 1979; Brunsson, 1989). It should not be surprising that a similar pattern is found among organized research workers. Nor should the pattern be routinely condemned. When we observe that an organization justifies a decision with information that has been gathered after the decision was made, we sometimes note that the information is probably more connected to the task of confirming important social norms than to the task of making a particular decision (Feldman and March, 1981). Similarly, in the present case, the tradition of honoring normatively approved principles of scholarly inference while violating them is a way of sustaining important values. At the least, it is probably more sensible than changing the principles to match the practices – which may be the primary behavioral alternative for achieving consistency.

The simultaneous embrace of the possibility of knowledge and the difficulty of achieving it can be a form of wisdom that sustains inquiry and skepticism in healthy confrontation (Meacham, 1990; Sutton and Hargadon, 1996). In particular, one of the complications of personal and organizational knowledge is that there are many ways of knowing, some of them individually compelling but impossible to confirm through acceptable procedures of inference from empirical observation.[3] Confronting the conflict between what is believed and what is demonstrable threatens either the belief or the standards of demonstration in a situation in which both may be worth preserving. Maintaining a formal pretense that the belief is consistent with the evidence sustains both the belief and the sanctity of scholarly standards.

Moreover, such a resolution occurs at the collective level without necessary consciousness. Principled observers who denounce the weak inferential base of studies attempting to explain variations in organizational performance and other features of ambiguous organizational histories provide inadvertent confirmation of the questionable practices. By affirming a collective commitment to high standards of scholarly interpretation, their audit legitimizes the system they expose. At the same time, those who weave a story of the organizational determinants of relative performance secure legitimacy and resources that protect their more fastidious brethren from the practical consequences of their scruples. As has been true since the beginning, the purities of the virtuous are subsidized by the accommodations of the sinful.

Whether we accept such an apologia for the emperor's tailors and the sycophants who proclaim the fineness of imperial garments depends on how we deal with the associated pathologies. The essential point is that scholarship is probably better served by maintaining a tension between saying more than we know and understanding how little we can know, rather than by a definitive resolution of the conflict; but maintaining the tension is vulnerable to the unquestioned temptations of imagining a resolution.

One danger is that the concrete rewards from pleasing the emperor may lead us to exaggerate both the advantages of seeing his clothing and the risks involved in confirming his nakedness. If reputations and institutions are to be maintained by proclaiming insights into history and the discovery of routes to sustained performance advantage, then it may become inordinately natural to characterize the niceties of inferential clarity as dispensable scholastic pretense. The tendency of many articles with a wide range of ideological, methodological, and disciplinary prejudices to subordinate issues of inference ambiguity to issues of practical recommendations and sweeping generalizations may be a symptom of that danger. A second danger is that the terrors of claiming unjustifiable knowledge will drive us from empirical discourse into the relatively safe activities of proving theorems, contemplating conundrums, and writing poetry. The tendency of many of our best minds to eschew empirical inference for the innocently elegant worlds of mathematics, formal logic, and literary theory may be a symptom of that danger.

Partial protection from the two dangers may be provided by consciousness of the ambivalences. If we remind ourselves, from time to time, that standards of inference, like standards of imperial fashion, are more temporary approximations than eternal verities, we do not demean our allegiance to them but we reduce the risk that we will overlook the occasional beauty of cloth woven from invisible threads. And if we remind ourselves, from time to time, that what we are doing is the work of sustaining a belief in the emperor's clothes as a social mythology and a confession of weakness, we do not demean that work but we reduce the risk that we will come to believe in the emperors clothes as a literal reality.

Ultimately, however, the pain of discomfort at failing to choose between the simultaneous imperatives of speech and silence is better endured than is the denial of either. There is no neat solution, for neatness itself would be a claim that an essential dilemma has been overcome, that virtue can be discovered and proclaimed, or that the trade-offs can be calculated and accepted. Scholarly virtue is more a struggle than an achievement, and seeking knowledge about historically ambiguous phenomena such as organizational performance is more a necessary form of disciplined self-flagellation than a pursuit of happiness.

Acknowledgments

We are grateful for financial and fellowship assistance provided by Hewlett-Packard, National Science Foundation (SBR-9022192), the Spencer Foundation, the Center for Advanced Study in the Behavioral Sciences, and the Stanford Graduate School of Business; and for various intellectual and professional contributions by Jerker Denrell, Thomas D'Aunno,

Robert Gibbons, J. Richard Hackman, Hans Krogh Hvide, Robert Kahn, David Owens, and Barry Staw.

Notes

1. We use the terms "performance" and "effectiveness" interchangeably. The problems with defining, measuring, and explaining the two terms are virtually identical.
2. Three of the more highly regarded journals involved in publishing empirical research on organizations – the *Strategic Management Journal*, the *Academy of Management Journal*, and the *Administrative Science Quarterly* – are particularly likely to focus on performance and performance as a dependent variable. For the issues published in 1993, 1994, and 1995, we counted all articles and research notes in these journals except for editorials, editors' remarks, introductions to special issues, and essays. Whether organizational performance (or effectiveness) was examined in a paper and the role it played in the author's analysis was gleaned from the abstract. If the abstract indicated that performance (or effectiveness) was considered but it was not clear whether it was portrayed as an independent variable, dependent variable, both, or in some other way (e.g., as only a control or intervening variable), we examined the text and tables to classify it. In these three years, these three journals published 439 articles and research notes. Performance appeared as a variable in 124 (28 percent) of the abstracts of those articles, 88 times as a dependent variable only, 15 times as an independent variable only, 13 times as both, and 8 times in some other capacity. At the other extreme, we counted only seven (7 percent) out of 98 articles published in *Organization Studies* in the same three-year period as having performance as a variable cited in their abstracts (five of those with performance as a dependent variable only). *Organizational Behavior and Human Decision Processes* and *Organization Science* locate themselves between the two extremes. Performance appeared as a variable in the abstracts of 57 (16 percent) of the 355 articles published in those journals over the same three years, 42 times as a dependent variable only, 5 times as an independent variable only, 8 times as both, and 2 times in some other capacity.
3. The idea of multiple ways of knowing goes back at least to Plato and keeps resurfacing, particularly in the hands of those who would challenge established epistemologies, thus is a useful, generic claim of exemption from recognized rules of intelligent inference. In the present case, the distinction is not between different kinds of scholarly traditions, each of which claims specialized capabilities for making knowledge assertions, but between the procedures of scholarship and the procedures of ordinary comprehension. The argument in favor of ordinary comprehension is, however, similar to the argument in favor of deviant scholarship in that it depends on the assumption that it provides variety. Since any established mode of thought tends to become less exploratory as it becomes more effective, variety is useful even though any particular idea generated from ordinary comprehension, like any particular idea generated by deviant scholarship, is likely to be inferior.

References

Academy of Management (1995) Academy of Management code of ethical conduct, *Academy of Management Journal*, 38, 573–7.

Adams, J. B., J. Adams, R. W. Rice, D. Instone (1985) Effects of perceived group effectiveness and group role on attributions of group performance, *Journal of Applied Social Psychology*, 15, 387–98.

Arthur, W. B. (1989) Competing technologies, increasing returns, and lock-in by historical events, *Economic Journal*, 99, 116–31.

Barney, Jay (1991) Firm resources and sustained competitive advantage, *Journal of Management*, 17, 99–120.

Brown, S. L., and K. M. Eisenhardt (1995) Product development: Past research, present findings, and future directions, *Academy of Management Review*, 20, 343–78.

Brunsson, N. (1989) *The Organization of Hypocrisy*, Chichester: Wiley.

Cyert R. M., and J. G. March (1963) *A Behavioral Theory of the Firm*, Englewood Cliffs, NJ: Prentice Hall.

D'Aunno, T., and R. I. Sutton (1992) Organizational responses to financial adversity: A partial test of the threat-rigidity thesis, *Journal of Management*, 18, 117–31.

DiMaggio, P. J., and W. W. Powell (1983) The iron cage revisited: Institutional isomorphism and collective rationality in organizational fields, *American Sociological Review*, 48, 146–60.

Edelman, M. (1964) *The Symbolic Uses of Politics*, Urbana, IL: University of Illinois Press.

Feldman, M. S., and J. G. March (1981) Information in organizations as signal and symbol, *Administrative Science Quarterly*, 26, 171–86.

Fischhoff, B. (1975) Hindsight/Foresight: The Effect of Outcome Knowledge on Judgment Uncertainty, in T. S. Wallsten (ed.), *Cognitive Processes in Choice and Decision Behavior*, Hillsdale, NJ: Erlbaum.

Fischhoff, B., and R. Beyth (1975) "I knew it would happen" – remembered probabilities of once future things, *Organizational Behavior and Human Performance*, 13, 1–16.

Greenhalgh, L. (1983) Organizational decline, in S. Bacharach (ed.), *Perspectives in Organizational Sociology: Theory and Research*, vol. 1, Greenwich, CT: JAI Press.

Isen, A. M., and R. A. Baron (1991) Positive affect as a factor in organizational behavior, in L. L. Cummings and B. M. Staw (eds), *Research in Organizational Behavior*, vol. 13, Greenwich, CT: JAI Press.

Jones, E. E., and C. Wortman (1973) *Ingratiation: An Attributional Approach*, Morristown, NJ: General Learning Press.

Lenz, R. (1981) Determinants of organizational performance: An interdisciplinary review, *Strategic Management Review*, 2, 131–54.

Levinthal, D. A., and J. G. March (1993) The Myopia of Learning, *Strategic Management Journal*, 14, 95–112.

Levitt, B., and J. G. March (1988) Organizational learning, *Annual Review of Sociology*, 14, 314–40.

Locke, P., and G. Latham (1990) *A Theory of Goals and Performance*, Englewood Cliffs, NJ: Prentice Hall.

March, J. G. (1988) Introduction: A chronicle of speculations about decision-making in organizations, in J. G. March (ed.), *Decisions and Organizations*, Oxford: Blackwell.

March, J. G. (1991) Exploration and exploitation in organizational learning, *Organization Science*, 2, 71–87.

March, J. G. (1994) *A Primer of Decision Making: How Decisions Happen*, New York: Free Press.

March, J. G., and Z. Shapira (1987) Managerial perspectives on risk and risk taking, *Management Science*, 33, 1404–18.

Masuch, M. (1985) Vicious circles in organizations, *Administrative Science Quarterly*, 30, 14–33.

McGuire, J. B., T. Schneeweis, and B. Branch (1990) Perceptions of firm quality. A cause or result of firm performance, *Journal of Management*, 16, 167–80.

Meacham, J. A. (1990) The loss of wisdom, in R. J. Sternberg (ed.), *Wisdom: Its Nature, Origins, and Development*, Cambridge: Cambridge University Press.

Miller, D. (1993) The architecture of simplicity, *Academy of Management Review*, 18, 116–38.

Padgett, J. F., and C. K. Ansell (1993) Robust action and the rise of the Medici, 1400–1434. *American Journal of Sociology*, 98, 1250–1310.

Pritchard, D., S. D. Jones, P. L. Roth, K. K. Stuebing, and S. E. Ekeberg (1988) Effects of group feedback, goal setting, and incentives on organizational productivity, *Journal of Applied Psychology*, 73, 337–58.

Starbuck, W. H., and F. J. Milliken (1988) Challenger: Fine-tuning the odds until something breaks, *Journal of Management Studies*, 25, 319–40.

Staw, B. M. (1975) Attribution of the "causes" of performance: An alternative interpretation of cross-sectional research on organizations, *Organizational Behavior and Human Performance*, 13, 414–32.

Staw, B. M., P. I. McKechnie, and S. M. Puffer (1983) The justification of organizational performance, *Administrative Science Quarterly*, 28, 582–600.

Staw, B. M., L. E. Sandelands, and J. E. Dutton (1981) Threat-rigidity effects in organizational behavior: A multilevel analysis, *Administrative Science Quarterly*, 26, 501–24.

Sutton, R. I., and A. L. Callahan (1987) The stigma of bankruptcy: Spoiled organizational image and its management, *Academy of Management Journal*, 30, 405–36.

Sutton, R. I., and A. Hargadon (1996) Brainstorming groups in context: Effectiveness in a product design team, *Administrative Science Quarterly*, 41, 685–718.

Tosi, H. L., Jr and L. R. Gomez-Mejia (1994) CEO compensation monitoring and firm performance, *Academy of Management Journal*, 37, 1002–16.

Weick, K. (1979) *The Social Psychology of Organizing*, 2nd. edn, Reading, MA: Addison-Wesley.

Zirger, B. J., and M. Maidique (1990) A model of new product development: An empirical test, *Management Science*, 36, 867–83.

CHAPTER NINETEEN

Science, Politics, and Mrs. Gruenberg

Not long ago, I spent a few hours with some colleagues, a small cluster of friends stranded in Washington. The occasion was indolent; the talk more Stoppard than Shaw; and the main topic the merits of passing on first down. Intruding on this quiet sonata of acquaintance, however, was a minor serious theme – complaints about the incompetence of scientists in politics, elaborated with vivid tales of exceptional foolishness. It was innocuous, and our pleasant sense of superiority was moderated only slightly by an awareness that the level of discourse was not quite the Vienna Circle and a small suspicion that somewhere else in Washington we ourselves were featured in someone else's favorite illustration of political infancy. It was not the kind of occasion that generates precise memory or clear conclusions, but most of my friends seemed to agree that the political innocence of scientists was unfortunate, that scientific advice related to public policy profits from political consciousness. The discussion elicited sentiments that were not unique to this group of friends. They were sentiments that have an impressive ancestry, are reflected in the attitudes of many smart people, and can easily be defended; but I think they are wrong.

On balance, I think political scientists and others who know about politics place too much emphasis on increasing the political sophistication of scientists involved in policy questions. We simultaneously underestimate the knowledge scientists already have about political life and overestimate the significance of it. By criticizing the naivete of scientific advisors, we encourage behavior that reduces the usefulness of science in policymaking. Capitals are the natural habitat of political voyeurs, people who enjoy the vicarious pleasures of contemplating politics and imagining their importance to it. They are harmlessly clever, like experienced pornographers, and contribute to the sweet ornamentation of life; but I do not think we should make them models for scientists who come to Washington. There is still room for specialization in life.

Science is a collection of ignorances. We want to know everything and count the lack of time, skill, and money that stand in our way as regrettable limitations. Nevertheless, we are specialists; and the illusions we have about our competences are mostly specific to small corners of the library. We have a vague sense of the appropriate balance between specialized and more general knowledge, as wary of those who would goad us into extradisciplinary embarrassment as of those who would confine us too much. We accept our ignorance while trying to reduce it. This comfortable sense of balance is lost when we turn to questions of public policy. Policy questions seem to confound ideas about scientific specialization that we have developed around the canons of more basic research. The contrast is manifest in the differences between the spirit and organization of the National Academy of Sciences as an honorific and scientific society and the spirit and organization of the National Research Council as a consultant on scientific aspects of public policy. The council is littered with multidisciplinary committees, the academy with disciplinary ones. When we work in the policy area, we seem to change our notions of what is tolerable ignorance.

Even more conspicuously, policy questions draw scientists near to politics, where most of them are not specialists at all. People active in political life commonly report that scientists are badly informed about the political system, and that, as a result, they frequently give advice that is irrelevant in a policy context or has perverse consequences. The belief is, as might be expected, persistent among political scientists; it is also frequent among policymakers, particularly experienced bureaucrats and politicians. The picture is plausible. Even for most behavioral and social scientists, the political process is an alien domain, distant in spirit despite its temptations. Although science politicians and agencies have prospered impressively in political systems around the world, many scientists find the rules of politics uncomfortable.

At the base of much of this discomfort is a conspicuous disparity between the rhetoric of science and the rhetoric of politics. Science presumes a process by which alternative theories are evaluated systematically against available data within a framework shared by "reasonable" (i.e., well-trained) people in order to rank ideas in terms of their plausibility. Politics presumes a process by which alternative policies are compared on the basis of the power of the people supporting them in order to rank programs in terms of their acceptability. On the surface, one process attempts to reduce subjectivity through standardized procedures designed to assure verifiable knowledge; the other attempts to organize subjectivity through a set of bargains designed to assure social stability. One process seeks data; the other seeks allies. The prototypic scientist engages in an experiment; the prototypic politician engages in a logroll.

Clearly, the differences can easily be overdrawn; and few observers of either science or politics would accept any simple formulation; but politics has a different logic and a different style. Because of the complications of creating coalitions of supporters, public policy is often ambiguous and intendedly inconsistent. Because of limitations on the attention of political institutions, "good" ideas that are not timely are largely ignored; and timeliness is a matter of political agendas, not scientific ones. Because of the importance of ideology and belief in politics, the symbols of governmental actions are sometimes more important than their substance. Because the constituencies active in shaping a policy in a legislature are often different from the constituencies active during its implementation by a governmental agency, policies seem to change in the course of their execution.

Political leaders calculate the costs and benefits of policy alternatives in terms of their consequences for popular support in the next few months or years. Technical expertise is often vital to such calculations, but it must fit a political frame. Policymakers frequently ask for scientific advice, but they also often seem to use scientific advice as an excuse for doing what they want to do on other grounds, or as a scapegoat for doing what is unpopular with some groups. They often seem to be inattentive to the cautions and fine details of scientific studies, and seem to have an inordinate confidence in the quality of scientific advice given by scientists living in their own districts compared to advice given by others. When scientists disagree, policymakers often seem to view the disagreement as justification for accepting whatever advice is convenient. Agreement among scientists, on the other hand, is likely to be treated as a symptom of conspiracy.

These features of the political process are elementary, familiar, and intriguing; but they can also be disconcerting. When scientists complain, politicians grumble something about getting out of the kitchen if you can't stand the heat, and political scientists give lectures on the nature of politics. Neither response is entirely foolish. It probably is sensible for people who are deeply offended, or bewildered, by the logic of politics to stay in their laboratories most of the time. It probably is sensible for almost anyone to know the rudiments of political analysis. Ignorance is not bliss. It would help if policymakers were better informed about science and scientists about politics.

However, few scientists are quite as ignorant of politics, or as antagonistic, as they are portrayed. They generally believe that it is responsible to obtain the best possible scientific and technical advice before making a public policy decision, and they think that one reason policymakers turn to scientists is to obtain information. They are aware, however, of other reasons for seeking advice and not overly surprised or offended by them. They know that agencies sometimes hold political hot potatoes in their hands and want to share or avoid responsibility for dropping them; that sometimes an agency knows exactly what it wants to do but needs a report from an outside consultant as an excuse, or basis, for action; that sometimes an agency does not want to do anything and hopes that a study will provide a delay adequate for burying a problem or proposal; that sometimes an agency wants the minor accolades that come from association with a distinguished, but undemanding, set of advisors; that sometimes some groups within an agency need allies in internal agency politics and hope they can recruit some scientists to their side; and that sometimes scientists and scientific organizations pursue contracts in order to sustain employment or permit growth, and give advice in order to lay the basis for subsequent favors.

Characteristically, the motivations are intricately intertwined. Personal ambition, interagency warfare, pressure tactics, and creative bureaucratic obfuscation are well-integrated parts of the political process. Congress, the White House, government agencies, and the National Academy of Sciences seek to pursue their visions of public interest in such a way that they prosper as institutions and the individuals within them thrive. They give and take advice; and if the giving and taking seems naturally to generate not only benefits to the nation through improved public decisions, but also increased wealth and the perquisites of power for themselves, they are not surprised.

Most scientists who are involved in advising policymakers know these basic facts of life. They do not suffer from unusual political myopia. They know that trades are made and promises kept in politics, that legislators want rewards for their constituents, that some people count more than others, that bureaus leak information, and that White House and congressional assistants inexorably become insufferable. Moreover, I think most of them are impressed with the general good sense of politics, of the way it reconciles claims, develops alternatives, explores consequences, and manages change. They concede that politicians have useful skills, and the political process a curious intelligence. Scientists, indeed, easily become actively infatuated with politics, enjoying the sense of involvement in vital decisions that attends even a minor role in the political scene. What is distinctive about many scientists is not that they are ignorant about politics, or alienated from it, but that they do not naturally act or think politically or strategically. And what is distinctive about many of the proposals for change is not that they urge scientists to learn more about politics, but that they advocate a greater explicit political consciousness on the part of scientists, greater sophistication, and less innocence.

Ignorance is not knowing the way life is; innocence is not attending to the way life is. It is possible that scientists should not be ignorant, that they should know something about politics, if they are involved in policy issues. It is also possible that scientists should not be innocent, that they should be more sophisticated in their tactics, less naive in their advice. But the two ideas are not equally compelling; the first seems unexceptionable; the second more doubtful. Indeed, innocence without ignorance is often a feature of wisdom. The case for abandoning innocence usually rests on two arguments: First, it is argued that science, as a distinct social institution with special interests, suffers in the political arena by not being organized properly to influence political decisions. Second, it is argued that politically naive scientific advice is bad advice, unlikely to be persuasive in policymaking. I think there is some sense in the first argument. Insofar as science and scientists have shared interests and wish to contend with other groups for resources and recognition, effective action probably requires political organization and conscious political tactics. The second argument, however, seems misleading to me. I think there are good reasons for urging scientists to stick to science.

A sharp distinction between science (the traditional realm of the scientist) and policy (the traditional realm of the politician) is impossible to sustain, either conceptually or behaviorally. Scientific knowledge clearly rests on values that regulate the way knowledge is organized and validated. The structures of theories are partly arbitrary and do not necessarily lead to the right questions, nor to the right answers. Like other people, scientists seem to find facts consistent with their policy preferences and to forget facts inconvenient for their hopes. Scientific judgments are not magically shielded from personal commitments and professional biases. In general, scientific purity, like other kinds, is a remote vision far from reasonable hope for attainment. The issue is not whether it is possible, or wise, to be a virgin scientist, for such simplicity is beyond our capabilities. Rather, we ask whether the effort to be sophisticated improves our collective lives more than a commitment to ordinary innocence. And that is a more difficult question.

Some years ago, there was a well-known child psychologist who talked to California parents on strategies for child-rearing. I never heard her, but I am told that at the end of each talk, someone in the audience would invariably ask: "Mrs. Gruenberg, do you really mean that we should never spank our children?" And Mrs. Gruenberg would reply: "Well, I suppose, if you keep reminding yourself every moment that you should never ever spank your children, you will end up spanking them just about the right amount." Mrs. Gruenberg reminds us that precepts are not made inappropriate simply by their impossibility. They are part of the process, not its outcome; and a strategic commitment to innocence is not made foolish by the fact we cannot achieve it.

Giving scientific advice usefully is inseparable from the problem of taking advice intelligently, and the central dilemma in taking advice is the simultaneous need for information and the danger of being victimized by dependence on it. Both as a society and as individuals, we alternate between ingenuousness and stubbornness, sometimes allowing considerable diminution of our independence in order to gain the advantages of expertise, sometimes refusing to listen to advice in order to retain our autonomy. Knowledge and information are sources of power with which a policymaker contends uneasily, and scientific advisors must accept the reality and legitimacy of that unease.

It is possible to argue that society is best served by scientists who self-consciously announce their personal prejudices and try to marshall evidence for them, that politics is the art of making judgments when everyone is probably lying. Consider, for example, the complications of securing scientific assessments in such areas as population control, ethnic or gender bases of behavior, nuclear energy, or family stability and structure. Scientists with strong feelings organize other scientists to assure that "truth" is told, and they confront other scientists with other strong feelings and other "truths." It is a feasible procedure with important elements of beauty in it. Much of the time, however, the giving and taking of advice depends on trust. Neither the fact that it is possible, and sometimes necessary, to function without much trust, nor the fact that trust is fragile destroys its general importance as a basis for exchange of information where some people know significant things that other people need to know.

Despite the difficulties, trust is often established and maintained in relations between scientific experts and policymakers. The process is too complicated for short description, but I would note three attributes of scientists that I suspect affect the trust extended to a scientific advisor by most policymakers: competence, reliability, and irrelevance. By competence I mean what any scientist would mean about technical competence in the field. Determining competence is not always easy, but there are clues, informants, and past experiences. You trust someone who is properly respected in the field. By reliability I mean the degree of congruence between the values and personal style of the scientist and the values and personal style of the policymaker. You trust an advisor whose values are close enough to yours that the motivation to mislead you is modest and whose personal style is familiar enough to allow you to understand one another. By irrelevance I mean the extent to which the advisor is politically unambitious, and avoids basing advice on guessing what the policymaker will do with the advice, what is wanted, or what others are thinking. You trust an advisor who leaves the politics to you, who yearns for neither influence nor martyrdom.

The implications are not complicated. Without question, the most competent scientists possible must be available to policymakers. But competence alone, however exquisite, is unlikely to be enough. On the one hand, we need to make science reliable, not in the sense of politicizing it, but in the sense of having a distribution of values and styles among competent scientists that encourages a pairing of competent scientists with policymakers who trust them. In a relatively homogeneous, relatively stable society, this is not a serious problem. In a heterogeneous society, however, it is possible that politically important groups (most conspicuously lower-status groups and nonestablishment social movements) will have difficulty obtaining scientific advice from competent advisors they trust.

At the same time, we need to innoculate scientists against the temptations of political awareness. It is possible for a knowledgeable scientist to give advice with consciousness of the nuances of its political meaning. To do so, however, is to enter a game of political maneuver in which the other players are unusually suspicious and exceptionally adroit. Policymakers, for whom the threats of manipulation through information are clear, are more likely to see political maneuver when it does not exist than to fail to see it when it does. As a result, they may often have unwarranted suspicions; but they rarely mistake cleverness for naivete. And they are unlikely to be fooled for long. The chance that a politically ambitious scientist will maintain trust as a scientist is modest. Moreover, from the point of view of society and science, success is no better than failure. Scientists unfortunate enough to be successful in political maneuver come to think of their role not as someone giving advice but as someone who has influence over policy. It is a tempting shift, by no means dishonorable; but by changing the frame of reference, it tends to compromise the quality of scientific information in the political process.

Innocence in politics, like innocence elsewhere, has its costs. There are personal costs, the embarrassment of naivete amplified by the patronizing amusement of friends. There are social costs, scientific and technical advice ignored because it is given at a bad time, or in an incomprehensible way, or so that it offends a key political or bureaucratic actor or belief. The greatest cost of innocence, however, is the awareness that not everyone is innocent. Politics is filled with sophistication, with people who know what is going on. For the most part, they do what sophisticated people do, look for hidden meanings, lay subtle traps, develop codes for distinguishing insiders, cover their flanks, and happily pull the feathers of any innocents who land in their garden. It is not a style unknown to ordinary life; and most of us, most of the time, would rather be the pluckers than the plucked. Knowledge, pride, and annoyance conspire against innocence, and we try to be clever. But cleverness is its own trap, and never more conspicuously than when scientists play politics.

Quixote said that all knights have their parts to play. We have ours, and we can try to play them. Not in ignorance of politics, for ignorance has no virtue; but in innocence. And when our friends say that the pursuit of innocence is futile, that there are exceptions, complications, and corruptions, and that obviously it would be better to find the optimal balance between innocence and sophistication, we may want to remember Mrs. Gruenberg and reply that, if scientists keep reminding themselves every moment that they should never ever think politically, they will think politically just about the right amount.

CHAPTER TWENTY

Education and the Pursuit of Optimism[1]

The history of education is a history of optimism, sustained confidence about the effects of education on individual and social well-being. This confidence has been shaken by indications that the consequences of education and educational investment are less certain than was once believed. The erosion of hope in education has led to a variety of renewed efforts to proclaim new programs and projects for education with new prospects of great consequences. These new hopes are, however, likely to be dashed by experience and awareness of the persistent difficulties in proclaiming human significance. They need to be supplemented by perspectives on the motivation of great action that are less linked to hopes for great consequences. One can imagine pessimism without despair or an acceptance of irrelevance without loss of faith, but perhaps the greatest tradition of education is that of optimism without hope, a commitment to the joyful unconditional obligations of participating in education.

i

Whoever crosses this street enters a more ancient and sterner world.

(Borges, 1962, p. 169)

ii

Friends and relatives paid him visits and, with exaggerated smiles, assured him that he looked fine. *(Borges, 1962, p. 168)*

The modern history of American education is a history of optimism. We have believed in the successes of our past and the good prospects of our future. We have had fancy buildings, good careers, popular support, and impressive students. New curricula, new schools, new successes. We have had ample self-evident grounds for optimism. Teachers, administrators, parents, legislators, and students have enjoyed a common enthusiasm for the social and individual values of education. We have claimed, and been granted, credit for significant contribution to twentieth-century growth in American power and wealth. Our society has supported the development of a massive educational establishment in the name of individual self-development and opportunity, and national pride and prosperity.

Prima facie evidence for the effectiveness of education and the importance of schooling has been impressive. The United States has educated more people for a longer period of time than other countries. We have produced an enviable and envied population with skills, particularly skills in the new technologies. American progress has been contemporaneous with the development of its educational system.

In addition, it has been obvious that education has had a substantial return for the individual. People with more education have held better jobs and earned higher incomes than those with less. The better and longer the education, the more successful the individual. Good jobs have been routinely associated with educational prerequisites. A good education clearly has been a profitable personal investment.

Finally, education has sustained a Jeffersonian dream of equality of opportunity and an aristocracy of talent. Through education and hard work, people have progressed. Inherited position has been seen as surrendering to position based on ability and training. The paraphernalia of free public education, objective assessment of ability, and an ideology of advancement through knowledge has seemed to produce considerable movement of individuals from lower social and economic groups into the middle class.

iii

> Of a sudden Dahlmann felt something brush lightly against his face. Next to the heavy glass of turbid wine, upon one of the stripes in the table cloth, lay a spitball of breadcrumb. That was all, but someone had thrown it there. *(Borges, 1962, p. 173)*

It is a sweet memory, fondly recalled. And like most memories, it has been cudgeled by sophistication. Revisionist historians of education have complicated the dream with alternative descriptions of what American education has accomplished and less romantic notions of why it developed as it did. Revisionist economists, political scientists, and sociologists have similarly identified the limitations of education as an instrument of social justice and equality. Revisionist psychologists have elaborated the difficulties of devising neutral measures of ability or achievement, and even of demonstrating that schooling affects educational outcomes.

The general spirit and some of the specific content of our new sophistication have been summarized in a report from the Rand Corporation (Averch et al., 1974). The report concludes:

> Input-output studies provide very little evidence that school resources, in general, greatly influence student outcomes. . . . On balance, there is little evidence that a student's classmates exercise a strong, independent influence on his educational outcomes. . . . (p. 166) The research on teaching approaches, teacher differences, class size, and the like shows no consistent effect on student achievement, as measured by standardized cognitive tests. . . . Work on instructional methods suggests no difference among methods. (p. 167) Organizational innovations that have so far been tried (decentralization, performance contracting) as yet show no significant improvement in outcomes compared with traditional forms of organization. . . . Without exception, all surveys of large, national compensatory education programs have shown no beneficial results on average. . . . There is considerable evidence that many of the short-run gains from educational interventions fade away after two or three years if they are not reinforced. (p. 169).

In general, the report concludes that previous studies have been unable to identify any variation in schooling that is consistently related to changes in student educational outcomes. There are positive results, but they are matched by negative results with the same practices. Careful studies seem to indicate no consistent, observable effect of teacher experience, teacher education, or class size on student educational achievement. The Rand report is not unique. It is representative of a growing mood of disappointment. Christopher Jencks (1972), in his well-reported study, reached similar conclusions with respect to the overall impact of education on equality in American society. Drawing the obvious economic implication of this record of doubt, the Rand group concluded that "there seem to be opportunities for significant reduction or redirection of educational expenditures without deterioration in educational outcomes" (Averch et al., 1974, p. 173).

The unthinkable is now being said. It is possible that American education is overpriced and overadvertised, unfair and complacent, fat and incompetent. It is possible that education is substantially irrelevant to – or at least currently a grossly expensive instrument for – social and individual prosperity, progress, and justice.

The message is especially discomforting because it comes from the voice of research and intelligence. Each of the classic claims of education has been subjected to the methods of research and analysis and found "not proven." Each of the instrumental grounds by which educators have justified optimism in education has become questionable. Within a decade, each of our hopes has been converted to a doubt. Although support for education as a social institution is still exceptionally strong in American society, it seems possible that the support stems from ignorance. It seems possible that society would support us less if it understood us better.

Indeed, it seems possible that our own commitment to education depends on a series of delusions. We have believed that education was important and that it could be improved by our professional intervention. Our optimism has had a solid base in hope. But as each hope has been undermined, the optimism has wavered. Recent educational literature portrays a world of falling hopes in which our enthusiasms are bewildered, and the pursuit of optimism is unrewarding.

iv

Perplexed, Dahlmann decided that nothing had happened, and he opened the volume of *The Thousand and One Nights*, by way of suppressing reality.
(Borges, 1962, p. 173)

Our efforts to recapture traditional optimism have begun with the search for new hope. We look for great hopes to sustain great action. Since the educational establishment seems to be somewhat discouraged by discovery of the limits of its past successes, great hopes are now more characteristic of outside reformers. These reformers profess a variety of ideologies and educational theories. They are still mostly excluded from control and discouraged, not by the failure of their ideas but by their failure to penetrate what appears to be a closed system of administrators, teachers, educational researchers, and schools of education.

They find confirmation of their beliefs in the failures of education. They define our current condition as stemming from our previous failure to identify and exploit the real, underlying factors in education. They are inclined to see evidence of previous failure as evidence for the effectiveness of some new alternative. For example, the Rand report (Averch et al., 1974) argues that "research tentatively suggests that improvement in student outcomes, both cognitive and noncognitive, may require sweeping changes in the organization, structure, and conduct of educational experience" (p. 175).

It is a process with which we are easily familiar. From any long perspective, our current despair is probably transient. We have had a history of hopes. When we felt successful, we discovered hope in our success; when we felt unsuccessful, we discovered hope in the things we were not then doing. The present softening of educational optimism is the usual Thermidorian reaction to great expectations in heroic social institutions. It seems reasonable to assume that if education faces no grand disasters over the next few years, optimism will return, built on hopes for new solutions.

There are some of us who will find hope in possible new curricula. Each month produces more work in developing new programs of study with prospects for improving the quality of what is learned in our schools.

There are some of us who will find hope in new learning methods or new teaching strategies. Ideas about how children learn are amenable to classical methods of research, and we know more now than we used to know. We have hopes for additional knowledge that might yield more improvements in education.

There are some of us who will find hope in extending education into early childhood. Because small differences among five-year-olds seem inexorably to become large differences among fifteen-year-olds, we look for a solution in a change of the pattern of educational experiences in the first few years of life.

There are some of us who will find hope in biochemical intervention or genetic control. Some features of the physiological and genetic bases of learning and other intellective processes are somewhat understood. It seems possible that further understanding would permit, if we wished, an educational pharmacology.

There are some of us who will find hope in a redefinition of educational goals. Perhaps education can be directed away from recent objectives and toward some alternative things that it *can* do. There are hopes for self-actualizing education or political education or career education or education in the basic three-R skills.

There are some of us who will find hope in new organization, in revising the organizational arrangements among students, teachers, parents, administrators, and public agencies. We suspect that our arrangements for governance and administration are susceptible to planned improvement.

There are some of us who will find hope in new personnel. The evidence seems persuasive that many people involved in education – parents, teachers, and school administrators – are imperfect instruments. They seem susceptible to improvement through education or replacement.

There are some of us who will find hope in deep structural changes in society and the relations between society and education. The role of education in any society seems linked to sustaining the major features of social structure. Perhaps a change requires, and can be effected only by, a revolutionary change in the social system.

Our history is a history of optimism dashed and optimism revived, and the cycle probably did not end in 1968. It is likely that our current malaise will be dissipated by belief in new discoveries, new revolutions, new heroes, and new mythologies. We will find ground for action in our plans for new successes. We will enjoy a renascence of optimism and the confidence that optimism imparts. We will reassert the fundamental axioms of hope: that if there is a problem, there is a solution; and if there is a solution, it can be discovered by human intelligence and implemented by human action.

Although this process appears to condemn us to a dubious cycle of false hope followed by disillusion, it is not to be scorned innocently, nor casually to be rejected in an orgy of realism. Education has traditionally attracted many good people whose commitment to the profession depended on a romantic retention of ideals for what could be accomplished. Their delusion of hope has stimulated optimism and action. In Ibsen's *Wild Duck*, Doctor Relling reminds us that "ideal" is a euphemism for "lie," yet he says: "Take the illusions away from an average man and you take his happiness as well" (Act 5).

In particular, we should prefer a myth of educational possibilities to the cynicism or self-indulgence that appear as major behavioral alternatives. Teachers, administrators, researchers, and students share a danger of responding to irrelevance with privatism and with an excessive concern for career, position, and the petty indulgence of personal pleasure. An ostentatious retreat into a private world is no more attractive for education than it is in everyday existence.

If we wish to continue to maintain broad enthusiasm within education, the same realism that leads us to question the mythology of hope will lead us to sustain it. The myth of human significance is a myth we cannot routinely eliminate. As long as our beliefs require that action be justified in terms of ambition for its consequences, many of us will need hope to sustain a commitment to the ordinary things that should be done. We will need to continue to discover useful expectations about ambiguous possible futures and to construct imaginative reinterpretations of dubious pasts.

v

> From a corner of the room, the old ecstatic gaucho – in whom Dahlmann saw a summary and cipher of the South (his South) – threw him a naked dagger, which landed at his feet. It was as if the South had resolved that Dahlmann should accept the duel.   *(Borges, 1962, p. 174)*

Doctor Relling's illusions sustain persistence in the face of difficulty, but they are dangerous. They encourage an exaggerated view of human control over human destiny and form a base for delusion and disillusion. Every educational past was once an educational future, and every educational future has been advertised as a dramatic solution miraculously discovered.

By insisting that great action be justified by great hopes, we encourage a belief in the possibility of magic. For examples, read the litany of magic in the literature on free schools, Montessori, Head Start, Sesame Street, team teaching, open schools, structured schools, computer-assisted instruction, community control, and hot lunches. Inasmuch as there appears to be rather little magic in the world, great hopes are normally difficult to realize. Having been seduced into great expectations, we are abandoned to a choice between failure and delusion.

The temptations of delusion are accentuated both by our investment in hope and by the potential for ambiguity in educational outcomes. To a substantial extent we are able to believe whatever we want to believe, and we want to believe in the possibility of progress. We are unsure about what we want to accomplish, or how we would know when we had accomplished it, or how to allocate credit or blame for accomplishment or lack of it. So we fool ourselves.

The conversion of great hopes into magic, and magic into delusion describes much of modern educational history. It continues to be a dominant theme of educational reform in the United States. But there comes a time when the conversion does not work for everyone. As we come to recognize the political, sociological, and psychological dynamics of repeated waves of optimism based on heroic hopes, our willingness to participate in the process is compromised.

Thus, contemporary disillusion with education is on two levels. The first is a recognition that there are severe limitations to our ability to understand or control the effects of schooling. This disillusion leads us to call for more and better research, new and more original alternatives. The second, and deeper, disillusion is a recognition that we are reproducing the history that we are condemning. It leads us to ask whether anything makes a difference, and whether we should care.

This deeper disillusion will not be overcome by persuasive promises of new magic solutions, or indeed by evidence for them; for it questions the classical procedures for establishing reality. Whereas the first level of disillusion creates a challenge for educators, the second level denies it. Each step in our understanding drives us closer to a view of the world in which human victory is uncertain and the consequences of human intervention are difficult to detect. Education has lost its innocence.

vi

They went out and if Dahlmann was without hope, he was also without fear. *(Borges, 1962, p. 174)*

Where do we discover optimism when hope is difficult to sustain? How is an educator to maintain commitment to his role when he suspects that his dreams for reform are mostly fruitless rhetoric? What are the alternatives for those who recognize and accept the limits of human intentional action, who find the mythology of magic unacceptable? Over the next few years, I suspect, it is the style of response among such intelligent skeptics that will determine important elements in the nature of our educational institutions. How do we confront our irrelevance? What are the prospects for optimism when hope is not permitted?

The questions are, of course, classic ones that touch every domain of human existence and are bases for major philosophical, literary, and artistic masterpieces in our cultural history. As a result, we will probably find more guidance from our literary and philosophical tradition than from contemporary social commentary, behavioral research, educational consultants, or even invited speakers. This is not an idle acknowledgment of the significance of important cultural artifacts; it is an assertion that the complications of confronting intelligent despair are recognized and explored more profoundly in our traditional literature than they are in our contemporary discussions of education.

Using great literature as a vehicle for examining the pursuit of optimism in education is probably pretentious, like using a Nieman-Marcus catalogue in an outhouse. Yet, I think we need to take our problems seriously; and to take them seriously involves recognizing that they are neither unique, nor new, nor solvable. As a result, I will be presumptuous enough to recall three classic responses to human irrelevance that seem easily to be forgotten in our search for hope. Each accepts the absence of hope as a fundamental condition of human life, yet argues for a meaningful human existence.

The first is *pessimism without despair*. We can adopt a pessimistic view of life, recognize our inability to change that life in its exterior characteristics, doubt the likelihood that the forces controlling life are reliably benevolent, and yet make no claim for pity. At the end of a day

> Shukhov went to sleep fully content. He'd had many strokes of luck that day: they hadn't put him in the cells; they hadn't sent his squad to the settlement; he'd swiped a bowl of kasha at dinner; the squad leader had fixed the rates well; he'd built a wall and enjoyed it; he'd smuggled that bit of hacksaw blade through; he'd earned a favor from Tsezar that evening; he'd bought that tobacco. And he hadn't fallen ill. He'd got over it. A day without a dark cloud. Almost a happy day. There were three thousand six hundred and fifty-three days like that in his stretch. From the first clang of the rail to the last clang of the rail. Three thousand six hundred and fifty-three days. The three extra days were for leap years. (*Solzhenitsyn, 1963*)

To compare education with a labor camp is a rape of metaphor, but Shukhov is an appropriate reminder that human spirit does not require optimism in order to embrace life, and that we may serve education well by marking stoicism as a virtue. There is little guarantee of pleasure, or dramatic hope, in many schools; but there is still a basis for commitment in our appreciation of the nonheroic efforts of minor lives.

The second classic response is the acceptance of *irrelevance without loss of faith*. When an educator can confront the fact that intentional control over educational outcomes is imperceptible without surrendering to professional cynicism, he is recreating General Kutuzov before the Battle of Borodino.

> Prince Andrew could not have explained how or why it was, but after that interview with Kutuzov he went back to his regiment reassured as to the general course of affairs and as to the man to whom it had been entrusted. The more he realized the absence of all personal motive in that old man – in whom there seemed to remain only the habit of passions, and in place of an intellect (grouping events and drawing conclusions) only the capacity calmly to contemplate the course of events – the more reassured he was that everything would be as it should. "He will not bring in any plan of his own. He will not devise or undertake anything," thought Prince Andrew, "but he will hear everything, remember everything, and put everything in its place. He will not hinder anything useful nor allow anything harmful. He understands that there is something stronger and more important than his own will – the inevitable course of events, and he can see them and grasp their significance, and seeing that significance can refrain from meddling and renounce his personal wish directed to something else. And above all," thought Prince Andrew, "one believes in him because he is Russian."
>
> (Tolstoy, 1952 ed., pp. 425–6)

Kutuzov represents three things. First, an acceptance of the minor role intention plays in battle: generals create a commentary on a play written by more powerful authors. Second, a confidence in the appropriateness of destiny: although not by man's will, there is virtue. And third, an embrace of traditional passions: the faith in Russia and the Russian people is not subject to reason.

Education is a collection of minor Borodinos. Educators are participants in a process they do not control; yet it is possible to believe in the intelligence of the historical fate that has brought us to where we are and will carry us somewhere further. And educators, like generals, may be better guided by faith in a few traditional commitments – to the future and the beauties of learning – than by the pursuit of evidence for instrumental meaning.

The third classic response is *optimism without hope*. We can acknowledge that hope for improvement in the human estate, either through our intentional action or through the operation of forces beyond our control, is unwarranted either by human experience or by human reason; that our present condition is not the result of human ignorance or human malevolence, but is in the nature of things; and yet we can deny the relevance of hopelessness for the spirit of optimism. We justify what we do, not by a belief in its efficacy but by an acceptance of its necessity.

> "No doubt, Señor Don Diego de Miranda, you set me down in your mind as a fool and a madman, and it would be no wonder if you did, for my deeds do not argue anything else. But for all that, I would have you take notice that I am neither so mad nor so foolish as I must have seemed to you ... All knights have their special parts to play ... let the knight-errant explore the corners of the earth and penetrate the most intricate labyrinths, at each step let him attempt impossibilities, on desolate hearths let him endure the burning rays of the midsummer sun, and the bitter inclemency of the winter winds and frosts; let no lions daunt him, no monsters terrify him, no dragons make him quail; for to see these, to attack those, and to vanquish all, are in truth his main duties. I, then, as it has fallen to my lot to be a member of knight-errantry, can not avoid attempting all that to me seems to come within the sphere of my duties. (*Cervantes, 1952 ed., p. 256*)

Don Quixote embraces the foolishness of obligatory action. Justification for knight-errantry lies not in anticipation of effectiveness but in an enthusiasm for the pointless heroics of a good life. The celebration of life lies in the pleasures of pursuing the demands of duty.

In a similar way, we may ask the educator to separate his optimism from his hopes. Neither the teacher nor the educational administrator has profound basis for hope. The world is probably cruel. But hope is not required for attacking educational windmills, only a commitment to the classical traditions of knight-errantry in schools – enthusiasm, intelligence, imagination, and devotion to the future. The roles we accept define the battles we fight; and we find optimism in the joys of that dependence.

Indeed, we can make a stronger claim. To be optimistic is the nature of education. The terminology is archaic. We have grown to accept the modern idea that human actions, institutions, and traditions are justified by expectations of their consequences; and we have come to view optimism without hope as an unfortunate surrender to Pollyanna. But education unconditionally celebrates life. It is an arbitrary assertion of optimism. It echoes an ancient conception by which I do what I do because that is what is appropriate to my nature; and my nature is not simply a tautological summary of what I do but an understanding of the essence of my destiny, an interpretation of my history, and an assertion of my humanity.

The vivid Argentine writer, Jorge Luis Borges, has written a story of arbitrary commitment to obligation without hope in his short parable, "El Sur." It is the story from which I have drawn the numbered quotations here. Borges portrays the way in which Juan Dahlmann, the grandson of a German minister on one side of his family and an Argentina soldier on the other, leaves city life after an illness and travels – physically and spiritually – to the plains in the Argentine South. When he reaches the South, he is led by a series of individually fortuitous but collectively compelling steps to acknowledge the unreasoning code of that world and accept an unprovoked challenge to a hopeless knife fight. Borges' portrayal is both rich and parsimonious, and it ends with a testament to the power of hopeless obligation.

> They went out and if Dahlmann was without hope, he was also without fear. As he crossed the threshold, he felt that to die in a knife fight, under the open sky, and going foward to the attack, would have been a liberation, a joy, and a festive occasion, on the first night in the sanitarium, when they stuck him with the needle. He felt that if he had been able to choose then, or to dream his death, this would have been the death he would have chosen or dreamt. Firmly clutching his knife, which he would perhaps not know how to wield, Dahlmann went out into the plain. (*Borges, 1962, p. 174*)

Like Juan Dahlmann, American education has a nearly forgotten tradition, one that we have kept idly alive while indulging in the fantasies of grand ambitions. Our recent utilitarian conversion obscures our heritage of soul. Teaching is a calling, and education is a faith. They need establish neither relevance nor effectiveness to claim us.

vii

> Firmly clutching his knife, which he would perhaps not know how to wield, Dahlmann went out into the plain. (*Borges, 1962, p. 174*)

It is, I believe, a good vision. But the metaphors of knight-errantry and hopeless fights are possibly misleading. The ordinary life of ordinary people is neither marked nor measured by opportunities for mortal confrontation. Rather, it is filled with numerous minor events calling for the exercise of minor talents in the service of minor obligations without apparent point or consequence. Schools have toilets that have to flush and buses that have to run. They have classes that have to be met and records that have to be kept. They are collections of little things, done mostly by little people. It is our destiny to seek joy in actions that are not only meaningless, but also cruelly mundane.

I do not think that it is easy to translate the dramatics of grand principles into the facts of another day at Public School Number 108. Certainly, I cannot do it. But I think they call for commitment more than ambition. As a result, I think we are led finally in our pursuit of optimism to ask what is essential to education. "Essential" not in the sense of being necessary for education to be more effective, for we know very little about that; but "essential" in the more classic sense of "that which constitutes the being of a thing – that 'by which it is what it is'" (*Oxford English Dictionary*).

Unfortunately, there is hardly any agreement in our modern tradition that the question is meaningful, and as a result, no serious help on the answer. Discovering "that by which education is education" involves recognizing and comprehending both some tradition in educational philosophy and the everyday expectations that we associate with educational roles. The technology is one of thought and discussion, and we have recently been more concerned with more utilitarian efforts to improve education than with trying to examine what "constitutes the being of the thing." As a consequence, much current talk of essences is more hyperbole than serious effort.

I am not sure I can escape warranting a similar charge, but I would begin with three key elements of the essence of education. First, *a faith in learning*. A belief in the beauty and grace of knowledge, trained intelligence, and scholarly competence. We seek educated educators, not primarily in order to have them know something that can be transmitted to their students, but to assure us that they share a fundamental personal faith in learning. We have a library, not primarily because it is needed or used, but because books are a symbol of our faith.

Second, *a commitment to adulthood*. Some might prefer to emphasize a love of children; but I think that is less essential. Education is a recognition that childhood is a precursor to adulthood, that children are tourists in adolescence. We declare that being an adult is different from being a child, that educators are adults, and that children should develop beyond childish things and childish beliefs.

Third, *a fundamental spirit of optimism*. Enthusiasm for life and pleasure in its manifest ambiguity. Education presumes not so much an outcome of success as a process of personal dedication and excitement. The injustice, pessimism, and cruelty of existence belong in the curriculum; but education is deeply optimistic. It proclaims a human will.

These three elements – faith in learning, commitment to adulthood, and fundamental optimism – are neither mysterious nor profound. They are elementary ideas recorded in a long tradition of simple dedication by ordinary people.

Borges calls the South of Argentina "un mundo más antiguo y más firme" – "an older and a harder world." Contemporary American education is such a place. There are empty school rooms and empty buildings; educators unable to find a job in education; careers dismantled by the end of rapid growth; students, teachers, and institutions confused about their futures. There is a profession in doubt about its contribution, a doubt widely shared among legislators, the intelligentsia, and a large number of parents.

It is a hard world and one that demands an older wisdom, in which optimism is not an assertion of hope, but a proclamation of humanity, of the pleasures of obligation, and of surrender to an unreasoning enthusiasm for life. The vision is Don Quixote's, and like the rules of knightly honor, may be listed as symptom of a curious madness. But there is beauty in it nevertheless. As we are tempted, over the coming decades, by the soft dangers of new sets of great expectations, we may want to shield the beauties of our quixotic optimism from the corruptions of hope. For all knights have their special parts to play; and as it has fallen to us to be educators, we can not avoid attempting all that comes within the sphere of our duties.

Note

1. This chapter is one of a number of efforts to explore the possibilities for action in modern educational organizations. Some additional perspectives are attempted in March's other works, including "Model Bias in Social Action," *Review of Educational Research* 42 (1973), 413–429; "Analytical Skills and the University Training of Educational Administrators," *Journal of Educational Administration* 12 (1974), 17–44 and *Journal of Education and Urban Society* 6 (1974), 382–427; "Commitment and Competence in Educational Administration," in Lewis B. Mayhew, *Educational Leadership and Declining Enrollments*, Berkeley, Ca.: John McCutchan, 1974, pp. 131–141; and in *Leadership and Ambiguity* (with Michael D. Cohen), New York: McGraw-Hill, 1974.

References

Averch, Harvey A., Carroll, Stephen J., Donaldson. Theodore S., Kiesling, Herbert J., and Pincus, John. *How Effective Is Schooling?* Englewood Cliffs, N.J.: Educational Technology Publications, 1974.

Borges, Jorge Luis. "The South," in *Ficciones*. Trans. by Anthony Kerrigan. New York: Grove Press, 1962.

Cervantes, Miguel de. *Don Quixote de la Mancha*. Trans. by John Ormsby. Chicago: Encyclopedia Britannica, 1952. (Part Two, Chapter 17)

Jencks, Christopher, Smith, Marshall,

Acland, Henry, Bane, Mary Jo, Cohen, David, Ginitis, Herbert, Heyns, Barbara, and Michelson, Stephan. *Inequality: A Reassessment of the Effect of Family and Schooling in America*. New York: Basic Books, 1972.

Solzhenitsyn, Alexander. *One Day in the Life of Ivan Denisovich*. Trans. by Ralph Parker. New York: Signet, 1963. English translation copyright by E. P. Dutton and Co., 1963.

Tolstoy, Leo. *War and Peace*. Trans. by Louise and Aylmer Maude. Chicago: Encyclopedia Britannica, 1952. (Book Ten, Chapter 16)

CHAPTER TWENTY ONE

A Scholar's Quest

Modern portrayals of human action are overwhelmingly drawn from Bentham. Action is seen as choice, and choice is seen as driven by anticipations, incentives, and desires. The ideas are important, but they are limited. They obscure another tradition, one that emphasizes action as stemming from efforts to fulfill identities and involves our willingness to act in spite of consequences rather than because of them. In such a view, universities are not markets or factories but temples, and they are maintained by those who are committed to higher education not as instrumentalities of their desires but as objects of beauty and affirmations of humanity. This chapter is from the Stanford Graduate School of Business.

INTRODUCTION

My topic is not what the future holds, nor what the implications of any future might be for business schools. Forecasting the future seems to me to be a fool's fantasy, and I have few illusions about the role of the old in shaping the decisions of the young. If I have anything to say, it is not about the decisions this school, or any school, should make but rather about how we think about taking action in our lives.

Modern portrayals of human action are overwhelmingly in a calculative and consequentialist tradition. Consequentialist reasoning is the basis for most of modern social and behavioral science, and preeminently for economics. Action is seen as choice; and choice is seen as driven by anticipations, incentives, and desires.

These ideas trace their roots at least to the Greeks, owe substantial parts of their modern manifestation to the formulations of Jeremy Bentham, and derive much of their contemporary power from the geniuses of L. J. Savage and John von Neumann.

It is no surprise that schools of applied economics (or business) teach such a consequentialist theology as a sacred doctrine and also address their own problems of decision and strategy in the same spirit. They evaluate their alternatives in terms of expected consequences, implement strategies with expected outcomes that appear attractive, and seek to manage the actions of others by assuming they are similarly guided.

Such practices honor ideas that are of enormous importance in human development. It is inconceivable that we would abandon them. Nevertheless, the ideas have their limitations. John Stuart Mill characterized Bentham, the patron saint of modern consequentialist thought, as having the "completeness of a limited man."

In particular, Mill wrote that "Man is never recognised by [Bentham] as a being capable of . . . desiring for its own sake, the conformity of his own character to his standard of excellence, without hope of good or evil from other source than his own inward consciousness."

Mill's comments on Bentham might as easily be applied to us. Our comfortable sense of completeness leads us, as it led Bentham, largely to exclude from our visions of human behavior a second grand tradition for understanding, motivating, and justifying action.

This tradition sees action as based not on anticipations of consequences but on attempts to fulfill the obligations of personal and social identities and sense of self, particularly as those obligations and senses are informed by the ethos and practices of great human institutions. It is a tradition that speaks of self-conceptions and proper behavior, rather than expectations, incentives, and desires.

This second vision has become somewhat obscured in contemporary life, and particularly in the halls of business schools; but it has a long and distinguished pedigree. It is captured classically in many major works of literature and philosophy but particularly in that great testament to the human spirit, *Don Quixote*. When challenged to explain his behavior, Quixote does not justify his actions in terms of expectations of their consequences. Rather, he says, "I know who I am." – "*Yo sé quien soy.*"

Quixote seeks consistency with imperatives of the self more than with imperatives of the environment. He exhibits a sanity of identity more than a sanity of reality. He follows a logic of appropriateness more than a logic of consequences. He pursues self-respect more than self-interest.

As Quixote's misadventures illustrate quite vividly, following a sense of self has its own confusions and limitations, but it celebrates a non-consequentialist view of humanity. Great enthusiasms, commitments, and actions are tied not to hopes for great outcomes but to a willingness to embrace the arbitrary and unconditional claims of a proper life.

Quixote reminds us that if we trust only when trust is warranted, love only when love is returned, learn only when learning is valuable, we abandon an essential feature of our humanness – our willingness to act in the name of a conception of ourselves regardless of its consequences.

The words are obviously a bit peculiar for this setting. But I think they have some mundane implications for those of us who claim to be educators. Our involvements in education undoubtedly have many consequences that we value, but we also pursue and venerate knowledge and learning as a manifestation of faith in what it means to be a human being. When we recognize ourselves as sharing a human identity that is intertwined with traditions of scholarship, we are led to view business schools in ways that are somewhat less consequentialist than are the ways that have become familiar to contemporary discussions.

Recently, our metaphors of business schools have become indistinguishable from metaphors of markets. The problems of business schools are pictured as problems of creating educational programs (or public relations activities) that satisfy the wishes of customers and patrons rich enough to sustain them. It is a conception that yields useful insights and is not to be dismissed thoughtlessly. But it fails to capture the fundamental nature of the educational soul.

A university is only incidentally a market. It is more essentially a temple – a temple dedicated to knowledge and a human spirit of inquiry. It is a place where learning and scholarship are revered, not primarily for what they contribute to personal or social well-being but for the vision of humanity that they symbolize, sustain, and pass on.

Søren Kierkegaard said that any religion that could be justified by its consequences was hardly a religion. We can say a similar thing about university education and scholarship. They only become truly worthy of their names when they are embraced as arbitrary matters of faith, not as matters of usefulness. Higher education is a vision, not a calculation. It is a commitment, not a choice. Students are not customers; they are acolytes. Teaching is not a job; it is a sacrament. Research is not an investment; it is a testament.

And when someone says, as they certainly will and do, that all this is romantic madness, that any such foolishness requires a consequential justification, perhaps one that discovers an evolutionary advantage in traditions and faith, the proper answer is Quixote's: "For a knight errant to make himself crazy for a reason merits neither credit nor thanks. The point is to act foolishly without justification."

The complications of confronting the ordinary realities of day-to-day life often confound such lofty sentiments, and I would not pretend that it is possible or desirable to ignore consequences altogether. But in order to sustain the temple of education, we probably need to rescue it from those deans, donors, faculty, and students who respond to incentives and calculate consequences and restore it to those who respond to senses of themselves and their callings, who support and pursue knowledge and learning because they represent a proper life, who read books not because they are relevant to their jobs but because they are not, who do research not in order to secure their reputations or improve the world but in order to honor scholarship, and who are committed to sustaining an institution of learning as an object of beauty and an affirmation of humanity.

I do not know whether any such thing is imaginable, much less possible. But if it is, then perhaps we can say that we, like Quixote, know who we are. And that would not be entirely bad.

INDEX

Note: 'n.' after a page reference indicates the number of a note on that page.